CHURCHES
AND THE CRISIS
OF DECLINE

CHURCHES
AND THE CRISIS
OF DECLINE

A HOPEFUL, PRACTICAL
ECCLESIOLOGY FOR A SECULAR AGE

Andrew Root

Baker Academic
a division of Baker Publishing Group
Grand Rapids, Michigan

© 2022 by Andrew Root

Published by Baker Academic
a division of Baker Publishing Group
PO Box 6287, Grand Rapids, MI 49516-6287
www.bakeracademic.com

Printed in the United States of America

Library of Congress Cataloging-in-Publication Data
Names: Root, Andrew, 1974– author.
Title: Churches and the crisis of decline : a hopeful, practical ecclesiology for a secular age / Andrew Root.
Description: Grand Rapids, Michigan : Baker Academic, a division of Baker Publishing Group, [2022] | Series: Ministry in a secular age ; 4 | Includes bibliographical references and index.
Identifiers: LCCN 2021035439 | ISBN 9781540964816 (paperback) | ISBN 9781540965332 (casebound) | ISBN 9781493434954 (ebook) | ISBN 9781493434961 (pdf)
Subjects: LCSH: Church renewal. | Church—Forecasting.
Classification: LCC BV600.3 .R659 2022 | DDC 262.001/7—dc23
LC record available at https://lccn.loc.gov/2021035439

Baker Publishing Group publications use paper produced from sustainable forestry practices and post-consumer waste whenever possible.

22   23   24   25   26   27   28   7   6   5   4   3   2   1

To Kara Root in gratitude for life together!

CONTENTS

PREFACE

The first draft of this book was composed in lockdown. Yep, it's a COVID-19 lockdown baby! As an introvert who is an avid indoorsman, I thought I was built for quarantine. But that ended up not being the case. I found it difficult, haunting, and at times depressing. To keep the darkness from getting to me, I'd drag myself out of bed earlier than usual to type away at this project. It helped. I spent my evenings watching TV (well, honestly, that was no change from before COVID—TV is kind of my jam). There were a few highlights to the hundreds of shows I watched during the months of lockdown.

Maybe it was the COVID effect, but I found myself falling deeply for *Dark*, a mind-bending German show about time travelers.[1] It's like if *Lost* had a cool German cousin who smoked cigarettes, was tatted out like Lil Peep, quoted Schopenhauer, and listened to emo rap. It's good! All the time travel is so confusingly awesome!

Another quite different highlight was *Hamilton*. My family was one of the millions who streamed it on Disney+ on the Fourth of July. I liked it more than I thought I would—or was willing to admit to my wife and kids. (Okay, I loved it! But I played it cool because I didn't need the "I told you so" refrain.)

This book is a little like those shows: part time travel saga, part contemporary musical update to a historical figure (without the music and costumes). I figure if Lin-Manuel Miranda can make Alexander Hamilton interesting, I can do the same for Karl Barth (I know, the hubris!). I'm not under any delusion that there is a musical future for this book. I'm not even suggesting that this book will be wonderfully entertaining (I'd take *mildly*). But I have tried to retell the story of Karl Barth in a way that looks more deeply at his

---

1. Thanks to pastor Matthew Codd for suggesting it.

ten years as pastor. I'll explore whether Barth's early theology gives us any helpful ways of thinking about the church and how his early theology calls us to address and live within the secular age we have inherited. I ask the reader to recognize that my focus is on Pastor Barth. I want to show how the great Karl Barth must be seen as a pastor.

This is where time travel comes in.

As my earlier projects (particularly the Ministry in a Secular Age series) have sought to show, we are living in a time when it's much harder to point to, and therefore build communities around, robust articulations of God's action in the world. The church and its local congregations appear to be in a crisis. We keep interpreting this crisis as the loss of people and resources, but it's really the radical transformation of belief itself. I contend, and I hope to show, that Pastor Karl Barth saw this in the early twentieth century. What Barth didn't have was Charles Taylor's deep description of modernity. Barth intuited much of this, but he didn't have Taylor's articulation of the immanent frame in particular (a culturally imposed map or frame we receive from culture that leads us to see things as mostly, if not completely, natural and material). Though Barth didn't have this language or description, the immanent frame was what Pastor Barth was seeking to address. Barth, through his pastoral ministry, was seeking to offer a new modern pastoral theology that could address the immanent frame. What I'll do in this book, all-time-travel-like, is import Taylor's descriptive language from the early twenty-first century back to Karl Barth in the early twentieth. Doing so will no doubt cause some jaggedness, but I'm trusting that it will be helpful. Ultimately, this book hopes to show that Pastor Karl Barth is a modern theologian addressing the immanent frame. Further, I hope that uncovering how Barth made a case for a living God inside this immanent frame can inspire the imagination of pastors and the congregations they lead.

The point of this book is not to offer a case for Karl Barth. The book's point is not even to make Karl Barth the gravitational center of the project. Instead, I hope that in using Barth's story I can offer some of my own theological construction. This book is a thought experiment that desires to present a constructive practical ecclesiology that draws inspiration and direction from Barth—not unlike Lin-Manuel Miranda's objective to not offer a historically defensible case for Alexander Hamilton but instead access Hamilton's story to push the imagination of his audience. To offer my own constructive ecclesiology, I'll be putting Barth's story and thoughts in conversation with others like Erich Fromm and Hartmut Rosa. To be clear, this project is not necessarily intended for those studying Barth but for those pastoring churches in a secular age. My objective in telling Barth's story is to explore what his theology means for the life of the church in our time and how it gives us a different vision for the church in a secular age framed in immanence.

Alongside Barth's story, I tell the story of a fictional local congregation. That fictional church closed, and the building became a microbrewery, but I will offer an alternate history, retelling their story to see what might have helped them find the life they needed to remain active. I've done this kind of fictional storytelling before to flesh out theological ideas. I suppose in some way it's become a genre I've embraced. It fits well into what Barth himself called "irregular dogmatics." I'll admit it's irregular to use this kind of storytelling, particularly in the academic guild, but I think it's advantageous. Since the beginning of my career, my focus has been on the church in its most concrete form. I've had the privilege of giving thousands of presentations to churches and church leaders. I've discovered that the best way to teach theology in the church is not through intricately laying out theologians' doctrinal differences but through stories of concrete people encountering a living God. Pedagogically, it's best to *show*, not *tell*, people theological ideas. Thus I've shaped this theological project around stories (showing).

Of course, I hope academic groups can wrestle with the ideas. I believe there are contributions to fields of study here. But my first audience is the church and pastors on the ground. Below you'll hear the story of Pastor Karl Barth told alongside the story of a small congregation, called Saint John the Baptist, seeking life amid its decline. I'll show that it's the immanent frame and the loss of a God who is God—not the loss of relevance and resources—that threatens the church. Against this backdrop Pastor Barth's own breakthroughs will be salutary. My hope is that the theology I build in dialogue with Barth (and its importance for our ecclesial moment) will become evident as it's placed alongside the story of this little church.

I'm deeply thankful for a handful of friends and colleagues who read parts or all of the manuscript, giving me invaluable feedback. David Wood, Jon Wasson, and Derek Tronsgard read the whole manuscript, providing insightful feedback on pastoral ministry. Wes Ellis, who knows my work better than I do, Dave Brunner, and Erik Leafblad offered helpful feedback as able constructive theologians. Christian Collins Winn read parts of the manuscript, offering important help on the Blumhardts. Kait Dugan provided insights on the first few chapters. My former student Amy Janssen ran down and photocopied dozens of articles for me. Blair Bertrand, who has been one of my closest friends and most trusted dialogue partners since our days at Princeton, helped with this work in multiple places. Bob Hosack and Eric Salo again have been amazing to work with. Bob's vision and Eric's skill have made this project so much better. Finally, i need again and again and even again to thank Kara Root for her patient reading and editing of this project. It was an added task inside COVID-19. She blessed me by wading through it while she so faithfully was leading her congregation through unprecedented times. Her person and skills are the greatest gift I've been blessed with.

1

When the Church Becomes a Pub, and the Immanent Frame Our Map

It was a haunted space. If I paused and blocked out all the ambient noise, I could hear it. The faint echoes of life and worship, a century of suffering and joy; it all dripped from the walls. You could feel it—if you let yourself. It reverberated, ever so softly but assuredly, with all those decades of prayers, sermons, funerals, and overall yearning for God's action.

But I'll admit it was hard to stay haunted when the wings and riblets were so amazing. They melted in your mouth. And the beats and flow of Lizzo filled your ears from the speakers above. The overall buzz in what was once a sanctuary—now filled with tables of conversation and laughter, waitstaff racing from table to table, trays of beer and credit card slips—made it hard to hear any past voices of praise for a God who is God in life and death, loss and hope. I had to work hard to hang on to the haunting. To remember, in this room full of good beer and good fun, that indeed God is God. It seemed an unneeded acknowledgment in this space of food, drinks, and commerce, even in this space that was once a place of worship.

According to the menu of the Church Brewhouse, yet *another* microbrewery in this newly gentrified midwestern city, the corporate entity that owned the Church Brewhouse had taken over the building in 2019. It framed the acquisition as a service. The church building, with its beautiful stained glass, had sat empty in this supposed "reviving" neighborhood for too long. As Starbucks, bike shops, loft apartments, and boutiques marched in, taking over block by block, shining the streets with their glossy rejuvenation, the church building sat awkwardly as the ghost of a past neighborhood, desperately needing a coat of paint and a roof repair. It represented an unwanted monument to a time before gentrification. Once the anchor of the neighborhood, it was soon out of place, both architecturally and functionally. In this high-tech neighborhood the church was as antiquated as a flip phone.

The church building was the last remaining sign of the century before. Even as the congregation dwindled in membership and funds, the denomination was frozen by what to do with it. Which makes sense: places of tragic death are often left abandoned for a time, people paralyzed by what to do with these spaces now that they've endured such an event. Yet it's no shame for a congregation to close—no failure, necessarily, for a pastor to journey with a congregation into death. Even when the church building has been turned into a pub, it's important to remember that the church isn't a building but a people.

Then again, we as people are bodies that live in spaces. Our spaces take on symbolic weight, for these spaces house our experiences and the narratives of our lives. To live is to be moving and acting in a space. Because we are bodies we can only live in a space, and so space bears the mark of our spirit of life. In the case of the church building, it marks our life in relation to the life of the living God. Churches don't need a building. God is never stuck in a building. But church communities, because they are the body of Christ, can't be without a space. Congregations inhabit space as the sure sign of life. For the human spirit to be alive, it must be in a space. For a church to be in Christ, it too must *be* alive in a space.

When Death Comes to a Church

This connection between space and life was the very reason the denomination was frozen about what to do with the church building. Both the church's physical shape and locale had witnessed a tragic death, even the bloody vocational murder of a few pastors. Admittedly, that's a dramatic way to put it. But the death that this church community encountered was indeed tragic, not because this community died before its time but because it stopped living long before its end.

There are two very different kinds of tragic deaths. There is the kind where the person or people are living so fully that when death enters the scene it comes screeching and snatching. It takes the person from our side. Their life was so entwined in ours, their spirit of life so connected to our own spirit, that our life had become not only our own but somehow the sum of us living with and in their life. Losing them creates a throbbing absence in our being.

The fact that this person's full life is no longer part of the orchestra of life is a thought too hard to bear. We painfully sense that they were right in the middle of a song when it was abruptly halted. The fact that they are no longer living takes some of our own life from us. This is a tragic death because it ends life. Mourners say things like, "But we had plans," "But her laugh . . . I need it to live," and "He was so full of life."

But there is another kind of tragic death. It's the kind where a person or a people stop living. Their absence, rather than throbbing, instead becomes a deeply uncomfortable awareness that one can live a life without truly living at all. We grieve not because this person is absent from the orchestra of life but because this person stopped playing long ago. They still sit in the orchestra pit, but for whatever reason they are unable to take up their instrument. They died forgetting or refusing to live. This actuality is hard for the human spirit to tolerate because we know that it could happen, and at times has happened, to us. We've slid into that rut, refusing to live while living. The thought that the rut could become too deep to escape, and we could die there, is painful to acknowledge.

It was this second kind of death that the community suffered by no longer living in the space now called the Church Brewhouse. The building was solemnly sold off to the corporation. Selling it felt like pawning Grandma's wedding ring after she passed. There was no reason to keep it. It represented nothing to anyone living. Grandma had put the ring in a box, along with her will to live, long ago. For years, the church had a building but no life. The denomination finally sold it after it had sat empty for so long. To liquidate one-time symbolic things that represent life (but are no longer imbued with it) produces a certain kind of heavy, icky unease.

What Happened?

As I read the three-paragraph history of the pub in the menu, I wondered what had happened. Google says that the Church Brewhouse was once a congregation called Saint John the Baptist. The congregation was formed in 1912 and erected the building in 1920, which now proudly boasts the sign "Best Wings in Town 2020." The same young men who worked the mills and factories just north of the city, and then gave their youth fighting in the trenches of France, built most of the sanctuary with their own hands.

When the stained glass was installed after World War II, it became the talk of all the surrounding churches. The beautiful stained glass became a space inside a space, a symbolic representation of life and death. Each boy who died in the bright blue waters of the Pacific or the menacing, cold waters of Normandy was placed into the biblical stories depicted in the glass. This connected their story of lost life with God's own lost life. The lost boys were given an ever-present space in the life of this community that had lost them and lived on without them.

It was boys who fought and died, but it was the women who lived without them who gave them a place in the glass. As the factories in the neighborhood were shifted to producing arms for the war, the women who worked in their husbands' absence picked up extra hours to fund the production of the stained glass.

After the Second World War the congregation ballooned in size, from about one hundred members to over two hundred. With the growth came a new education wing and an expansion to the sanctuary. The neighborhood began to change in the latter part of the century. African American families joined European immigrant families. The congregation reflected this change, though not quite on par with the demographics of the neighborhood as a whole. Nevertheless, this church punched above its weight as it fought for civil rights in the city. The final stained glass panel erected by the congregation showed John the Baptist pointing to Dr. King preaching in Chicago in 1967.

I was intrigued, so I sent a few emails to former pastors to learn more about the congregation's story. The two world wars had imprinted themselves on the congregation, first in the impetus to build the sanctuary and then in the choice to imbue it with the stained glass of remembrance and hope. The war in Vietnam didn't imprint itself on the congregation so much as strike and wound it. The divided opinions and multiple pains around the war resulted in a quiet but sure distrust that never left the congregation. As the 1980s and 1990s came and went, the congregation's size hovered around a hundred members. Children of those who placed the stained glass still drove in from the suburbs, intent on having their own children involved. Yet people slowly peeled off as the factories closed and the drug trade entered the neighborhood, and churches in the suburbs (or no church at all) seemed more logical and convenient. The congregation grayed.

There is no shame in graying: it's part of life. It may be culturally uncomfortable, but it's nevertheless a sure sign that you're alive and that you've been living. Saint John the Baptist was aging, but there was still life. Yet the church had far less access to resources. And this concerned the denomination. The congregation had always made, but never exceeded, its budget. Just enough new members arrived to offset the losses to funerals and long-term-care centers. Saint John the Baptist was as steady as the beams that the boys from the Great War had used to build the sanctuary. But the church's flat growth worried some.

With no real sustainability plan, the church proposed hiring a new young pastor when the neighborhood began to shift in 2005, bringing in tech companies, restaurants, and single young adults. It was assumed that having someone who could attract the new residents of the neighborhood was important. And it was. But something seemed to be amiss.

From 2008 to 2017 the congregation had three pastors and two different names. A young church planter took over in 2008. I imagine that his heart was in the right place, but I also know it's hard for young church planters to work inside existing structures. Inheriting a congregation with a hundred-year history has its problems for those looking to move fast. I'm not completely sure what happened, but it appears he burned hot and then burned up. The congregation became known as Thrive (officially Thrive at Saint John the Baptist). It littered the neighborhood with advertisements and used many of the new church growth and network building strategies. By 2011 the young church planter was gone, moving on to a much bigger (and boldly stated) doctrinally orthodox congregation with multiple sites. It's hard to know, but reading between the lines it seems that this young church planter who was equally committed to correct doctrine and church growth burned bridges within the congregation by the flames of his own ambition.

In early 2012 a new young pastor took over. He seemed to stabilize things, keeping Thrive going, but perhaps not racing full throttle toward expansion (and protection of pure doctrine). The new pastor's ambitions were not quite as high as the church planter's. His goal was a growing church connected to the neighborhood, as opposed to a multicampus church that planted other churches. But in 2014 the tone of things seemed to change. Community organizing rather than church planting became the metaphor and focus. As the denomination entered debates around sexual identities and as social media galvanized people around identity issues across the country, Thrive at Saint John the Baptist, or at least its pastor, weighed in.

The congregation boldly positioned itself as a critical voice in the denomination, even taking a critical stance against the Christian tradition itself. This was quite a change from the church-planting predecessor. This new young pastor even questioned whether the Christian church as a whole hadn't done more evil than good in the world. He was now calling the church a community of post-Christians seeking to live right in *this world*—not for heaven. This focus seemed to fit the ethos of the neighborhood hand in glove. Whether it fit the congregation itself is hard to know, but the congregation's decline provided at least some justification for that not mattering. The congregation needed to be relevant in order to attract new people. To this pastor, nothing seemed more relevant (and I suppose true) than to critique the church and its tradition as a whole. Not surprisingly, even when Thrive was renamed Thrive for Justice, few young people from the neighborhood participated. Somehow songs of justice sounded offbeat to those in the neighborhood. After the 2016 presidential election the young pastor left the congregation and Christian ministry (and one might assume Christianity) altogether.

In the spring of 2017 the congregation welcomed its third pastor since 2008. Remaining were only a handful of members whose participation stretched back decades. The congregation returned to just Saint John the Baptist, seeing no reason to retain Thrive. The congregation was now terminal, though it ignored the diagnosis until the fall of 2018. But I imagine you would have had to have been in a coma to not feel it. All of its life had been burned up in the ambitions and initiatives of the previous two pastors. No matter what this new pastor did, she couldn't revive it. By the summer of 2018, fifteen people sat in a sanctuary built in 1920 for one hundred and expanded for two hundred in the 1950s. Again, fifteen is no shame. A community of fifteen people seeking the *living* Christ is beautiful. What makes a congregation beautiful is its life, not its numbers, programs, or access to resources. A community that is alive is beautiful, whether six or six hundred. The problem was the lack of a pulse. These fifteen people never interacted and rarely said much of anything to each other. The aura of lifelessness was so heavy it felt suffocating. On Christmas Eve 2018, Saint John the Baptist held its last service. Everyone knew it would be the last, and yet no one said much except the pastor. As the congregation concluded its final worship gathering, there was no visible emotion. People just disappeared into the cold winter night. It ended with no sign of life. It was just over.

Eight weeks later the corporate entity that was opening microbreweries across the Midwest took control of the building. They'd been in conversation with a member of Saint John the Baptist and with the denomination for over a year. The pastor had been surprised to find a handful of people in executive attire standing in the middle of her sanctuary on a weekday pointing at the ceiling. No one had told her a thing.

It was a good building with good bones. Never mind that those good bones were built by the bones of lives lived before God.

For nearly one hundred years it was a church building—once full but now empty. In just fourteen months the Church Brewhouse was open and full. Thanks to commerce and capitalism, life again spilled from the building's every corner. Where once young women sat grieving the loss of brothers and husbands on faraway beaches, pleading with God to remember them and minister to their own sorrow, now sorority girls sat laughing and business meetings took place. The boys in the stained glass were now forgotten, though still present. Where once people came seeking God, to find life in this space, now others came who rarely thought about God and had no discernible need for sacraments, words of salvation, or life in the Spirit.

The Church and the Secular

Charles Taylor reminds us that we live in a secular age. It is perhaps easy to herald a church building being turned into a pub as a victory (maybe a stark one) for the secular. After all, it's easy to imagine a medieval priest or a Puritan elder shocked to learn that a consecrated space of worship has become an alehouse. But Taylor reminds us that "the secular" is always multivalent. It's a word, concept, or reality that we all sense but can't clearly define. In conversation, our definitions have enough overlap to lead us to assume we're on the same page. But there is also enough slippage to wonder if we're really discussing the same thing.

For instance, if we were to say that a church building becoming a pub is an issue of the secular, we could mean this in at least three different ways. The first would sound like this: "Yes, indeed, this is a victory for the secular. There should be laws against sacred spaces being bought and owned by secular institutions. This is a direct sign that the public institutions that run our societies have no concern for religion and faith."[1] Staying inside this same definition of the secular, another person might rebut, "Oh, I don't know. I don't think our political and public institutions should get their hands in religious matters. To them it should just be a building. If the entity that owns it can't afford it, then it should be sold, bought, and used just like any other building. Whether the building is used for religious purposes is a private matter, not a public one. As long it's in compliance with zoning laws, who cares?" The above are two different expressions of one way of thinking about and defining the secular. This one way is what Taylor calls the divide between the public and the private (or secular 1).[2] Both statements above operate out of this public/private divide.

A second, more common way of thinking of the secular goes like this: "Can you believe that Saint John the Baptist is now a pub? I guess that's what happens when people just stop going to church. The secular has clearly won

---

1. In some societies there are such laws. But those societies justify such laws, unveiling other definitions of secular, not because old churches are sacred holy places but because they are heritage sites. Their age and history, not their definition as spaces for encounter with the living God, is what leads public institutions to protect them.

2. For more on this, see the introduction to Charles Taylor, *A Secular Age* (Cambridge, MA: Belknap, 2007).

ground, turning churches into bars. It would have never happened if people still cared to go to church and gave their offerings. But those young people in that neighborhood just don't care about church or religion." This second definition assumes that the secular is defined by fewer and fewer people committing to religious institutions, to the extent that sacred spaces can be stripped empty and made into pubs. Taylor calls this secular 2. The church-planting pastor had visions of beating back the secular by giving Saint John the Baptist a radical makeover. He imagined that if he could rebrand it as Thrive, the church would be more relevant and therefore win a victory over secular 2.

But it didn't work. And while there were, I imagine, many reasons why it didn't work, one reason was that he took little account of the third definition of the secular. Taylor explains that to live in a secular age means, and therefore feels like, having all belief contested and thus made fragile (secular 3). We live in a secular age because we can imagine living, and at times do live, as though there is no transcendent quality to life at all. Most of us in the West (and the West may be an outlier here) can live our lives as though there is no living God who enters into history and speaks to persons. Westerners hold on to the *idea* of God (most of us "believe" in God, at least in America), but few of us are sure we can *encounter* this God. We find ourselves even doubt-ing the experiences we have of God. Most of us have major doubts about whether we can encounter, or be taught how to encounter, a living God in our churches. Most people, even in our churches, would not claim that church is for encountering a living God who speaks and moves in the world.

Inside secular 3, the ligaments that connect church life and the encounter with a living God have been culturally severed. The pastors who preceded the church planter at Saint John the Baptist ignored the severing, focusing on business as usual. The church planter, to his credit, sought to stabilize the church despite the severing. He contended that the severing would take care of itself if the church was relevant and doctrinally pure. The pastor following the church planter saw the severing and believed there was no way beyond it. He even came to believe that the severing was necessary. The only way forward was to forget about divine action and the eternal reality our ancestors sought. He instead embraced a world without direct communication from God. The way forward was to engage in the politics of identity. The church was admit-tedly no longer a place to encounter a living, eternal God. Who even knew how to do that? And whether they even believed that was anything more than just an idea? The church's only task was to make the world less awful. This gave him a sense that his action could matter. He wasn't sure whether arcane practices or the ebb and flow of life in the community could lead people into transcendence (he wasn't even sure there was such a thing as transcendence). But he could imagine making a difference by being an activist, by making the church about activism.

The perceived life that animated the church shifted over the last fifteen years of the congregation's life. Before the church planter, in the 1980s and 1990s, *business as usual* was the animating force. The church planter thought that *growth and relevance* would infuse the church with life by giving it access to resources. The pastor after him shifted the animating life to *critique*. He believed that what would energize the church and bring it life was not encounters with the living God but critique of the hidden ways that the church and Christianity supported all the awful parts of the world. Yet nothing worked. Rather, like an air mattress with a small puncture, the life just steadily and surely leaked from the congregation.

A Frame of Reference

The church cannot produce its own life. Actually, nothing in the created realm can. Everything comes from something else. All life is the result of relationship, and therefore life is fundamentally contingent. There is no such thing as a relation of one.[3] Both science and faith believe this. Plants are the contingent relations of sun, soil, and seed. The seed results from a relation between a bud and a bee. No bees, no buds. No buds, no bees. Life is in the relation. *But the question is: what kind of relations bring life?*

Contingent relations are all around us. We exist inside webs of such relations. Being conscious of consciousness, we are compelled to make sense of this thick web of contingent relations within which we live, particularly because we know our own being is itself a contingent relation. Therefore, we believe these relations have meaning, and we are thereby moved to make judgments about the kind of life we're living. It's never enough for a human being to just breathe and eat. We do more than just accept our relationship with air and food. Breathing and eating must mean something. We're the strange kind of creatures who can reflect on life and worry that, though we're alive, we're not really living. We believe there is a *right* way of breathing and eating, as mindfulness, meditation, and cooking shows reveal. We need to

3. Actually there is: the one true God's triunity as Father, Son, and Spirit. Profoundly and marvelously, the Christian tradition has claimed that God is a relationship of one, uniquely and singularly the one *ousia* in a relation of three *hypostases*. God is creator because God is free of contingency. We (and all other things) are creatures/creation, because we have our being not in ourselves but through the gift of relations outside us. We ultimately, and finally, have our being in the relation of God, who is a relationship of three in one.

have at least some implicit sense of what it means to have life (to really live!) in and through all these necessary contingent relationships.

This drive for meaning comes with a problem: there are just too many of these relations. These relations are always and everywhere, too many to dissect each for its own individual meaning. We need to have some sense of these relations to live fully, but ironically we cannot live (are driven quite literally out of our minds) if, in our own computing power, we have to give meaning to each relation we encounter, each second of each day. It would be like having to name each pebble of sand on the seashore before making it to the water for a soak and a swim.[4]

This drive for meaning exponentially escalates the number of contingent relations within which we have our being. The drive for meaning and purpose in contingent acts like eating, sleeping, and others creates culture. Culture both helps and hinders us in dealing with these relations. In one sense it expands the number of relations, giving symbolic meaning to things like eating and sleeping that connect to moral visions. But to assist us in handling the escalating number of contingent relations, culture gives us an important device to conceive of (almost) all these relations. Though culture exponentially adds to our contingent relations, giving us a thicker sense of being alive by making even common creaturely acts mean something significant, culture also gives us a necessary device to deal with all the contingent relations before us.

The device that culture gives us is a frame of reference for understanding almost all of these relations. This frame of reference allows us to escape the need to reflect on every strand of the contingent relationships we encounter every second of every day. This frame of reference gives us unthought—implicit—interpretations of the contingent relationships that make up our life. These contingent relations are so numerous and important and layered so thickly that we need some kind of shortcut reference map to make quick sense of them to live. We avoid crashing like an overworked hard drive by uploading most of this interpretation and meaning making to culture. We do this to avoid being shut down by the relations and to instead live and act within them. Without a reference map, without some framework, we'd go catatonic. This cultural frame of reference becomes a shortcut for interpreting and weighing the massive surplus of relations each of us encounters each day. Importantly, this frame prepares us for what to expect from the relations we live within and that give us life.

It is with this in view that we can return to discussion of the three seculars.

---

4. Hans Joas explains this framework in *The Genesis of Values* (Chicago: University of Chicago Press, 2000), 131.

The Immanent Frame

We live in a secular age—our secular is set at 3—because the frame of reference we inherit from our Western culture(s) is a fully immanent one (i.e., a world closed off from transcendence). It doesn't matter whether we're believers in a church full of life or part of a dying church. We all inherit a frame of reference that sees the relationships of life as mostly (if not completely) immanent. Some of us may not welcome this, but it is hard to avoid. Sometimes it's easier for us to believe in blind luck than the hand of God. It is easier to believe in scientific explanations for certain occurrences than to see them as an act of the living God. It is easier to conceive of God only as a flat concept—a kind of final contingent relation behind the curtain of all other explanations—than to conceive of God as an acting and speaking agent in the world. It's difficult inside this framework to live as though God is ever present and ever active in each and every one of the contingent relations that make up our lives.

We can see this framework in operation within social media controversies around "thoughts and prayers." When a tragedy hits, particularly around *another* mass shooting in America, some people tweet, "My thoughts and prayers go out to . . ."[5] And others respond, "To hell with your thoughts and prayers. We don't need thoughts and prayers. Prayers don't stop bullets." Inside our shared frame of reference this is hard to argue against. Those who tweet "thoughts and prayers" mostly agree that the God we pray to doesn't act. The first tweeters believe this as much as the second. Yet, inside this shared frame, the first tweeters often assume that God can be conceived of as an idea that gives comfort when we can't understand a negative contingent relationship—like that between a child and a shooter (or a child who is a shooter). The second tweeter finds such sentiment a waste of time, a distraction from *real* action. Real action consists of humans, not God, willing to act. These "thoughts and prayers" pacify the necessity to willfully act.

Both tweeters reveal our shared operative framework. A God prayed to may positively affect our psychological constitution (and this isn't nothing). But we have a harder time imagining that our nonmaterial prayers, words uttered to an invisible being who may or may not exist, actually affect the world. Inside a framework based on transcendence, as opposed to immanence, to

5. Of course usually the ones who tweet "thoughts and prayers" are politicians, who are at the same time unwilling to change laws. This allows for a whole other layer of cultural interpretation that I simply can't go into. For the above paragraph I ask the reader to put that aside and remember that other people besides politicians also tweet "thoughts and prayers."

say "thoughts and prayers"[6] wouldn't be assumed to be empty sentiment or vapid encouragement. In this other framework, to call for prayer would be to expect the living God to act in the world, bringing judgment and grace. This God would be assumed to participate in, and therefore shift the contingent flow of, relations in one direction or another. But this is hard for us to believe. Even when we want to believe, it's hard to imagine.

Belief becomes fragile because our shared frame of reference[7] sees the order, direction, and meaning of our contingent relationships as almost completely natural and material. Our framework (our cultural shortcut map) buffers us from assuming that a transcendent force directs and orders our relations in and to the world. The source of life is imagined as relations without transcendence.[8] We inherit a world that creates its institutions, practices, and narratives around immanent explanations for the relationships that give us life. Put another way, the shortcut map we all inherit from our culture interprets nearly all of our relations as immanent contingencies, rather than next to or inside a transcendent reality. Relations that give life are bound in natural and material interpretations. This frame of reference, this shared shortcut map placed in our consciousness by the culture we share, is what Charles Taylor calls the immanent frame.

The immanent frame assumes that these relations that give us life have no supernatural force (no relation with that which is outside the created contingencies). To live inside an immanent frame is to assume that all the contingent relations we meet in the world have their source and significance in immanence, not transcendence. Unlike our ancient and medieval ancestors, our frame of reference is not supernatural but natural. For good or ill, our ancestors believed that most of their relations were directly fused within

6. You probably wouldn't say only "thoughts." "Thoughts" is a signal word that does two things for those operating within an immanent frame. (1) It witnesses that prayers are equal to thoughts, meaning prayer is mainly sentimental, not really anticipating divine action in the world. (2) The "thoughts" are an inclusive signal that shows that the tweeter knows she or he is living in a frame where others don't believe in prayer. These others can agree to "thoughts" even if they're not prayers. In the end, inside this immanent frame, thoughts and prayers are basically the same thing.

7. Our shared frame of reference and therefore our social imaginary. The discussion in this chapter is dependent on Charles Taylor's sense of social imaginary. To find more on social imaginary, see Taylor, *Modern Social Imaginaries* (Durham, NC: Duke University Press, 2007); and Andrew Root, *The Pastor in a Secular Age* (Grand Rapids: Baker Academic, 2019).

8. Whether or not it is fair to the science, this was the cultural impact of Darwinism. We can see this clearly in New Atheism's use of Darwin and its commitment to Darwinism. Evolution by natural selection gives us a way of understanding the change in the flow of contingent relations without the necessity of a transcendent force moving them into being. For discussion of this cultural impact, see Ronald Osborn's *Humanism and the Death of God: Searching for the Good after Darwin, Marx, and Nietzsche* (London: Oxford University Press, 2017).

the economy of God. The sun rose and set because of God's grace. Children lived or died because of God's hand. Crops failed and children acted oddly because of demons. Not so for us. Some of us have outgrown such explanations and interpretations. Others just find themselves not believing it in their day-to-day practice.[9]

Living in the immanent frame requires *a lot* of work for us to see beyond the prescribed cultural map. It's hard to assume that these contingent relations, which give us life, have any direct source in God's own action. It takes a great amount of work for most late-modern Western people to assume that God acts and speaks. Confrontation with a great amount of doubt and suspicion is simply our context, the direct by-product of our frame of reference.

What Gives Life?

This framework (the immanent frame) shapes how we interpret Saint John the Baptist's death. We return to our earlier statement: *The church cannot produce its own life.* As a created thing, it cannot do so. Nothing created can produce its own life by its own will and energy. Everything in the created world needs some relation from outside in order to be. But what is this outside relation that gives the church life?

The dogmatic answer, found in most every ecclesiology, is God. The church has life only because of its relationship to the triune God. It is the body of Christ. Jesus of Nazareth, who is the Christ, is the church's head (Col. 1:18). Without this head it has no life. Bodies without heads tend not to live. If they do, they live as (headless) monsters. This is a kind of living death, which is exactly how the final pastor of Saint John the Baptist described the congregation.

The dogmatic answer might continue: for the church to live, its life must be seen as a gift from the Holy Spirit. Such statements are certainly true. And I'll need to make some similar statements below. But the danger with these important dogmatic statements is that they never seem to confront the concrete and practical experience of congregations. Such dogmatic statements never seem to discuss how the challenges of the immanent frame make these dogmatic answers seem stale and abstract.

9. A much different kind of thinker than Charles Taylor, David Bentley Hart offers a poignant articulation of the late-modern immanent frame: "Late modernity is thus a condition of willful spiritual deafness. Enframed, racked, reduced to machinery, nature cannot speak unless spoken to, and then her answers must be only yes, no, or obedient silence. She cannot address us in her own voice. And we certainly cannot hear whatever voice might attempt to speak to us through her." *The Experience of God: Being, Consciousness, Bliss* (New Haven: Yale University Press, 2013), 312.

The final pastor of Saint John the Baptist couldn't shake off the heavy lifelessness of the congregation by just repeating dogmatic formulas. There were no incantations, even those chanted in dogmatic orthodoxy, that could have awakened her church. Perhaps she tried, but even if so, it didn't help free the congregation from the cold grip of lifelessness. She needed the strength and wisdom to do what must be done to the living dead: to mercifully put it down (allowing the dead to be dead). The pastors before her, and even the denomination itself, believed many of these dogmatic statements. But when it came to the practical life of the church, they believed something quite different about what produces life.

The immanent frame led the denomination and congregational leaders to make particular claims about what produced life: neither the church's commitment to dogmatic formulas nor experiences of the living, transcendent God could produce life. Rather, it was the church's relation to resources. The slow depletion of resources in the 1980s and 1990s first led the denomination to prematurely declare this steady congregation as flat and declining. Though the congregation was steady and alive, it was unable to grow its resources: members, budget dollars, and cultural relevance. This inability was diagnosed as a terminal cancer, a diagnosis that seemed obvious from deep inside the immanent frame (though it may have been a misdiagnosis stemming from the frame's bias).

The inability of the congregation to expand its resources gave many the impression that the church was leaking life—becoming the living dead before the denomination's eyes! They assumed it to be a dying church because it could not accrue new and growing resources. The immanent frame, and modernity's assertion that God is no real source of life, was tacitly accepted by the denomination.[10] What's more, it was used as a powerful evaluative measure for what can be considered living. The church was dying, it was assumed, not because the leadership was corrupt, evil, or faithless but because that trajectory simply seemed obvious. Immanence set the terms for evaluation. And this congregation's stamp of death was its lack of resources.

The next pastors were hired *not* because of their ability to speak a Word from God; *not* for their vision of God's act and beauty; and *not* for their ability to communicate this to others. Rather, they were qualified because of their vision for drawing younger populations to the church. This vision was

10. There is a longer conversation here about how modernity has seen religion. I simply don't have space to rehearse it; however, one can find this important discussion in Hans Joas's books *Do We Need Religion? On the Experience of Self-Transcendence* (London: Routledge, 2008) and *Faith as an Option: Possible Futures for Christianity* (Stanford, CA: Stanford University Press, 2014).

based in innovation and entrepreneurship, not necessarily transcendence.[11] Transcendence on the one hand and innovation and entrepreneurship on the other need not be conflicting opposites.[12] But to keep them from contentious conflict we have to be ever aware of the unthought cultural map imposed by the immanent frame. More importantly, we have to be conscious of how innovation and entrepreneurship, if not deeply reimagined, lean hard toward a closed-world structure, as Taylor calls it.[13] A closed-world structure directly asserts that a personal God is meaningless. If the immanent frame is not acknowledged, innovation and entrepreneurship will do their work against transcendence itself. Why wouldn't they? Innovation and entrepreneurship are the children of an accelerated late modernity. The denomination's immanent vision for resource growth qualified the young church planter and then the activist pastor to lead: it was never their sensitivity to transcendence and obedience to a living God that qualified them.

It's clear: resources create life, or so it's assumed. This is its own late-modern dogma, bound in the immanent frame. Many in leadership accept the dogma that a church full of life is a church full of resources, and vice versa. The capacity to harvest these immanent realities sustains the congregation (not sacraments, visions, and encounters with the divine being). This is logical, almost self-evident, inside the immanent frame. We consider almost every big church with a big budget and many resources to be "alive." We are shocked when we so often learn of intimidation and spiritual abuse that was allowed to fester and feed in such "alive" churches.

The dysfunction of such a church is allowed because of the assumption that resource accrual is what gives life. How can we possibly see the toxicity in leadership, let alone call it out, when resources just keep gloriously accumulating? When we assume that resources bring life, then resource accrual forms our moral vision and overall sense of a good and faithful church (and pastor). The reasoning then easily slides into statements like, "I hate how

11. These realities of innovation/entrepreneurship and transcendence don't have to be conceived as opposites. But work has to be done on how innovation and entrepreneurship can bear the weight of transcendence. In our time, Silicon Valley has owned the discourse on innovation and entrepreneurship. And Silicon Valley has a deeply held commitment to close the immanent frame from any openings to religion and an acting, personal God. I've fleshed out this argument more fully in *The Congregation in a Secular Age* (Grand Rapids: Baker Academic, 2021).

12. For Taylor, the immanent frame is not devoid of transcendence. There are ways to be open to transcendence even while living deeply in the immanent frame. It's possible for innovation and entrepreneurship to have an openness to transcendence, but this openness will have to be intentionally cultivated. One cannot simply assume it will happen, ignore its lack, or presume that it is possible to escape immanence.

13. Taylor discusses closed-world structures in *A Secular Age*, chap. 15.

Pastor Bud intimidates people that oppose him. And his personal boundaries seem so fuzzy. But he's the one who took this church from three hundred to three thousand. I guess that's what you need to have such a lively church."

The Chasm Between

There seems to be a chasm before us. Our dogmatic statements stand on one side. We believe them, at least theoretically. Many of us affirm that the church is the body of Christ, and therefore the church's life is found only in the life of the resurrected body of Jesus himself. What gives the church life is the gift of participating in this body of Jesus by receiving the Holy Spirit who is the Spirit of Life.[14] This Holy Spirit, who raised Jesus from the dead, is given to the gathered at Pentecost. The church lives because the same Spirit who raised Jesus from the dead by the will of the Father now lives in the very space of our gathering. But this profound reality is hard to access when your church is in living-dead mode and the denomination has sent executives to assess where best to put the bar and high-tops.

On the other side of the chasm from our dogmatic statements is the practical life of the congregation. The chasm is so wide because the practical life of the congregation has been driven by the assumption, thanks to the immanent frame, that resources sustain life. The chasm is an expanse because the dogmatic statements seem to have little to say to the practical life of the church. But the fault line doesn't rest *just* on the obscurity of the dogmatic statements and their abandonment of the practical life of the congregation (though that is part of it).[15]

Rather, what significantly enlarges this chasm is how the practical life of the congregation has been allowed to drive so intensely for resources. Resources, not the Holy Spirit, have been imagined as the source of life. In this drive for resources, pastors and congregational leaders have been happy to shed dogmatic language, creedal commitments, and theological visions so they might be light enough to move fast, chasing down resources and therefore (presumably) life. As much as dogmatic statements have felt disconnected from the life of congregations, congregational leaders have been happy to throw off the concepts, commitments, and cumbersome vocabularies of the dogmatic in order to go fast in harvesting resources and assuring themselves of life.

14. See Jürgen Moltmann, *The Source of Life: The Holy Spirit and the Theology of Life* (Minneapolis: Fortress, 1997).

15. Nicholas Healy has made a similar assertion in his book *Church, World and the Christian Life: Practical-Prophetic Ecclesiology* (London: Cambridge University Press, 2000), 3–4.

The immanent frame separates these two into their own corners, divided by a deep, jagged chasm. Dogmatic ecclesiology and practical congregational life never meet, or meet only in seminary curriculum to never again come together in any direct practice. The story of modernity and its imposing of this immanent frame is the source of this separation. As the immanent frame burrowed its way deeper into our imagination, clouding our vision for a living God who speaks and moves in history, it imposed a dual reduction on both dogmatics and practical congregational life.

Ironically, what divides the dogmatic and practical shape of the church is the same source. Or, better, they broadly inherit the same interpretation of that source. Both dogmatics and the practical life of the church, at least in classic Protestantism, conceded that the loss of transcendence is a reality. Both seem to admit, without protest, that transcendence is over. In a modern world (inside modernity), respectability, or even life itself, can be achieved only by embracing the immanent reductions. Therefore, we must peel off the transcendent foci and qualities of both dogmatics and practical church life. Both sides grant that the immanent frame, and its tendency to close off transcendence, is a reality.[16]

Granting and conceding this point meant that dogmatic theology could no longer make its object of study the living God.[17] Nineteenth-century European theology, particularly, needed to pivot hard away from directing its attention to a living God and focus instead on religious consciousness (the Schleiermacherian school), or the historical development of creeds (the Harnackian school), or the value judgments of faith (the Ritschlian school). Into the twentieth century, scholars of dogmatics had conceded to do their work

16. A good argument can be made that Pentecostalism and other church forms tracing their history back to Azusa Street have sought ways beyond this reduction in practical church life and even dogmatics (though the dogmatic reflection took much longer in coming). But because these forms of practical church life are a response to modernity and are therefore born in its womb, there is always the risk of reduction. We can see this in some Pentecostal theologies in which there is the temptation to turn the living Christ into an idea.

17. The Kantian noumenal (the transcendent) and phenomenal (the immanent) break was too complete. Of course, this is much more complicated. Kant imposes a noumenal/phenomenal divide, asserting strongly that human knowledge has no access to the noumenal. This essential commitment brings the immanent frame. Kant did, however, have ways for us to access the noumenal, particularly through the oughts of ethical imperative. If traced back we can see that these ethical demands came upon us from some noumenal reality, and we could still access them if we obeyed them. But there is no access to direct knowledge of a personal noumenal reality that moves in phenomenal space, changing and directing it. Karl Barth understood this better than most and sought to answer Kant. But, as I'll say in the text, Barth never did so without affirming that the problems Kant named were real, and therefore Barth was not looking to do something other than offer a modern response to our conundrums in modernity.

inside the reductions of the immanent frame. If dogmatics wanted a secure place in the modern university, it would have to embrace the closed-world structure of those who saw no room for transcendence in the sciences of the cultural frame of modernity.[18]

For very different reasons, practical congregational life also conceded to immanence (closed to transcendence). The temptations to embrace a closed-world structure were not nearly as direct and acute for the congregation as they were within the university. Nevertheless, as the church started to feel losses toward the end of the twentieth century, all the answers to beat decline were borrowed from hypercapitalism. For example, congregational life turned not to prayer, confession, sacramental ontologies, and discernment of the Spirit as much as to direct marketing, business structuring, customer focus groups, efficacy budgets, and spaces that feel like malls. These hypercapitalist perspectives function as closed-world structures. Efficiency and optimization are frames that see the world as a resource, time as money, and the good life as inseparable from constant and continued growth.

To bridge this chasm we need what has so rarely been offered. We are not in need of another monograph on dogmatic ecclesiology. Nor do we need another conference, consultant, or series of books on practical steps congregations can take to accrue resources. Rather, we need to pursue the more difficult task of exploring how, even though inextricably resting inside modernity and its immanent frame, the church might return to transcendence, finding its life in revelation itself.

Moving Forward

The rest of this book seeks to do exactly that: to show that congregational life is connected to revelation, and revelation is only encountered in relations in the world. *The relations that bring the church life are relations with revelation.* These encounters with revelation cannot be described strictly dogmatically. They must also be witnessed in the concrete life of the church (and the concrete experience for Christians in the world). The challenge before us is to see if the return to transcendence through revelation can bridge this chasm. The ecclesiology that arises from this will be directed toward dogmatics as much as toward the practical life of the congregation. It will offer us a full 360-degree sense of what gives the church life.

18. "Closed-world structure" is Taylor's language. He believes that certain locales, like the university, fight for an interpretation of the immanent frame that sees *no* place for transcendence. See *A Secular Age*, 551–92.

The only way to do the kind of work that possesses both dogmatic depth and practical attention is to embed the process in stories. Therefore, two stories will lead us forward.

The First Story

One of these stories will be the narrative of Pastor Karl Barth. This may seem an odd choice. Barth has been accused by many of being the über-dogmatician. If the dictionary included a picture of an obsessed dogmatician caught in a thought experiment (it doesn't, I just checked online), it would be of Karl Barth. Some have even gone so far as to argue that Barth's focus on doctrine makes any direct attention to the actuality of practical congregational life impossible in his work.[19] He's been derided as a deeply "impractical" theologian.[20]

It can't be denied that Barth worked within the field of dogmatics. By the mid-1920s he identified himself as a dogmatician. Yet his road into dogmatics was undeniably paved by direct experience with practical congregational life. It was not the currents of PhD studies and seminar rooms that pulled Barth into dogmatics. Rather, it was the strong pull of the grave task of mounting a pulpit and seeking a Word that might bring life to his small congregation.[21] In turn, it was the fight for his congregants (and citizens) to receive fair treatment in mills and factories that pulled Pastor Barth into dogmatics. Or maybe it's better to say that it was the Swiss socialist movement that pushed Pastor Barth into dogmatics.[22]

Unlike our assumptions of socialist movements today, the Swiss socialist movement of the early twentieth century possessed deep theological commitments. The movement's leaders, such as Hermann Kutter and Leonhard Ragaz (though disagreeing with each other), mutually contended that socialism was

19. See Don Browning, *A Fundamental Practical Theology* (Minneapolis: Fortress, 1991), chap. 1.

20. See also the beginning of Joyce Ann Mercer's *Welcoming the Child: A Practical Theology of Childhood* (St. Louis: Chalice Press, 2005). Mercer goes to lengths to apologize for using Barth, feeling the need to repent both as a feminist and as a practical theologian. Both perspectives seek to attend to concrete praxis, and her apology shows that Barth is assumed to be an enemy of such practical action.

21. "The ten years Barth spent as a pastor were a period of intensely concentrated development, and most accounts of his work (including those from Barth himself) make much of how the realities of pastoral work, which were brought home to him during this decade, led to his abandonment of theological liberalism and his adoption of a quite different set of commitments." John Webster, *The Culture of Theology* (Grand Rapids: Baker Academic, 2019), 3.

22. For more on this, see Gary Dorrien, *The Barthian Revolt in Modern Theology: Theology without Weapons* (Louisville: Westminster John Knox, 2000), 34–40.

a way of participating in the coming kingdom of God.[23] Socialism was anticipated as a concrete way to find an acting God inside the immanent frame,
although this promise would never come to fruition. The presumptions of
modernity—that history itself was closed to God's action—were just too
entrenched.

Pastor Barth recognized this more than anyone else. He saw clearly that
nineteenth-century dogmatics had conceded too much ground to the closed-
world structures of the immanent frame. This immanence, and the unthought
reduction that God cannot move and speak in history, kept the church from
obedience. The church was merely following a theological establishment who
stopped talking about a God who acted in modernity, believing it impossible.
Yet, through both the frustrations and possibilities of the socialist movement
and the experience of his small congregation, Pastor Barth began to doubt
the impossibility. Maybe, even in the immanent frame of modernity, the act
of God—the still-speaking God of the Bible—was the impossible possibility.
Barth became assured, as we'll see, of this impossible possibility through his
experience with pastors Johann and Christoph Blumhardt. The Blumhardts'
ministry convinced the young Barth that the immanent frame, to give them
Taylor's language, was not closed off from the transcendent arrival of the God
of the Bible, as all Barth's heavyweight theology teachers across Germany
presumed.

In the early 1920s, with his surprise *Epistle to Romans* unpredictably awakening theology across the continent and with his own burning anger for the
theological establishment's support of the Great War still hot, Barth stood
at a crossroads. He could either engage more fully in the socialist movement
or turn to dogmatics, taking a position as a lecturer in Göttingen. To Kutter and Ragaz's disappointment, Barth chose the latter. They, like others,
misinterpreted Barth's project. They believed he was choosing the dogmatic
over the practical side of the chasm. Yet this isn't quite right—especially if
we keep Barth's experience with the Blumhardts close. If we can explore this
story of Barth and the Blumhardts, I believe we will see something different.
Barth, though he indeed turned to dogmatics, did so for the sake of being able
to speak to the practical and concrete action of God in the immanent frame.

Barth's disappointing experience within the socialist movement led him to
recognize that there was no way back from modernity. Barth was no nostalgic
revisionist wishing to turn back the clock to a time before modernity. Barth
was happy to be a modern theologian, living inside the frame of immanence.

---

23. Eberhard Jüngel discusses this in *Karl Barth: A Theological Legacy* (Philadelphia: Westminster, 1986), 84–88.

Barth admitted that the immanent frame was now our context (his theological teachers had already taught him this), but he also admitted that the socialist movement's manner of talking about God could not stand up to reductions of modernity and the closed-world structures of the immanent frame.[24] Barth recognized that what upended the closed spin of immanence was not will, practical know-how, or even resources, but rather the inability to speak of and therefore see the action of the living God moving, even in modernity and its immanent frame.[25] To give it Taylor's language, Barth turned to dogmatics not to avoid the practical world but to find a way to speak boldly and directly about God's action inside the immanent frame in which the church now inextricably existed.[26]

The story I tell about Barth is the account of a pastoral theology for the immanent frame.[27] Barth gives us a way, even inside modernity, to encounter the living God. I contend that our present congregations need more than pure doctrine or a busload of resources.

The chapters that follow will contend that, though the fact is often unnoticed, Karl Barth has a deep pastoral theology. Sure, he takes on the cadence of a dogmatician, but I believe he does so for the sake of the pastoral. He uses dogmatics for the sake of giving us pictures and visions of how the living God moves in our immanent-bound modern world. To see the veins of this pastoral theology in Barth we'll have to recognize the concrete centrality of the Blumhardts' ministry to Barth's thinking.[28] The Reformers give Barth the language, the Blumhardts the concrete assurance. The Blumhardts' ministry is Barth's case study, or touchstone, or maybe even empirical verification,

24. "It is evident that Barth's theology of the Word is indeed modern and not a return to the distant past, yet without proving a sellout to modernity." Paul Louis Metzger, *The Word of Christ and the World of Culture: Sacred and Secular through the Theology of Karl Barth* (Grand Rapids: Eerdmans, 2003), 226.

25. For more on this, see Webster, *Culture of Theology*, 52–54.

26. The following quotation by Jüngel shows both Barth's commitments to the work of a pastor and how the work connected him to socialism: "For, Barth continues, he became a socialist and a Social Democrat precisely because he is glad to be a pastor, not because he is more or less bored with his calling. The 'great cause' for which he lives, and for which he works as a pastor, is also that which allowed him to become a socialist. The path which leads into the Social Democratic Party does not lead away from that cause, which 'is and remains the main thing' for him." Jüngel, *Karl Barth*, 90.

27. I'm seeking to explore in depth the following assertion from Christoph Schwöbel: "At Safenwil, Barth's theology became a theology of a preacher for preachers, challenged by the task of being minister of the Word of God." Schwöbel, "Theology," in *The Cambridge Companion to Karl Barth*, ed. John Webster (New York: Cambridge University Press, 2000), 19.

28. Kenneth Oakes argues that Barth's famous *Epistle to the Romans* (*Römerbrief I* and *II*) is primarily a pastoral text. See *Reading Karl Barth: A Companion to Karl Barth's "Epistle to the Romans"* (Eugene, OR: Cascade Books, 2011), 3, 29.

that indeed the God of the Bible still moves even in modernity. To recover a way of speaking of God inside the immanent frame, this story of Pastor Barth and the eccentric Blumhardts will be our doorway into a theological vision for the church.

The Second Story

Willie James Jennings, an appreciative reader of Barth, states that ecclesiology starts with fantasy.[29] Ecclesiology takes place in the genre of fantasy. If it's to be free of the reduction of the immanent frame, ecclesiology must be an imaginative operation. But like all good fantasy, there is a backstory and rules to the world in which the fantasy is set. We need some sense of the dogmatic. But no one wants just backstory (this is why George R. R. Martin's *The World of Ice and Fire: The Untold History of Westeros and the Game of Thrones*, as a book of backstory, isn't nearly as popular as his other books). For fantasy to thrive it must connect with our concrete lives and say something to our context and experience. Backstory and rules bridge the chasm between dogmatics and practical congregational life. Both the dry dogmatic and the hyperconsumeristic practical, disconnected from one another, lack a sense of fantasy.

To avoid this trap, the second story needs to be a fantasy. But instead of being like *Game of Thrones* or *The Witcher*, this fantasy needs to be set in a world that is more like our own. We need something like *Watchmen*: a fantasy set in a world very much like ours but nevertheless with some major differences. Perhaps the best version of fantasy would be an alternate history. Our ecclesiological construction needs to be something like the recent screenplays and films of Quentin Tarantino, such as *Inglourious Basterds*, *Django Unchained*, and *Once upon a Time in Hollywood*. All three movies are set in a firm historical moment. Yet all three play with an alternate history.[30] *Inglourious Basterds* is set in Nazi Europe, but the end of the film alters history by killing off the leading figures of the evil regime in a Parisian movie theater. In *Django Unchained* an alternate history is offered to American slavery. And *Once upon a Time in Hollywood* imagines an alternate history to the savage killing of Sharon Tate in 1969 by the Manson family. Like the Nazis and slave traders, the Manson family is thwarted, Tate is saved, and history is different.

29. See Willie James Jennings's essay "The Desire of the Church," in *The Community of the Word: Toward an Evangelical Ecclesiology*, ed. Mark Husbands and Daniel J. Treier (Downers Grove, IL: InterVarsity, 2005).
30. Officially, they're alternate histories more than true fantasy.

In homage to such storytelling, our second story offers an alternate history for Saint John the Baptist. We'll fantasize about what could have kept the congregation from losing life, shifting into zombie mode, and being extinguished for the sake of chicken wings and $3 happy hour draft beers. In its place, we will tell the story of the Saint John the Baptist that might have been.

2

Brother Trouble and Meeting the Exorcist's Son

The Beginning of Karl Barth

In our family we often remind our daughter Maisy that she's the only one of us who knows what it's like to have a brother. My wife Kara grew up with three sisters. I grew up with one sister. And Owen, our oldest, has Maisy. Only Maisy knows what it's like to have a brother.

Growing up, I always wished I had a brother. Watching my friends with brothers was always intoxicating. I couldn't take my eyes off them in those moments where a duality as old as Jacob and Esau burst to the surface. There is something about sisters too. I see it with Kara and her own sisters. It's a kind of closeness that leads to war. The brothers I watched growing up seemed to collide like immovable objects. Their violent emotional (and at times physical) tussles were equal parts loyalty and rivalry, companionship and competition, love and pure rage. I wanted that at fifteen. Such aggressive opposition mixed with devotion was bloody but beautiful to my adolescent mind. It's just something that seems less common between brothers and sisters.

Karl Barth was the oldest of five children born to Anna and Fritz Barth. Karl (or Karli, as they affectionately called him) was followed by two brothers.[1] And it appears that those boys fought like hell. Actually, we don't have much

---

1. Barth also had two sisters; one died in childhood.

documentation to prove it. But we do know that, as adults, Karl Barth and his brothers were never that close, often finding occasions to fight. We know that in childhood Karl was not an easy boy. He was trouble for his parents. He even organized a street gang in his Bern, Switzerland, neighborhood. The only thing that captured his imagination more than the troublemaking of gang life was confirmation (that last line will make any confirmation teacher take notice!). Barth's confirmation class led him to follow in the footsteps of his father.

The Backstory to Karl Barth and His Sibling Rivalry

Fritz and Anna hailed from Basel, Switzerland. Actually, they were products of Basel to their core. Major parts of the immanent frame's intellectual scaffolding were constructed in Basel. In the sixteenth century, for example, humanism was developed and distributed to all of Europe from Basel through the pen of Erasmus. In the late nineteenth century, Basel housed thinkers who made cases for the closed-world structure of modernity. Frans Overbeck made a frontal attack on religion. And Friedrich Nietzsche, a young and shy classical philologist at the University of Basel, would (eventually) herald the death of God. Overbeck and Nietzsche are two great examples of those setting the intellectual scaffolding for immanence.

Perhaps it's more accurate to say that Overbeck and Nietzsche inherited, described, and ultimately questioned the closed-world structure of the immanent frame (without retreating from it). Both recognized, almost to their horror, that the world was now closed and we must bear the uncomfortable hollowness. We must bear the fact that God is no more. But what meaning is left once the illusion of God and religion itself are gone? Both Overbeck and Nietzsche, in different ways, felt and described modernity's lifelessness and Christianity's vapid state in modernity. Both wondered whether—now that religion and God had been maimed by modernity, dying and disappearing, stripping us of the illusion of a great task—we were now without anything to live for at all.

Fritz Barth found himself taking classes taught by both Overbeck and Nietzsche. In Fritz's student days, Nietzsche was just a painfully shy young professor, not yet the antichrist raiding against the slave religion of Christianity and doubling down on immanence. Fritz's orthodoxy was unshaken. Like the father of Carl Jung, another great Basel intellectual of immanence, Fritz would pastor in Basel.

Eventually, Fritz was invited to Bern, the Swiss capital, to teach at a missionary school. The occasion of his father teaching pastors and missionaries would release the budding gangster Karl Barth into the streets of Bern. If it weren't for confirmation—and the teaching of Pastor Robert Aeschbacker[2]— Barth's name may have become more synonymous with Al Capone or John Gotti. (This, of course, is *not* quite true, but it's fun to think of a Scorsesean version of Karl Barth.)

Student Days

Confirmation made such an indelible impact on Karl Barth that he began studying theology. He quickly set his eyes on the University of Marburg. But Fritz forbade it because the ethos of Marburg, and its heavy commitment to neo-Kantianism, was not in line with Fritz's own theology.[3] A compromise was struck and Karl was off to Berlin. Freed from his father's house, he deeply breathed in the air of liberal Protestantism. Berlin, and Adolf von Harnack's contention that theology was now the history of doctrine, didn't break the fever for Marburg. Instead it spiked it.

After his year in Berlin, Barth spent a compromise year in Tubingen—a place where Fritz's brand of theology still existed. Finally, after this year in Tubingen, his father relented and Karl went to Marburg.[4] It seems many sons of Swiss conservative pastors were making their way to Marburg. They seemed drawn to the liberal ethos, a dramatic step away from the stiff theology of their fathers. There is a picture in Eberhard Busch's biography of Barth that shows a group of fifteen young men, wearing hats and holding canes, posing under a Swiss flag. Busch tells us it's a picture of the Swiss theological students at Marburg, taken in 1908.[5]

Friendship and a Crisis

One of those sons of a conservative Swiss pastor was Eduard Thurneysen. Thurneysen was from Basel, the place of Barth's birth and family heritage.

2. Eberhard Busch discusses Karl Barth's confirmation experience in *Karl Barth: His Life from Letters and Autobiographical Texts* (Philadelphia: Fortress, 1975), 30–32.

3. Marburg was home of the great Jewish philosopher Hermann Cohen, considered one of the great interpreters of Kant. While Cohen wasn't alone in his Kantian commitment at Marburg, he had a deep impact on the school. Karl Barth received a rich understanding of Kant, never departing from his divide of reason from revelation. In many ways, Barth's whole project is a response to this divide. Kant was a major force in constructing the immanent frame, and Marburg was committed not only to the system but to the ramifications of the Kantian project.

4. For more on Fritz Barth, see Bruce McCormack, *Karl Barth's Critically Realistic Dialectical Theology: Its Genesis and Development, 1909–1936* (Oxford: Oxford University Press, 1997), 36–38.

5. Busch, *Karl Barth*, 48.

Barth and Thurneysen eventually became the closest of friends, remaining so for the rest of their lives.[6] In Marburg they were just acquaintances. Nevertheless, they both waded deeply into the German liberal theology of Marburg. Their eventual friendship solidified when they both took pastorates in the Aargau region in Switzerland, just a bike ride away from one another. Their acquaintance turned into a lifelong friendship thanks to a crisis.

The crisis started personally for Barth. He had been installed as pastor in July 1911. "Like my father before me, I came to the Aargau as a pastor, to Safenwil, an agricultural and industrial community," Barth said.[7] Just six months later his father was dead, taken by blood poisoning. In his student days, Karl had revolted against his father and his seeming premodern theological commitments. Now Karl was back in Switzerland, following directly in his father's footsteps. Even with liberal theology pulsing through his veins, Karl may have been seeking peace and his father's approval. But now, just six months after Karl had followed the trail worn by his father's footsteps, Fritz was dead. The raised voices and desperate pleas for Marburg were now an empty echo, making the pain of his loss throb with regret. Karl had sought theology beyond his father, even in opposition to him. But with Fritz gone, the theology of a living God, which Karl had once resisted, now called. Barth acknowledged that the death of his father and the direct tasks of the pastorate were the first pressures that brought a significant fracture to his commitment to liberal theology.[8]

Before coming to Safenwil, Barth had spent a year as an intern in Geneva. He had decided against a PhD and chose instead to preach from Calvin's

6. Busch does not mention whether Thurneysen was in the picture described earlier. One would assume he was not. It would be a whole different argument to explore the necessity and importance of friendship for theologians like Barth and Bonhoeffer. Both of these epoch-making theologians had a very close relationship with a friend who served as a sounding board, anchor, and support as each carved out their theology in a changing context. Bonhoeffer's close friend was Eberhard Bethge. Bonhoeffer and Bethge were so close that some—mainly Charles Marsh in *Strange Glory*—have stated that this relationship was romantic. Bethge, a married man, said on record it was not (and we have no direct evidence indicating otherwise). But it is of little regard whether the relationship was romantic. More interesting is that the theological work Barth and Bonhoeffer were doing was lonely, and therefore it necessitated a close, loyal, and even intimate friendship. No one has ever made an assertion about a romantic relationship between Barth and Thurneysen, mainly because the role of intimate companion in the process of theological thinking was already filled for Barth by Charlotte von Kirschbaum, his secretary (and intellectual equal—although it's also important to mention that his wife, Nelly, was no dim bulb; it is well documented that he leaned heavily on her in writing *Römerbrief I*; she had a significant handle on Greek—far better than his).

7. "Autobiographical Texts I," in *Fakultätsalbum der Evangelisch-theologischen Fakultät Münster* (1927), quoted by Busch, *Karl Barth*, 60.

8. See Busch, *Karl Barth*, 68.

pulpit. He wielded his modern liberal theology that year from the famous Reformer's raised lectern. Barth doubled down on the divide between reason and revelation, giving his people a theology for an immanent frame without an acting God. None of it seemed to land for the congregation. These dogmatics worked in Marburg, but not in practical congregational life. But that didn't matter, because the theology was solid. The young pastor was able to hide from the people's longing behind the seawall of his theology.

Yet, now in Safenwil, to truly follow his father's footsteps would require more than just preparing sermons that made the whitebeards at Marburg nod in approval. Barth had to be a pastor connected to the life of his people. He could no longer just exposit university theology from the pulpit, judging his sermons by their faithfulness to the hermeneutics of liberal theology. He was *their* pastor now. His sermons and pastoral acts needed to meet people directly in their lives. Barth's congregation's concerns and yearnings added pressure to the cracked ice of the modern liberal theology he'd been taught. Barth says, "My position in the community [as a pastor] led me to be involved in socialism, and especially in the trade union movement."[9]

By spring of 1912, Fritz was dead and Karl, in seeking to be a faithful pastor like his father, was active in the socialist movement fighting for workers' rights. On June 1, Thurneysen—whose father had been friends with Karl's father— was installed as pastor of Leutwil. The two pastors had known each other in their student days but could not yet be called friends. Barth walked over to be present at Thurneysen's installation. Walking, or bike riding, between Safenwil and Leutwil became common for Barth. The conversations between them became the beginning notes of a different kind of modern theological vision. It would become a modern theological vision that sought a way to return to revelation rather than extinguish it as the dead relic of a past age.

Thurneysen offered much to Barth personally and intellectually, but perhaps his greatest gift to Barth was his contacts. Thurneysen's connections far outstripped Barth's.[10] As the two young pastors discussed socialism and sermons, Thurneysen introduced Barth to Hermann Kutter. Thurneysen saw Kutter as a paradigm for the kind of pastor he wished to be. Kutter's sermons, children's classes, and involvement in Social Democracy were inspiring to the young pastors. Kutter proved to be much different from their German teachers. Attending to the pastoral task led Kutter into action, catalyzed by

9. "Nachwort," in *Schleiermacher-Auswahl* (Siebenstern Taschenbuch, 1960), 292, quoted by Busch, *Karl Barth*, 69.

10. Barth talks about the importance of Thurneysen for the development of his thinking. See Barth and Thurneysen, *Revolutionary Theology in the Making*, trans. James D. Smart (Richmond: John Knox, 1964), 72.

a God who spoke and moved in history. Barth says about him, "From Kutter I simply learnt to speak the great word 'God' seriously, responsibly and with a sense of its importance."[11] To speak the great word "God." The immanent frame, and modernity itself, made such speech more difficult. Both reason and romanticism sought meaning and purpose beyond the language of a living God. Barth himself had wanted to move beyond such talk when he fought Fritz to go to Marburg. But as a pastor, now knee-deep in ministry to actual people, he wondered whether speaking this word "God" was just what the circumstances called for. But the question became, How can we speak this word "God" inside modernity, and not naively against it? Marburg had convinced both Barth and Thurneysen that modernity and its framework (its immanent frame) could not simply be ignored or guilelessly opposed.

For the next few years Barth and Thurneysen talked about, imagined, and wrestled with what it meant to be a pastor. They visited Kutter, and Kutter visited them. Both Barth and Thurneysen wanted to be pastors like Kutter, inspired again to take the word "God" seriously.

But how could they synthesize "taking God seriously" with the liberal theology they'd been taught? It was one thing to take God seriously; it was a completely other thing to imagine that this God of the Bible could act in the modern world. Could a world that had constructed an immanent frame, lodging it so deeply in our imagination, really take God seriously and with a sense of importance?

Barth knew that beating his chest about the seriousness and importance of God—as American fundamentalists were doing—was no way forward. He wasn't interested in being anything but a modern pastor with a modern theology. Barth knew that wishing for the demise of modernity, seeking a theology outside modernity, was also no way forward. This was especially true if he was going to truly minister to his people living inside the modern immanent frame. To do theology outside modernity would only lead to a hatred of modernity, while ironically completely investing in modernity. To try and say the word "God" again by hating modernity, despising its immanent frame, would only create untenable contradictions (which has been the unfortunate legacy of American evangelicalism since the modernist–fundamentalist split).[12]

11. "Nachwort," 293, quoted by Busch, *Karl Barth*, 76.
12. We should remember that the liberal (or modernist) objectives have been just as bankrupt—or, better, defeatist—as the contradictions of fundamentalists/evangelicals. The latter have sought to return to something before modernity, hating modernity while investing in modernity to win over modernity. Liberal theology has accepted modernity to such a degree that it has struggled even to talk of God. Unlike Kutter, it has not taken God seriously and instead entered

The conundrum for Barth was that modernity needed to be taken seriously. The only theologies that took modernity seriously no longer took God seriously—at uttering the word "God" they became mute at best, dismissive at worst. As a pastor in Safenwil, observing people's struggles in mines and factories, he simply could not abide this second option. The closer Pastor Barth got to his people, the more they wanted him—needed him—to speak to them about God. They needed their pastor to say this great word "God." Inside the immanent frame, there is a sneaky temptation for the pastor. She is often tempted, and somehow invisibly formed, to take God less seriously than her people do. The pastor can feel embarrassed to say the great word "God" or to even see the word "God" as a great word. Inside the invisible immanent frame, the word "God" feels meaningless, even immature. The pastor feels the temptation to run the congregation as a small business, even a little self-conscious of all the enchantment and dogma. But her people, who more directly bear the contradictions of modernity, and at times spit out the dry sawdust of the immanent frame, yearn to know that God has a purpose for their lives. They yearn to know that God can still speak. Secretly, and maybe with a little shame, the pastor finds herself doubting this, wanting at least one foot to rest squarely inside modernity, fearing she'll be overtaken by superstition. The moral vision of immanence becomes more tempting for her than for her people.

The Fracture and the Great War

The utopian visions of modernity's progress began to unravel on August 1, 1914, and with violence never seen before. With Kaiser Wilhelm II's declaration and the commencement of the Great War, the inhuman elements of the immanent frame—the dehumanizing parts of reason and its industrial logic—were exposed. No straight line could be drawn between reason and peace. There was no truth to the assumption that an immanent frame would de facto release us from using transcendence, and our God's wishes, as a justification for war.[13]

For Pastor Karl Barth, even more was exposed. Following the declaration of war, ninety-three German intellectuals published a memorandum in full support of the kaiser's war policy. To Barth's shock, almost *all* of his German

---

into social engagement. To win ground in social engagement it has given up on God-talk. For an interesting discussion on this mutual bankruptcy and dual idolatry toward political imaginations, see Nathan Hatch, "The Political Captivity of the Faithful," *Comment*, February 13, 2020, https://www.cardus.ca/comment/article/the-political-captivity-of-the-faithful.

13. William Cavanaugh has explored this misguided assumption—which is still with us—in *The Myth of Religious Violence* (London: Oxford University Press, 2009).

teachers signed their names to the memorandum.[14] There they were! The names of the very teachers Barth had begged to learn from. Years earlier, he had argued furiously with his now-deceased father, passionately claiming that these theologians, who now reveled in war, held the theological truth for a modern age. Their kind of modern theology, which moved beyond speaking the Word of the living God, was the answer.

Barth now knew—as his father had known long before—this was not the case. The practice of ministry had assured Barth that indeed a wholly other theology,[15] a very different kind of modern theology from that of his teachers, was needed. The concrete lives of those he pastored, not the academic holes in his former teachers' systems, had convinced him something was wrong with liberal Protestantism. Liberal theology was no help to workers, farmers, and families across Europe.

Immediately after the declaration, Safenwil citizens, members of Barth's congregation, were called to guard the frontier. Busch adds that "Barth helped farming families for weeks on end with haymaking."[16] For months, in *every* sermon, Barth spouted righteous indignation against the war. Barth says, "I felt obligated to let the war rage through all my sermons, until finally a woman came up to me and asked me for once to talk about something else."[17] Cultural criticism, even for those so diabolically affected, couldn't nourish his people. Yet, to Barth's dismay, nor could movement politics. Following Kutter, Barth had entered the socialist movement, joining the Social Democratic Party. He had believed that the socialist movement could do what liberal theology had denied: participate in bringing the kingdom of God to earth. Kutter taught Barth to speak the name of God again, resurrecting the belief in a living God even in modernity. Following these socialist movements—in Switzerland and Germany—Barth believed he had found the answer. The way God moves inside the immanent frame is not necessarily through the spirit or *Geist* of history, as his Ritschlian teachers had taught him, but through the movement politics of socialism (Barth would eventually see that all such human constructs, political or historical, would need to come under the judgment of God).

But now the war revealed, to Barth's despair, that socialism could not be the answer.[18] "For Barth the outbreak of the World War was 'a double

14. See Gordon Craig, *Germany, 1866–1945* (New York: Oxford University Press, 1978), 361–64.
15. It was actually Thurneysen who uttered these words about needing a "wholly other" theology. For Barth it became the seeds of his wholly different modern theology that had its very starting and ending point in claiming God's own wholly otherness.
16. Busch, *Karl Barth*, 81.
17. *Homiletik* (1966), 98, quoted by Busch, *Karl Barth*, 81.
18. Although Barth came to this realization, he did remain a loyal party member his whole life, even joining the party in January 1915 after this realization. Barth held that socialism was

madness,' involving not only his theological teachers but also European socialism."[19] Barth said, "We had . . . expected that socialism would prove to be a kind of hammer of God, yet all along the national war fronts we saw it swinging into line. . . . Many of us were completely flabbergasted. Our bold criticism began to recoil on us."[20] Neither the criticism of the theology coming from his theological teachers nor the criticism of societal structures coming from movement politics could stand up against the negative forces of modernity.

Back to Brother Conflict

With Europe in a bloody tussle, we return to the sibling rivalry and conflict of the brothers Barth. For nearly a year after the start of the war, Barth stood in front of his congregation trying to preach. He wondered how he could do this, standing in the rubble of the dual failures of liberal theology and socialist movement politics. The call of ministry kept him from conceding to or retreating from one or the other of these failed perspectives. Barth was brave enough to *not* try to resist one or the other. Yet pastoral ministry demanded he find something to say to the practical, concrete lives of his congregants. Being a pastor, he needed some way forward. Barth knew, as news came of his brother's coming wedding, that he was in need of a much different starting point. But where that point might be, he was unsure.

Carrying this confusion, Barth returned to the scene where he had grasped with both hands the liberal theology that now melted between his fingers like hot wax. Karl made his way back to Marburg for the wedding of his middle brother Peter.

Peter was marrying Helene Rade. Seeking both rivalry and companionship, his younger brother Peter had followed Karl's footsteps to Marburg for his own student years. Karl had been the blunt object that won passage for both of Karl's brothers, Peter and Heinrich, to matriculate at Marburg. Peter one-upped his older brother by falling in love with a woman of Marburg theological royalty. Helene was the daughter of the famous theologian Martin Rade. When Barth had earlier traced his finger down the page of the memorandum supporting the war, looking for the names of his teachers, he had found Adolf von Harnack and his favorite teacher, Wilhelm Herrmann. But he had noticed one name conspicuously missing—Martin Rade. Karl had

---

still the best political system (and the most faithful to Christian teaching), but he would not and could not confuse it for God's action.

19. Busch, *Karl Barth*, 82.

20. "Lebenslauf," in *Schweizer Köpfe* (1945), 4, quoted by Busch, *Karl Barth*, 82.

no hesitation, then, in traveling into wartime Germany to celebrate with his brother and the Rade family.

Karl had grown close to Professor Rade in his student days, remaining in contact with him as he returned to Switzerland. But now Peter would be Rade's son-in-law. Peter seemed to always play the middle child. A Calvin scholar, he had much in common with his older brother but nevertheless found reasons to quarrel with him. If Karl was Greg Brady, always in charge and demanding, then Peter was, well, Peter Brady. Generally he was loyal to his older brother and of good spirits, never seeking conflict. Yet at times he could be unrelenting in his opposition to his older brother's strong will. It was the youngest brother, Heinrich, who more directly affected Karl's thinking. Heinrich never tired of wrestling with his oldest brother. Heinrich, too, found himself at Marburg, but to study philosophy. When Karl rewrote his *Epistle to the Romans (Römerbrief II)*, it was Heinrich's tutoring in Plato that helped him more clearly make his argument (more on this later). But it seems this help would forever be held over his head.[21]

I'm sure the speeches at the wedding reception proved interesting. Here was Peter outdoing his older brother by marrying Marburg royalty. Karl did not even take his own wife with him to the wedding in Marburg, choosing Thurneysen instead as his travel partner.[22] The youngest brother Heinrich stood next to his older brothers. While the oldest had chosen not to get a PhD and the middle had pursued a PhD and studied Calvin, the youngest considered himself the true intellectual, doing what his older brothers could not: study philosophy. This tension and competition never left the Barth brothers.

Karl may have been "just a pastor" in his brothers' eyes, but he was nearing an epic insight. Rubbing shoulders again with those in Marburg—and butting heads with his brothers—pushed him further toward finding this new starting point. Little did he know, as he toasted Peter and Helene at the night's close on April 9, that he was about to find it.

Meeting the Younger

On the morning of April 10, Barth and Thurneysen left Marburg for the town of Bad Boll. It's not easy to explain Bad Boll. It sits in the southern part of Germany, in the Württemberg region. In the late nineteenth century

---

21. Bruce McCormack also interprets this relationship as tense. See McCormack, *Karl Barth's Critically Realistic Dialectical Theology*, 222–25.

22. This may say less about the state of Barth's marriage than about the fact that it was wartime in Germany. But it's hard to ignore this detail, knowing that Barth's marriage had more than a little peculiarity to it.

Württemberg witnessed a kind of revival brought about by an exorcism (yes, you read that correctly).

A young Lutheran pastor named Johann Blumhardt was struggling along in his pastoral duties in Möttlingen, a village in Württemberg. Nineteenth-century liberal theology was sweeping through German churches. Blumhardt, a pietist, was no Schleiermacherian liberal. Blumhardt had previously taught in a mission school in Fritz Barth's fair Basel. Now back in the parish, Blumhardt was plodding along when a young woman began manifesting the strangest of behaviors. She saw figures in the room and started speaking in voices not her own. Though a pietist, Blumhardt was unashamedly modern, living squarely in the immanent frame that has little room for (and can make less sense of) such realities. When strange behaviors occur, the immanent frame asserts they are psychological or medical. Period. No need to look further. Science—not spirituality—must make sense of them. So Johann Blumhardt tried every doctor and medicine he could to help the young woman. But none of it worked. Only prayer and the name of Jesus brought her relief and eventually healing—and all in a very *Poltergeist*-y way. (I'll share this story and its ramifications in chap. 15.)

When word of this spread, it was like a midsummer downpour on land parched by the beating sun of immanence. People began traveling to Möttlingen, seeking prayer and healing. It was an experience of the New Testament come to modernity. The demands for this new ministry were soon too much for the Möttlingen congregation. When a spa became available in Bad Boll, Johann Blumhardt made it the new locale of his healing ministry. People from across Europe came for prayer and rest. For those with pietist leanings it became a kind of retreat center, a famous place to visit.

Karl Barth had been there before during his student days, but never with Thurneysen.[23] Thurneysen, with his deep contacts, got them a room and an

---

23. Christian Collins Winn adds some detail: "Anecdotal evidence abounds that Barth had encountered many of the rudimentary elements of the Blumhardts' thought prior to 1915. Karl's father Fritz Barth was one of the last students of the . . . theologian Johannes Tobias Beck (1804–1878), who had been a classmate of Johann Christoph Blumhardt and would later be Christoph Blumhardt's most important theological influence, outside of his father, while studying at Tubingen. . . . Aside from Fritz Barth, Karl also mentions that his mother's sister, Elizabeth (Aunt 'Bethi') made a deep impression on him. Barth noted that, 'She often went to stay in Bad Boll, and especially as a result of meeting Pastor Blumhardt, she increasingly developed an eye for signs of the coming of the kingdom of God." *"Jesus Is Victor!": The Significance of the Blumhardts for the Theology of Karl Barth* (Eugene, OR: Pickwick, 2009), 159–60. Collins Winn continues, "During the winter semester 1907 to 1908, while a theological student at the University of Tubingen, Barth visited Bad Boll on three separate occasions, having the opportunity to meet Christoph Blumhardt at least once. In his autobiographical reflections, Barth notes that his 'eyes were not fully open,' during this first encounter" (160).

audience with Christoph Blumhardt. Johann Blumhardt (or, as Barth often calls him, "the Elder") had led the exorcism of the young woman and moved the ministry to Bad Boll. His son, Christoph ("the Younger"), followed his father, overseeing the ministry at Bad Boll after his father's death.

Christoph was no weak imitation of his father. He possessed his own unique genius. He was loyal to, and indeed continued, his father's ministry. But he also pushed things in a new direction. As Barth and Thurneysen spent those five days in April with Christoph, his unique voice was evident. They heard his homilies and had many occasions to sit personally with him in conversation. These conversations provided Barth with the starting point he'd been seeking.

The New Starting Point

During those April days, Barth and Blumhardt the Younger may have seen something of themselves in each other's eyes. The Younger, like Barth, had just lived through the double madness of the Spirit of August 1914 and the first months of the war.[24] The Elder's mission was to release people from spiritual bondage. The Younger continued this, but he saw that the spiritual bondage grasping people manifested itself in the oppressive structures of society. As with Barth, ministering to people led the Younger into the Social Democratic Party.[25] Going far beyond Barth, the Younger became an elected deputy in the party.

The Younger moved in this direction for pastoral and theological purposes. He'd experienced the Protestant churches, in both their liberal and pietist forms, as idolatrous. These pastors and theologians were more concerned with their own survival than with encountering the living God. But now with the Great War, the Younger recognized that the Social Democratic party too sought its own party's survival over the humanity of its neighbors. In the years before the war, the Younger, like an early social-media-adopting pastor in 2009, spoke of the grand possibility of socialism for church and faith, only to recognize just a few short years later that socialism had its shortcomings (the same realization as that of the social media pastor in 2018). The Younger Blumhardt naively entered the party believing it was a new thing that would

24. For more on the Spirit of August and how and why the German church embraced it, see Philip Jenkins, *The Great and Holy War: How World War I Became a Religious Crusade* (San Francisco: HarperOne, 2014), 72–78.

25. For a helpful overview of socialism in Germany in the nineteenth century, see Robert Wuthnow, *Communities of Discourse: Ideology and Social Structure in the Reformation, the Enlightenment, and European Socialism* (Cambridge, MA: Harvard University Press, 1989), chap. 12.

deliver a good life, drawing society nearer to the kingdom of God. Yet, like Barth in the war years, the Younger experienced only the excruciating double failure of both the church and the political party.

Sharing the burden of this double madness and the failures it produced gave Barth eyes to see something rich in Blumhardt the Younger's homiletical thoughts. Unlike all of Barth's teachers in Marburg, the Younger was clearly no academic theologian. He was unashamedly a pastor. Barth now had two models of pastors who seemed to outstrip his academic teachers—Hermann Kutter and Christoph Blumhardt.

As Barth and the Younger talked, Barth recognized a rich theological vision that had the potential to indeed say something to modernity. Blumhardt the Younger was sowing seeds in Barth that would eventually grow into a thick forest of a completely different modern theology than had been found in the German-speaking world. Kutter was important to Barth as a congregational pastor by encouraging Barth to again speak the word "God." But through conversations with the Younger in Bad Boll, Barth was beginning to see how to do so. Barth began to see that it could be done even inside the immanent frame, opening the immanent frame to the possibility of encounter with the divine.

Karl Barth had journeyed to his brother Peter's wedding knowing he needed a wholly other modern theology, one that could speak again the great word "God." But he had few examples of anyone doing so. Now here was Christoph Blumhardt, who though standing squarely in modernity, began and ended every discussion with God. He talked of this God not as an idea but as an actuality, as one who acts even in the immanent frame of modernity. The Younger spoke again and again of an acting God. His father's experience in Möttlingen was an empirical, concrete case of this actuality. The Younger had seen this act himself and was part of the event of God's arriving, time and again, in Bad Boll.

Eberhard Busch tells us that when Karl returned home from Peter's wedding and his days in Bad Boll, he devoured Friedrich Zündel's book on Johann Blumhardt the Elder and his Möttlingen experience.[26] Zündel's book is a kind of journalistic report, with interviews and investigation, mixed with an ethnography of what had happened in Möttlingen.[27] Barth's fascination with

---

26. Busch, *Karl Barth*, 85.

27. See Friedrich Zündel, *The Awakening* (Rifton, NY: Plough, 2000). Zündel was the godfather of Emil Brunner. It's interesting that these sons of conservative pietist fathers are the ones who broke from liberalism and found a uniquely new theological position. Simeon Zahl offers this tidbit: "Emil Brunner was the godson of Friedrich Zündel, author of the well-known biography of the elder Blumhardt, and close friend to both Johann Christoph and

the Elder's pastoral experience would never leave him. He constantly returned to it throughout his career (even giving the Elder a chapter in his book on the great nineteenth-century theologians).[28] The reason for this continued interest, I believe, is that Blumhardt the Elder's ministry became the concrete case for Barth that indeed the God of the Bible could act—and does act!—even inside modernity. The Elder's pastoral experience was sure testimony that even in modernity and its immanent frame, the acting God could *not* be shut out. The Elder's ministry revealed that modern liberal theology was misguided in seeing the immanent frame as closed to transcendence.

The dogmatic theology that followed from Karl Barth's pen would always rest, I believe, on the pastoral experience of the Elder and the organic pastoral theology of the Younger Blumhardt.[29] In thought and life, the Blumhardts assured Barth that the God who acts in the Bible can still act in a modern world. But the Younger Blumhardt did more. He not only modeled to Barth what it looked like to take Kutter's advice and utter again the word "God," unwaveringly remembering that *God is God*; he also gave Barth hints on how to do this.

Barth recognized that the Younger spoke the word "God," contending that God acts in modernity by holding together seeming opposites.[30] "Blumhardt combined an active and eager search for signs and 'breakthroughs' of the kingdom of God with a tranquil, patient 'waiting' on God, and the decisive action which [God] alone could perform."[31] Barth began to see this tension as productive, as a possible way forward. Having witnessed the failures of the Social Democratic Party, the Younger recognized that waiting, as much as

---

Christoph." Zahl, *Pneumatology and Theology of the Cross in the Preaching of Christoph Friedrich Blumhardt: The Holy Spirit between Wittenberg and Azusa Street* (London: T&T Clark, 2010), 135.

28. See Barth, *Protestant Theology in the Nineteenth Century* (Grand Rapids: Eerdmans, 2002), chap. 28.

29. That is, Barth's theology is essentially dogmatic theology inside pastoral theology. Barth himself saw his theology as a theology for pastors—not for the academic guild but for those like the Blumhardts. I wonder if there is a missing school of Barth interpretation that has recognized in Barth this deep pastoral DNA. Thinkers who may have seen this are the likes of Andrew Purves and Ray S. Anderson. As far as I can tell, Anderson, particularly, never seems to quote the Blumhardts and never comes close to drawing out this genealogical connection between the Blumhardts and Barth. But Anderson still sees more clearly than most the pastoral depth in Barth's project. I believe that Anderson is picking up on the Blumhardtian DNA in the genome of Barth's project. I hope this project draws out the pastoral focus in Barth's thought.

30. Barth says, "Blumhardt always begins with God's presence, power, and purpose. He starts out from God. He does not begin by climbing upwards to him by means of contemplation and deliberation." Barth, afterword to *Action in Waiting*, by Christoph Blumhardt (Farmington, PA: Plough, 1998), 219.

31. Busch, *Karl Barth*, 85.

doing, was needed. Waiting and doing needed to be held in tension, a dialectic. Opposites in tension—Barth saw this as the direct way that the Younger spoke from start to end about God. Inside the opposites he could not only speak of God in modernity but also recognize God's direct action in the immanent frame.[32] As Busch says, these productive opposites in tension stretched even deeper for the Younger Blumhardt, affecting Barth. Busch says, "Even more important was the fundamental connection in Blumhardt's thought between knowledge of God and the Christian hope for the future; through this [Barth] learnt to understand God afresh as the radical renewer of the world who is at the same time himself completely and utterly new."[33]

Seeking and *waiting*, *hoping* and *suffering*, and recognizing God's *attainability in the world* and *complete otherness from the world*: these tensions (let's call them dialectics) that rested so deeply in the pastoral vision and wisdom of Christoph Blumhardt would become, as Busch says, "the starting point for [Barth's] further development."[34]

Into an Alternate History

Luther was once asked, "What would you do if you knew tomorrow was the end of the world?" Luther, who was prone to an anxiety that could quickly shift into a debilitating depression, responded assuredly and joyfully, "Plant a tree."[35]

It's an odd response. If you knew the world was ending, all of it melting away in twenty-four hours, the clock ticking away, you'd carefully prepare soil? You'd take a small seed that would take days to germinate, weeks to break the soil, years to grow a thick trunk, and decades to be strong enough to climb, to shelter in its branches, and to eat its fruit? You'd plant a tree? Really, you weirdo?

Luckily, this is a hypothetical question. But what if we shifted it slightly by asking, "What would you do if you knew tomorrow was the end of your . . . church?"

32. I believe that the Younger played an important practical role in moving Barth in this direction. But Barth would find the more intellectual depth of this dialectical approach in the Reformers, particularly Luther. The Younger was returning to Luther's *theologia crucis*, and through the Younger and then far beyond him, Barth was returning to the Reformers and Luther's *theologia crucis* as a way of speaking of and seeing God's activity inside modernity.

33. Busch, *Karl Barth*, 85.

34. Busch, *Karl Barth*, 85.

35. It is debated whether Luther said this. For instance, Martin Schloemann, *Luthers Apfelbäumchen? Ein Kapitel deutscher Mentalitätsgeschichte seit dem Zweiten Weltkrieg* (Göttingen: Vandenhoeck & Ruprecht, 1994), 246–51, argues that he did not. But it is often quoted as one of Luther's most famous sayings.

3

A Funeral for a Church— a Funeral That Remakes a Church

December 24, 2018, was the end for Saint John the Baptist. The church disappeared with hardly a whimper. No one seemed to care. The life had so completely left the congregation that there was nothing to do other than walk away. The closure had somehow already been sealed. There was no reason for a cessation ceremony, no sense that the space itself needed to be deconsecrated. Everyone forgot (or didn't care to remember) all those who had lived and died in that space. The keys were unceremoniously handed over to the new corporate owner.

This is where we step into our alternate history. Let's rewind a bit to explore an ecclesiology for the immanent frame by going Quentin Tarantino—but without the blood and profanity. This is the story of the Saint John the Baptist that might have been.

The Way It Could Have Gone

It was late summer 2011. Adele's song "Rolling in the Deep" could be heard everywhere. It leaked from every cafe and shop in the neighborhood. Just months earlier, Michael Scott had sadly left *The Office* and Ned Stark had shockingly lost his head in the season one finale of *Game of Thrones*. Obama's reelection campaign was gearing up. The cultural divides, which would become a gorge, were already obvious. The economic recovery had been set in motion, but most people still bore the deep bruises of the sharp 2008 downturn.

Saint John the Baptist had just lost its pastor. Without much warning, Luke Evans had announced his departure. Pastor Luke had worked hard to revitalize the congregation, or rather to forge a new congregation inside the old one. When he arrived in 2008 he saw the church as a diamond in the rough. What better place for a church plant than a newly gentrified neighborhood filled with young adults? Though this *was not* a church plant, Luke treated it as such. He rebranded everything, even renaming the Sunday worship gathering, calling it "Thrive."

Treating an established congregation as a shell for a church plant is never easy (or wise). Conflict and tension started immediately. But the fear of further decline, and an awareness that the neighborhood had indeed changed, led the personnel committee to hire Luke and led most of the rest of the congregation to give him a shot. They had to admit he exuded energy. Luke was always ready to act. To listen, not so much.

Things were not easy, and Luke was hard to follow. Yet the majority of the congregation supported him. Luke's promise of exponential growth had not yet come to fruition, but no one could doubt that he was grinding. So it came as a shock when he announced in early May of his third year that he would be leaving by June 1. It was a punch in the congregational solar plexus. They all felt as if they were role players in Luke's game. And now Luke was taking his ball and going home.

Luke announced his departure with little concern for what Saint John the Baptist would do without a pastor. They felt jilted and rudderless. Though not well loved, Luke did scratch an itch that many in the congregation shared. He wanted the congregation to survive, even return to its golden era. Most were willing to do all sorts of things to get to this end—even allowing the church to be called Thrive.

But now Luke had abandoned them for another church, taking a position as teaching pastor at a nondenominational megachurch across town. In his introduction interview (which appeared on the megachurch's blog—remember this is 2011), Luke stated that he left Thrive and Saint John the Baptist because of his conscience. He just couldn't pastor a church in a denomination that had turned so hard left. He wanted to return to a denomination that cared about the Bible. Luke never mentioned these concerns to anyone at Saint John the Baptist. Reading them now stung.

———

By June the congregation opened a search for a new pastor. It would be months before this new pastor, whomever he or she would be, would arrive. The only option was for the elders to lead the congregation through the summer and early fall. All of Luke's flashy branding and hip programming soon disappeared. The congregation could only manage a simple worship service, an all-generations Sunday school class, and a midweek Bible study. The brew group, knitting night, and slide-filled sermons were all casualties of Luke's departure.

The silver lining in this painful summer of transition was that a few of the older members, who had quietly disappeared during Luke's tenure, returned. One was eighty-five-year-old Jean. As a young woman, Jean had given money for the stained glass, working extra hours at the factory. She was one of the last living souls who had placed those beautiful panels of remembrance on the church walls. She had lost her husband, her high school sweetheart, in France. When she was pregnant, he left for the war, never to return. Saint John the Baptist saw her through. The church helped with her newborn while she worked. Out of gratitude and grief she gave what to her was a significant amount to have her Harry placed in the stained glass and remembered. Now, in June 2011, she was back, sitting in the third row, straight across from Harry's panel. An oxygen tube connected her to a metal canister. Through June and July she came every week, even attending the midweek Bible study.

One Wednesday night in early August, she told the Bible study, in a matter-of-fact way and to their surprise, that hospice would be coming to her house that week. She revealed that she had been battling lung cancer for over a year. It was now the end.

She grieved that she'd be leaving her house more than she grieved her impending death. She had lived there over seventy years. She never could have imagined what would become of the neighborhood or of her home value. She'd been in the neighborhood long enough to watch housing prices bottom out in the late 1980s and now skyrocket. She could sell and turn what had been a $5,000 investment in 1940 into a $550,000 return in 2011 (it would have been closer to $700,000 in 2007).

Yet, she told the Bible study, she had decided against this. Instead, she'd chosen to pass the house along to her youngest grandson, Philip. He'd bounced between colleges and dead-end jobs, and at one point even found himself with some drug troubles. Philip was always full of ideas but short on follow-through. Philip had convinced Jean to allow him to move in with her. Jean had imagined that she would be taking care of him. Even at twenty-four, he seemed to be a child in need of care.

But Jean's cancer diagnosis changed everything, and radically so. Something flipped in Philip. Philip was now taking care of his grandma, driving her to appointments, overseeing her medication, calling doctors. Jean told the Bible study that sometimes she even thanked God for the cancer, because it gave Philip a purpose and produced a bond between them as strong as Jean had ever known. She told the Bible study, "I haven't felt this cared for by someone since Harry left and never returned from the war."

Philip was exactly the kind of young adult Luke was trying to reach but never could. Philip pieced together two half-time jobs: fifteen hours a week in the bike shop and another fifteen to twenty hours a week in a neighborhood coffee shop. But Philip's true passion was trivia. Teddy's Tacos had a Tuesday night trivia contest with half-off tacos. Philip never missed and never failed to help his team place, winning free drinks and free tacos. Most weeks, particularly after the cancer diagnosis, Jean could be spotted at Philip's side, surrounded by young adults huddled for answers, Jean a happy onlooker as Philip's team debated how many number one hits were on Michael Jackson's *Thriller* album. Jean even participated once in a while. She was the trivia team's go-to for 1930s and 1940s movies. She knew all the actors. "I love those pictures," she told the Bible study.

In the decade before Philip arrived, Jean had been slowly fading away—disappearing, forgotten, and overlooked by her neighborhood and congregation. She was dying before she was dying, losing life, searching for a reason to live. But now that she was truly dying, the cancer eating the life out of her, she came alive. With Philip at her side she became the queen of trivia night. Philip called Grandma Jean their good luck charm. The two of them could be spotted walking home arm-in-arm from trivia night, tippy on tacos, as dusk fell.

———

As the summer slid into the dog days of late August, it was over. First her seat was empty on Sunday. Then she was absent on Wednesday night. Finally, Jean's son called Bert with the news that Jean had died. A funeral needed to be planned.

Bert was a fifty-five-year-old African American man. He ran a successful law firm in the neighborhood and had been a member of Saint John the Baptist since he was a child. His parents had moved into the neighborhood in the mid-1960s. As an ordained lay leader and the chair of the church council, Bert took on most of the pastoral duties after Luke's departure. Having been a child during the civil rights movement, Bert always felt drawn toward ministry, the role of the pastor important to him. But in the end, law seemed the better route in doing his part.

Now, at this late stage in his career, he found himself stepping into pastoral ministry after all—even if just for the short term. Bert had always considered his lay leadership to be ministry. He led the church's Stephen Ministry (a lay care-giving ministry) for years, taught confirmation, and signed up for a number of ministry conferences at the local seminary. He was kind of a pastoral ministry aficionado, a bit of a church junkie. For decades he even sat on the local seminary's board, loving those long meetings. But things were different this summer. Bert did most of the preaching and pastoral care. There were just too many Sundays to fill with pulpit supply.

Bert jumped in with a nervous excitement. The pulpit was a holy place for him, and he did not take his responsibility for the summer lightly. To prepare, Bert took an intensive online seminary course on preaching. He also joined a local pastors text study group. But funerals were beyond his self-study, so another pastor from across town was asked to officiate.

It was a moving funeral. Bert felt the heaviness as he realized Jean was one of the last of the ladies from the generation who gave the church the stained glass. Nevertheless, the funeral had the feeling of a somber celebration. Luke's departure gave the congregation another opportunity to know Jean. They were able to grieve and bury her in the knowledge that her final years had been full. Her final months were a return, like the prodigal, to the congregation that sat at the center of her life story.

After nearly everyone had departed from the simple gathering of coffee and cold cuts after the funeral, Bert got to tidying. There were still a few people talking and milling around. But it seemed more than appropriate for Bert to move some chairs and put the leftovers in the refrigerator. It'd been a long day for Bert. He hadn't officiated the funeral, but he had prepared the building, done the welcome, and read Scripture. Just a few more tasks and he'd go home to his recliner.

With the last table wiped, Bert briskly began shutting off the lights. As he flicked off the lights in the narthex, he glanced into the sanctuary. That's when he saw him. A young man stood in the aisle at the front row looking up at the stained glass. He was tall, maybe six-foot-three, wearing khakis that seemed too small and a dress shirt that was too big. Bert was sure the outfit was borrowed. The shirt was so big it wouldn't stay tucked in. His hair was shoulder length and his beard red and unkempt. His askew tie was breaking hard right as if it were trying to escape the whole scene. Clearly none of this was his usual attire.

"Hi there," Bert said as he approached, breaking into the young man's moment of solitude.

"Oh—hi," returned the young man. His face was painted with sadness, even as he smiled a cheerful return to Bert's greeting. "I'm Woz," he said with his hand extended.

"Nice to meet you," Bert said as they shook hands.

They stood together in silence for a few seconds that felt like more. Bert decided for some reason that silence was the appropriate response.

Finally Woz, looking at the stained glass and altar, said, "I can't believe she's gone. It's hard for me to face. You know what I mean?"

Bert understood, but he wasn't sure about the context of this statement. More silence met them.

Finally it clicked for Bert. "Wait, are you Philip? Are you Jean's grandson?"

"Yeah . . . sorry," Woz said. "No one calls me Philip. Only my grandma does . . . or did . . ." the words getting snagged by the sadness in Woz's throat.

He continued, "I'm Philip Wozniak, but everyone, like even my family, calls me Woz. It's just a name from high school that stuck."

Pausing for a few seconds and collecting himself, he continued, fighting back the tears, "Only Grandma called me Philip."

Reaching for Woz's shoulder, Bert said, "Well, it's so nice to meet you, Woz." And he meant it. Bert was genuinely happy to meet Philip after hearing about him so often at the midweek Bible study.

Silence again descended. The longer it sat between them the heavier it became, the bitter loss of Jean's absence stinging. But Bert's presence was nice.

Bert finally broke the silence, saying, "Well, Woz, you're welcome to stay as long as you'd like, and let me know if there is anything I can do for you."

Bert assumed that this statement, though genuine, would end their conversation. It would give Woz the space he had sought when he entered the empty sanctuary. Yet, to Bert's surprise, Woz responded almost immediately, "Actually, there is."

"Oh, what's that?" Bert returned.

"Well," Woz said, "after Grandma's diagnosis she always said she had three pearls of wisdom she wanted to pass on to me. She told them over and over to the point that I just stopped listening. But now that she's gone, I think I owe it to her to try, don't you think?"

"What were they?" Bert asked, now genuinely interested.

"She said her three pearls of wisdom were, 'One, take care of your teeth.' The day after she died, it was weird, I called the dentist to make my first appointment in like three years. Grief, man, it's crazy."

Bert laughed.

"Second, she said, 'Save some money.' Right after she died and the hospice people took her body," Woz paused to collect himself, "I went to Teddy's for a drink. I just couldn't be alone. I've known the owner Teddy since high school. He said he'd help me with saving money. I don't know what that means, maybe like an IRA thing or whatever. He knows about that stuff. So I have the first two covered."

"What's the third?" Bert asked.

"The third is 'Find God.'" They shared a look and Woz continued, "See, I think I have a bead on the first two, but the third one . . ." A pregnant silence returned.

Eventually Woz continued, now more earnest, "See, *that* one I have no clue about. I'm not even sure it's possible. If you asked me two months ago, I'd have told you it was stupid. I'd have told you there is no God, or at least no God who cares to care about me and my feelings or whatever. And I was sure no church could help me find God. But now that she's gone, I guess I just feel like I should give it a shot. But honestly, I have no idea how to even start."

Bert was at a loss for words. He didn't know how to respond. Luke had said that young adults would come for the cutting-edge relevance. Woz seemed to be looking for something very different. Bert couldn't quite name it.

"So I guess my question is," Woz continued, "what time is the Wednesday Bible study?"

For the next few days Bert couldn't get Woz out of his mind. He thought about Jean's three pearls and Woz's earnestness to follow her wisdom. Bert wondered whether it was just the funeral talking. After a few tacos, maybe Woz's energy for his search would redirect itself elsewhere. Always a realist, Bert figured that Woz would never show up to the Bible study. After all, Luke had had a hard time getting young adults like Woz to show up to anything. And Luke, Bert reasoned, was way cooler and younger than Bert. The Bible study was just an old-fashioned study, no brew kits or promo videos. Why would a trivia champion like Woz be interested in an old-school Bible study?

By Wednesday night, Bert had as much as forgotten about Woz until Woz awkwardly entered the fellowship hall about ten minutes after things had begun. Bert's shock was twofold: he was surprised that Woz had shown up and surprised at how surprised Bert found himself. Bert felt frozen by this double surprise.

Woz emanated a gawky unease as he approached the gathering. He moved briskly but jaggedly, hunching his shoulders as if to make his six-foot-three lanky frame smaller. He found an empty chair in the circle, his face now bright red. This conspicuous entrance, and the shade of red on his face, made it impossible for everyone not to stare. Feeling all the eyes, Woz could only muster a shy and whispery "sorry."

Bert snapped back into the moment. He quickly jumped in to introduce Woz to the group. Their confused faces transformed immediately to bright smiles. Woz smiled back, his face returning to a more normal shade.

"Do you want to introduce yourself?" Bert asked Woz.

"Sure," Woz said with an excited nod, a naive confidence straightening his back. "So I guess you all know my grandma Jean who died. Before she died, she told me to find God."

After pausing and thinking, Woz continued. "I'm here because, well, I'm trying to find God. And I hope you all at this church and in this Bible study can help me. My grandma told me to find God and I guess I decided to start where she found God. I haven't been to church much, haven't really ever been. But I'm assuming you all know how to find God."

Now the embarrassed shade came over the rest of the group. Sue, one of the other lay leaders, looked around the circle with shrugged shoulders and said, "Do we?"

God Is God

When Karl Barth returned from Peter's wedding, the Blumhardts had nestled deeply under his skin. "[Barth] found that he was extremely moved by what he had encountered in Bad Boll."[1] He devoured Zündel's book on the Elder (Johann Blumhardt), who was a concrete example that God could and still does act in the immanent frame. And the Younger (Christoph Blumhardt) became a kind of indirect mentor for Pastor Barth, standing even above Hermann Kutter. The Younger possessed a kind of spiritually sagacious maturity that Barth admired but which, to be honest, he had failed to attain in his own life.[2]

Barth says about the Younger, "He simply passes over dogmatic and liberal theologians. . . . He is friendly, but quite uninvolved. He does not contradict anyone, and no one needs to feel rejected, but at the same time he does not

1. Eberhard Busch, *Karl Barth: His Life from Letters and Autobiographical Texts* (Philadelphia: Fortress, 1975), 85.
2. Though he did try. For instance, Bonhoeffer's experience of Barth is worth pointing out here. It shows both Barth's failures to have this disposition and at the same time his nearness to it. Bonhoeffer reports that when he went to visit Barth for the first time, Barth was very standoffish, even skeptical. This was because the young German from Berlin was now in his classroom. But once Bonhoeffer asked a good question, Barth was won over. He met and had a meal with Bonhoeffer. Bonhoeffer was impressed with how much he listened and wasn't defensive about his positions, really seeking to learn and understand. One can assume that what Bonhoeffer experienced of Barth in summer 1931 is a little bit of what Barth experienced of Blumhardt the Younger in April 1915.

agree with anyone's views."[3] Barth too would decide to pass over everyone's views, finding his own unique theological voice. Like the Younger, he would move beyond the liberal and dogmatic (call it high orthodoxy) theologians. In this sense, he followed in the Younger's footsteps. But Barth had a much harder time following the Younger's even-keeled spirituality.

Barth never really possessed the friendly, uninvolved spirit where no one felt rejected. His passion ran too hot. He entered into life and ministry in the same way he related to his brothers, with nose-to-nose passion, never ducking a fight but always loving the life of his opponent. By the 1930s Barth's passion would strike a match and burn to ash the bridges between him and many of his friends. Barth saw such a narrow path beyond the reductions of the immanent frame that patient sensitivity without feelings of rejection became impossible. In the 1930s Barth burned down the *Zwischen den Zeiten* theological movement. Then he famously incinerated his friendship with Emil Brunner. He struck Brunner with a disposition opposite to that of the sanguine Younger. Going toe to toe with a friend who had been as close as a brother, he shouted a bold *Nein*! But I suppose in Barth's mind this is what brothers do: "Brothers gotta fight."

In 1915, the most important thing that Pastor Barth had taken from the Younger was how every conversation with him started and ended with God. Kutter had reminded him that a pastor says the word "God." The Younger showed how to start and end all your thoughts with God. God was the centering frame for the Younger. But more than just a frame, God was an agent. All thought about the world, society, and church was inextricably God-talk. It was God-talk because the Younger so deeply held—and indeed experienced—that God acts in the world. For the Younger, Barth said, *God is still God*. This is a deeply important statement. For Kant, God is God, but our only access to this God is through a moral categorical imperative. For Harnack, God may be God, somewhere, but our only access is through the history of the church, not God's direct agency. For Schleiermacher, in a sense God is lowered from being God so that the romantic human spirit can be raised.

For about a year Pastor Barth contemplated his experience with the Younger. Over that year of 1915 Barth made his break with liberal theology. He talked it through with Thurneysen. Finally, in March 1916, almost one year after Peter's wedding and his time with the Younger, Barth preached a sermon on Genesis 15:6 ("[Abram] believed the LORD; and the LORD reckoned it to him as righteousness"). In this sermon, Barth, following the footsteps

3. "Auf das Reich Gottes warten," in *Der freie Schweizer Arbeiter* (1916), n47, quoted by Busch, *Karl Barth*, 85.

of the Younger, uses the phrase "God is God." Barth preaches that to have
faith, to believe at all, means "to acknowledge that God is God."[4] This assertion that God is God would be the first note of a very different modern
theological symphony. God is God would become the gravitational center of
Barth's famous *Römerbrief*.

The question for us is, Could a "God is God" ecclesiology have some coherence in the immanent frame of late modernity? Does it give us a different
vision of the church or set the congregation's gaze toward a different sense
of what is good? The challenge is that the phrase "God is God" sounds incoherent inside the immanent frame, like hearing someone speak a language
different from your own. Its weighty incoherence is the core of Barth's modern theology for the immanent frame. The salvo of Barth's theology for the
coherence of God's sure action, even in modernity's closed immanent frame,
is itself incoherent and irrational. It must be so, because the immanent frame
itself claims that any *super*natural (i.e., above or beyond) phenomenon is
itself incoherent and irrational. Instead of making talk of God submit to the
logic of immanence and therefore be seen as coherent by the closed-world
structures of the university, Barth chooses to start with incoherence. Pastor
Barth is wagering that the only way toward a coherence that attends to God's
action is to embrace incoherence.[5]

What Does "God Is God" Mean?

When Woz stumbled into the Bible study, he put the group off balance. It
wasn't necessarily his presence. They'd been hoping and thirsting for a few
young adults to arrive. Rather, they were knocked off balance by Woz's naive
assumption that they should know how to find God. He didn't show up
looking for companionship, entertainment, morals, or religion. He may have
needed some measure of each, but that's not what he was seeking. Like no
one else before him, Woz came looking for God.

Woz assumed that the church possessed knowledge of God, some direct way
to find God. He trusted his grandmother. She claimed that God was knowable,
but Woz doubted it. The immanent frame seemed closed to him. But with his
grandma gone, it opened ever so slightly. Love and loss made the unforgiving

---

4. Eberhard Busch, "God Is God: The Meaning of a Controversial Formula and the Fundamental Problem of Speaking about God," *Princeton Seminary Review* 3, no. 2 (1986): 101.

5. This is not much different from the romantic philosophical response to rationalism. In
some sense, Barth was always a lover of Schleiermacher, even as he attacked him. Barth loved
Schleiermacher even though he was ultimately trying to turn him on his head.

beams of the immanent frame seem too cold. Woz was willing, at least for a time, to try. Trying meant starting where his grandma had ended, in a small community of persons gathering around a sacred text. Woz would have preferred a hike in the Rockies or a trip to Thailand or just a good blunt.[6] But his grandma didn't tell him to find his spiritual center: she said to find the God who got her through the loss of Harry, the God who freed Israel from Egypt.

This Bible study gathered for reasons that may have been beyond them. If asked, they might have said they were meeting for the benefit of being together or because religion is important or because of their own interest in learning about the Bible. These indeed are all good reasons; there is nothing wrong or bad about them. But all these reasons for gathering mesh with the coherence of the immanent frame.

The immanent frame declares that togetherness, religious literacy, and intellectual interests are in bounds and therefore coherent. Less accepted is the idea that the God of Israel who stands outside the universe could enter into it, judging and redeeming it from death for life. The immanent frame renders incoherent the commitment to a personal God who moves as an agent in action, and even intervenes in history. It is incoherent at the intellectual level for those in universities (even theology faculties in Marburg and Berlin). For others, like those at trivia night at Teddy's Tacos, it is incoherent at the level of cultural imagination.

The Bible study avoided incoherence by making their hidden assumptions for gathering match immanence. They studied the Bible not because it held knowledge of the transcendent God of Israel who speaks but because it was interesting. Or it's just what religious people do. Their reason for gathering was not because their persons in relation, narrated through the stories of Scripture, were a kind of sacrament. Their gathering was not intended to become an event of the divine arriving in the history of persons. They gathered because it was nice to be together. If they didn't gather together, the institutional church would disappear, and that would be a shame.

There would have been no unease if Woz had come because he was interested in learning about the Bible or because he was lonely and needed something to do on Wednesday nights. That would have been coherent, matching the norms and assumptions of the immanent frame. That *wouldn't* have been weird.

But what Woz did was very weird, even in a church. His reasons for coming couldn't be bound in immanence. He stated boldly that he was searching for

---

6. This is to point to Taylor's discussion of the nova effect. See Taylor, *A Secular Age* (Cambridge, MA: Belknap, 2007), 299–313.

God, the God of his grandmother, the God who arrived and led her through the hell of 1946, the God who saw her and her baby through those times just as God had so many centuries before with Hagar and Ishmael. Woz wanted the practices and visions to experience God as God, just as his grandmother had, just as the Younger taught Barth to seek.

This struck the whole group as incoherent. Not in an angry or disgusted way, but as if they had been exposed, as when Nathan told David that David was the man who had taken what was not his (2 Sam. 12). This unveiled judgment of assumptions and actions led Sue to ask, or confess, "Do we?" We also might wonder: Do we have any sense of how to encounter this God of Israel who arrives even inside this immanent frame?

Woz seemed to be asking whether this little group, at this nondescript, declining congregation, possessed the vision for finding the God of Israel, the God of Grandma Jean, even in an immanent frame. They were shocked that this might indeed be their purpose.

4

An Apple Tree and the
Incoherence of "God Is God"

In early June 1916 Karl Barth spent a few days with Thurneysen in Leutwil. The occasion surrounded marriage and weddings again; this time it was Thurneysen's. Shortly before Barth's visit, Thurneysen married Marguerite Meyer. She was a talented young woman from Basel. Like Barth's wife, Nelly, Marguerite was professionally trained as a musician. The two women hit it off swimmingly, spending hours playing music together. When he wasn't overtaken "by the Spirit . . . to join in making music with them in the wildest of ways,"[1] Karl was in deep conversation with Thurneysen. The two men tried to crack the inner logic and necessity of the Blumhardtian commitment that "God is God." Barth had already taken the first step in his sermon on Genesis 15:6 a few months earlier.

Inspired by their conversations, Barth returned to Safenwil, grabbed a notebook, and sat under an apple tree to sketch his reflections on the book of Romans. "Romans under an apple tree": it all feels too crafted, too contrived, to be accepted. Nevertheless, it's true.

In the summer of 1666, Isaac Newton sat under his own apple tree, sketching out the laws of motion in the natural world, giving the West a new way of seeing the world without the necessity of God's act.[2] His laws represented some of the first firm planks used to close the world off from God's action.

---

1. Barth, *Briefwechsel Karl Barth–Eduard Thurneysen, 1914–1925* (1966), 110, quoted by Eberhard Busch, *Karl Barth: His Life From Letters and Autobiographical Texts* (Philadelphia: Fortress, 1975), 97.

2. See Richard S. Westfall, *The Life of Isaac Newton* (London: Cambridge University Press, 1993), for an engaging biography of Newton.

Newton, whether intentionally or not, was one of the architects of the immanent frame.[3] Now, in the summer of 1916, Barth sat under his own apple
tree crafting an attack on the assumption that God could not act inside the
immanent frame. Barth did this not as an attack on modernity but to show
that modernity's immanent frame, even with its natural laws, was not so firm
as to keep the God of Israel from acting.

And Romans? This too seems too perfect. Twice already in the history
of Western Christianity it was Romans and its ramifications that shifted the
theological imagination. In 386, a young man as lost as Woz heard God speak
through the voice of a child, saying, "Pick up and read." What this young
man was told to pick up and read was Romans. From this event, Augustine
converted to Christianity.

In 1505, an anxious young man, new to the monastery and as awkward
and as earnest as Woz, tried to find God. But he found himself only locked
in his own mind, unable to please a God of righteous virtue. In his anxiety
and despair, he found it most coherent to wonder whether God was good at
all. It was then that Martin Luther reread Romans and found the words of
salvation. He discovered that the Holy God does the incoherent act of justifying sinners, even becoming sin for us (Rom. 3).

Picking up Romans and reading it under his own apple tree, Barth was not
consciously following Augustine or Luther's footsteps. He was following the
advice of his confirmation teacher: "I had already learnt in my confirmation
instruction that this book was of crucial importance. I began to read it as
though I had never read it before. I wrote down carefully what I discovered,
point by point. . . . I read and read and wrote and wrote."[4]

Barth did this writing really only for the eyes of Thurneysen.[5] Under that
apple tree, Barth put down on paper what he and Thurneysen had been

3. See Jason A. Josephson-Storm's *The Myth of Disenchantment: Magic, Modernity, and
the Birth of the Human Sciences* (Chicago: University of Chicago Press, 2017) for a discussion
on the disenchantment of Newton and others. There is no doubt that Newton wasn't a pure
materialist, and while Josephson-Storm makes some good points, I think he overasserts his point
and misses how deeply disenchantment has burrowed its way into our institutional imaginations. Nevertheless, his discussion of Newton does give us some nuance, showing that Newton
wasn't a radical raider for immanence. His thought inevitably built the immanent frame, even
with his interests in alchemy and other magical beliefs. See also Jane Bennett, *The Enchantment
of Modern Life: Attachments, Crossings, and Ethics* (Princeton: Princeton University Press,
2001); and Courtney Bender, *The New Metaphysics: Spirituality and the American Religious
Imagination* (Chicago: University of Chicago Press, 2010).
4. Barth, "Nachwort," in *Schleiermacher-Auswahl* (Siebenstern Taschenbuch, 1968), 294,
quoted by Busch, *Karl Barth*, 98.
5. "In the first instance, I wrote the book only for myself and for the private edification
of Eduard Thurneysen and other concerned people." Barth writes this in *Karl Barth–Rudolf*

discussing on their long walks between Safenwil and Leutwil and deep into
the night in Bad Boll. He wrote the notes of their mutual voyage from sons
of conservative pastors to students of liberal theological giants to pastors of
real people searching for a living God inside the hell of a great war.

The writing was a way for Barth to synthesize and make sense of this journey, to work out what was at stake for him, to finally make peace, if not with
his brothers then with his father. Barth says, "Only now [in writing under my
apple tree] did I begin to think of my dead father 'with reverence and gratitude,' as I indicated in the foreword to the first edition of *Romans*."[6] More
than likely these were words Karl was never able to say to Fritz in person.[7]

Bombs and Bells

Barth's notes under an apple tree, when published as the *Römerbrief*, were
like a bomb falling on post-WWI Europe. It shook the theological establishment, leaving cracks, even gaping holes, in its foundations. German liberal
theology was never the same. Its foundation was so compromised that its theological edifice was ruled unsafe for habitation. Or to say it all with less violent
imagery, Barth explained that he was like a village pastor who at midnight
stumbled in the bell tower of his church. To keep from falling to his demise,
he reached for the rope, only to accidentally ring the church bells, awakening
all the countryside. Pastor Barth's *Römerbrief* was his own desperate attempt to steady himself and find a way to pastor in the spirit of Blumhardt
the Younger, in a place where God is God.

When the *Römerbrief* appeared in 1919 it awakened pastors and professors
alike. Yet not everyone had the same reaction to being shaken from a slumber.
Pastors in particular found something exciting, sensing that a much different
modern theology had arrived. They awoke enthused. Others, particularly
Barth's own professors, awakened from their slumber angry. They were annoyed they'd been stirred awake by such an unintelligible racket.

Adolf von Harnack, the professor Barth had loved in Berlin when he left
his father's house in conflict, read the *Römerbrief*, not necessarily because he

---

Bultmann Letters, 1922/1966, ed. Bernd Jaspert, trans. Geoffrey W. Bromiley (Edinburgh: T&T
Clark, 1982), 155.

6. Barth, "Nachwort," 295, quoted by Busch, *Karl Barth*, 98.

7. Here Barth provides affectionate words about his father: "The man to whom I undoubtedly
owe the presuppositions of my later relation to theology was my father, Fritz Barth (1856–1912),
who by the quiet seriousness with which he applied himself to Christian things as a scholar and
as a teacher was for me, and still is, an ineffaceable and often enough admonitory example."
In *Karl Barth–Rudolf Bultmann Letters*, 157.

wanted to but because it was a bomb that had fallen too close to the theological building he'd helped construct. Harnack's response was that the *Römerbrief* was incoherent and irrational. It seemed to Harnack, and his great peers, to be some kind of odd gibberish that had somehow put congregational pastors in a trance.

Leaning into Irrational Incoherence

Harnack isn't wrong. The *Römerbrief* is the fruit of what Barth first preached in the spring of 1916. The *Römerbrief* is centered on the claim that "God is God." The statement "God is God," which shows up many times in the first and second editions of the *Römerbrief*, is indeed strange. It must be. There is no other way, Barth believes, to witness to God's direct involvement in the immanent frame.

The immanent frame had shut down and barricaded all other avenues to the action of God. Barth is deeply skeptical from the beginning to the end of his career that apologetics (making a coherent case for the Christian story) can make any real impact in the immanent frame. Trying to make a case for God by the rules of rational coherence set by immanence will either flatten the Christian confession to some disconnected orthodox banality or strip it of its evangelical spirit, creating a theology palpable only to philosophers.

Only in following incoherence, a reality modernity had sought to smother, can a way forward be found.[8] Inside the immanent frame, the acting God of Israel is indeed strange and incoherent. The immanent frame's rational laws and natural philosophy can make no sense of a God who personally enters history. In turn, the immanent frame's romantic disposition of freedom from constraints, whether natural, historical, social, political, or religious, can make no sense of a God who directly judges us for the sins that bring war and death into God's good world.[9]

8. In this sense Barth is following others who have gone before him, particularly Johann Hamann. Hamann birthed the beginnings of Romanticism by standing against French rationalism and embracing the incoherent longing of the human spirit. For more on Hamann, see Oswald Bayer, *A Contemporary in Dissent: Johann Georg Hamann as a Radical Enlightener* (Grand Rapids: Eerdmans, 2012).

9. In discussing both these rationalist and romantic elements in the immanent frame, I'm drawing from the great Isaiah Berlin. For more on this, see Berlin's *The Roots of Romanticism* (Princeton: Princeton University Press, 1999); *Three Critics of the Enlightenment* (Princeton: Princeton University Press, 2013); and *The Crooked Timber of Humanity* (Princeton: Princeton University Press, 2013). I'm convinced by Berlin's analysis that to be modern is to find ourselves with these two logics of rationalist and romantic deeply in our DNA. So, too, is Berlin's student

Harnack is right to state that "God is God" makes no sense. But Harnack misses the genius of Pastor Barth's embrace of incoherence. Harnack had breathed too deeply the air of the university and its closed-world structure to grasp how only incoherence bears the visions of an acting God inside an immanent frame. Barth, too, would have missed it if he had not been a pastor, preaching and ministering inside the madness of the Great War. Ministry for Pastor Barth, as it did for the Younger, revealed that only incoherence could make some coherent proclamation of God's act inside the immanent frame. The incoherence Barth seeks *isn't* illogical. It's not a claim without some logic. Rather, Barth is asserting that the only logical way to find the acting God of Israel in the immanent frame is in and through the logic of incoherence and strangeness.

Then what is it about the illogical logic of incoherence that Barth thinks can return us to an acting God in the immanent frame? How does the claim that "God is God" do this? Eberhard Busch admits that Barth's claim that "God is God" is meaningless. But Busch's words shouldn't be read as a slight. Busch explains, "That is to say that the sentence is an explanation that does not explain anything; it is an explanation that works by *refusing* to explain."[10]

Modernity, and particularly its closed-world structures of the immanent frame, demands explanation.[11] Modernity's power is in its ability to explain natural and social phenomena.[12] Meaning, belonging, ritual, and even peace are not necessarily modernity's strong points. Its strength is explanation. Modernity claims that it can explain both the largest infinities, like galaxies, and the smallest, like cells, bacteria, and quarks. The logical currency of the immanent frame is explanation. The immanent frame seems obviously closed when we can explain everything. Modernity demands some rational or romantic form of reason. A system of explanations for all natural and social phenomena creates what Peter Berger calls the "plausibility structure." Explanations of phenomena create a structure for what we assume is plausible. These explanations

---

Charles Taylor. Taylor even more directly states these conflicting realities in his book *Hegel and Modern Society* (London: Cambridge University Press, 1979).

10. Eberhard Busch, "God Is God: The Meaning of a Controversial Formula and the Fundamental Problem of Speaking about God," *Princeton Seminary Review* 3, no. 2 (1986): 107 (emphasis original).

11. For more on this, see Alexander Schmemann, *For the Life of the World* (Yonkers, NY: St. Vladimir's Seminary Press, 2018), 115–20.

12. John Milbank, drawing from Catherine Pickstock, says, "Modernity is metaphysical, for since it cannot refer the flux of time to the ungraspable infinite, it is forced to seek graspable, *immanent* security; hence, as Catherine Pickstock has pointed out, its characteristic project is one of 'spatialization,' a *mathesis* or measurement of what is, which can master that which merely occurs." *The Word Made Strange: Theology, Language, Culture* (Oxford: Blackwell, 1997), 44. This is the heart of the drive for explanation.

that modernity has given us make the acting and speaking of the God of Israel incoherent. In other words, incoherence is that which stands outside or in direct contrast to the explanations that make up our plausibility structure.

And yet, Barth claims, "God is still God." Pastor Barth is taking the tact of neither knocker of theology nor booster of modernity.[13] He's doing something genuinely unique. Instead of accusing modernity of overlooking the explanation of God (common among American fundamentalists) and instead of conceding and therefore correlating all explanations for God to the explanations of modernity's immanence (what Barth accuses Schleiermacher of doing), Barth just refuses to explain at all! The refusal to explain becomes the starting point of a different way of speaking of God in the immanent frame.

The Hidden God

The statement "God is God" is considered incoherent because it refuses an explanation. It refuses an explanation *not* as concession but as construction. Barth's refusal to explain is not a cheeky way to avoid some trap but a constructive way forward inside the immanent frame. "God is God" is a fundamental claim of a pastoral theology. It's a move to return theological reflection (contemplating and proclaiming God's *real* action) to the pastor and her people in the congregation.

The pastor is stripped of importance and purpose when God is subordinate to explanations and the world is stripped of mystery. Theology can have no real connection to the church and can only be locked inside the university and its closed-world structure when explanation is the objective. The pastor, then, has no knowledge, practices, or visions that are not subordinate to those of the philosopher or (in our time) the business manager, nonprofit CEO, therapist, or social media political movement specialist. Without the incoherent claim "God is God," the pastor has no center to her ministry and the church has no real reason (that couldn't be achieved by some other social collective) to exist. Explanation is not capable of producing life in the church. My point, following Barth, is that only when we claim "God is God" do the pastor and the church have a purpose that can escape the flattening of modernity and its immanent frame. Only the claim "God is God" can direct us to life. Modernity's drive for explanation cannot lead to life. Pastor Barth is convinced of this because of the injustice heaped on workers and the evil of the Great War.

---

13. "Booster" and "knocker" reference Charles Taylor's language in *The Ethics of Authenticity* (Cambridge, MA: Harvard University Press, 1991). Taylor says he refuses to be either a booster or knocker of modernity. I think Karl Barth holds to the same sensibility.

Barth's contention is that starting with the nonexplanation, even meaningless assertion, that "God is God" creates a cavity inside the immanent
frame. Inside this cavity, the pastor and her people can again speak of God.
The church takes hope in the possibility of truly encountering God's actual
(real) presence as its very life. But this encounter can occur only in a backward
way. Without such backwardness we'd return to explanations and logical
coherence, therefore doing our part, even over and against our desire, to close
the immanent frame. This cavity can only exist if we enter the hidden logic
of incoherence. The meaningless statement "God is God" explains nothing
but nevertheless reminds us that to speak of God is to witness to one who
cannot be explained. To say "God is God" is to claim that God is beyond
explanation. It is to seek to name the one who takes no concern for human
constructs of explanation. To assert that God is God is to assert that God
is beyond, and even in opposition to, all human frames, explanations, and
structures.

Speaking of God is *not* the same as speaking of humanity in a loud voice.[14]
"God is God" means that no cultural construct, logic, or explanation can possess God. To find God and God's act will call for a much different vision from
that given by modernity. Busch adds, "God is God means: God is *unknown,
hidden, deus absconditus*."[15]

Under that apple tree in Safenwil, Barth writes out what he learned from
the Younger. He gives shape and depth to the statement "God is God," which
the Younger embodied but couldn't himself extrapolate. As the wind blows
through the tree's branches and the conversations with Thurneysen come
back to mind, Barth fleshes out the statement "God is God" by asserting
that God is beyond. God is beyond all constructs we have of God. Barth's
point is that when we say "God," we are not talking about God if we assume
this God is simply furniture inside our immanent frame. When we talk of
God, we are talking of one who cannot be known through human reason
and methods.[16] We are proclaiming one who is beyond us and other than
us, the one who is fundamentally beyond the frame of immanence and all
its explanations.

14. This is a paraphrase of Barth's famous words in a lecture titled "The Word of God and
the Word of Man," in *The Word of God and the Word of Man* (New York: Harper, 1957).
15. Busch, "God Is God," 107 (emphasis original).
16. This is what Harnack finds so absurd. How can you have a science—which the immanent
frame demands theology be—without having a method and process of knowledge gathering?
To say that the object of theology is unknowable is to cut the modern science of theology at its
knees. It is absurd and incoherent, especially when the young Barth claims that theology, even
inside this claim that God cannot be known, can still be a science. Barth would work out how
in *Church Dogmatics* I/1 (Edinburgh: T&T Clark, 1936).

What Kind of Transcendence? From Orgies to Acts

Starting again with "God is God" shows that the immanent frame cannot be as closed as some think. "God is God" is a fundamental reorientation. To claim that God is unknown, hidden, and unable to be captured by our cultural or intellectual pursuits not only gives us different visions of God but also opens up reality itself. To lean into the claim "God is God," that God is unknown and beyond, has the potential to open the immanent frame. Barth, ninety years before Charles Taylor, is showing us that there can be a kind of openness even in the immanent frame (Taylor calls this an open take).[17] The immanent frame is opened to transcendence.

When we hear "transcendence," we tend to think of otherworldliness. And as modern people we feel a stab of skepticism because we tend to see transcendence as that which *is* outside or beyond the world. Modernity has a strong bias against anything outside the world. It trips the alarm of our modernist-imposed plausibility structure. Some modern thinkers even claim there is nothing, *no thing*, outside natural and social phenomena.[18] Or at least there is nothing worth contemplating (because there are no methods and tools—forgetting over six thousand years of spiritual practices—for discovering things outside the world, and therefore no real way to enter into explanation). In this kind of thinking, transcendence is lost.

Transcendence is lost because it is defined *in toto* as that which is otherworldly (outside the world). Modernity believes humanity has outgrown the concern for the otherworldly. By setting up explanation as a high good, modernity redefines transcendence as that which is outside the world.[19] Transcendence is understood to be otherworldly because it cannot be expounded by the methods and tools of explanation. Modernity, in its hubris, believes it can (or eventually will be able to) explain everything in the world. Thus,

17. I'm not necessarily claiming here that Barth and Taylor are in complete agreement. The two work out their claims to a transcendent quality of life in much different ways. But I do think that Taylor's use of transcendence has been misunderstood and that the final part of *A Secular Age* shows some points of congruence.

18. Kant, however, acknowledges a noumenal reality, but it can't be explained. We know it's there because we somehow have moral imperatives that land in our consciousness. But there is no way to explain a noumenal reality, so while we should acknowledge its existence, we should move on. The modern world is run by the reason of science, and science has no way to explain noumenal realities. So for all intents and purposes, they don't exist.

19. Not everyone defined transcendence this way, William James being one important example. See his *Varieties of Religious Experience* (New York: Penguin Classics, 1982). For discussion of James's significance, see Charles Taylor, *Varieties of Religion Today: William James Revisited* (Cambridge, MA: Harvard University Press, 2002); and Hans Joas, *Do We Need Religion? On the Experience of Self-Transcendence* (London: Routledge, 2008).

if it can't be explained, it must be otherworldly (and a delusion). Rational people in their right minds don't spend time on otherworldly things that have no correlation to explanation. Having redefined transcendence in this way, modernity can rail against it. Modernity can claim that the desire to escape the world and even explain the world by some unexplainable logic from outside the world turns the stomach (and is dangerous).[20]

Barth refuses to concede to these definitions of transcendence. Otherworldliness is not necessarily how the Bible understands the God who is God. We should not forget that Barth is a modern pastor seeking a modern theology as neither a knocker nor a booster of modernity. His openness to transcendence cannot be found outside the world but rather more deeply in it. When Barth sits under the apple tree, sketching out his notes on Romans, he is *not* seeking to make a case for transcendence per se. Nor is he arguing for transcendence opposed to immanence (and the immanent frame). Barth's theology seeks not to attack the immanent frame but only to show that the presumption that the God of Israel is excluded from acting in the immanent frame is misguided. The Elder and the Younger's ministry reveals concretely that God cannot be excluded. Even in modernity, the God of Israel acts.

Barth seeks *not* to return to some orthodox affirmation of an otherworldly transcendence. Nor is Barth's objective to find the soft spots in modernity, unmasking its fetishizing of immanence. Barth is not Karl Jung, nor the more radical Russian Grigori Rasputin. Both are examples of an intellectual and religious leader seeking transcendence by returning to a kind of otherworldliness in order to make a case for transcendence, not to recover an imagination for the God who is God.[21]

From 1907 until the time Barth wrote in Safenwil, Jung, a fellow Swiss national also from Basel, worked to show Freud and the other psychoanalysts that reality isn't as closed as they had assumed.[22] Jung's point is that psychoanalysis and the contemplation of the working of the mind are not just part of an immanent science but touch on something transcendent and otherworldly. Freud could not stomach this thought. Freud believed his own legitimacy was dependent on a science that supported only a closed commitment to the immanent frame and its explanations.

---

20. This kind of thinking is radicalized (or popularized) in the work of the New Atheists such as Richard Dawkins and others. See Dawkins, *The God Delusion* (New York: Mariner, 2008).

21. "After 1900, and especially after the First World War, mysticism came into fashion in Germany, with or without God." Joachim Radkau, *Max Weber: A Biography* (London: Polity, 2011), 536.

22. For more, see Philip Jenkins, *The Great and Holy War: How World War I Became a Religious Crusade* (San Francisco: HarperOne, 2014), 152–55.

In the same year that Barth began writing under the apple tree, Rasputin was at the pinnacle of his power. Rasputin was a Russian Eastern Orthodox mystical peasant who used sexual ecstasy (orgies) and magical spells of healing to experience transcendence. His electric, otherworldly practices of magic and ecstasy somehow made it all the way to the court of the czar. He became a beloved source of counsel to Czar Nicholas II's wife Alexandra. When Nicholas marched his armies to the eastern front in WWI in 1915, Rasputin helped Alexandra rule the Russian Empire. Six months after Barth started his notebooks on Romans in 1916, Rasputin, assumed to be a witch, was shot three times and killed by Russian nobles.

There were others, both intellectuals and spiritualists, who sought to show that modernity was not absent of a transcendent quality. *But this was not Barth's objective.* Barth's objective was more pointed. He was not interested in making a case for a generic transcendence inside the immanent frame, but was seeking an encounter with the God of Israel. The visions of the Younger and experiences of the Elder had shown Barth that the challenge is not in claiming a spiritual dimension within modernity but in claiming, more boldly, that the God of Israel, who is witnessed to in the biblical text, acts in modernity, penetrating the immanent frame.

Barth pushes for something deeper and more difficult than simply showing that the immanent frame is open to *transcendence.* Barth seeks to show that the immanent frame is open to encounters with *the transcendent God who is God.* This God who is God is known not outside the world but deeply within it. God acts in the world, and only through God's acts can a human being come to know the God who is God. Barth explores how the immanent frame is open to encounters with the one who, though outside the world, nevertheless enters the world. The one who is unknowable nevertheless comes near enough to be known in and through his acts. Inspired by the Younger, Barth explores how it is that God who is God, and therefore transcends all created categories, nevertheless acts in the world. My assertion, in following Barth and claiming "God is God," is that the immanent frame cannot keep out this wild God of Israel who acts in history and speaks directly to persons. The pastoral experience of the Elder proves this, Barth believes.

Unlike Rasputin, Barth is not interested in transcendence that escapes the world. He wants to find a way to encounter God who is God *in the world.* Barth seeks transcendence in the world, a historical transcendence.[23] The transcendence that I'm seeking, following Barth, is inside the immanent frame and

23. This phrase comes from Ray S. Anderson, *Historical Transcendence and the Reality of God* (Grand Rapids: Eerdmans, 1975).

therefore not bound in some metaphysical ether world.[24] This transcendence is bound in and through encounters with God's act in the time and space of the real world. We could say that transcendence can be found within the apophatic character of the immanent frame.[25]

Apophatic Frames

In mobilizing "God is God" as a nonexplanation for a God who is beyond, Barth no doubt reveals the apophatic element in his early theology. The apophatic is the practice of describing something by naming what it is not. When thinking of Barth's statement "God is God," the apophatic is used because the object being described renders human language (and therefore our mental composites) incapable of knowing and expressing the object and its reality.[26] In this apophatic vein, Barth is seeking to speak of God by stating what cannot be said of God.[27] The statement "God is God" claims that the essence of God cannot be known apart from God's act to make Godself known.

In a much different sense, the closed-world structures of the immanent frame have believed this all along. They affirm this not because they believe God is God, confessing that God stands beyond and above the explanations of modernity, but rather because modernity's explanations reveal there is no direct reality for God at all.

The immanent frame is closed off from God, and God is shut out of it but not necessarily through a frontal attack on God. Descartes, Newton, Locke, and even Spinoza never directly sought to eliminate God from the dawning modern world. That would have been unthinkable.[28] Their profound and impactful efforts had the effect of not only constructing the immanent frame but also installing hinges that would slam it closed to the witness of the act and

24. For further discussion on this, see Kevin W. Hector, *Theology without Metaphysics: God, Language, and the Spirit of Recognition* (London: Cambridge University Press, 2011), 34–37.

25. Barth discusses this historical transcendence in *Church Dogmatics* I/1, 325–31.

26. For more on this, see Timothy Stanley, *Protestant Metaphysics after Karl Barth and Martin Heidegger* (Eugene, OR: Cascade, 2010), 98–104. Not surprisingly, the apophatic approach to thinking predates modernity, going back to the church fathers and mystics of the tradition.

27. John Webster says something similar: "All through his early writings, Barth struggled to express an idea of God's transcendence as more than mere comparative superiority, more than some observable, exalted aspect of creaturely existence. 'God,' he wrote, 'is pure negation.'" *Karl Barth* (Edinburgh: T&T Clark, 2004), 25.

28. Ethan Shagan points in this direction when he says, "The transformation of belief, rather than the rise of unbelief, propelled Western thought into modernity. The resulting configuration has shaped the conditions of religion in a secular age." *The Birth of Modern Belief: Faith and Judgment from the Middle Ages to the Enlightenment* (Princeton: Princeton University Press, 2018), 2.

being of God.[29] These thinkers crafted methods of explanation that moved God far from the center of understanding. They eliminated God, not as a religious and personal confession but as an explanation![30] The earth spun and the seasons came and went *maybe* because God willed it. But that was no longer a real explanation. Instead new explanations arrived that had no need for transcendence. These new explanations revealed the mechanics (deduced from mathematics) that moved planets (Newton).[31] These methods could even reveal the conditions that allowed for just rule and economic advance (Locke).

Unlike with the medieval imagination, God's willing and doing could no longer explain the ways of the world. For the modern architects of the immanent frame, medieval thinking was too cloaked in mystery as a legitimate explanation.[32] Mystery could no longer serve as an explanation. Only reason could overcome mystery (Descartes).[33] And only contemplation and discovery could mobilize reason. The value of any method of contemplation and discovery was how widely it reached in explanation. The more it explained, the more it rested on reason (and usefulness). Ultimately, the more it rested on reason, born from methods of explanation, the more it cast out mystery.[34] Barth pointed to modernity's aversion to mystery, and the belief that explanation can cast out all mystery: "The mysteries of the world are of such a kind [in modernity] that someday they can cease to be mysteries. God is always a mystery."[35]

With mystery cast out, we were given a world framed by immanence thanks to the methods of explanation. This immanently framed world was appealing because it explained *almost* everything. Even the unexplainable was no longer considered to be a witness to the transcendent quality of reality and our own inability to know something greater than us.[36] It was rather just a puzzle, a

29. For more on this, see Terry Eagleton, *Culture and the Death of God* (New Haven: Yale University Press, 2014), 42–45.

30. See Dominic Erdozain, *The Soul of Doubt: The Religious Roots of Unbelief from Luther to Marx* (New York: Oxford University Press, 2016), 65–72.

31. Hannah Arendt adds texture to this in *The Human Condition* (Chicago: University of Chicago Press, 1998), 268–72.

32. John Thornhill adds, "It may well be argued that the essential concern of the culture which succeeded the Middle Ages was an affirmation of the legitimate autonomy of the secular order." *Modernity: Christianity's Estranged Child Reconstructed* (Grand Rapids: Eerdmans, 2000), 4. See also Bruce Ward, *Redeeming the Enlightenment: Christianity and the Liberal Virtues* (Grand Rapids: Eerdmans, 2010), 6–10.

33. Arendt offers a rich discussion of Descartes in *Human Condition*, 275–80. See also Shagan, *Birth of Modern Belief*, 207–8.

34. For a rich discussion of disenchantment, see Eva Illouz, *Why Love Hurts* (Malden, MA: Polity, 2012), 156–60.

35. *Church Dogmatics* I/1, 322.

36. This has been an emphasis in Bhaskarian-based critical realism. See, e.g., Andrew Collier, *Critical Realism: An Introduction to Roy Bhaskar's Philosophy* (London: Verso,

conundrum, which the methods of reason had not quite *yet* explained. Soon enough we would be able explain the riddles and puzzles yet to be solved.[37] We just needed a little more time to hone the method.

Inside the closed-world structures of the immanent frame there are no longer open spaces that allow mystery to encounter us. In such a closed world, where mystery has been excommunicated, it becomes almost impossible to hold to the biblical truth that the God of Israel arrived in time and at a place, speaking words that enter and overcome death with life. This commitment to such a God could only be chalked up to an antiquated belief held before the immanent frame and its rational-based methods expelled mystery. Inside the closed immanent frame there is no place for even an apophatic sense of modernity, let alone God.

The modern project's obsession with explanation sought to expel any and all space where reality could escape human knowledge and slide back into mystery.[38] Had the immanent frame become a land so mapped by reason that there were no longer any realities that might outstrip explanation? Could it be true what modernity seemed to be peddling: that reality itself had escaped any apophatic element? Was there really nothing inside reality that escaped human forms of knowing? Was mystery (that which could not be explained) dead?

Bringing Together the Apophatics

As a student, Barth came to believe something like this. To his father's disappointment, he looked to embrace a theology for a closed world of complete explanation. As a student, Barth thirsted to follow the theologians who no longer had time for mystery and even threw shade on those who did, such as Fritz Barth.[39]

1994). Critical realism claims that parts of reality—of the world—are beyond the capacity of human knowing.

37. This is the fundamental progressive nature of modernity, this sense that modernity is always leading to progress. This sense of progress is linked to a desire to eliminate mystery. The progress modernity seeks is not just technological, economic, or even in the area of rights. Rather, it can imagine progress in all areas because it seeks to conquer mystery itself. For a much longer conversation on this, see Taylor, *A Secular Age*, 365–68. For more on my sense of this, see *Exploding Stars, Dead Dinosaurs and Zombies* (Minneapolis: Fortress, 2018), chap. 6.

38. Of course, some romantic philosophers understood this as a problem from the start. But their impact was not expansive enough for them to be considered architects of the immanent frame. People like Hegel and Kant tried to synthesize their concerns with the drive toward reason. They placed a romantic sensibility in their thought (Kant, thanks to Hamann), giving the immanent frame a sense of this romantic concern.

39. This reference to shade is not just a clever adaptation of a hip cultural euphemism, but actually the words of Barth himself. After finishing the *Römerbrief* he says, "And I do not want

But as a pastor, Barth saw his father's wisdom. In the practice of ministry, it became impossible to believe that reality was absent of mystery and completely closed. Following both the Younger Blumhardt and the overlooked wisdom of his father, Barth believed that starting with "God is God" signaled a new starting point for theology and for interpreting modernity.[40]

Because of his pastoral experience, Barth could not contend that reality itself was closed to mystery. He could not believe that humanity had outgrown a longing for salvation that would come from outside the world (though found within the world). Barth knew this because he pastored people who were breaking their backs in mines, longing for freedom both spiritually and materially. Barth sensed that reality was indeed more open, parts of it unable to be mapped and controlled, because he witnessed the evil Spirit of August sweep Germany into aggressions and into a world war. These realities, birthed in the womb of modernity's immanent frame, assured Barth that there were indeed elements of modernity that could not be explained.

The immanent frame possessed its own apophatic character. Elements of reality, even wrapped by this immanent framing, escaped explanation. No science or power of explanation could truly wrap its arms around the longings and sinfulness of the human spirit and the cultures it created. In *Römerbrief II*, Barth entered into dialogue with Overbeck, Dostoevsky, Kierkegaard, and Plato (thanks to the tutoring of little brother Heinrich) to show that the immanent frame had more openings, conundrums, and inconsistencies than had been assumed. The Great War revealed that modernity was unable to produce its own salvation. Modernity could not eradicate sin through reason. It even created all sorts of its own evils. By dismissing transcendence, modernity was unable to give hope. Yet it's important to say that this apophatic character of modernity was no point of contact for Barth. The fact that mystery still had a place in modernity (over and against modernity's denial) did not mean there was an easy apologetic for God. Modernity's apophatic character, revealed by the Great War, made *no* case for God. Perhaps there were no atheists in foxholes, but there was also enough hell to make anyone doubt a good God. "God is God" stands beyond easy explanations, because God stands beyond *all* understanding. The apophatic character of modernity—the Great War as an irrationality born from the rational systems

to conceal the fact that for a moment . . . the idea came into my head that now I could and would get my own back on those who had put my father in the shade, although he knew just as much (but in a different way)!" Busch, *Karl Barth*, 98.

40. This is the critically realist part of Barth's approach that Bruce McCormack has so importantly explicated. See McCormack, *Karl Barth's Critically Realistic Dialectical Theology: Its Genesis and Development, 1909–1936* (Oxford: Oxford University Press, 1997).

of modernity—only proves that the immanent frame is not nearly as closed as some would think.

Starting with God who is God, Barth revealed that the immanent frame was open. When Barth said so in the first edition of *Römerbrief*, pastors across the German-speaking world recognized it too. Professors like Harnack couldn't see it, but congregational pastors could. The incoherent assertion that "God is God" unveiled the incoherence of a closed immanent frame that imagined it could shut out a God who is God. And if the immanent frame proved to be open, then a theology that sought God's act inside modernity was possible.

Yet this kind of modern theology that sought God's act inside an open modernity needed to be located not in the university and its tendency toward a closed-world structure but in the church. The church was the right locale for reflection on God who is God, for the church has life only by proclaiming that God is God.[41] The church can find life only by embracing the dual apophatic character of God and reality. The church confesses to be in the world, but only so as to encounter the one who transcends the world as a God who is God never without the world. The church is in a position to witness to the world that the strange God of the Bible still indeed acts. This is what the church is for!

———

Somehow Saint John the Baptist had forgotten this. Woz told the Bible study he'd come looking for help in finding God. Woz assumed they knew how to find God. Sue responded, "Do we?" Her response was both correct and misguided.

41. Barth would have a more implicit sense of this in 1916 and into the 1920s. It was only after his failed *Christian Dogmatics* in Göttingen that Barth more clearly saw that such a modern theology of God's act would unequivocally have to be located in the church. Stanley Hauerwas discusses this powerfully in *With the Grain of the Universe: The Church's Witness and Natural Theology* (Grand Rapids: Baker Academic, 2013), 146–47.

5

The Church *Can't* Know
How to Find God

Sue was the yin to Bert's yang. Sue and Bert were the true lay leaders of Saint John the Baptist, both dedicated and able. Though they had mutual respect for one another, they saw things differently. Bert was an optimist. Sue was a pessimist. Bert lived under the belief that the next pastor would move the congregation onto strong footing, securing new membership. He still believed this despite Luke's limited success and early departure. Sue, on the other hand, thought that the congregation needed to face its financial struggles.

Sue often reminded the congregation that the financial fundamentals were anything but solid. Bert thought it harsh and too painful to even entertain the thought of the dissolution of Saint John the Baptist. But they both agreed that the congregation needed something new.

Yet confusion arose because they couldn't really name what they meant by "new." If pushed, Bert would say "new" revolved around a new direction and some new members. For Sue, "new" could be explained as new money, new stability, and a new direction. They especially found themselves in conflict over this "new" direction. This conflict did not arise from one of them protecting a past and another aiming for a new horizon. Both wanted the new, but they were missing each other's meaning even in their shared desires for this nebulous new. This need for the "new" (to do something new, to find new money, to attract new members) became a red herring, more misleading and distracting than helpful.

To discover whether the new was really a red herring, you'd need to start with the opposite of the new (an apophatic method). To name the opposite of the new—old, stale, existing, hackneyed—would reveal that Sue or Bert were not truly after the new. Neither would describe the present state of Saint John the Baptist as outdated. Luke, unlike Bert and Sue, would have. He tried to bring the new by exorcising all stale elements of the congregation. He did this so that new, exciting, and hip young adults would attend. But that wasn't really what Bert or Sue were after. In the end, they weren't really looking for the *new*. They were looking for *life*.

In a consumer society, we too often equate the new with life. The new does have within it a dynamic of life, but life cannot be synonymous with the new—no matter how much late-modern consumer society tries to equate them. Sue and Bert both worried that life, *not* the new, would elude the congregation. They both wanted the church to experience a fullness of life. How to secure that life was the source of their contention. Through the summer months, that contention moved into tension and then grew.

———

Over the summer, Bert took on many of the pastoral duties while the congregation searched for a new pastor. Sue researched more radical models for their future. Sue even argued that they should suspend the search and more directly entertain a merger with another congregation.

Bert was a civil rights lawyer, Sue a corporate real estate agent. Both were a decade or so away from retirement. Sue's company helped chain restaurants find new locations for their budding franchises. Sue had always respected Bert, but their impasse in these moments of transition was wearing. Clearly the momentum had gone in the direction of Bert's position. The search for a new pastor had commenced and résumés were being reviewed. Sue found the naivete nauseating.

The two were becoming entrenched in their positions. They misunderstood each other's desire for the new. Both thought the new could somehow save the congregation. Though Bert had more people behind him, Sue did garner some support. Her backing was a small but mighty vocal minority. This vocal minority reminded everyone in the congregation that Saint John the Baptist needed to think differently. They asserted that the new that Bert sought wasn't new enough, wasn't radical or novel enough. In the months after Luke left, Sue never failed to remind everyone that despite Bert's optimism, business as usual wouldn't work. It wasn't really new.

Sue's mighty vocal minority fluctuated between seeming poles. They advocated for sweeping and creative changes, like renovating the church building for office rental space to attract tech startups from the neighborhood. Sue even formed an early business plan. It included a $500,000 renovation project. Sue had floated such a plan to Luke late last year, but he'd dismissed it. Luke had boldly asserted that they'd need all that space soon enough. Luke had visions of a $5 million renovation to match the wave of growth that would soon crest from his talent and persistence.

That wave never arrived. Now Luke and his fantasies were gone, so Sue found it advantageous to float this plan more widely to the congregation. Bert resisted, though he was not sure why. There seemed to be too many unknown variables, and few people in the congregation seemed to have energy for it. It could bring in revenue, but Bert worried about the risk to the congregation. And he wasn't sure how it connected to the mission of the church. Sue declared that the church was already well beyond the point of financial risk. They could hold on for *maybe* a decade if they were lucky, but without fundamental change their situation was terminal.

And the mission? Sue wondered what that mission even was. Luke's mission was for Thrive to reach post-Christian young adults. That disappeared with Luke's departure, as made clear by the dropping of the name Thrive. Sue thought the time for flashy mission statements was over. They were in a Darwinian fight for their life (revealing again that this wasn't all about newness but life).

Yet, at other times, Sue and her small group were the opposite of ambitious. Their fight would turn from business plans to concessions, perhaps another winning strategy in a Darwinian fight for life. You either beat 'em and eat 'em or join 'em. The congregation's long-term instability led to speeches about selling the building, sharing a pastor, and moving in with another ailing congregation. This seemed to Bert like a sure way to die and lose all life. Two drowning people can't save each other.

Sue found that metaphor to be a stretch. She reminded the congregation, "We could eliminate so much overhead." But Bert sensed, without being able to form it into words, that this congregation could not exist without a space that connected it to a history. To eliminate the overhead and displace the congregation would suck the life out of it. Sure, the congregation would be doing something new. But this new thing would snatch life from them by pushing them apart. The new doesn't always promise life. (For instance, a new virus may spell our doom.) The overhead would be cut, but so too would the spirit that held the community together.

The tensions had turned into conflict when Woz awkwardly entered the Bible study. Sue was there only because of her growing contention with Bert, which was turning into distrust. Knowing that some of her strong vocal minority faithfully attended the Bible study, Sue worried that, without her presence, Bert would persuade them to his side. It was a small case study on how well-intended people who both want what's best can spin a conflict into potential dysfunction.

When Woz shared why he came, he didn't mention any interest in finding something new or stable. He came to find God. His grandmother had told him to find God, not necessarily to join a church. He simply started the journey where she had ended it. When Woz said, "I'm assuming you all know how to find God," Sue's response was "Do we?"

Sue's question was born from a depth she had never accessed before. She had never thought that the church could have a purpose beyond surviving to do churchy things—like gathering for worship, having Sunday school, and getting a few people to join a Bible study. Sue thought Luke had failed to reach the young adults and take them into the activities of the church because he was apolitical. "Young people are socially conscious," Sue often stated. "We need to show that we are too . . . if they're going to come." Yet Woz was not looking for political consciousness either. He was looking for help in finding God.

"Do We?"

Woz's presence and his direct plea for help shifted something in Sue, at least for that moment. The presence of a pilgrim in their midst, seeking assistance on a journey, on his clumsy way in a spiritual quest, led Sue into a moment of honest reflection. She wondered out loud, "Do we?" Do we, this unstable, passive-aggressive, little church, forgotten by our denomination and one roof repair from closing, know how to "find God"? Do we, this little church that is fighting a silent but growing war against each other, even know how we'd start?

Sue's question was as much a confession as an inquiry. They didn't know how to find God, and worse, they'd forgotten they were supposed to be looking. Their attention and interest had shifted to other things that were somehow found more important. Squeezed by decline and institutional vulnerability, Saint John the Baptist found that the immanent frame had spun closed. This hidden but acute danger exists for many midsize-to-small congregations. The closed immanent frame had sucked the life from the church.[1] Saint John the

1. Liberal mainline churches are always flabbergasted as to why evangelical churches, which are less socially conscious and more disconnected from the intellectual tradition of Christianity, seem to be far better at growth and retaining members. There are complicated reasons for this, of course. But one reason seems to be that the more conservative congregations *seem*

Baptist kept diagnosing other problems: no clear new vision, no new sustainability plan, no new programs to get new members, no new branding to bring relevance. But the real illness was the heavy immanence that, like cancer, was attacking the congregation's living cells. Saint John the Baptist had forgotten, or somehow become disinterested in (even embarrassed about), the longing for transcendence. They wanted something new, something stable. But Woz wanted to be taught a way to see so that he could live in the way of his grandmother.

Yet Sue's "Do we?" was more than just an admission of something forgotten. It was also a confession, and therefore it was also the first step into theological reflection. Her question was an openness against an unthought closedness. Sue had never made a deliberate choice to close the immanent frame, seeing her own life and the church's life as bound in immanence. It just happened. Woz's inquiry revealed Sue's own presumptions. This revealing felt like being cross-pressured, like a strong current washing over her hidden presumptions, unmooring them from their stable place.[2] Sue's assumptions about the church and its needs were cut across by another vision, intercepted by another strong evaluation of what was important and good.[3] Seeing Woz seek the fullness of life by trying to find God, asking the Bible study for help, tripped up Sue. It caused her to see something different from what she had when she arrived at the Bible study that night.

"Do We?" Meets "God Is God"

Finding her presumptions judged and left wanting by a new vision shifted Sue nearer to the same (il)logic as Barth's "God is God." Sue's question, while

---

more alive—*seem* to have more life. What seems to give them more life is not better doctrine or smarter pastors but a refusal to concede to a completely closed immanence. They are still open to transcendence. Of course, certain elements of conservative Protestantism, even those coming from an anti-immanence perspective (which is misguided in its own right), have nevertheless diabolically conceded to immanence by seeing the world's salvation in and through political power brokers. For more on this, see John Fea, *Believe Me: The Evangelical Road to Donald Trump* (Grand Rapids: Eerdmans, 2018), esp. chaps. 1 and 4. Chapter 4 on "Court Evangelicals," those evangelicals who found their way into Trump's court of influence, is particularly interesting and enlightening on the brief point this note is trying to make.

2. For more on cross-pressure, see Taylor, *A Secular Age* (Cambridge, MA: Belknap, 2007), 595–600.

3. Taylor's philosophical anthropology argues that we always act from some sense of the good. Our identities—at both an individual and a collective level—are bound in strong evaluations of what is good and brings fullness. For more, see Charles Taylor, *Human Agency and Language: Philosophical Papers 1* (London: Cambridge University Press, 1999), 34–36. See also Andrew Root, *The End of Youth Ministry?* (Grand Rapids: Baker Academic, 2020), 51–66.

fully the confession of immanence and its crossed-up presumptions, became the first step to actually finding God inside the immanent frame. To find God, if it is the wholly other God we seek, begins with the confession that we have no way of knowing this God. To ask "Do we?" is to assert that no human being possesses the way to know God. This God who is God is beyond all knowing. The God who is God cannot be captured by any epistemological structure. This God is unknowable, escaping all the ways that the immanent frame seeks to capture this God.

Woz was mistaken if he thought he could stumble into his grandmother's church, get a few quick lessons on God—like a golf pro would give to a beginner at a country club—and move on. Woz was wrong if he thought he could take those lessons and use them to place God nicely in some mental category, now having God as a resource to add to his life. Woz wouldn't find the God who is God even if he stuck around the church for more resources and tips. A church that promised Woz resources in coping with his busy, dull, and lonely life would be a church dangerously close to missing that God is God. This provision of resources, and packaging of God as an idea consumable in the immanent frame, is exactly how churches position themselves. The church is imagined as the provider of tips and lessons on God, making your membership worth the cost.

But a church that confesses "Do we?" moves closer to seeking a "God who is God." A church that confesses "Do we?" offers its people a different invitation, an invitation to gather and seek a God who cannot be known. This invitation finds ways to worship and obey a God who is so other than us that this God whom we seek cannot be known or explained. The God who is God cannot be known, because the God who is God cannot be possessed, most particularly by our ideas of God.[4] While the closed structures of the immanent frame have sought to cage God, making God knowable through institutionalized religion or individualized "spiritualties,"[5] the God who is

4. For how most of the great religious traditions have held to something like this, see David Bentley Hart, *The Experience of God: Being, Consciousness, Bliss* (New Haven: Yale University Press, 2013), chaps. 1 and 2.

5. Barth, again following Blumhardt the Younger, roars against the Protestant establishment in the *Römerbrief II*. Religion is set over and against God, for religion, following a reworking of Overbeck, makes God a knowable object inside the immanent frame. Barth could not see what we cannot help but see now: that the immanent frame, particularly after 1968, creates a nova effect of a surplus of third-way spiritualties disconnected from classic forms of religion but that nevertheless concede that God (now impersonalized) is a piece and part of the immanent frame. The new spiritualities are an attempt to cope with the reductions of immanence without ever having to encounter a God who stands outside the immanent frame, judging it and the self within it.

God, the God of Israel, cannot be known. This God is not an object that (thanks to methodological explanations of modernity) can be categorized within immanence.

To find God (not just to find an idea of God) in the immanent frame starts with the paradoxical confession that "God is God" and therefore unable to be known, the confession that we *do not* know how to find this God. This counterintuitive confession is necessary, for the more we encounter this God who acts in the immanent frame, the more God transcends our categories. God is encountered, but this encounter reveals that this God who acts cannot be known and therefore possessed.

The incoherent and irrational confession that "God is God" couples with the other confession "Do we?" Do we really know how to find this God? These coupled confessions claim that *we can encounter God only when we confess that we cannot know God.* These dual incoherent dictums ("God is God" and "Do we?") remind us that the one we seek is beyond and radically other than us. In this first proclamation to the world, the church boldly announces to the world that it *does not* know how to find God, because the God it seeks (the God it has encountered) is true God of true God. God is not an idea or a concept, not a therapeutic salve but the God of Israel who brings judgment and grace, the God who speaks a Word such that what is not *is* and what was dead *is* made alive. This first move helps those in the immanent frame find God, because only in confessing that we have no way to find God are we assured that we seek God and not just our own echo.

For the people of Saint John the Baptist to help Woz find God, they must first confess to Woz, as fellow pilgrims seeking God, that they do not know how to find God. *God finds them; they never find God.* For the God they seek, with all their lives, is beyond knowing. Woz's search for the God of Israel must begin with the confession that the closer he gets to finding this God, the less he'll know (or possess) this God. God's unknowability (his wholly otherness) judges the church, reminding the church that it must always enter the world and make its proclamations in humility. Nevertheless, the church is the community that reminds the world that God is God, seeking to commune with a God who is other than us. The church seeks connection to a God who stands outside the immanent frame but nevertheless enters into it, seeking to find us.

This confession that we cannot know God becomes the base immunization against the closed-world structure of the immanent frame. To confess that God is beyond knowing, because God is God, is to claim that the immanent frame cannot be *in toto* confused for reality. The God of Israel is no simple object in the immanent frame. The God of Israel is no idol. We do not know how to find this God, because we encounter this God—particularly in the immanent frame—only when God chooses in freedom to act within it.[6] We can ready ourselves for this act by remembering that "God is God" and confessing that we do not know how to find such a God who is God.

So Much Knowing, So Little Being

Not until we make this confession—"Do we?"—can we escape the temptation to close down the immanent frame, trapping God like a puppy in a pen of immanence. Only when we confess that we cannot know God can we take our first step in seeking the God who is God.

But I can feel the readers' unease. Some of us have the habit of equating *knowing* and *intimacy*. Even some translations of the Bible have this tendency. For instance, Genesis 4:1 says, "Adam knew Eve," meaning that they entered into an intimate (and erotic) encounter. This knowing is related to mystery and even transcendence, bound first in the encounter of being. But the rational elements of the modern project—which set the foundations for the immanent frame—have instead seen knowing in a very different way.[7]

For modernity, knowing fuses with explanation. And ambitious explanation seeks to cast out all mystery, in effect endangering transcendence. This kind of knowing becomes ambitious because it's bound in a method, which is understood as a kind of thought machine that can dissect and eventually explain everything (with enough methods).

But, as thought machines, the methods of this dissection are both operational and methodological. The methods of explanation dissect because they often cannot take a phenomenon as a whole. A phenomenon is usually too big to take into the thought machine without breaking it down into parts (which is why the natural and social sciences are broken up into disciplines

6. As we'll see, God always acts within it for the sake of life, for the sake of communion in the life of God, or what we might call salvation for all of creation.

7. The romantic elements of modernity have pushed against this sense of knowing since the days of Johann Hamann. And no doubt the romantic elements have made their impact, but they've been unable to upend the dominant version of knowing as bound in explanation and therefore the casting out of mystery. As modern people, we feel some level of discomfort with modernity's sense of knowing, but this sense of knowing has given us amazing technological and industrial breakthroughs; our whole economies are built on it in the West. So while we're uncomfortable with parts of it, we can't escape it. We want rationalized forms of knowing when it comes to disease, airplane schedules, and even mental illness. For an important piece that offers a differing view of knowing, see Michael Polanyi, *Personal Knowledge: Toward a Post-Critical Philosophy* (Chicago: University of Chicago Press, 1962). For a less well-known but nevertheless interesting alternative epistemology, see James Loder, *The Transforming Moment* (Colorado Springs: Helmers & Howard, 1989).

and subdisciplines). The methods of explanation necessitate reduction so that a phenomenon can be known. Inside modernity's methods of explanation, phenomena are reduced in order to be explained.[8] The parts are knowable, because disconnecting them from the whole reduces them. Taking the phenomenon by its parts gives the knower a sense that the thing they are seeking to know can be possessed (all the more reason the parts as opposed to the whole are important). In modernity, knowing and possession (and therefore control) become tightly entangled.[9]

Taking apart a phenomenon and knowing it through the reduction of its parts produces the stiff temptation to forget the mystery (even the miracle) that the phenomenon *exists* at all. We forget the wonder that there are brains that can think about thinking, whales bigger than school buses, and an aspect of material we call "magnetic" that pulls things toward or repels them from one another. The astonishment that such phenomena *are* is obscured by our drive to know and have them. By ignoring being, we believe knowing equals having. In this thinking, being becomes subordinate to having. Having knowledge of something becomes more important than having an encounter with the being of something.[10]

A God who is reduced to something that can be known is not a God who is God. A God who in a little conflict-stricken church can easily be found and therefore possessed is not God. A God who is subordinate to the methods of knowing is not God. This is Barth's point in both his early sermons in 1916 and in *Römerbrief I* and *II*.

A God who can be known through a method of explanation is a God who is subordinate to theology. In this obsession with the methods of knowing, theology and its methods become more profound than God himself. Barth thinks this is what happened.[11] In different ways, both liberal and positive (hyperorthodox) theology have done just this. Their distinct theological methods

8. For more on this, see David Bentley Hart, *Atheist Delusions: The Christian Revolution and Its Fashionable Enemies* (New Haven: Yale University Press, 2009).

9. Explained further in Alec Ryrie, *Unbelievers: An Emotional History of Doubt* (London: William Collins, 2019), 50–55.

10. This is essentially Martin Heidegger's argument in *Being and Time* (San Francisco: HarperSanFrancisco, 1962). He contends that modernity's drive to explain elevated epistemology to such a height that ontology was nearly forgotten. Heidegger sought to return philosophy to ontology by freeing it of obsession with explanations and the possession of knowledge.

11. I'm not arguing that Barth does not have a method. He indeed has a method. At a certain level, all knowledge is dependent on some sense of a method. But Barth's method is to start outside method. It claims that God is God, and therefore all theological methods are rendered impotent in knowing God. Barth's method—of starting with God and God's act—opposes the idolatry of method. It remains a science, because it seeks intricate and disciplined reflection, but it refuses to kneel to the closed tendencies of the immanent frame. It claims that its method,

have outstripped God. Both have chosen methods of knowing over encounters with the very being of God. They have theology but not encounters with God (which is a tempting strategy inside an immanent frame).

Barth contends that theology has become obsessed with methods because theologians have failed to give attention to a God who is God. Bonhoeffer, in *Creation and Fall*, makes the provocative statement that the devil—represented as the serpent in the garden—is the first theologian.[12] The serpent reduces God's Word into parts, methodically examining it. The serpent tempts Eve with theology by asking, "Did God really say . . . ?" Sin enters the world because Adam and Eve are tempted to make knowledge and knowing more important than being. They encounter God's being in the cool of the garden, but they are tempted to make knowledge through theological method—represented in the tree and its fruit at the center of the garden—more important than being.[13]

Barth fought with his father to go to Marburg because he sensed that the positive and pietist theology his father followed had turned theological commitments into idols. Positive theology did not require a living God, because it had pure doctrine. But this commitment to pure doctrine as method was shabby science. It proved hard to justify that doctrines and creeds were as legitimate instruments for knowing as other scientific methods. Positive theology (and more radically North American fundamentalism) mistakenly equated its normative sources with the immanent-bound tools of knowledge possession.

This was confirmed for Barth as he sat through lectures at Tubingen. Fritz punched the ticket for matriculation at Marburg after a year in the air of Tubingen's positive/orthodox theology. But this year sent the young Barth running deeper into the arms of German liberalism. When the two methods of explanation faced off, positive theology became no match for liberalism. German liberal theology had much better methods of explanation, stretching far deeper into the sciences.[14] Liberal theology was both more scientific and

---

while important, has no power to possess the object it seeks to study. The more the object of theology is studied, the less it is known.

12. See Bonhoeffer, *Creation and Fall: A Theological Exposition on Genesis 1–3* (Minneapolis: Fortress, 1997), 135.

13. This fits into Eberhard Jüngel's interpretation of Genesis 1 and 2 and his overall hamartiology. Jüngel contends that Adam and Eve desired to be like God by having knowledge that would place them beyond nothingness. They chose to possess God by possessing knowledge of what God knows. See Jüngel, *Justification: The Heart of the Christian Faith* (Edinburgh: T&T Clark, 2001), 110–19.

14. This is particularly true when considering the American scene and the fundamentalist–modernist controversy of the 1920s.

therefore more directly connected to the ethos and pathos of society. It was modern! This appealed to Barth. Until he was a pastor.

As a pastor, Barth saw clearly the wisdom of Fritz. Deep in pastoral ministry, Barth saw that the liberalism he loved had also made its methods of explanation an idol. German liberal theology made God into an immanent object knowable through the methods of modern science (or, realizing it couldn't, pivoted away from making God the object of theology). The methods of explanation of both positive and liberal theology and their sure confidence that they could know God, Barth came to believe, were a sure sign that both attended to a God who is *not* God. Right before Peter's wedding, Barth was stuck. The liberal theology he had chased sought scientific methods of knowing over God. But the positive theology of Tubingen also made idols, turning doctrine and the Bible itself into pseudoscientific methods of knowing God and possessing truth.[15]

Not until those days in Bad Boll with the Younger did Barth see another way. Barth saw that the Younger's ministry boldly sought not to know God but to encounter the very acting and being of God. Inspired by the Younger, Barth heralds from under his apple tree that we must start all over again. The Younger's pastoral theology was a prime impetus for the restart that sought to encounter God. For Barth, what made the Blumhardts different was not necessarily their intellect or pietism but their uncompromising commitment that the God of Israel is living and acting even in the immanent frame. In their ministry they sought not to have God by knowing God but to encounter the being of God by first claiming there is *no way* to know God. There is no way to know God unless this God of Israel, as God did with Abraham and Moses, arrives (Gen. 17; Exod. 3).

The *Is*

Sue's question was the right response to the recognition that God is God. Woz's quest to find God, his request for Saint John the Baptist to help in this finding, gave Sue the startling vision. Sue couldn't quite articulate it, but she could see it. When Woz asked for help in finding God, Sue recognized that God is God and therefore cannot be found. Recognizing that God is God, she could only respond with "Do we?"

15. For Barth, the Bible is deeply normative, but not because it is a pseudoscientific text. Turning the Bible into a "scientific" text was the strategy of fundamentalism. The Bible for Barth is a strange book that must remain strange. Its normativity rests in its strange ability to speak about God, even penetrating an immanent frame, not in some idea of it as a tool to possess God.

But what really startled Sue into her confession? What crossed her up? Or, to turn these questions in the direction of Barth's story, what is so important about the statement "God is God"?

The statement has only two unique words: *God* (repeated twice) and *is*. Eberhard Busch reminds us that it's a simple statement, bordering on absurd. Yet, sensing it crossed Sue up. What hit her in a way that had never before was *not* the word "God." She would certainly have agreed that the church was about God. She wasn't looking to turn the church into a religious support group. Most people, even in the mainline churches, aren't looking for congregations that no longer have a concept of God. Sue believed in God . . . most of the time. She expected some kind of God-talk in the church. It wasn't Woz talking about God that crossed Sue up but that he so poignantly stated that he wanted to find God. Sue recognized that this meant not God as an idea but the very God who is God.

As the immanent frame took shape in the eighteenth century, a radical experiment was tried. Right after the storming of the Bastille and the commencement of the French Revolution, a group tried to expunge all God-concepts and God-talk completely from the immanent frame.[16] These revolutionaries pulled priests from cathedrals and killed them. They stripped Notre Dame's altar, changing the building's name to the Temple of Reason. In the 1790s these revolutionaries sought to shape the immanent frame with no space or tolerance for God-talk. But this violent excommunication of God-talk from the immanent frame did not last long. Within a few years, Napoleon Bonaparte reinstated the Catholic Church, allowing the altar to be redressed in the Notre Dame Cathedral. It was advantageous for Napoleon to do so.[17] Most people in Paris were uninterested in excluding all God-talk from the immanent frame. Most were happy to live in the immanent but not without some space for God-talk. For some, God-talk was tolerated, for others it was comforting, and for still others it was despised.

Since the eighteenth century, the concept of God has not been forbidden or precluded from the immanent frame (with a few exceptions). True, even today, a small group of intellectuals, such as the New Atheists, work to eliminate God-talk from the lexicon of the inhabitants of the immanent frame, but they'd never imagine storming Westminster Abbey, overtaking it, and calling it the Temple of Darwin. For most, the concept of God remains. Charles Taylor has explained that our secular age is one in which American

16. This same pursuit was undertaken after another revolution in 1917. The Soviet view of Marxism led to its own pursuits to expunge God from society and turn the immanent frame completely and fully over to material objectives.

17. See Andrew Roberts, *Napoleon: A Life* (New York: Penguin, 2014), esp. part 1.

presidents conclude speeches with "God bless America." Even European citizens hold vigil, offering prayers outside a cathedral, when tragedy strikes. These prayers, they assume, are to "God." Our secular age is not absent the concept of God.[18] Since the 1790s, it is not the concept of God that the immanent frame has attacked. The "God" part of the statement "God is God" is not what's staggering.

Rather, the immanent frame opposes or obscures the *is*, which in turn delivers us into a secular age. The *is* makes Barth's statement important. The immanent frame retains the concept of God but disconnects "God" from the *is*.[19]

When Woz stated that he wanted to find God, in his naivete he was asking something bold: he was asking for help encountering the God who *is*. To her own surprise, Sue saw that Woz wanted the *is*. The stark realization of the *is* led Sue to confess, "Do we?" Do we know how to encounter (even see) a God who *is*? Does this church worship an *idea* of God or does it worship the God who *is*? This question changed things for Sue. For Barth, it changed the direction of his ministry.

Ministry is about the God who *is*. The preacher must speak of the *is*, drawing near to her people as pastor with a presence that proclaims that God *is*. Barth sensed that his people wanted to know who God *is* when they were strenuously laboring at their work and when war was invading their lives. The challenge of theology, against the backdrop of this kind of ministry, is to reflect on the *is*. What was so profound about the Younger when Barth sat with him in 1915 was not that he used the word "God" but that he never wavered from thinking through every issue from the angle of the *is*. The Younger never wavered in his commitment that God *is* the one who speaks, who heals, who acts. Even in this world of immanence, God *is* God, because God *is*. The *is* confesses that God is not a concept but an agent moving in history, penetrating the immanent frame, coming to those in the immanent frame with judgment and grace.

The church is central for *is* theology, because this theology is not concerned with the concept of God (the theology of the university) but with the God who *is*. A God who *is* spills over all categories and concepts and therefore

18. Taylor's *A Secular Age* is an attempt to explain this weird Western phenomenon. Many misinterpretations of Taylor arise among those who often hear this talk of God and think we're not in a secular age (which they understand as a world without any talk of God or gods) but a postsecular age. Taylor understands the shift to be more complicated than just a movement from presecular to secular to postsecular. He thinks there is more than just one imagination that exists in many of us. Our secular age is one where we can still hold on to a concept like God but in a very different way from our ancestors.

19. For the importance of the "is" in Barth's thought, see Timothy Stanley, *Protestant Metaphysics after Karl Barth and Martin Heidegger* (Eugene, OR: Cascade, 2010), 123–24. Stanley provides a nice discussion of how Barth is drawing on Luther for this argument.

can only be found in the context of the world. The church is the collective that encounters and proclaims that God *is* in the world. The church does not simply gather around a concept of God and seek to survive as an institution or defend religion against cultural misappropriation. No, the church is only the church when it seeks the God who *is* and when it proclaims to the world that God *is*. The church is called to help those in the world, like Woz, to encounter the God who *is* to Israel, witnessing that, even deep in the immanent frame, God *is* acting, speaking, judging, healing, and electing.

———————

Through Woz's request, Sue had encountered something she couldn't quite name: she had been encountered by the reality (the realism) that God *is* God. Even though she was unable to name this clearly, something about it swept her up and shifted everything.

6

The Church Is Not the Star
of Its Own Story

Over that month of August, something changed at Saint John the Baptist. Before Woz had stumbled into the Bible study, armaments had been moving and coalescing at the borders. The border between Sue's contingent and Bert's seemed to be readying for a war. The coming battle would be for the future of the congregation.

The question "Who will Saint John the Baptist be?" seemed to hover over everything during those summer months. It exhausted those on the front line, as well as the rank and file. Wrestling both implicitly and explicitly with the question "Who will Saint John the Baptist be?" sucked the energy out of everyone.

Truth be told, this question had been central for some time. It was Luke's main focus. But Luke functioned like a centralized empire. For good or ill, no one else needed to worry about answering the question, because Luke was obsessed with it. Anyone not named Luke just needed to help gather resources so Luke could succeed in making Saint John the Baptist into what he thought it needed to be. Little did anyone, including Luke, know that enduring this question was sucking the life right out of him. With Luke's departure, his ambitious rule ended, and the empire that he had tried to build fell to pieces. As with a real empire, its failure allowed smaller factions and tribes to rise, fighting with each other over who Saint John the Baptist would be. Now the congregation found itself facing the high probability of civil war. Bert and Sue were the opposing generals. They never wanted the fight, but they figured someone had to answer the question "Who will Saint John the Baptist be?" especially now that Luke had departed and they were in the middle of calling a new pastor.

This civil war would suck the life out of them all. It was a race on both sides to outrun apathy. No one seemed to have the energy to wrestle with whether Bert's or Sue's answers were better. The only way to find the energy was to use fear and anger.[1] The question somehow became so lifeless that the only way to muster the drive to address it was to tell yourself or your contingent that you would lose if you didn't rise up and fight for your definition of who the church would be. This produced an unavoidable temptation to characterize, even demonize, the other side. Neither Sue nor Bert wanted that, but it was slowly happening as the calendar turned to August.

The day before Woz stumbled into the Bible study, the pastor search committee had interviewed its first candidate, sooner than anticipated. They didn't expect to review résumés until mid-September. But Bert was concerned that the war would soon burst to the surface, leading to hard feelings and frustration, making it unpleasant and difficult to convince anyone to take the job. This early candidate didn't wow Bert. The committee as a whole was lukewarm. The candidate discussed social and political engagement and mentioned websites Bert had never heard of. Something called Tweeter maybe (remember this is 2012). Bert wasn't excited about him, but the candidate checked several boxes that Sue had been trumpeting. So, wanting to extend an olive branch to Sue, Bert went into the Bible study deciding to throw his weight behind this early candidate. Bert figured, without really admitting it to himself, that it was better to settle than be thrust into conflict. This candidate would give Sue a politically conscious pastor who understood the internet. Maybe that would cast out the malaise that had fallen like the August humidity on the congregation.

But Bert's plan was quickly scrapped after the Bible study. A different vision had dawned. With the plan jettisoned, his anxious concern about the question

---

1. This hints at my own sense of the culture war that swamps the US. It is partly brought on by a lifeless fatigue due to the acceleration of modernity. Life is going too fast and we feel too lifeless to really enter into discussion and conversations. It's easier to just follow your tribe. But still, following the tribe lacks life and meaning unless you can mobilize the tribe through rhetoric—and internet memes—of anger, outrage, and fear. See the following books, which point in this direction: Hartmut Rosa, *Alienation and Acceleration: Towards a Critical Theory of Late-Modern Temporality* (Copenhagen: NSU Press, 2014); Amy Chua, *Political Tribes: Group Instinct and the Fate of Nations* (New York: Penguin, 2018); Douglas Murray, *The Madness of Crowds: Gender, Race and Identity* (London: Bloomsbury, 2019); Ezra Klein, *Why We're Polarized* (New York: Avid Reader, 2020); Julia Ebner, *The Rage: The Vicious Circle of Islamist and Far-Right Extremism* (London: I. B. Tauris, 2017); Jia Tolentino, *Trick Mirror: Reflections on Self-Delusion* (London: 4thEstate, 2019).

"Who will Saint John the Baptist be?" also disappeared. That question shriveled next to the implications of Woz's quest.

––––––

When Sue responded with "Do we?" the room fell silent. Woz's direct appeal for assistance in finding God, coupled with Sue's direct inquisition in response, made everyone stop and think. The pregnant silence finally broke when Helene, a woman in her early seventies who was part of Sue's vocal minority, responded, "I think we can."

The silence fell heavier. Helene paused. Sensing the disquiet, she looked at the group. Recognizing the confused terror on their faces, she prodded with an earnest plea to their silent unease, "Well, I think we should! I think we should help him find God."

Though Helene was aware of the group's uneasiness, Woz was oblivious. He took Helene at her word, not recognizing the meaning of the group's silence. Woz's eyes opened wide, his head bounced with an excited nod and a big toothy grin appeared, framed by his unkempt red beard. "Great! That's great."

Like a sudden August downpour that breaks a suffocating humidity, Helene's naive affirmation and Woz's equally naive response brought a downpour of laughter. It was the first time in weeks, maybe since Jean was in the Bible study, that Bert remembered them laughing. But it was more than laughter. Bert also felt a tangible feeling of anxious energy come over them, startlingly different from the spirit that had hovered over the congregation since Luke's last few months. That anxious exhaustion was a feeling of dullness that worried people with a dreaded discomfort about the congregation's future. That experience of alienation had birthed despondency. This new feeling was an anxiousness of connection and possibility. This anxious excitement felt as if they were standing on the precipice of something important. They felt insecure but alive. They all smiled, which made Woz smile back with his big, goofy, wide grin. The group smiled because Helene had implicated the Bible study, really the whole congregation, in something they weren't sure they could do but felt alive trying. Woz smiled because he wasn't alone.

––––––

From that moment, the question "Who will Saint John the Baptist be?" was pushed to the periphery. In a sense, it disappeared. This important question remained present somewhere, but it seemed much less pressing. No one, not even Sue, thought it a question that needed much attention anymore. Their concerns had shifted. For the first time in a long time, they weren't primarily concerned with how they'd survive. They didn't care much about their own future. Of course they wanted a future, but they were just too occupied with living to be concerned about it. That's the odd thing about life. The more you try to procure it, particularly in some coming future, the quicker you lose it. Life is a gift. To try and hoard it, holding on to it ferociously, corrupts it from the core. It changes life from a gift to a possession (from a *being* to a *having*, as we'll see below). Life as a possession, as something you *have*, as opposed to a gift of being, becomes a heavy burden.

With the Bible study's affirmation to help Woz find God, the very sense of why Saint John the Baptist existed shifted. For the first time in decades, their attention moved off themselves. They weren't racing to possess life, watching it leak out as quickly as it was attained. This was exactly Luke's problem. The more buckets of life that he poured into Saint John the Baptist, the more life leaked out the seams of the congregation. The finding and filling of life over and against its steady draining pushed Luke and the whole congregation to pour faster and faster, eventually exhausting them all.

In its place arrived an odd and welcome relief to stop thinking about themselves and just be alive. Questions of their own existence didn't seem to matter as much. Woz's arrival made their existence matter, while taking their attention off themselves.[2] Saint John the Baptist's existence mattered all the more now, but not in itself. When they stopped thinking about themselves and their need to survive, surprisingly they found life.[3]

Your Story Is No Longer Your Own

Saint John the Baptist was able to stop focusing on itself by recognizing that the story it was now invited to live as a congregation shifted toward two other primary subjects, neither of which was itself! Saint John the Baptist realized that *they*, as a church, were no longer the main character of their own story. Their story was about awkward Woz and the God he sought to encounter. The main characters of their story were Woz (as a representative of the world) and the God who is God.

2. Woz put a call on Saint John the Baptist. This call gave them life. Colm O'Grady, in *The Church in the Theology of Karl Barth* (Washington, DC: Corpus Books, 1968), 250–53, discusses the centrality of call in Barth's ecclesiology.

3. "When the Christian community believes that it exists for the world, it knows what it believes. What it says in this regard, therefore, can be said only with unconditional, assured and joyous certainty if it is really made as a statement of faith." Karl Barth, *Church Dogmatics*, IV/3.2 (Edinburgh: T&T Clark, 1962), 785.

This construct is similar to the ecclesiology that Barth imagined in the decades after his encounter with the Younger.[4] Both the Elder and the Younger Blumhardt recognized that Jesus Christ—not the church—was profoundly the Victor, whose ministry was in the world.

The world itself was the object of God's love. The Younger boldly lived out this commitment. In 1915, the Younger impressed upon Pastor Barth the importance of starting and finishing every contemplation with God, because God is God. But he also taught Barth that because God is God, we are called to love the world. Barth confronted the world in the same way he did his brothers, taking no prisoners. The Younger encouraged Barth to keep that fierce passion but to remember that love for the world is essential. The Younger broke the mold of most pietist healers. Most dynamic pietist preachers and healers spoke with venom toward the depravity of the world, calling people out of the world. They tended to see the church as a shelter, a haven in a sinful world. The church was in the world but not of it. These passionate pietists tended to preach that God hates the world but loves the church.

Thanks to the inspiration of the Younger, Barth flips this script, provocatively stating that God judges the church and loves the world. In God's love for the world, God does judge the world in order to redeem the world. But it's the church, not the world, that has refused to be faithful. With all its shiny religion, the church has failed to seek a God who is God. The church has idolatrously made *itself* the subject of its own story. The church's story has become about the church and its possession of its religion, *not* the God who is acting in and *for* the world. The target of Barth's attack in *Römerbrief II* is not the world—not even a modern, immanent-bound one. He's attacking the church and its religion. Religion is the corrosive issue, because religion deceives the church into believing it is the subject, even the star, of its own story.

Beyond the Religion of Immanence

When Barth met the Younger, the Younger had just come through a humiliation. Frustrated with the churches in Württemberg and their own self-interest, the Younger had turned to socialism. We'll discuss this more in a later chapter, but for now it's important to know that the Younger did this because he

4. I'm referring here to the ecclesiology that Barth sketched in *Church Dogmatics* IV. I find Barth's formal ecclesiology in IV less captivating than the thought in I/1 and his earlier theology. That said, I see continuity (dialectical continuity) even in this more formal ecclesiology, particularly as it relates to the church and the world.

understood God's great love for the world. He believed God was acting in the world, working to save not the church but the world. Socialism, against the background of the church's obsession with itself, seemed like a tool for God's use.[5]

Pastor Barth saw something similar in socialism. Hermann Kutter, through Thurneysen, had shown Barth how to think about socialism in relation to the great word "God." As the Younger made it far into the heart of the socialist party in Germany, he sensed disease, to his great disappointment. This disease eerily resembled the one he smelled in the churches of Württemberg. The socialist party, as much as the church, cared not for the world and those suffering in it but only for its own survival. The party, like the church, wanted to be the star of its own story. As the stars of their own stories, neither the party nor the church could love the world. Without loving the world, they were blind to the act of a God who is God.

Barth learned from the Blumhardts that God acts in the world. If God acts in the world, God does not abandon the world but instead seeks its salvation. *God's acting in the immanent frame means that God acts in the world, not just in the church.* If this crucial point is missed, so too is the profundity of the modern theology Barth seeks to construct for the church.

As mentioned, Barth takes the radical and distinct step of claiming that God acts within the totality of the immanent frame—in all of it, not just a part of it. To claim that God *is* God means that God cannot be excluded and kept from acting in any part of the immanent frame. There are no zones or structures inside the immanent frame that can exclude God (though this exclusion of God is a central goal for some architects of the immanent frame).[6] God acts in the world, as the world is constituted, because God acts not in an ideal world but in the real/actual world.

To state that God acts in the totality of the immanent frame, and therefore in the world as it is constituted (not in its ideal form), is an incredibly radical move. Both liberalism and pietism, in their own distinct ways, have conceded to the wishes of the immanent frame and would not say this. The immanent frame allows God a place in its structures, but only a single place that is itself bound in immanence: religion.

Most other modern theologies, Barth believes, have done their work by conceding that God can be known only in the zone of private or institutionalized

5. Christian Collins Winn discusses this further in *"Jesus Is Victor!" The Significance of the Blumhardts for the Theology of Karl Barth* (Eugene, OR: Pickwick, 2009), xvi, 144–46.

6. According to Taylor, this exclusion of God is what first brought our sense of the secular. Secular 1 is the exclusion of God from the public structures of society, planting God in only the private realm.

religion (or some variation thereof).[7] The immanent frame imposes a temptation that most modern theologies before Barth succumbed to. It pushes God from the center of life to the edge, as Bonhoeffer said, caging God in religion.[8] The immanent frame, wanting mystery and transcendence out of the center of life, makes a space for religion on the fringes, consequently planting God there. A God planted in religion cannot act. Most other modern theologies are theology without God.[9]

As a pastor, and a theologian for pastors, Barth knew that a theology without God would not suffice.[10] It weakened the practice of ministry and imported a narcissistic idolatry into the church. It led the church to become obsessed with the church, thereby no longer concerning itself with a God who is God by ministering to the world. It lost the kenotic (self-emptying) nature that conforms the church to the crucified Christ, who has been raised from the dead and acts even now in the whole world through the Spirit. Most denominational churches and congregations have succumbed to the temptation to make themselves the star of their own story. They've made themselves their own idol by holding their own survival (or growth—really the same thing) as their deepest longing.[11]

The immanent frame, by creating a zone for religion and equating God with religion (by putting an immanent shell around God), allows a space for the church, at least in most contexts. This space for the church is the concrete institutional form of religion. In modernity, religion becomes the church as an immanent institution. God is in the church, and the church even controls God, because the only place where God can exist in the immanent frame is in the zone of religion. No wonder the alluring temptation for the church to

7. This makes Kierkegaard so important to Barth's *Römerbrief II*. The statement above is also a slight overstatement: Others had pushed at the edges of this, such as Barth's favorite teacher Wilhelm Herrmann. But no one could name this as forcefully and as creatively as Barth, because in my mind none were doing this thinking as deeply inside the practice of ministry and inspired by ministers such as Christoph Blumhardt.

8. See Bonhoeffer, *Letters and Papers from Prison* (New York: Macmillan, 1953), 327–28.

9. "Religion—and Barth is here speaking pre-eminently of Christianity—is at its heart, an exercise in self-delusion." Bruce McCormack, *Karl Barth's Critically Realistic Dialectical Theology: Its Genesis and Development, 1909–1936* (Oxford: Oxford University Press, 1997), 133.

10. Here is an example of how Barth's theology was assumed to be for pastors. Konrad Hammann, in his biography of Rudolf Bultmann, mentions that Barth was second on a list of possible hires for a new position. But Barth was passed over because his work was assumed to be for pastors and not academic enough. Hammann writes, "Bultmann thereupon presented his own candidates of choice: Friedrich Gogarten, Karl Barth, and Friedrich Karl Schumann. Although he recognized the excellent theological work that Barth had carried out 'with dazzling intuition,' he could only place him second behind Gogarten. For in Barth's case, scholarly interest trailed behind orienting theology to the church." *Rudolf Bultmann: A Biography* (Salem, OR: Polebridge, 2013), 167.

11. Protestantism has become its own worst nightmare.

make itself the star of its own story. If you tacitly contend that you possess God, survival very easily becomes the most important thing.[12]

The logic that equates God and religion, and the church as the concrete form of religion, benefits those wanting to shut down the immanent frame to any sense of transcendence. With God caged in religion, and religion pushed to the fringes, resources can be shifted to other institutions and state bureaucracies. This shifting of resources to other institutions leads the church to misinterpret the dependence of their existence, *not* on God who is God, but on the accruing of resources. The church becomes the center of its own story, because its highest longing is to accrue enough resources to survive (or to thrive as a star in its denomination or synod). These other institutions that resources are shifted to are believed to deserve the resources, for they're more central to our lives. This has the advantage of keeping religion weak enough that it will have little reach to return to mystery or reinstate itself within political or economic orders.[13] This resource-shifting will in turn make religious institutions more anxious about who they are than about where God is acting in the world.

The Church as Supporting Actor

Yet, if the church is not the star of its own story, who or what is? Following Barth, we're not after a modern theology beyond the church. Ironically, modern theologies that concede to the immanent frame's planting of God in religion tend toward a theology *without* the church. For Barth, attending to a God who is God is impossible outside the church. The church is the context for reflecting on and knowing a God who acts as God. As the servant of the world and not the primary subject of God's action, the church holds the story, proclaims the story, and embodies the story of God's action in the world for the sake of the world's salvation.[14]

---

12. Alexander Schmemann adds to this in his own way: "Nowhere in the New Testament, in fact, is Christianity presented as a cult or as a religion. Religion is needed where there is a wall of separation between God and man. But Christ who is both God and man has broken down the wall between man and God. He has inaugurated a new life, not a new religion." *For the Life of the World* (Yonkers, NY: St. Vladimir's Seminary Press, 2018), 27.

13. This attempt to grab political or economic power is one odd peculiarity of late modernity in America, but it is also popping up across Europe as the continent deals with the immigration crisis. Religion is seeking to reinstate itself in political orders. This has been done to a corrupting level in America. The major problem with this logic is that these fundamentalist groups can't see that they fight not for a God who is God, but for religion to not be at the fringes of society. This just cements their view of God deeper into institutions of religion. Even over against their rhetoric, they are not fighting for God but for religion. They've fallen into the idolatry of not having a God who is God and instead are seeking their own political wishes.

14. "The World and the Church are what they are only because they are related to one another. Neither can say that the other is excluded absolutely. What is absolute is simply the fact

The church is not the primary, or even the secondary, subject of the story. The story is God's act (first subject) in and for the world (second subject).[15] In relation to Saint John the Baptist, the subject of their story is Woz (the concrete representation of the world) and the God who is God that Woz seeks.[16] Woz's plea reminded—or maybe informed for the first time—the congregation of its mission to witness to the God who *is*. The question "Who will Saint John the Baptist be?" was replaced by "Who is God and where do we find God?" Or more specifically, "In what ways can we help Woz find the God who *is* God?"

Barth is after specifically a *church* dogmatics (reflection on this God's act), because the church, as a supporting subject of the story, is in position to narrate, hold, and in humility proclaim the story. The church is the narrator, not the star. The narrator serves the story and the primary characters in the story. Though the story is not about the narrator, the narrator is crucial. Paul proclaims only Christ and him crucified (1 Cor. 2:2), not the answer to "Who should the church in Ephesus or Corinth be?" Paul is clear on who God is for us in Jesus Christ and the shape of this crucified God's act for the salvation of the world. Paul is less clear, because he's less direct, on his ecclesiology.

The church can only proclaim the story—particularly inside the immanent frame—when the church remembers it is not the primary subject or star of the story. The church has its ministry, mission, and purpose when it forgets itself. Its mission and purpose is to concern itself with the ministry of God who is acting in and for the world. Vladimir Lossky says beautifully, "The Church exists in the world, . . . [and when she does] the world cannot contain her."[17] Saint John the Baptist becomes flooded with life because their attention is given to the God who is God and to the world, coming to them in the person of Woz seeking to encounter this God.

But this didn't free Saint John the Baptist from a crisis. It only heightened the crisis.

---

that both are opposed to God. Seen from God's point of view, the church is done with—but then, so is the world. Israel and the world are both done away." Karl Barth, *The Epistle to the Romans* (London: Oxford University Press, 1933), 401.

15. Barth's ecclesiology in *Church Dogmatics* IV/3.2 is built around this sense of the church not being the star of its own story. By serving the world, the church is a community in and for the world.

16. The Woz event made Saint John the Baptist the church. For Barth the church is event before institution.

17. *In the Image and Likeness of God* (Yonkers, NY: St. Vladimir Seminary Press, 1974), 183.

7

Welcome to Crisis Mode

After Karl Barth finished his musings under his apple tree on Romans, Thurneysen and others encouraged him to publish them. But no publisher agreed. Pastors in small, rural, working-class villages tend not to get book deals. Such deals were easier for pastors like Hermann Kutter and Leonhard Ragaz, who mounted the pulpits of important urban churches. Three publishers said no (to one of the most important books in the history of Christian thought!).[1] Finally, with the financial help of a friend, a small Bern publisher took a shot on the odd book.[2]

Barth was reading the proofs of the forthcoming book when the Great War came to an end. Its end came with little celebration and even less relief. The end of the war wasn't quite like jumping out of the frying pan and into the fire, but it was nowhere near the ticker-tape parade in New York City after victory in World War II. Across the whole continent, but particularly in central Europe, the war ended but the dread continued. In some ways, the dread of a crisis even mounted. After the war's conclusion, new troubles arose. The war's confusing and bloody end only seemed to multiply the problems. The Great War was promised to be the war to end all wars. But with its end came economic calamity, further strife and hatred between nations, and a terrible influenza (the Spanish Flu).[3]

---

1. Barth had published before. He'd contributed numerous pieces to magazines and academic journals (at a time when such publications were important). He'd also published a short book before this with Thurneysen. But this was different. This was a substantive piece of his own theological making. Therefore, it was much harder to find a publisher.
2. Eventually a German publisher would get the rights and distribute it widely.
3. The flu came in July and returned in the fall. Barth had to cancel services and was even bedridden. As I write these pages, the world is in the middle of its own COVID-19 crisis. In-person

On New Year's Day 1919, Barth held the published *Römerbrief* in his
hands. It bore a 1919 publication date, but Barth had already received his
copies before Christmas 1918. The satisfaction of the book's release brought
no relief from the crises that rudely seemed to be accosting Europe in the
new year. Psalm 23 seemed to be the only appropriate text to preach this
New Year's Day Sunday. Hope in the valley of the shadow of death felt like
the right text for the moment. (Though, in reading the sermon, hope is much
harder to see than the darkness of the valley.) In Barth's sermon the crisis is
ripe. Toward the end, Barth says that the psalmist invites us—the listeners
up against a crisis—to transformation. But to find this transformation, we
need to become the kind of persons who confess the depth of a crisis and
seek God in the midst of crisis. On this New Year's Day 1919, after the Great
War and with the economy crumbling and workers striking, Barth says this
kind of person "would speak with us like this":

> Yes, as I go into the New Year, I too am burdened with serious cares and con-
> cerns. I do not see the world through rose-colored glasses. I do not think people
> are better than they are. I know that for all guilt the penalty must be and is paid.
> I except from this guilt neither myself, nor my family, nor my country. I antici-
> pate difficult, serious, and confused times to come for me and my children. I no
> longer rely on my small amount of money, nor on what is now called law and
> order, nor on my good intentions, nor on the goodwill of those around me. I
> know that we live in a time when everything is unstable: churches, states, the
> crowns of kings. Even less stable is the small frame of rights and duties that
> has until now held and protected me.
>
> But in all this I perceive the hand of God, and certainly God's hand of judg-
> ment, which perhaps touches a great deal that is dear to me, and yet it is God's
> hand and not the hand of the devil. Whatever may fall under God's judgment
> must fall under it, and it will involve me as it must; but God is dearer to me
> than all else that is dear to me. In good times I forgot God long enough; I do
> not intend to lose God anew in evil times. I understand God, and I want to
> understand God. I see God pronounce judgment, because God will reveal God's
> grace on earth. I see God destroy, because God wills to build. I hear God say
> "No," in order that God's great "Yes" can be heard again. My hope is in God,
> and therefore I am safe in the middle of the storm. I look forward to and await
> God's light, and therefore all the darkness of the present can have no power

---

church services have been shut down for months and the economy is in free fall. The economic
crisis of the influenza also affected Barth in 1919. The workers in Safenwil took the step to
socially distance, striking for the sake of safety. This influenza-caused strike pulled Barth into
the conflict. It would eventually lead to major issues with some members of his congregation.
For more on this, see Eberhard Busch, *Karl Barth: His Life from Letters and Autobiographical
Texts* (Philadelphia: Fortress, 1975), 106. Busch doesn't give us a lot of detail, however.

over me. "The Lord is my shepherd, I shall not want. He makes me lie down in green pastures; he leads me beside still waters; he restores my soul." Yes, we can sigh and yet still be blessed.[4]

These words are the first sign that the book, which on this New Year's Day had not yet even been released, would need to be rewritten. The crisis and its relation to a God who is God will need to be sharpened. Crisis is already starkly present in the first *Römerbrief*. But a clear articulation of how God acts inside such a crisis, how God's action itself *is* a crisis, is not clear enough. The Great War and the crises that followed show two things to us unequivocally. First, the immanent frame cannot save us from the crises of war, famine, oppression, and disease. Second, the immanent frame, though unable to save us, still stands. Even after this buffet of post–Great War crises, the immanent frame *is*.

The crisis is stoked. It asks how a God who *is* acting in the concrete *is* of the immanent frame. Barth knows that a modern theology for the church will need to more clearly claim, inside these crises, how God *is* God. For all the crises that Pastor Barth faces, the crisis of all crises is the reality that God *is* God. Inside an immanent frame that *is*, the God who *is* is a crisis. But a church in the immanent frame has not embraced this sense that God is a crisis. More to the point, the church has directly opposed such a view of God. Let's see why.

The Crisis of Relevance

Saint John the Baptist felt the exhausting necessity to answer, "Who should Saint John the Baptist be?" because they thought they were at the precipice of a great crisis. If they couldn't answer who and why they were, they wouldn't survive. They would have no life unless they could find it for and within themselves.[5] The crisis the congregation felt was the viability of their existence.

With Luke's departure they were in this crisis because they no longer had a grip on being the star of their own story. They lacked money and new members. But more, they lacked relevance (after all, it's assumed that only relevance attracts new money and new members). Truth be told, Saint John the Baptist had about the same amount of money and members as when Luke left. But Luke did seem to take relevance with him. To be the star of

---

4. Karl Barth, in William Willimon, *The Early Preaching of Karl Barth: Fourteen Sermons with Commentary by William H. Willimon* (Louisville: Westminster John Knox, 2009), 92–93.

5. Michael Horton's *People and Places: A Covenant Ecclesiology* (Louisville: Westminster John Knox, 2008) discusses this temptation of the church inheriting modernity's concern for the self by looking inside the self, never coming out of the self. Horton offers a number of interesting points about the eccentric nature of the church.

your own story, you need to feel relevant for the now, but even more so for an anticipated future. To really shine as the star of your own story, you need to be accruing more and more future relevance (and receiving recognition for your relevance).[6]

In trying to find relevance without Luke, the church started by answering, "Who should Saint John the Baptist be?" This question really wanted to know, "What would make Saint John the Baptist relevant?" Saint John the Baptist was facing a crisis of their viable existence because they were feeling a crisis of relevance. If they couldn't find relevance, and therefore find the confidence to be the star of their own story, their future was bleak. Without relevance, they surmised, there would be no life and only the crisis of their decline.

Sue's argument for change was always dually mobilized by discussions of financial runways and the need for a politically engaged pastor. Political consciousness was somehow assumed to solve the issue of a short financial runway. This seems contradictory: how would a pastor who speaks against the excesses of capitalism, for instance, create more capital to secure the institutional viability of the congregation? These don't seem to go together until you add relevance into the equation. Sue imagined that a politically conscious pastor would be relevant (even more relevant, or at least differently relevant, than Luke).[7] Through this hypothetical pastor's relevance, new resources would be accrued, which would extend the financial runway of the church—by extending its relevance and ability to secure resources.

Saint John the Baptist is far from alone in chasing relevance. It's not difficult to convince church leaders that they stand before a crisis. But it is hard for this crisis *not* to be understood as a crisis of relevance. Some denominations and congregations attempt to secure relevance through models of attraction, others through social consciousness. The tension between these two groups can fracture a denomination. But in the end, even despite their animosity, they agree that they are facing a crisis of relevance. The loss of the church as the primary subject of its own story is the problem. The question that violently divides them is whether programs or doctrinal protectionism or political attentiveness or the rhetoric of identity justice will win the relevance to ease the acute inflammation of crisis.

---

6. I lean particularly on Alex Honneth's social theory in *The Struggle for Recognition: The Moral Grammar of Social Conflicts* (Cambridge, MA: MIT Press, 1995). Honneth makes a case that recognition is a significant piece of identity and purpose in late modernity.

7. Political consciousness as being equal to relevance is a legacy of the 1960s. For more on this, see Christopher Caldwell, *The Age of Entitlement: America since the Sixties* (New York: Simon & Schuster, 2020).

But the presumptions here may not be true. This way of thinking assumes the church can exist beyond or outside crisis, as if some strategy could move the church beyond the uncomfortable place of crisis, relieving the swelling imposed by crisis. "The church just needs to get back to the Bible," or "The church just needs to stop being unwelcoming."[8] These statements insinuate that the crisis can be solved and done with, giving the church a footing beyond crisis. But this can only be presumed if the church has wrongly been thought of as the subject of its own story. If the church is the subject (star) of its own story, it should be able, in its own power, to solve the crisis that meets it in the second act of the tale it is living. Because the church is the star of its own story, the crisis it confronts is its own crisis, one that challenges the identity and viability of the church alone. In this way of thinking, the church ironically both narrows and at the same time catastrophizes the crisis.

The church narrows the crisis by matching it to the reductions of the immanent frame. The crisis becomes only as wide as a congregation or denomination's viability to win resources through relevance. This reduced ability to possess the relevance that wins resources is catastrophized to mean that the Christian confession can and will disappear. "If we don't change, the church is sunk, and Christian faith will vanish." Without new ways to get new resources through relevance, the gospel will be lost. A church could only believe this if it has replaced Jesus Christ with itself (which may indeed have occurred).

Pastor Barth does not think that this narrowing or catastrophizing is the essence of the crisis. The crisis he sees cannot be solved by church ingenuity, because the church is not the subject of its story. And the crisis is much bigger than the loss of relevance. In fact, trying to evacuate the crisis may be the height of the church's disobedience, showing it has replaced a living God with dead religion. A church that wants to be outside the crisis is not the church (or is the church of Esau, not the church of Jacob, as Barth says in the rewritten *Römerbrief II*).

Pastor Barth contends that the church can never solve the crisis because the crisis is not escapable. This inescapability is what caused others to label Barth and his friends as theologians of crisis, and their thought the "theology of crisis," originally intended as a slight. It would eventually become a positive (or at least neutral) descriptor of the work of Barth, Friedrich Gogarten, Emil Brunner, and Rudolf Bultmann.[9] Crisis, particularly in Barth's theology, had

8. Samuel Wells offers these insightful comments about "welcoming" as a high good in relation to the congregation. See *A Future That's Bigger Than the Past: Catalysing Kingdom Communities* (Norwich, UK: Canterbury, 2019).

9. For more on this, see Gary Dorrien, *The Barthian Revolt in Modern Theology: Theology without Weapons* (Louisville: Westminster John Knox, 2000), 72.

become so inescapable it was dizzying. And this crisis was so inescapable it could never be confused as a crisis of relevance. But this is exactly how most modern churches, big and small, think about the crisis before them. The crisis is an immanent-bound loss of relevance, *not* the crisis of the encounter with a God who is God. To explore why both big and small, liberal and conservative, traditional and contemporary congregations believe the crisis they face is one of relevance, we need to look again at the immanent frame.

The Crisis of Relevance inside the Immanent Frame

Because of the shape of the immanent frame, it is hard *not* to be deceived into understanding the church's crisis as a crisis of relevance. The immanent frame inflicts upon the church a predicament of relevance by pushing the church (and transcendence) from the center of life to its fringes. Being moved to the fringes is not *the* crisis.[10] This red herring allows the immanent frame to impose on our imagination that the church's deepest crisis is its loss of relevance (which is problematic only in the immanent frame, not in transcendent reality). We feel this crisis of relevance deeply. But if we go deeper, beyond the loss of relevance, we can spot the real crisis and understand what Pastor Barth sees and pushes us to confess.

As mentioned, the architects of the immanent frame were not necessarily looking to eliminate God from the universe. But they were eliminating mystery as an explanation for what was and could be.[11] Devaluing mystery pushes the proprietor of mystery, the church, from the center of control. René Descartes, for instance, never directly attacked the church. As a good, Jesuit-educated man, he never made a frontal attack on any ecclesial power or structure.[12] But the ramifications of his thought dislodged the church from the center of our social imagination. His thought caused us to move past mystery and into mathematics as true explanation.

10. One could interpret Stanley Hauerwas's theology as a response, even an embrace, of this ecclesial reality. Hauerwas has been of significant help in thinking theologically about how the church should embrace being at the fringes and existing as an alternative community.

11. Providential deism was a kind of halfway point in removing mystery from the center of life. Mystery no longer provided an explanation, but mystery without presence could still be felt in the imaginary. Providential deism claimed that all explanations were bound within the methods of natural discovery. But to mitigate the longing for mystery, it could claim a watchmaker God was the first cause that set these laws of natural explanation in motion. Eventually the imaginary would shift enough that the halfway point of deism became unnecessary, and the belief arose that people could live without mystery, pushing deism into an artifact of the eighteenth (and early nineteenth) century.

12. This point is made very clear in A. C. Grayling, *Descartes* (London: Pocket Books, 2005).

The church was deeply relevant when mystery was central to both our social imagination and social order. When mathematics took mystery's place, the church became de facto less relevant, unmoored from the center and eventually pushed to the fringes.[13]

Mystery being upended as a viable explanation introduced the possibility of the church as irrelevant.[14] Before modernity, the thought of an irrelevant church was nearly impossible. In the early medieval period, the mystery of the infinite participating in the finite was too central to everyone's imagination to *not* make the church deeply pertinent. This imagination was solidified less through treatises and doctrinal exposition than through the practice of the Eucharist.[15] The people routinely participated, or at least watched, as the mystery of the Mass brought the infinite into the finite realities of bread and wine. Witnessing this mystery allowed the finite creatures watching or tasting to trust that their own vulnerable souls would also be given an infinite home in heaven through the consumed body of Jesus and the loving embrace of his mother.

The Crown and Its Crisis

When Descartes was sitting in his Jesuit classroom, the church and the crown shared the center. When mathematics unbolted the church from the center of relevance, the crown wasn't all that upset. Most monarchies across Europe were not sad to see the church slowly dislodged and pulled outside the center.[16]

13. This is as operational in Europe as America. However, America is an exception in some sense because the accruing of relevance by religion has still somehow been possible. Those in France, for instance, have given up on such assumptions. For more on the American exception, see Charles Taylor, *Dilemmas and Connections: Selected Essays* (Cambridge, MA: Belknap, 2011), chap. 8.

14. There is some slippage here. These few sentences read too much as a home run or as a "subtraction story," as Taylor calls it. I'm deeply committed, here and in my other works, to Taylor's assertion that there is no one thing—no home run of sole change—that completely shifts an imaginary. I wish to avoid falling into this trap. The scope of this project is a discussion between Karl Barth and a lived ecclesiology. I ask the reader to forgive me for not developing this push to the fringes with enough zigs and zags, as Taylor has taught.

15. For more on how the Eucharist framed the social imaginary of people before modernity, see Regina Mara Schwartz, *Sacramental Poetics at the Dawn of Secularism* (Stanford, CA: Stanford University Press, 2008).

16. It's around this time that the divine right of kings is developed as a viable concept, something not previously developed or even thought about before. The church and the crown were too interconnected. But with the church unbolted from the center, the king sought to fill the vacuum. Someone like Louis XIV could view himself as far more powerful than even the church (as if he, himself, were France). He became the fullness of mystery, the Sun King who needed a palace in Versailles that directly reflected heaven itself.

The crown now had sole ownership of the center. The sovereign was able to do what he wanted without those pesky bishops and cardinals being strong enough to oppose his power (think Louis XIV). But the crown's monopoly on the center was only a short pause before it too would be (even more violently) pushed from the center (Louis's great-great-great-grandson meeting *Madame la Guillotine*).

After all, the crown secured the center through the mystery of the lineage of blood, symbol, and ritual. The monarchy smelled like mystery as well, and soon it too was under attack. The relevance—or centrality—of the crown could no longer be won by mystery. But if its power was not in mystery, where was it? When the church was dislodged by the rationalistic thoughts of the enlightened, the crown didn't realize its own dislodging was soon to follow. John Locke was already starting the wrenching, which decades later (in 1776) colonists in the so-called New World would accomplish.

To give us some perspective (and to help us recognize that relevance can't really be our crisis), we need to see that the crown, even more than the church, has borne the brunt of the loss of relevance inside the immanent frame. For instance, outside England it's nearly impossible to name a royal. Most European countries, like France and Germany, have long buried the crown. Though the church was first to be pushed from the center, the crown was even more violently excommunicated. In countries like France and Germany, the crown disappeared and the church continued. No one outside the Scandinavian countries can name the king of Norway or Denmark. Visitors might be shocked to find that Oslo has an inhabited palace.

Even in England the crown has faced a number of crises. Most of them, especially in the twentieth century, have revolved around relevance (consider the plot of the movie *The Queen* and season 1 of the TV series *The Crown*). The population might rightfully wonder about the relevance of the crown on their lives. The English royals on occasion have been severely critiqued for their own irrelevance and ignorance of the life of common citizens. What has kept the crown secure in England is not a return to the mystery of blood, symbol, and enchanted ritual, but instead a shift to equate the crown with celebrity. This is the direct legacy of Diana, Princess of Wales (though even Queen Victoria was moving in this direction). Before her death, Diana recognized that her relevance as a royal rested in celebrity. Diana embraced celebrity, as opposed to being above it, making her "the people's princess." Diana knew that the way for even celebrity to free itself from biting satire, which can turn to disdain, is to show your relevance by using your celebrity to support causes and charities (which has its nineteenth-century antecedent in Prince Albert, Victoria's able husband who began moving in this direction).[17]

Inside the immanent frame, celebrity is a powerful reality, because though it is not mystery, it gives off a low buzz of mystery's transcendent quality. Celebrity can combine a feeling of mysterious transcendence with a strong commitment to immanence. It feels otherworldly to meet a celebrity, because a celebrity is so relevant (marked by a high level of achieved recognition) that she affects how you dress, talk, and even think about the drought in Sudan.[18] The celebrity's relevance is bound in her personification of the realities that now rest at the center, replacing church and crown. The celebrity is the personification of commerce and consumption. The celebrity becomes the immanent frame priest, giving the new center of commerce and consumption a feeling of weight and yet effervescence.[19]

What is relevant wears the marks of commerce and consumption, because these realities are at the center of our imaginary. These realities stretch so deep they land even in the lap of a small church like Saint John the Baptist. This congregation's imagination is so framed by commerce and consumption, without really even knowing it, that they're led to think a relevant pastor can win them resources. Or, at the very least, they think they need to answer "Who should Saint John the Baptist be?" to stave off decline and win resources. These won resources, it's imagined, will secure for the congregation more members and a longer financial runway.

A Crisis Made for the Immanent Frame

The crisis the church faces, in this logic, is the crisis of relevance. If the church could gain relevance, it could win resources in a world centered on commerce and consumption. But this kind of thinking implicitly concedes that the immanent frame is closed and God cannot *personally* act in it. This leads congregations to think they must, themselves, become the subject of their own story if they hope to survive.

Those in big churches are particularly tempted (having tasted an amusebouche of relevance) to speak of God as an object or possession of the church. Without intending to, this just occurs, because the church makes itself so

17. For an insightful, practical theology on celebrity, see Pete Ward, *Gods Behaving Badly: Media, Religion, and Celebrity Culture* (Waco: Baylor University Press, 2011).

18. Taylor discusses some of this and particularly the grieving of the death of Princes Diana in *A Secular Age* (Cambridge, MA: Belknap, 2007), 50, 482, 517, and 715.

19. This points to William Cavanaugh's argument about how consumerism becomes a form of enchantment. See *Being Consumed* (Grand Rapids: Eerdmans, 2008).

much the subject of its own story that God plays only a supporting role, and a depersonalized one at that.[20]

The congregation begins to resemble a company. As a company, the church must understand itself as the star. There is nothing wrong with a congregation or denomination learning from business and the practices of companies.[21] But while doing so, the church must be careful. For the goods that shape the practices and imaginary of businesses are bound in a closed immanent frame substantiated by the logic of commerce and consumption. God can be imagined as a depersonalized object that is assumed to be the church's product.

Products are important to companies, but not as important as the story the company tells about itself. The story of a company always outstrips the story of a product. The account of a product is contingent on the narrative of the company. Just watch *Shark Tank*. A common critique of a pitch is "This is a good product, but not yet a company." Sharks invest in companies, not products, because products don't make money until they exist within the story (and structure) of a company. It's nearly impossible to tell a story about *just* a product. Such stories are antistories. We call them "user's guides."[22] User guides are boring to read! But before racing too far ahead, let's step back and think about all this in relation to a specific company: Apple Inc.[23]

It's hard to tell the story of Apple Inc. without mentioning products like the Mac or iPod. But ultimately the company's story is something beyond the products. At times, Apple has even stopped selling iPods, and the Mac is now far from the center of their business. The product itself can never be the star of the story, because the product is depersonalized. The best story we can tell about the product is the user's guide—which is no story at all.

20. The most radical example of such logic is the American prosperity gospel. In such churches God is talked about a lot, but not as a God who is, not as God who is the subject of the church's own story. The church or its ministry is star of the story. God is the device that wins the church or ministry the resources to be über-relevant.

21. For how a congregation can do this, see Wells, *A Future That's Bigger Than the Past*. Wells is a significant theologian who has reflected deeply on this.

22. Which, not surprisingly, is what North American fundamentalism made the Bible into. It made sense that this would happen, because God was made into an objectified product, not a person. It became necessary for the church to worship relevance by cleaving to commerce and consumption, to "evangelize" the unbelieving world. See further my *The Congregation in a Secular Age* (Grand Rapids: Baker Academic, 2020).

23. I have a small obsession with using Apple as an analogy. I've done so in many of my other books, most substantially in *Bonhoeffer as Youth Worker* (Grand Rapids: Baker Academic, 2014), chap. 15 (on discipleship). I'm not sure why. Probably because at this moment I type on a Mac, to my immediate right is an iPhone, an Apple Pencil, and AirPods, and to my left is an Apple Watch on the charger, resting next to my iPad charger (the iPad is upstairs). Commerce and consumption frame my imagination as much as anyone's.

What makes stories both captivating and formational is their personal nature. It's captivating to hear about *who* came up with the idea for the iPod and how others built off the success of the iPod to further Apple Inc.'s story of expanding relevance and growth. The immanent frame depersonalizes God by blinding us to God's action. The immanent frame leads us to tacitly accept that God cannot act. Implicitly conceding this, the best the church can do is make God into a depersonalized object. The church's story as a company must become central, making God the church's product, at best.

This reductive way of thinking proves tempting because it is so advantageous. Making God into a product allows us to put the church and its God-product back into the center of our lives, which achieves relevance. This can happen only if we make God into a depersonalized product that can stand squarely on our new center of commerce and consumption. The church's gravest temptation in the immanent frame of late modernity (in a neoliberal age) is to turn God into a product so that the church can be the subject of its own story. This ever-present temptation in the immanent frame tells us that only the relevant survive. The celebrity pastor of a relevant congregation may speak of God ad nauseam. But often God is not spoken of as a God who *is* God, but as an object of consumption. Such pastors speak of the mission, vision, and future of their congregation with more passion than they speak of the God who *is*. Not to sound snarky, but they might find better company with business executives and marketers than with theologians (or maybe that's just because theologians are boring).

The televangelist, without pretense or shame, lives out this sense of God as a depersonalized product. The rest of us angrily ridicule them on Twitter. We feel hot rage toward them because ultimately somewhere down deep we know we're not that different from them. We have also exchanged a God who *is* God for a God who is a product shaped for commerce and consumption. They're selling God as a product on TV. We're selling the relevance of our congregation. For them and us, relevance has been made into salvation, and the church made into the star of its own story. Instead of seeking God, we both seek survival through resources. The televangelist is just willing to more crassly connect it all with superstition and manipulation. We feel superior because we've done our resource-obsessive hunts for relevance with less kitsch, obnoxious personality, and cocksure bad theology.

We've all been tempted to chase resources, because doing so seems to have a direct benefit. Making God into a product, and the church the subject of the story that sells (or offers) that product, gives the church a plan to escape the crisis of relevance. The congregation with a compelling story and a relevant (even celebrity) pastor is assumed to be free from crisis, and therefore safe, because they have won a surplus of relevance.

Becoming Clear about the Real Crisis

True, many churches have built up a stockpile of relevance. These churches are indeed beyond crisis; their budgets and buildings seem to prove it. But this desire to be beyond crisis reveals our idolatry. To use Barth's language, it shows that our churches belong to the church of Esau. To be beyond crisis is a sure sign that we seek a God-product that we can parlay into survival. This makes the church, and not the God who *is* God, the object of faith. We've cashed in our ecclesial birthright of encounter with the God who *is* God for a bowl of the hot porridge of relevance. To choose the porridge of relevance over the haunting crisis of encounter with the living God is particularly tempting inside the immanent frame.

On the one hand, avoiding crisis by procuring relevance seems tangible, applicable, and straightforward. These values are highly honored in a legacy that has sought the evacuation of mystery. God's action, particularly inside the immanent frame, on the other hand, can be known only in confession, doubt, and dialectics (tensions and conflicts). This is the crisis! And this crisis cannot—and should not—be avoided. In an immanent frame, centered on commerce and consumption, avoiding all crises is a high good. But the faithful church cannot affirm this good. To lose, avoid, and disdain crisis is to wish again for the fleshpots of Egypt (Exod. 16:3). It is to want religion more than an encounter with the living God.[24]

The crisis the church must embrace to be the church of Jacob is one reality in two parts: (1) that there is a God who *is* God and (2) that we can know the God who *is* God only through a dialectic. This is particularly true inside an immanent frame that we cannot escape (developed more deeply in the coming chapters). The crisis is inescapable and must be embraced by the church. Building off Barth, I believe that the church that looks to avoid crisis has chosen religion over the living God. Such a church has relevance but not transcendence.[25] The church seeking to avoid crisis may *have* something like a "God," but it cannot encounter the *being* of the God who *is*. It cannot *be* a community receiving the speaking and acting of the God who *is* (whose very *being* is present in the world).

24. A central point for Pastor Barth. See *Epistle to the Romans* (London: Oxford University Press, 1933), 68–70.
25. Although relevance becomes a kind of faux transcendence honed by the logic of consumption.

We must embrace crisis as both the *context* and the *manner* in which we encounter the living God. The church's only purpose is to proclaim to the world that God (the prime subject of the story) acts in the world (the other subject of the story) for the sake of the world's salvation. God seeks salvation for the world, not for the church.

Though the church is not the primary subject of its own story, it does have life. This life is a deep resonance with both the being of God and the being of the world. It obtains this life in confessing that it is commissioned to steward and proclaim the distinct and cosmic significance of the story of God's act in the world. This story is not, and can never be, primarily about the church. The church is responsible for caring for, treasuring, and proclaiming the story of the God who *is* God acting in the world. To do this, the church shares with the world the absurd manner (especially absurd against the backdrop of immanence) in which to encounter this living God. If the church wishes to encounter a God who *is*, it must live unavoidably in the crisis as both *context* and *manner*.

The *context* of the crisis is God's real presence inside the immanent frame. God is not present as an idea but as a living person who speaks and acts. This deep crisis inside the immanent frame has made such encounters of *real presence* unbelievable. The church must bear the crisis of being the people inside the unbelievability imposed by the immanent frame who nevertheless proclaim that we encounter the real presence of God. As we'll see, this is never without doubt. To make this claim is itself a crisis, making the crisis of context inescapable. Once the church says it encounters God's real presence or witnesses to God's real action in the world, it is thrust into the crisis that the church is not promoting a product, concept, or religious idea but claiming to relate with the very God who *is* God. The church is claiming to come up against the one who *is*—who *is* above all else, who *is* true God of true God.

The crisis is this: at the same time that the church claims to witness to the real encounter with *the* living God, it is also claiming that the church is sinful and weak (not even powerful enough to be the subject of its own story). For the church to insist that it encounters the very God who is God thrusts the church always and necessarily into a state of constant doubt. The church must always be in this constant crisis of doubt lest it seek to turn God into its product and, like the sons of Zebedee, demand the honor of its own story (Matt. 20:20–23). If the church wishes to encounter the God of Israel and not run back to the fleshpots of Egypt, it must live day to day in the crisis that the One it knows and serves is unable to be known. The church must claim that its only reason for being is to witness to God's life-giving encounter with the world. But this witness is never absent doubt.

If the context is the inescapability of unavoidable and necessary crisis, in what *manner* does the church operate inside this crisis? In what *manner* does the church embrace doubt as obedience? The only way to operate inside such a crisis is to take on the manner of crisis as the way of being in the world. The crisis is everywhere. The crisis fills everything. The church not only lives in crisis but is also shaped by crisis. Living in crisis, the only way to encounter the God who is a crisis, with the double crisis of our own inability to encounter this God, is through a dialectic.

The dialectical nature (the way of finding truth through opposing realities) of Barth's theology is *not* an intellectual idea primarily but a pastoral one (unpacked more fully in chap. 16). The dialectical shape of Barth's theology (which I'm inspired by in building this ecclesiology) is his concrete way of helping his people encounter the real presence of the God of Israel who is acting in and for the world. Following Barth, we bear the crisis by seeking this God in the crisis of the opposite. A God who truly *is* can be known only as this God in freedom chooses to be known: in the opposite. It's in these opposing realities that we find the God who *is*. In confession of our sin, alienation, death, and despair, we are moved from trusting in our own story to seeking the living God.

Barth makes this dialectical pastoral move in his sermon on New Year's Day 1919. This sermon foreshadows the coming rewrite of the *Römerbrief*. The sermon asserts that the *manner* of living in the crisis is to embrace the crisis as the way to see, know, and proclaim God's action in the immanent frame. The crisis of the dialectic spills from the sermon when Barth says hope is found in despair; God's building is in God's tearing down; God's grace comes through God's judgment; God's loving "yes" is encountered in God's "no." These are not just intellectual theological assertions; this is a pastoral theology. The *manner* of this lived dialectic is not placed in the mouth of a theologian or even a church professional. It comes from the mouth of a man with a family, watching the structures of work and law crumble before him.

The dialectic doesn't crack an academic theological code. It is the practical *manner* in which to live, particularly in the immanent frame. The dialectic Barth begins honing in his rewrite will take him back to the experience and work of the Younger, giving shape to how the Younger's own pastoral theology, while lacking the precision Barth offers, was also based on the *manner* of a lived dialectic. In the crisis of these dialectics, the church can begin to trust that it seeks and hears the God who *is* God, not the echo of its own voice. In and through the manner of the dialectic, the church can be assured that its life comes from the God of Israel and not from its own relevance.

This single crisis with two parts is what Woz represents to Saint John the Baptist. Woz threw the congregation into crisis: not by challenging them to be more relevant or to open his unique identity but by asking them to help him find God. Woz's direct pursuit to encounter God, and his need for the congregation to help him, threw the church into a crisis it couldn't escape. They confessed "Do we?" and then wondered "How do we?" Ironically (call it dialectically), this crisis gave them life rather than threatening their life.

This true crisis moved the church into the ultimate Christian practice of confession. This confession moved Saint John the Baptist away from the concerns for its own story and future and into the present event of serving this one in the world who was seeking to know the God who is unknowable. Their confession that they did not know how to find the God who *is* God was the first step to truly (really!) encountering the living God—even inside the immanent frame.

8

Wedding Blunders and Brotherly Love

By early 1919 the first edition of *Römerbrief* was out in the world. The dedication to his father, Fritz, gave Barth a tangible sense of returning home. He had returned as his own man, with his own theological vision that no longer collided with his father's. In Barth's mind, though distinct, it supported the legacy of his father's own ministry and theology. The publication of the *Römerbrief* seemed to give Barth a period of peace with his immediate family. But there was to be no peace from writing—or from conflict with his extended relatives.

Throughout 1919 Barth wrote just as furiously as he had in his notebooks under the apple tree. In the winter of 1919, he scribbled out thoughts on Acts and 1 Corinthians. Then he wrote reflections on Ephesians, which were inspired by his confirmation class the year before.

This writing, along with sermon prep and some lectures, kept the freshly published pastor occupied, but not occupied enough to avoid conflict with his extended family. Since childhood, poor Barth seemed unable to avoid some kind of tussle. In this case, the tussle came with some of his more conservative relatives. The origins of the fight, at least to me, seem to be completely Barth's fault—Barth admits that he was tactless. The *Römerbrief* had led him starkly away from his liberal teachers and back, in some sense, to the arms of his deceased father. But just to make sure no one confused him for a conservative pietist, Barth decided to throw a right cross to his conservative relatives' chin.

The occasion was another wedding. Barth's uncle Ernst Sartorius (from his pietist mother's side) was getting married in Basel. Pastor Karl was asked to give an after-dinner speech. Like the epic fails of YouTube best man toasts, Barth decided, *at a wedding*, to make remarks against family life both as an idea and as a way of life.[1] There is no mention whether he'd been overserved or tipsy on wedding wine, or even if his remarks were prepared. But we do know the room turned on him quickly. Barth says, "I can still see the devastating look which uncle Hans Burckhardt directed against me." But that was nothing in comparison to Uncle Fritz Sartorius. He leaned hard against the side of his armchair and, Barth says, "announced his utter disapproval with a long drawn out 'ay-ay-ay-ay' and what seemed to me to be a particularly impressive shaking of his double chin."[2]

The moment was such an epic blunder and the relatives' anger so hot that it seemed to melt away all the conflict he had with his brothers. It's easy to imagine Peter, Heinrich, and their brother-in-law Karl Lindt (a pastor in Bern of whom Barth was particularly fond) dying of laughter, stomachs aching, at Barth's predicament and expense.[3]

This conflict with the larger family may have brought the brothers back together, moving them past the competition and rivalry that had filled the air of the Marburg wedding in 1915. This, of course, is informed speculation. But we do know that cheerful letters and good times for the immediate family followed. A joyful peace came between Karl and his brothers. The 1919 wedding proved no less fraught with conflict than the 1915 wedding, but this time the brothers Barth were on the same side.[4]

As the year unfolded, "links in the family were further strengthened when Barth became godfather of Peter's son Ulrich and [his sister] Gertrud's daughter Hanni."[5] Heinrich was now living in Basel, the location of Ernst Sartorius's wedding and Karl's epic fail. Heinrich had moved there the year before to teach philosophy at the girls' high school. Anna Barth, the siblings' mother, moved from Bern to Basel to live with Heinrich. She figured her bachelor son needed

1. I refuse to get too far into this, but it's hard not to think of Barth's own unusual family life in relation to this event.
2. Barth, letter to Ernst Sartorius, December 14, 1944, quoted by Eberhard Busch, *Karl Barth: His Life from Letters and Autobiographical Texts* (Philadelphia: Fortress, 1975), 108.
3. I concede this may be a stretch, but Barth's own humorous words about chins swaying and dirty looks lead me to imagine that this was a story reviewed often.
4. These stories are a good window into Barth. In 1915 he was in conflict with the liberals. In 1919, in some ways now known (or soon to be known) as the liberal slayer, he entered into conflict with the conservatives. Barth was seeking the narrow path between what he saw as these two ditches. He just didn't always do it with tact, at least not at weddings.
5. Busch, *Karl Barth*, 108. His sister was married to Karl Lindt.

her company. Her companionship was clearly helpful: by 1920 Heinrich was installed as professor of philosophy at the University of Basel.

For the story of Pastor Karl Barth, all of these experiences coalesce in an important way. They set the conditions for an influential moment. This season of brotherly closeness gave Barth the ears to hear something from his youngest brother Heinrich that would significantly deepen his theological and pastoral vision. It would mold the shape of the coming rewrite of the *Römerbrief*.

Brothers against Givenness

At the Aarau conference in the spring of 1919, Heinrich offered a lecture called "The Knowledge of God" (*Gotteserkenntnis*). In it Heinrich struck a bellowing, prophetic note. But unlike with his older brother, it came not in the tone of a Hebrew prophet or apostle but that of a philosopher. In a completely different way than his older brother, Heinrich too was seeking to strike a blow against what we've been calling the assumed closedness of the immanent frame. The atmosphere of Fritz and Anna's home clearly affected the way these boys saw the world. Even before the Great War, and surely after it, Heinrich, like his brother, challenged the presumptions of immanence (but for philosophical, not pastoral, reasons). Heinrich was not looking to be something other than modern. Like his brother, he was not seeking a return to a lost world. But he nevertheless observed a slippage in many of modernity's presumptions.

As we've said throughout this project, the immanent frame eliminates mystery. Mystery can no longer be a productive category within modernity, not even for knowledge of God. What strikes at the heart of mystery is modernity's belief that reality itself has a complete "givenness" to it. Reality, from top to bottom and everywhere in between, is assumed to be knowable. All we need is the right method to know it completely and entirely. What escapes us is not reality (it is given) but the methods necessary to possess its givenness.

If transcendence is understood as that which is beyond us, that which escapes all givenness, then modernity seeks the elimination of transcendence. It frames everything as immanent because it contends that everything is given to be known. This elimination of mystery just happens, thanks to the presumption of givenness. Once reality is assumed to be completely given, direct concern with something transcendent is both unimportant and unnecessary (or at least inaccessible).[6]

6. Any leftover residue of transcendence gets captured in religion. For theology to find any new footing, it must embrace the givenness of reality and therefore move beyond talking

The architects of the immanent frame assume that *all* of reality is know-able, because all of reality is given. It is knowable through something like the methodologies of mathematics (rationalists) or the ways of historicizing (romantics). They all presume, inside the immanent frame's commitment to the givenness of reality, that there is simply no place or only a fringe place for transcendence. Transcendence is dead not necessarily because transcendence has been attacked. Transcendence is dead because reality is assumed to be completely knowable and given without hindrance to the one who wields the proper methods.[7] This sense that reality is completely given and therefore knowable has often been called *positivism*, which is the radical form of given-ness. Heinrich, having written his dissertation on Descartes, understood this as well as anyone.

In his lecture at the Aarau conference, with his older brother listening, Heinrich challenged the presumption of reality's givenness. The younger brother made a strong case, returning to the philosophy of Plato, that real-ity has a distinct element of nongivenness to it.[8] Like Karl, Heinrich was not intent on blowing up the immanent frame. But he did want to show that the immanent frame could not be totally and completely closed. The immanent frame could not be tightly locked down by givenness. Even the romantic (and, Karl would later add, pietistic) ways of conceiving of modernity and their yearning for something more than the rigidity of rationalism fell into the same traps of givenness and closed immanence. Yet Heinrich saw that the immanent frame's closedness could only be assumed if reality was believed to be completely given.

If major elements of reality continue to escape knowledge (as they will con-tinually), reality cannot be closed down and assumed to be completely given. The immanent frame, then, must remain open because there is an inextricable sense of nongivenness to reality. This doesn't prove transcendence, but it shows that there is a space for it. Pastor Karl Barth, though never trying to prove

---

about a God who is beyond givenness. These are the twin enemies that Karl Barth attacks in his project.

7. Of course, the romantic revolt against the rationalist sense of knowing through method is also important to remember. But even the most romantic of this perspective believed that reality was given and broadly knowable. They just doubted that rationalist methods were the way into this knowledge. For them, a deeper knowledge of feeling was experienced not through rationalist methods but through poetry and song.

8. This point about Plato comes out more in a different lecture Heinrich gave in November 1920. This lecture wasn't just another lecture; it was Heinrich's inaugural lecture at the Uni-versity of Basel. Karl Barth attended this lecture as well, telling Thurneysen how important it was to his own thinking. See Bruce McCormack, *Karl Barth's Critically Realistic Dialectical Theology: Its Genesis and Development, 1909–1936* (Oxford: Oxford University Press, 1997), 119–22, for a discussion of this.

that God or even transcendence exists, asserts that even in a modern world of immanence there is space for the living Word and act of God to encounter us. Heinrich's lecture, which traced out the elements of nongivenness in reality, sharpened his older brother's (and constant rival's) vision. Karl Barth saw even more radically that there were indeed parts of reality that transcend all ways and methods of knowing. Now he was more convinced that human epistemology had its limits—even in its religious forms—most particularly when it came to knowledge of God.[9]

But what Karl learned from Heinrich proved to be even more radical.

Wholly Other Eschatology

It wasn't Heinrich's philosophical notions themselves that appealed to Karl. Barth was as able as any pastor—maybe even any theology professor—to wrestle with philosophy. Most of the thoughts we've just explored from Heinrich could be extracted from Kant. Karl's ability in philosophy has often been overlooked (and perhaps Karl's ability was the source of the tension that returned to Karl and Heinrich's relationship after 1919 and never departed).[10] In fact, Karl is held by some to be one of the best twentieth-century interpreters of Kant. That must have bothered his little brother. But sitting in his chair at the conference, Karl was grabbed by more than just the philosophy. It was the pastoral implications. Karl Barth never wavered from his pastoral commitments, and these pastoral concerns made Heinrich's words so evocative.

The Great War had been over for four months, and the crisis had only mounted. People were looking for solutions. They were looking for hope from within the givenness of reality, though it had been this drive to possess reality as given that had brought this hell upon the world. We can spot Heinrich's prophetic edge in this vicious cycle that seeks to escape from the despair delivered by the assumptions of givenness—and which seeks more givenness as a way out of the despair of givenness. True hope in the midst of this crisis, Heinrich believes, will never come from any ingenuity of the methods of knowing. It cannot be born out of givenness itself. The structures and forms of the closed immanent frame cannot produce our salvation from within themselves. Heinrich says boldly that salvation is needed. And who

9. Though critical realism has its problems, I've found it to be helpful, particularly for constructing a practical theology that places divine action and revelation as central. I've sketched this out in part 3 of *Christopraxis: A Practical Theology of the Cross* (Minneapolis: Fortress, 2014).

10. Gary Dorrien adds some texture to Barth's relationship with his brother. See *The Barthian Revolt in Modern Theology: Theology without Weapons* (Louisville: Westminster John Knox, 2000), 106–8.

would deny that after the war? But true salvation will not come from within the givenness of reality. It can come only from the nongivenness, only from something radically outside the structures that are part of the given.

Perhaps without intending to, Heinrich was now preaching. And his sermon was deeply edifying to Karl. Heinrich was saying something that Karl wished he'd said even more clearly in his *Römerbrief*. Heinrich's thoughts add important texture to Karl's pastoral commitment that we must encounter a God who *is* God. Heinrich's assertion that there is an element of nongivenness in reality, and that our hope must come from this nongivenness, adds weight to the crisis Karl sees. Theology and church ministry are inescapably bound within crisis because the church's attention and life must always be on the nongivenness of reality, *not* the givenness. To preach and minister hope in suffering and despair within the givenness of reality is to witness to a God who comes acting out of the nongivenness of reality. We must embrace this crisis. Our hope comes not from within us or anything inherent in society or nature but from the one who is wholly other than us.[11]

The church, by recognizing that it inhabits a crisis, is given a gift: to wait with the world for God's arrival coming out of the nongivenness of reality. Heinrich tells his listeners that this nongivenness of reality means that hope must come from some wholly other source than the methods we use to assume reality is bound in givenness. God cannot be thought of as some part (or even an analogy) of the givenness of the world. What Pastor Karl Barth recognizes, now even more poignantly thanks to Heinrich's lecture, is that God enters the world giving Godself to the world.

Heinrich helps Karl see that a God who *is* God is a wholly other God. A God who *is* God is completely beyond and outside the givenness of reality. *Römerbrief II* significantly sharpens this point over its fuzzy insinuations in *Römerbrief I*. God is wholly other because God encounters humanity from the nongivenness of reality. God is wholly other *not* because God is unable

---

11. The commitment to the wholly otherness of God that comes from the nongivenness of reality has often been fodder for critique of Barth. It feels like fideism to some or a means of attacking positivism with a positivism of revelation. But it's important to see that most post-WWII philosophy and theology saw similar issues. Barth is unique because he sees this earlier, after WWI, and addresses it inside a fully developed biblical imagination. Others also pushed hard against the givenness of reality and its ramifications and moved toward contemplating the element of nongivenness. To my mind, Emmanuel Levinas is the best example of this. But Levinas is a post-WWII thinker who is following others like Franz Rosenzweig. These two think in uniquely Jewish ways, but nevertheless, like the brothers Barth, they are seeking to move beyond the closedness of givenness. Levinas sees ethics as revelation and therefore an invitation into elements of nongivenness. See Emmanuel Levinas, *Totality and Infinity* (Pittsburgh: Duquesne University Press, 1961); and Franz Rosenzweig, *The Star of Redemption* (Notre Dame, IN: University of Notre Dame Press, 1970).

to be encountered but because any encounter with God reveals the crisis that the immanent frame remains open and we cannot escape the nongivenness of reality. The inescapable elements of the nongivenness of reality remind us that we are not God. We can never possess reality by totally enclosing it in immanence. Hope can come only from a radically transcendent (eschatological) other who is beyond all givenness. In the context of Europe's rebuilding efforts from the war, righting those wrongs cannot come from within our own ambitious methods to know and control reality. It must be other. It must come from outside, eschatologically, having no correlation with or connection to what is given.

How we encounter and therefore access this nongivenness of a God who *is* God will be the task of Karl Barth's rewrite of the *Römerbrief* and what follows it. It is the essence of all pastoral theology. The task is to articulate how human persons can encounter a God who is wholly other, having God's own being in nongivenness that is nevertheless given to us.

––––––––––

This is the challenge now facing Saint John the Baptist. The encounter with God as the nongiven within the givenness of reality is the place where theology and ministry meld and are unable to ever be separated.

9

Say Goodbye to Being and
Give Me More Busyness

In June 1919, Heinrich's thought can be spotted directly in one of Karl's presentations. In a lecture on Christian life given at the Student Christian Movement conference in Aarburg, Switzerland, Pastor Karl Barth said boldly, channeling Heinrich, "The kingdom of God is the kingdom of *God*. We cannot conceive of the transition from the analogies of the divine reality to human reality radically enough."[1]

Heinrich's bold line between givenness and nongivenness becomes clear in Karl's thought. The blurred lines between the kingdom of the givenness of reality and the kingdom of the God who *is* wholly other, seen in *Römerbrief I*, are now drawn bold and thick. These kingdoms will never again be confused one for the other in the mind of Barth. A God who *is* God comes into the givenness of reality by way of the nongivenness.

In this conference lecture, Barth showed that the hope for the newness of life cannot come from within what has been. Further channeling Heinrich, Barth said, "The pattern of development is a failure. . . . The new Jerusalem has not the least to do with the new Switzerland. . . . Of course this hope does not sap 'courage and strength . . . for things of today and of this world,' it supplies them."[2]

1. Barth, "Christian Life" (lecture, Student Christian Movement conference, Aarburg, Switzerland, June 1919), quoted by Eberhard Busch, *Karl Barth: His Life from Letters and Autobiographical Texts* (Philadelphia: Fortress, 1975), 109.
2. Barth, "Christian Life," quoted by Busch, *Karl Barth*, 109.

Courage and Strength

Waiting for a God who enters reality, but who is never to be confused as part of the givenness of reality, demands courage and strength. Living with this bold line between givenness and nongivenness proves very different from Nietzsche's slave religion. It is actually quite the opposite of it.

Nietzsche imagines the Judeo-Christian commitment to the rights and nobility of the weak as a sneaky strategy to pry power away from the powerful (whom Nietzsche called the *blond beasts*), from those who seek to confront the world in its givenness and shape it forcefully to their own will. These blond beasts embrace the givenness of the world, contending that there is *only* givenness. Recognizing only givenness, the blond beasts never concede to defeat but see the givenness as a call to raid this givenness for themselves. They unashamedly thrust their fingers violently into the flesh of the givenness of the world, contouring it for their own kingdom. This is one way—and Nietzsche thinks the better (i.e., more courageous and strong) way—of embracing reality as only and finally givenness.[3] The other way to deal with givenness, which Nietzsche thinks is personified particularly in late-nineteenth-century European Christianity, is to cope with the totality of givenness by deceptively making the values immoral that allowed the blond beasts to shape their kingdoms and dominate givenness. Nietzsche thinks the Christian religion makes cowardliness and timidity a sly and slithery way to cope with and conquer givenness.

Barth doesn't spend much time in dialogue with Nietzsche (though, as we mentioned, his father took a class under him).[4] Yet Pastor Barth would agree, but only in part: Religion is a problem. It can impose a cowardly timidity because it disobediently concedes that givenness is all there is—not because it uses passive-aggressive strategies to win in givenness. Religion as a closed structure of the givenness of reality is often led into believing its own existence is the highest good. It uses whatever deception necessary to achieve its survival. Religion should know better, but it nevertheless blurs the lines between the givenness and nongivenness of reality. To its peril, religion accepts that reality is only and finally givenness.

Right before Woz arrived at the Bible study, Saint John the Baptist had accepted reality as given. When religion uses the language and practices that

---

3. In a world where God is dead.

4. Busch says, "Jacob Burckhardt, Emil Kautzsch and Friedrich Nietzsche were among Fritz Barth's teachers; he remembered all three of them well. And especially the last. 'Personally, I can only speak of Nietzsche with great respect, since he was my teacher at school, and did not have the slightest unsavory influence on me.'" *Karl Barth*, 3.

orient one to nongivenness for the sake of winning space and power in given-ness, it has stumbled into a particularly hideous kind of disobedience. This temptation becomes especially strong inside modernity and its immanent frame. Both Bert and Sue were tempted to imagine that the congregation's life depended on them finding a way or method to turn givenness in their favor.

In *Römerbrief II*, even more than in *Römerbrief I*, Barth attacks religion. Religion is not inherently bad, but it becomes an idol factory with patheti-cally fragile cowards when it forgets or ignores the nongivenness of reality. For Nietzsche, the religious are cowards for their sketchy deception to win power. But for Barth, it's their unwillingness to confess and seek for the non-givenness of reality.

It takes courage and strength to stand inside the immanent frame and seek an encounter with nongivenness. It's a treacherous swim against the current to stay open to nongivenness amid an immanent frame whose attention is so squarely on givenness. Pastors need courage and strength to proclaim and lead their congregations by pointing to the bold line that divides the givenness and nongivenness of what is, to say to the people that their only hope is found in a God who comes from nongivenness and therefore is a God who *is* God. This bravery showed up in Sue, who, after Woz arrived, saw the bold line separat-ing the givenness and nongivenness, and confessed, "Do we?" The strength of true courage is to confess the crisis that what we yearn and hope for has no correlation or contingency with the kingdoms of the givenness of reality. Even the church has no secure place in nongivenness, no shortcut to God's presence. We need courage to seek encounter with the one who is wholly other.

Unconfused Kingdoms

There is another dimension particularly important for our own time that must be mentioned. Barth's drawing of this bold line between givenness and nongivenness has led some to believe erroneously that he is advocating a de-parture from the praxis of the world. Pastor Barth appears to be turning from political engagement in the shape of givenness to theological navel-gazing that peers into the glossy eyes of nongivenness. When Barth says "the new Jeru-salem has not the least to do with the new Switzerland," it appears to be the end of the red pastor, a kind of burying of Barth's socialist political interests.

From the day Pastor Barth started his pastorate in Safenwil in 1911, he was moving deeper and deeper into socialism, getting his hands dirty in shaping givenness. At the beginning of his ministry he was reading more sociology and political science than theology. His interests in socialism served as the

first steps in returning to his father. Fritz had always seen an important connection between the Christian life and care for the poor.

The friendship with Thurneysen wore both of these marks. Though Karl
didn't know Eduard particularly well before Thurneysen's installation as
pastor in Leutwil in 1913, it made sense to reach out to him. Not only was
Thurneysen also interested in socialism, having much deeper connections to
the movement, but Thurneysen was also connected to Barth's now deceased
father. Thurneysen's father and Fritz Barth had been close friends.[5] Fritz had
been dead about a year when Karl and Eduard's friendship blossomed. A
friendship with the son of Fritz's friend was a tangible means for Karl to stay
connected to his father. But the friendship would be much deeper than serving that moment of grief. Thurneysen connected Barth to Hermann Kutter,
who affirmed Barth's fusion of pastoral and political concerns. Barth's early
ministry, all the way into 1919, cannot be separated from his engagement in
socialism and the desire to shape the givenness of reality.

For example, in the first months of 1919, Pastor Barth led the workers in
striking against the factory owners (awkwardly, some of these owners were
part of Pastor Barth's congregation; Barth never ducked a fight). But now
just some five months later, Barth says, "The new Jerusalem has not the least
to do with the new Switzerland." Is this a sign of the end of Barth's political
and social concerns? Is the red pastor changing his colors?

I don't think so. Rather, it appears just the opposite. Barth recognized
that without a bold line between the givenness and nongivenness of reality,
justice has no mobilizing referent that can sustain and keep its objectives
from imploding on itself. The romantic-inspired historical hermeneutic of
seeing everything as power and therefore as a struggle between oppressed and
oppressor, while important, will fall in on itself without a transcendent (or
nongiven) referent. When reality is only and finally imagined as givenness,
those who are oppressed and fight against oppression will eventually, when
winning a power bound completely in givenness, become oppressors. This
becomes the only way to operate in givenness. This repeating back and forth
cannot be broken from within a closed immanent frame.

---

5. How close this friendship was is not clear. It appears to have been fairly close, but obviously not close enough to nurture a friendship between Eduard and Karl in childhood. And
not close enough to fuse them together when they overlapped in Marburg. But Fritz was in the
elder Thurneysen's wedding. See William Klempa, introduction to *A Unique Time of God: Karl
Barth's WWI Sermons*, by Karl Barth (Louisville: Westminster John Knox, 2016). Busch says,
"Karl's father, who was born on 25 October 1856, was a somewhat shy and sickly boy, who had
to be treated gently. From 1871–74 he went to the grammar school in Basel, where he happened
to sit next to Eduard Thurneysen (1856–1931), who became a friend for life. Thurneysen's son,
who had the same name, later became a friend of Karl Barth." *Karl Barth*, 3.

This is the problem Pastor Barth sees with Soviet-style socialism. It violently rids its society of transcendence, seeking to smother any sense of nongivenness in reality.[6] Without a referent to the nongivenness of reality (to some normative moral vision that goes beyond the resentment of the lack of power),[7] cycles of violence are almost impossible to interrupt. Bound within a closed givenness of the immanent frame, a system that seeks the end of class hierarchy and complete egalitarianism of the workers becomes totalitarian and hyperhierarchical.

In a similar way, a system seeking to unmask and act against the oppressor who eventually wins some power will simply reverse the roles. There must be a vision or a dream, like that of the prophet Micah or Martin Luther King Jr., which is bound in the nongivenness of reality. The nongivenness of reality breaks the cycle of the kingdoms of givenness. The problem with these systems of closed power structure or Soviet-style socialism is that they confuse themselves for a new Jerusalem produced from within givenness.

Pastor Barth's point in this lecture is that the new Jerusalem is not bound or contingent on a new Switzerland or a new America or a new human woke consciousness. It is bound totally and completely on the act of God. This act comes to us not as the givenness of our political action but as a proclamation of and participation in the nongivenness of God's being through God's act. The cycle of violence can never be broken inside the structures of givenness. WWII is concrete proof of this. There must be some kind of continued attention on the reality of nongivenness (like, in Martin Luther King's thought, the dignity of all human persons as bestowed by God, or the *imago Dei* in Desmond Tutu's thought)[8] to bring about reconciliation on earth (givenness) as it is in heaven (nongivenness).

But there are even deeper ramifications to Barth's bold line separating the new Jerusalem and the new Switzerland. These ramifications lead toward more direct engagement in the world. This bold line drawn between givenness and nongivenness is as much God's yes as it is God's no. Holding this no and yes together, Barth believes, is important for faithful engagement in the world.

6. I should be clear: Barth never saw Soviet communism as even half the problem he saw National Socialism to be. After WWII Barth was asked to raise his voice and pen against communism. He refused. He saw it as problematic but not nearly to the same degree as National Socialism.

7. For more on resentment, see Max Scheler's important book *Ressentiment* (Milwaukee: Marquette University Press, 2007). See also my piece "Pastoral Leadership Lessons from Bonhoeffer: The Alt-Right, the Twitter Mob, and *Ressentiment*," *Dialog* 59, no. 2 (2020): 82–92.

8. For a discussion of this, see Michael Battle, *Reconciliation: The Ubuntu Theology of Desmond Tutu* (Cleveland: Pilgrim, 2009).

Willie James Jennings, in his award-winning book *The Christian Imagination*, has provided a genealogy that traces the theological construction and justification of whiteness and the long history of oppression of black and brown bodies. The major takeaway from Jennings's intricate argument meshes with Pastor Barth's words here.[9] Jennings sees the heart of the colonial impulse as justifying itself theologically. Theology is wielded, Jennings shows, to make whiteness righteous and black/brownness less than. The confusion behind this theological idea festers in the Spanish, English, and Portuguese belief that they were bringing the new Jerusalem to the New World. These crowns assumed they were bringing the new Jerusalem because they believed their own nation was the new Israel. In other words, colonialism's justification was achieved on the devastating theological misunderstanding that new England and new Spain were the new Jerusalem. This misunderstanding, which led to incalculable amounts of suffering and evil, was embedded in the misconception that new England could be the new Jerusalem because reality itself is given.[10] The bold line between the kingdoms of the world and the kingdom of God became so blurred that Israel could be superseded and replaced with Spain, Portugal, France, or England.[11]

Mobilized with bad theology, the crowns of these nations interpreted themselves as Israel. As Israel, they felt justified in seeing the lands of the New World as *their* new Jerusalem, *their* promised land. This confusion propagated because the bold line that separated the givenness of reality from the nongivenness of reality was blurred and confused. These monarchies failed to understand that they were not the new Israel building the new Jerusalem: they were part of the givenness of reality, and the new Jerusalem was born out of the nongivenness (it was eschatological). Because the new Jerusalem

9. Willie James Jennings is a top-flight Barth interpreter, and he dialogues with Barth at points in *The Christian Imagination: Theology and the Origins of Race* (New Haven: Yale University Press, 2010). Jennings also draws from Barth's most famous student in the English-speaking world, T. F. Torrance, to make his most constructive argument. Jennings draws from Torrance's *Mediation of Christ* (Colorado Springs: Helmers & Howard, 1992).

10. For more on how great a role givenness plays within "discoveries" of the New World, see Daniel Boorstin, *The Discoverers: A History of Man's Search to Know His World and Himself* (New York: Vintage, 1985). This book is an insightful articulation of the period and the way it shifted cultural imaginaries.

11. Jennings traces the deep and long history of this move, beginning around the end of the *ancien régime*. It starts when the church is waning and the crown is made stronger. This waning is not just caused by the Enlightenment and its mathematics but by the church itself. The Reformation has the effect—and historical correlation—of strengthening the crown to the point that its ambitions for growth and power in the given world outstrip its commitments to nongivenness. In turn, the crown is allowed to theologically misinterpret itself as Israel and the "New World" as its Jerusalem to possess, missing that it is actually gentiles invading a land not their own.

will come only from the nongivenness of reality, these nations could never enter the world triumphalistically, turning the lands of the New World into something they could possess. These crowns failed to recognize that not everything had been given to them, that not all of reality is foreclosed in givenness.

To confess that there are indeed elements of reality that are nongiven reminds us, Jennings believes, that we as Christians are always gentiles in a strange land not our own.[12] The land itself can never be ours.[13] The church can never be the star of its own story, can never be Israel. The church's calling is to enter the world as a stranger, loving the lands and people it meets, free from needing to own them.[14] Jennings explains that as gentiles, not Israel, those coming to the New World could have recognized that they were always strangers in a land not their own, seeking not to *have* the land but to *be* in it with the being of others as guests who together await the coming of God.

Jennings helps us see Barth's point.[15] Drawing a bold line between the givenness and nongivenness of reality allows for engagement in the world that truly honors Kutter's desire while also seeing human beings in their full and complete value. To speak for justice by speaking the great word "God," as Kutter desired, Pastor Barth would say (thanks to Heinrich) you can never conflate the structures of the givenness of reality with nongivenness. The new Jerusalem has nothing to do with the new Switzerland!

To Have or to Be

If we fail to draw a bold line between the givenness and nongivenness of reality (either by blurring the two as colonialism and consumerism do or by seeking to smother nongivenness as Soviet communism did and scientism does), we can easily confuse *to have* with *to be*. We can even be tempted into believing that *to be* means only *to have* (as seen clearly by the stated good life of many late-modern people, "If I just *had* more money, *had* more time, *had* more recognition, *then* I'd *be* happy"). If all of reality is given, having reality is assumed to be possible. It can be had either through the methods

12. For more on this point, see Jennings, *Christian Imagination*, 274–76; and Jennings, "Theology and Race," in *The Routledge Companion to Modern Christian Thought*, ed. Chad Meister and James Beilby (London: Routledge, 2013), 786–87.

13. The heart of Jennings's project here in *The Christian Imagination* and beyond is focused sharply on land. Jennings has done very insightful work on the theological importance of land.

14. See Jennings, *Christian Imagination*, 61–63. See also Jennings, "Being Baptized: Race," in *The Blackwell Companion to Christian Ethics*, ed. Stanley Hauerwas and Samuel Wells (West Sussex: Wiley-Blackwell, 2011), 280–82.

15. Jennings discusses Barth in *Christian Imagination*, 60–62.

of knowing or through the supposed valor and spirit to brazenly take and possess it.[16] Whether you're Descartes, Locke, Nietzsche, or the composer Richard Wagner, almost everything can be possessed because reality itself is given in toto. *To have* eclipses *to be*.

This eclipsing of *to be* with *to have* is the diagnosis of the late-modern condition given by Erich Fromm, who was the only child of Orthodox Jewish parents in Frankfurt, Germany. His studies commenced during the Great War. In the years between the wars, he became a prominent figure in the famous Frankfurt School of cultural philosophy. As World War II arrived, he immigrated to the US to escape Nazi Germany. In the aftermath of the deep pools of blood that soaked the first half of the twentieth century, Fromm wrote his most famous book, *To Have or to Be?*

One of the most insightful discussions in this classic text comes under a heading called "Activity and Passivity." Fromm explains that something odd has happened inside modernity. Activity, or what it means to be active, has been radically redefined. In the modern sense, activity means "a quality of behavior that brings about a visible effect by expenditure of energy."[17] With this definition, modernity makes all human activity equal. It's *all just* behavior, which expends energy.

Modernity can equalize all activity, giving such a definition, because it picks up where the Reformation left off. The Reformation revolutionized activity, upending and ending both antiquity and the Middle Ages' sense of activity. In these earlier periods activity was fused with *what* you did.[18] What you did was greatly determined by *who* you were. Whether priest or peasant, your activity was determined by and even revealed your being, leading to a hierarchy of activity. The activity of the priest was believed to be higher than that of the peasant because the priest was a consecrated *being* whose activities (the Mass) crossed the line between the givenness and nongivenness of reality.

16. This is similar to Taylor's contrasting of Enlightenment and Counter-Enlightenment thinkers. He sees possession through knowledge and valor as two options, with a third being those who hold to a transcendent referent. Next to Barth, we could call this third option the contention that there is a nongivenness to reality. See *A Secular Age* (Cambridge, MA: Belknap, 2007), chaps. 17 and 18.

17. Erich Fromm, *To Have or to Be?* (London: Bloomsbury, 2018), 77.

18. Fromm is making a similar argument, referencing antiquity and the Middle Ages, but I'm more directly leaning on Charles Taylor here. In *The Sources of the Self: The Making of Modern Identity* (Cambridge, MA: Harvard University Press, 1989), Taylor speaks at length about how the Reformation changes activity from what you do to how you do it. Ruth Abbey helpfully discusses Taylor's argument here in *Charles Taylor* (Princeton: Princeton University Press, 2000), 88–93. I discuss the ramifications of this point in relation to pastoral ministry in *The Pastor in a Secular Age* (Grand Rapids: Baker Academic, 2019), chap. 5.

Yet, once it became clear that those with consecrated being were misusing their activities, the revolution began. The Reformers shifted the focus from *what* you did to *how* you did it. This had the effect of making all activity equal before God—whether giving the Mass or changing a baby's diaper. All activity, obediently done before God, revealed our *being* as sinners justified by faith. All activity, in one way or another, played out the drama of redemption. All activity was equal, but still revealed being, because all activity was done by sinners needing justification. Because *no* human activity could save your finite being, *all* activity became cosmically equivalent.

Modernity was happy to continue this commitment to the equalizing of activity. But this equalizing needed a different purpose and objective, one that would eventually screen us off from being itself. Being got sidelined when modernity became less interested in God and any nongivenness as the force that equalizes activity. Inside the construction of the immanent frame, activity needed to attend only to the givenness of reality, finding its equalization in immanence. What equalized activity shifted from God to something given.[19] The Reformation equalized activity so that all human *beings* could participate directly in their salvation (receiving the gift that comes from nongivenness). Modernity and the immanent frame continued with the equalizing but for very different immanent ends.

But even this immanent equalizing of action, bound only in givenness, wasn't all bad. It offered technological breakthroughs and even representative governments. Unfortunately, it also allowed activity to be equalized in such a manner that it became much harder to recognize how the *being* of persons encounters the *being* of God, or even how the *being* of a person connects with being alive. It became hard to know how our activity sweeps us up into life itself. It was assumed that the will of an actor was free to act upon the world as he or she wished. It was even assumed that *being* had little to do with *acting*.

19. I'm unfortunately being somewhat vague here on purpose. This is a complicated story that would need more space to rehearse. What replaces God is a sense of what Taylor calls "mutual equal regard." This high mutual equal regard is born out of Protestant—particularly Calvinist—Christianity, but eventually modernity disconnects this mutual equal regard from the nongivenness of God. The idea of mutual equal regard is that all people must be respected so that all people can work out their own salvation but not be blocked from doing whatever activity they do faithfully and passionately. All this remains, but what is lost is that this faithful, hardworking passion for, say, button making is eventually disconnected from the God who elects. What remains in the commerce and consumption of the immanent frame is that all activity is equal and that there should be some respect (mutual equal regard) for others' activity. See Taylor's discussion of the modern moral order in *A Secular Age*, 195–200.

The objective or end of all human activity was now primarily for the new centers of commerce and consumption. The ramifications are that activity is often seen as only the spent energy to possess and have. Ultimately, Fromm sees that modernity equalizes activity so the world can be owned in its givenness. Fromm lucidly shows that this kind of equalizing means all activity is the *same*. Fromm shows that activity is not as much equalized as it is *samed*. This is the danger to the human spirit of losing a lived sense of the nongivenness of reality. (It is also a major part of the modern illness Taylor calls "the malaise of immanence.")[20] When this happens, an activity like mundane data entry is made the same as painting a landscape. Organizing your sock drawer is ultimately the same as teaching a class of eager fifth graders to write a poem. Action is merely the expenditure of energy, and thus all action is the same. If organizing your sock drawer and teaching poetry to fifth graders are shown to be equal expenditures of energy, these activities are the same.

Of course, even to us late-modern people, something feels wrong about equating two such activities. We find more resonance with the likes of teaching poetry; we want those activities to mean more. We feel something deeper in them that escapes the flat reduction of givenness. But we have no reason, inside the immanent frame, for why. Particularly if we collapse the givenness and nongivenness of reality, it's difficult to justify why these second activities are substantially *different* from those listed first.[21] Inside a world without nongivenness (or in a world where givenness and nongivenness are confused), these activities are all the same because they are all reduced to behaviors that expend energy. An activity can have no greater referent.

Fromm's point is that when activity is allowed free reign to have the world, we lose a sense of being. We make all actions finally and completely behaviors, becoming blind "to the person behind the behavior."[22] Because reality is

20. See Taylor, *A Secular Age*, chap. 8.

21. Any justification ultimately can be won only through the logic of commerce and consumption. Some activities are better than others because they're either popular or make money. All activities are the same in the sense that they all can win recognition or dollars. The pointy prongs of the winnowing fork are made of the flat immanent realities of commerce and consumption. This is why some have discussed the end of art. See Boris Groys, *Art Power* (Cambridge, MA: MIT Press, 2013).

22. Fromm, *To Have or to Be?*, 77. Interestingly, around the time that Fromm is writing, behaviorism enters into philosophical anthropology, contending that it can explain every behavior in total. B. F. Skinner and others offered behaviorism as the philosophy of true rationalist modernity. It went far and had a major impact. Skinner was opposed to any sense of the nongivenness of reality. Coming from a conservative Protestant background and having to deal with the death of a brother—and the bad theology that justified it— Skinner wanted a science that could eliminate all nongivenness. In the 1950s and 1960s (and

conceived to be completely bound in givenness, activity can be disconnected from being.[23] Inside the immanent frame we are tempted to disconnect act from being, because encounters with being have been replaced by the desire to own inside a reality that is only givenness.[24]

Why Does This Matter?

Okay, but what real difference does this make beyond the splitting of philosophical hairs? Fromm thinks it makes an important difference, which will connect us back to the story of Pastor Barth and point us forward in our Saint John the Baptist alternate history. Fromm believes that when activity takes no account of being and seeks only having, there is then "no distinction between activity and busyness."[25] This is very important and relevant for our time!

Fromm's point is that when all activity is the *same* and intended for the sake of having, activity and busyness become synonymous. Because of the loss of being, the only measure of activity, as we've said, is the expenditure of energy. The more energy expended for the greater gain, the more the activity has value. Inside this logic busyness becomes a kind of nobility, because busyness witnesses to the actor's reach toward all sorts of having. Living a good and full life is equated with the amount you have. It supposedly shows how much return you've received back for the investment of the expenditure of your energy. Only such logic could justify giving tax cuts to billionaires. Somehow (in some dark corner of our social consciousness) we believe they deserve it. Their billions and their ability to have all they wish were earned through an extraordinary expenditure of energy. In this logic, the best actors are hurrying to expend energy to have. This means the best actors are busy

---

during Fromm's 1970s work), thinkers would expose behaviorism. One of most important texts is Charles Taylor's dissertation, *The Explanation of Behavior* (New York: Routledge & Kegan Paul, 1970).

23. David Bentley Hart adds to these thoughts in *The Experience of God: Being, Consciousness, Bliss* (New Haven: Yale University Press, 2013), 328–29.

24. This is a significant point for Barth. Barth's ontological actualism contends that we know being through action. This can be an anthropological commitment, but Barth uniquely and beautifully makes it a theological one. As a good modern theologian, Barth doesn't think that the being of God comes disclosed. Rather, inside the immanent frame being is revealed (unveiled) in act. God is free to act in the immanent frame, and God acts—which Barth's project seeks to show—unveiling God's being (being for us in Jesus Christ). But what is important to see next to what I'm saying above is that act must be connected to being. If modernity can separate act from being, then the immanent frame is closed completely. Fromm and many others are pointing out that modernity's inclinations to separate act and being and to fuse act with having are deeply problematic.

25. Fromm, *To Have or to Be?*, 78.

and constantly getting busier. The pace of life on Wall Street or Instagram seems to prove this.[26]

Inside the immanent frame there is a pull for all forms of action to be seen as busy activities used for the sake of possessing and having something found only and finally in the givenness of reality. Activity is ultimately for *having* money or experiences, or even *having* a unique identity.[27] The late-modern life—a life inside the immanent frame—is fundamentally well lived when it is a busy life. Yet what Fromm sees is that *busyness is dangerous*.

It Matters Because of Busy Alienation!

Fromm doesn't spend much time discussing in depth the modern phenomenon of busyness (that will become the task of a future Frankfurt School theorist, Hartmut Rosa).[28] Rather, Fromm goes right to the implications, where he shows the danger of busyness. Fromm explains that activity fused with busyness can't really hold. As hard as modernity tries, an activity's value can't really be judged by the expenditure of energy. Modernity seeks to equate activity and busyness all for the sake of having, but when looked at more closely, busyness reveals a distinction in activity. To explain what it reveals, Fromm uses a word that has had a place in socialist movements like the one Pastor Barth found so important: *alienation*.[29]

Fromm's point is that busyness is a form of activity caught in, and therefore trying to escape from, alienation. "In alienated activity I do not experience myself as the acting subject of my activity; rather, I experience the outcome of my activity . . . as something 'over there,' separated from me and standing above and against me."[30] Busyness speeds up my life to the point where I feel like I'm no longer in my life. Busyness alienates me from living. My activities

---

26. For more on busyness, see Arlie Russell Hochschild, *The Time Bind: When Work Becomes Home and Home Becomes Work* (New York: Metropolitan Books, 1997).

27. I go into this cultural phenomenon much more deeply in *The Congregation in a Secular Age* (Grand Rapids: Baker Academic, 2021), chaps. 1 and 2.

28. I'll be picking up on Rosa's ideas in the next few chapters. However, I won't be dealing with his earlier work on acceleration. I've been in deep conversation with this thought in my *The Congregation in a Secular Age*. That book deals with Rosa's two primary texts: *Social Acceleration: A New Theory of Modernity* (New York: Columbia University Press, 2015); and *Alienation and Acceleration: Towards a Critical Theory of Late-Modern Temporality* (Copenhagen: NSU Press, 2014). An interested reader can find in these works a discussion of the late-modern phenomenon of busyness.

29. For a discussion of how deep alienation slides into our lives, feeding even (primarily) on economic realities, see Daniel Bell, *The Cultural Contradictions of Capitalism* (New York: Basic Books, 1996), 35–45.

30. Fromm, *To Have or to Be?*, 78.

keep accelerating until my busyness disconnects me from my action, alienating me from the life I'm living.

There is a deep irony here. Modernity closes down reality, making it all given. Inside this givenness it tells me my activity is free of any divine or transcendent responsibility or consequence. The point of my actions is to have as much of the world as I can expend my energy to possess. I'm Charlie in the chocolate factory. But here is the irony. To get (and keep) this *having*, I must continue and never decrease my pace of more and more expended energy. I'm forced to always accelerate my activity to keep what I have. Standing still, or even taking a break, is no option. To decelerate energy expenditure is to risk the loss of what I have. To not grow in my having is to be dying. Activity, after all, has zero value until it procures (and keeps) what we want to have. Saint John the Baptist believed this as much as any modern institution.

Yet the irony stretches deeper. I'm given the world because reality is assumed to be only givenness. But I can only *have* it by accelerating my activity to a level that alienates me from the world I can supposedly have. That's deviously ironic! With enough expended energy, I'm told I can possess the world. But the more energy I expend, becoming busier in my activity, the more I'm alienated from the givenness of the world. Soon the exhaustion of this expenditure of energy, to have as much of the givenness of reality as I want, alienates me from myself. And, worse, being alienated from myself, I'm alienated from the world.

Inside the busyness to have, the world is no longer a place to encounter life. I've moved dangerously close to no longer having love and joy in being alive. Love and joy escape me because my racing to expend energy alienates me inside a closed world of givenness. The world has been made into a dead and lifeless object. As an object, it just seems obvious that the world can no longer be the second subject in the story of God's action. Building off Pastor Barth, the heart of this project is to show otherwise.

The Red Pastor Never Changes His Colors

We can see this when we look more closely at Barth's story. In February 1919, Pastor Barth resumed his engagement with the workers' union. He had taken a respite from direct engagement while recovering from the heavy workload of finishing *Römerbrief I*. But with the economy crumbling, Pastor Barth saw the need to reengage. The factory owners in Safenwil believed the only way forward was to speed up their workers. They demanded more expenditure of energy in more hours so that more capital could be had. The workers were expending so much energy that they were alienated from their own action. Particularly concerning for Pastor Barth was how both workers and factory owners (though Barth clearly cared more for the workers) were therefore alienated from their own action.[31]

To lose act, in Barth's theological vision, is to lose the doorway into being. And to lose being is to lose a living connection to the world. Without this living connection, the world is made flat by immanence, and the living God of the Bible who speaks is pushed out of the world. We are then deceived into assuming the world can no longer be the place of God's unveiling. Accepting this flat immanence, as so many churches tacitly do in our day, means the church can *only* assume that it's the star of its own story. There is no other story than the story of an immanent-bound institution's expenditure of energy to have enough to survive.

When we're alienated from the world by our busyness, the world is made too flat to be the location of the event of God's arrival. This alienation dually disconnects us from the world and from God's action. Alienated from the two primary subjects of the church's story, both God and the world, the church can only turn inward, believing, as all late-modern entities do, that its life is dependent on itself. Particularly, life depends on going faster to expend more energy through activities to have enough resources to be at all. To be alienated from the world through busyness makes the closed spin (a way that has no place at all for transcendence) of the immanent frame appear obvious.

After Uncle Sartorius's wedding, and just a month before Barth gave his lecture at the Student Christian Movement conference (which was inspired by Heinrich's own lecture), "he marched with workers behind the red flag of Zofingen. This was the last straw for many of the people of Safenwil. Others joined the manufacturer Hochuli in leaving the church."[32] In August the congregation cut Barth's salary.[33] But this made no difference to him. It only proved that this tendency to accelerate activity was ripe in the church as much as in factories. This is why, in my mind, Pastor Barth must come down so hard against religion in *Römerbrief II*. Like modern factories, churches built for modern religion alienate people by accelerating their actions, making even their religious activities about the expenditure of energy. Unable to recognize

---

31. Stanley Hauerwas discusses Barth's involvement in socialism in *With the Grain of the Universe: The Church's Witness and Natural Theology* (Grand Rapids: Baker Academic, 2013), 150–51. See also George Hunsinger, *Karl Barth and Radical Politics* (Eugene, OR: Cascade, 2017); and Eberhard Jüngel, *Karl Barth: A Theological Legacy* (Philadelphia: Westminster, 1986), 92–93.

32. Busch, *Karl Barth*, 106–7.

33. For more context, see Thurneysen's words in Barth and Thurneysen, *Revolutionary Theology in the Making*, trans. James D. Smart (Richmond: John Knox, 1964), 21–22.

the event of the living God's encounter in a living world, instead of asking its people to seek a God who is God, the church anxiously asks them to expend energy in activities that will keep the congregation afloat. We need more (we need to have more) volunteers! We need more new members! We need more young families! More young adults! More really committed people!

Throughout 1919, Pastor Barth saw how necessary it was to maintain the bold line between the givenness and nongivenness of reality. Only by keeping this line bold and returning to a God who is God (who Barth emphasized is wholly other) can we be free of the alienation of the busyness of labor and religion. The bold line needs to be drawn thick so we can again encounter the God of life. Barth may be using the cadence of the dogmatic theologian, but these are inextricably practical pastoral concerns. Pastor Barth wagers that theological and biblical contemplations and frames of reference, as opposed to those of philosophy, psychology, or business management, can address alienation. Only theology embedded in a church that is not the star of its own story can take the step of inviting the modern world back into participation in life, by waiting and seeking the God of life who comes from nongivenness.

This is exactly what happened to Saint John the Baptist.

10

A Shady Obituary and the Need to Wait

It wasn't so much that Bert and the pastor search committee had changed their minds. Their minds just shifted toward something else. This made the decision for them. They decided that the young, socially conscious and internet-savvy candidate, whom Bert was willing to support as a token of peace to Sue, wouldn't be offered the position. There was no debate or deliberation. It was just clear to everyone that they'd been taken in another direction. Somehow this new direction had found them. How this new direction came, or where it would lead, no one knew. At least they didn't know where it would lead in the long term. In the short term, they were convinced this was where to go.

They were going in the direction of helping Woz find God. That's all they were worried about now, which in itself was a transformation. This huge challenge somehow released them from the necessity to expend more energy than they possessed. This congregation had been worried about its future for decades. It had exhausted itself in worry. Concern for the congregation's future had been so consuming it had turned friends like Bert and Sue into enemies (or at least moved them in that direction).

But now all of that was gone, at least for the core of the congregation. For those who met at the Bible study or were nominated to the pastor search committee, concern for the future was placed on a back burner for the first time in decades. Now only helping Woz find God was deemed important.

No one, particularly not Bert, had any idea what that looked like. Especially after Sue's confession ("Do we?"), it was clear that the God they were seeking to encounter was the God who is God. To find the God who is God, Woz would need to come up against an element of the nongivenness of reality.

The church would have to lead him into an encounter with nongivenness. The God they were seeking was not just the echo of their own voice or enervated spirit of religion but the God who is wholly other.

But this overwhelming challenge oddly didn't seem to expend energy but to produce it. They didn't need to produce this energy within themselves: it came from outside of them. There seemed to be enough life in that concern to trust that the congregation had some future. Energy didn't need to be expended and directed toward the future; the future could just be. The congregation needed instead to live now, helping this pilgrim on his absurdly difficult journey. They owed that to Jean, Woz's grandmother. The crisis of the future melted and was replaced by the crisis of a God who is God. This crisis did not take them out of the world by making them anxious for the viability of their life in the future. It simply allowed them to be.

Yet this ability to be didn't keep Bert from a few moments of freaking out. He wondered more than once whether they were making a mistake in not hiring a pastor when they had the chance. Worry for the future is a persistent rash that always threatens to return. One evening when the worry returned, Bert decided to go back to the congregational assessment that the denomination stipulated each congregation must conduct before opening a search for a new pastor. Luke's tenure had been short enough to allow Saint John the Baptist to skip the assessment before opening this most recent search (which is why they could move so fast). But Bert had the paperwork from the assessment they had done before hiring Luke. To pacify his worry, Bert decided to review it.

Before Luke arrived, the denominational assessment had clearly stated that Saint John the Baptist was in crisis. This was not the crisis of the impossibility of a finite creature like Woz encountering the infinite God who is God. No, the crisis was all bound in *having*. The assessment showed that Saint John the Baptist did not *have* the resources it needed. And therefore it *had* no future. It could achieve a future only if it hurried and changed. Saint John the Baptist's thriving, or even surviving, was assumed to be contingent on its ability to *have* resources. Because it presently didn't *have* enough resources, it could only *have* a future if it expended its energy (maybe all its energy) on activities that procured these resources. The congregation's crisis was measured and assessed almost completely by the logic of having. Its next pastor, the assessment communicated, would need to *have* the skills and energy to move the congregation out of the crisis of *having* depleted resources.

Luke fit the bill perfectly because of his capacity to expend energy. Congregations with a deficit of energy usually have a hard time finding a pastor ready and able to expend large amounts of energy. Following the logic of the crisis laid out in the assessment, Luke was the perfect hire, and Saint John the Baptist was lucky to find him. His energy seemed limitless.

It may have been. Luke didn't leave because he ran out of energy to expend (that was probably coming at his next congregation). Luke left because he resented that the rest of the congregation couldn't keep pace. His expended energy made the congregation busy. They weren't too busy for Luke (the busyness giving him a warped sense of value), but they were too busy for most of the rest of the congregation. Older people with less energy, like Woz's Grandma Jean, simply disappeared. They never had the energy to keep pace with Luke's busyness. They never thought it necessary. Without this ability and willingness, they had little value. They lacked the energy to be an asset in expending the energy to *have* more resources. Such people became alienated from their own congregation. Luke framed this lack of energy as a resistance to change. But they weren't resistant to change; they were tired. They were resisting the way change was fused with *having* and how *having* was bound to expending more and more energy they honestly didn't possess. They were resisting how change had been captured by busyness. They were opposing a form of change that alienates one from *being*.

The more energy Luke expended to procure the resources Saint John the Baptist needed to *have*, the more alienated the congregation was from *being*. They were alienated from just *being* in the world, alienated from just *being* alive, even from *being* vulnerable. The need to *have* meant the necessity for more expended energy, which produced for Luke, as well as the whole con- gregation, more alienation from *being*. The alienation was their loss of belief that the actions taken by those in the congregation mattered. Luke's action mattered. Theirs didn't, because their action couldn't reach the level of Luke's energy expended. They were passengers, not participants, in the life of their own congregation. As Bert reviewed the assessment, he began to see that the denomination's prescribed treatment to keep Saint John the Baptist from dying might have been worse than the disease.

While Bert was reviewing the assessment, Sue was in the middle of her own review. She was trying to figure out how they'd actually help Woz. What would it look like to even do so? It was one thing to say they would help. It would be another to actually do it. Sue didn't doubt anyone's intentions. They all wholeheartedly wanted to help Woz, and this turning to Woz's search drew them back into being. They were now more concerned with helping the being of Woz encounter the being of God than with having enough resources.

Saint John the Baptist was no longer the star of its own story. And this was life-giving! But Sue was nonetheless stumped by how they would actually do it. How would they help Woz find God?

Sue wasn't one of those abstract kind of people. She despised everything abstract. That's why she liked corporate real estate. There's no abstraction. Usually, there's not even the abstraction of the feelings of buyers, which you always get in residential real estate. When people buy their own house there is so much abstract psychology to it. Most of that is blunted in corporate real estate: the property either works or it doesn't. The price and location fit or they don't.

Yet Sue hadn't known how much she really despised abstraction until she traveled to Europe. About three years ago, Sue and her close friend Magda went to Paris. Sue was celebrating twenty years sober, and Magda was celebrating a decade of being cancer-free. They planned to swallow whole the city of lights. They mapped in detail every cafe, museum, and cathedral they'd visit. Sue didn't want to miss a sight. But fifteen minutes into the Picasso Museum she was out. Those damn cubes agitated her. She kept muttering to her friend, "What is this? What's the point? My granddaughter could do this!" To keep from ruining their trip, Sue found a cab. Fifteen minutes after her foray inside Picasso's abstract mind, Sue was sitting in the grass near the Eiffel Tower. She expunged the abstraction from her nerves by reading about how many bolts were in the bold beamed structure.

Sue felt, as much as anyone else at the Bible study, that helping Woz find God was right. It changed something important, but hard to name, for them all. It shifted Saint John the Baptist in a new direction. But Sue couldn't settle for some abstract commitment. She now felt obliged to concretely help this unkempt pilgrim on a voyage. But she had no idea where to start. Sue even googled "How do I find God?" It didn't help. It was worse than Picasso's cubes.

A 1919 Obituary with Traces of 1915

As we've seen, 1919 was an important year for Pastor Barth. In the first weeks of 1919 *Römerbrief I* was released. In February Pastor Barth marched with the factory workers. In the spring Barth gave his terrible reception speech at Uncle Sartorius's wedding. Also that spring, Barth heard his brother Heinrich give a lecture that inspired him to draw a bolder line between the given and nongiven elements of reality. In June those thoughts made their way into Barth's own Student Christian Movement lecture. Barth saw that he needed to more boldly state that God is wholly other. This signaled that, in time, the

whole of the *Römerbrief* would need to be rewritten. A month before that
lecture, Pastor Barth marched even more valiantly with the workers in the
socialist movement. This led to some important departures from his congregation, and those who stayed voted to cut his pay. This doubling down on
both a God who is God and direct advocacy for the workers seemed to place
Pastor Barth more fully in the pastoral mold of Christoph Blumhardt (or the
Younger, as we've called him).

It was sad news when, in August 1919, Barth received word that the Younger
had died. To honor him, Barth picked up his pen, writing an obituary. But,
of course, from the pen of the early brawling Barth, it was a front for a fight.
Barth's genius outpaced his tact. This was a year of bad wedding reception
speeches and contentious obituaries. This contentious obituary fits the shape
of Pastor Barth's development through the first half of 1919, highlighting
how Barth had doubled down both on his commitment to a God who is God
and on his direct engagement for workers in the world. This obituary spoke
about how to fit together these two seemingly distinct commitments, and also
how *not* to fit them together.

It just so happened that Friedrich Naumann also died in August. Barth had
met both Naumann and Blumhardt within twenty-four hours of each other.[1]
Barth had met Naumann at his brother Peter and Helene Rade's wedding
back in 1915. Naumann was the father-in-law of Martin Rade—Helene's
father and Barth's teacher. Naumann was a parish pastor turned political
activist. Barth, also a pastor moving into political engagement in 1915, had
read Naumann's work and was interested in talking with him. Yet, over a
beer, things went sideways. The conversation, not surprisingly, turned quar-
relsome. The point of contention was Naumann's assertion that theology, in
any particularity, did not matter. Naumann, nursing his beer, told the young
pastor that it didn't matter one way or another how we talked or thought
about God. What mattered was that we use religion to survive the war and
build the party to change Europe. Naumann was giving up one side for the
sake of the other, losing the otherness of God for a kind of political action.
Naumann believed it necessary to evacuate concern for a God who is God so
that the world could be reshaped.

For Naumann, the immanent frame was indeed closed. Any place for talk of
God within the world was only to serve immanent political ends. Party politics,
not the act of God, was Germany's only hope. Naumann was presenting a
way to be a pastor after the concession to the closedness of the immanent

1. Barth had had small interactions with each before this, but April 1915 was the first time
he had had substantial interaction with both Naumann and the Younger.

frame. Once God is closed out completely from the world, the pastor must pivot and become a political activist. This was essentially what Naumann was telling Pastor Barth over a beer.

Barth couldn't agree. And he didn't have a problem telling it to the older, well-established, and well-known man. For Pastor Barth, any political engagement was not entered as a concession to the closed immanent frame. It wasn't a way of recreating a vocation now that God was inaccessible. Rather, engagement, for the workers, was a movement deeper into the confession that God acts in the immanent frame.

One day after meeting Naumann, Barth was shown by the Younger what this looked like. The Younger boldly and beautifully lived it out before him. He revealed to Barth how a God who is God is essential to taking the pastor *not* out of the world, as Naumann assumed, but deeper into it. Barth's love for the Younger was clearly heightened due to his collision with Naumann the night before. The Younger's ministry was the answer to the disturbing questions that the beer with Naumann threw open in Barth.

Back to 1919

When both Blumhardt and Naumann died in August 1919, Pastor Barth couldn't pass up the chance to write an obituary (it's titled *Vergangenheit und Zukunft*, or "Past and Future").[2] As the title hints, in classic early Barth form, this obituary pitted the two deceased men against one another. Only one would be able to hold the belt for helping us shape a theology for the future. Coming up on a year since the end of the Great War, and over five years since the Spirit of August had swept the world into a vicious self-destructive act, Pastor Barth asserts in the obituary that Naumann is clearly a man for the past whose ideas need to pass away. Barth explains that there is no way to synergize Blumhardt and Naumann; our only choice is to say yes to one and no to the other. Barth explains that he will say no to Naumann, leaving him for the dustbin of the past.[3]

2. Barth is flowing with praise for the Blumhardts. Find the obituary here: Karl Barth, "Past and Future: Friedrich Naumann and Christoph Blumhardt," in *The Beginnings of Dialectical Theology*, ed. James M. Robinson (Richmond: John Knox, 1968).

3. For further discussion on the obituary and its contents, see Paul Chung, *Karl Barth: God's Word in Action* (Eugene, OR: Wipf & Stock, 2008), 154–61; and Paul Silas Peterson, *The Early Karl Barth: Historical Contexts and Intellectual Formation, 1905–1935* (Heidelberg: Mohr Siebeck, 2018), 151–58. However, the reader should know that the latter book has been controversial in Barth scholarship. Many question the full historical scope of the book.

This seems harsh, but Barth isn't simply settling old scores. If we were to follow Naumann, Barth sees great problems for the world. Naumann had conceded to the closed structure of the immanent frame, asserting that the only hope for Europe revolved around industry (which now dehumanizes workers) and military might (which had killed millions). Naumann had so severely blurred the lines between the kingdom of Europe and the kingdom of God that the kingdom of God disappeared from his thought. The result of this disappearance wasn't peace and a deeper love for the world but the arrival of hell on earth, maiming and wounding the world.

The Younger, on the other hand, embodied a lived theology in which such lines were drawn boldly and reinforced again and again. The Younger believed only God, who enters into the world, could save the world. This commitment to the complete otherness of God's kingdom counterintuitively but truly kept him loving the world, seeking God's act to save the world, keeping him from visions that impose violence on the world. The Younger stood against the war and for workers' rights because he contended without wavering that God lives and acts. The Younger unswervingly was committed to the world, because he was committed to the bold line that separated the givenness from the nongivenness of reality.

This love for the world, born from an unswerving commitment to a God who is God, impressed Pastor Barth. In a letter from 1916, Barth says, "Blumhardt can do something which most of us cannot do: represent God's cause in the world yet not wage war on the world, love the world and yet be completely faithful to God, suffer with the world and speak a frank word about its need while simultaneously going beyond this to speak the redemptive word about the help it awaits. . . . Is that not the highest and most promising thing a person can do—if he or she can?"[4]

Barth sees a deep and important paradox between these two pastors, leading him to audaciously say that we should all remember the Younger and forget poor old Naumann. We should forget Naumann because in blurring the line between the kingdom of God and the kingdom of Europe, he produced a hate for the world. Naumann didn't mean to hate the world, but his ambition forced his finger sharply into the world, wounding it. Naumann might have believed he was embracing the world, becoming relevant to the world by eliminating the bold line between the kingdoms. But this embrace was really clawed fingers grasping for the world's neck. It was seeking to shape

4. Barth, afterword to *Action in Waiting*, by Christoph Blumhardt (Farmington, PA: Plough, 1998), 218. (Original from *Der Freie Schweizer Arbeiter*, September 1916, in response to Blumhardt's *Morgen-Andachten*).

the world in human power, which takes no account for transcendence and nongivenness. In other words, to lose the bold line between the kingdoms and to concede that God cannot act in the immanent frame allowed for the hells of the trenches and continued agonies of the factory floors.

Blumhardt the Younger, on the other hand, embraced the world by drawing boldly the lines of difference between the kingdom of God and the kingdoms of Europe.[5] This line of distinction leads to a loving embrace of the world. This loving embrace, rather than a rigid fist, results from the patient humility to see the world always as before God, trusting the shape of the world as God's own responsibility. The Younger was able to act for the world because he truly loved the world, believing God loved it by acting in it. Christoph Blumhardt believed God so loved even the modern world that God spoke in it. Barth shows that the Younger died a true lover of the world, willing to advocate for the world's freedom from war and dehumanizing work. Between these two men there was no choice, Barth believed: we must follow the Younger.

These are undeniably practical pastoral concerns, and I believe they serve as the bedrock to Barth's theology. In the 1920s and 1930s, Barth took on the cadence of a dogmatician, seeking to give theological shape to these pastoral and practical concerns that have their origins in the life and ministry of Christoph Blumhardt and, of course, Fritz Barth. Karl Barth may have become a dogmatician, but the origins of his unique theological voice were fully pastoral. And though long volumes filled with doctrine would be his future, they never abolished his deeply practical concerns and love for the world.

Welcome to Waiting

With the contentious obituary aside, and if these practical concerns are true, what does this actually mean? What does it look like to love the world while holding to the bold line between the kingdoms? It means just one main thing: to *wait*. Period. We love the world as God commands by waiting with the world for God's act to come to the world (not to the church).[6]

The only way to both love the world and hold to the bold line that separates the kingdom of God from the kingdoms of Europe (or of the US) is to wait. Inside the immanent frame, the only way to even find a God who is God at

5. Eberhard Jüngel discusses what Barth learns from the Blumhardts. See Jüngel, *Karl Barth: A Theological Legacy* (Philadelphia: Westminster, 1986), 30–33.

6. Bruce McCormack discusses the place of waiting in Barth in *Karl Barth's Critically Realistic Dialectical Theology: Its Genesis and Development, 1909–1936* (Oxford: Oxford University Press, 1997), 121–22.

all is to wait. This means that the only way for the church to remember that it is not, and cannot be, the star of its own story is to wait. The church is the church of the living God only when it waits.[7] Only in its waiting can the church love the God who is God by serving the world. And only by waiting can the church serve the living God by loving the world.[8]

The pastor leads her congregation into waiting. Barth says, "One of the deepest impressions I get from Blumhardt is that here we meet a priestly person."[9] In other words, here we have a pastor's pastor. In the Younger, we have a pastor not seeking to expend energy and have for himself a big church, winning back a shine for religion. No, in Blumhardt the Younger, we have an exemplar pastor who unflinchingly waits. The Younger leads the church *not* to do and to have but *to be* by waiting.[10]

Why Wait?

Yet, let's be honest, this focus on waiting is more than a little bit disorienting. For some it's annoying, and for others, worrisome. We find something within ourselves resisting it. To wait is to go against the grain of modernity. As Erich Fromm taught us in the previous chapter, modernity redefines action as the expenditure of energy. Modernity asserts that "good" action stands in opposition to waiting. Inside modernity's desire to speed up the expenditure of energy (so the world also can be had), modernity initiates an attack on waiting.

Particularly when commerce and consumption take their place at the center of our imagination, waiting is turned into a problem to overcome. For instance, consumerism (and the credit markets that support it) seeks to take the waiting out of wanting.[11] Homer Simpson is the epitome of the late-modern man seeking a world where all waiting is defeated and gratification

---

7. "In a 1911 letter to Ragaz, Blumhardt summarizes the latter point somewhat bluntly: '[God] is leading me into stillness. Whatever is true, whatever is from God, has to come through on its own; this is the "New Age." I am holding fast to this, and have no desire to be the kind of person who "accomplishes" things.'" Simeon Zahl, *Pneumatology and Theology of the Cross in the Preaching of Christoph Friedrich Blumhardt: The Holy Spirit between Wittenberg and Azusa Street* (London: T&T Clark, 2010), 133.

8. Barth discusses waiting in his later theology in *Church Dogmatics* IV/3.2 (Edinburgh: T&T Clark, 1962), 719–21.

9. Barth, afterword to *Action in Waiting*, 218. (Original from *Der Freie Schweitzer Arbeiter*, September 1916, in response to Blumhardt's *Morgen-Andachten*.)

10. For more on this, see Christoph Blumhardt, *The Gospel of God's Reign: Living for the Kingdom of God* (Eugene, OR: Cascade Books, 2014), 75–77.

11. "Taking the waiting out of wanting" is a phrase Zygmunt Bauman uses in describing late modernity. See *Globalization: The Human Consequences* (New York: Columbia University Press, 1998), 79.

is instant. To say it more dramatically, late modernity seeks to assassinate waiting. Most of the innovations of Silicon Valley, which are sold to the Homer Simpsons of the world, are driven by seeing waiting as a problem to overcome and eventually to eliminate completely. (Amazon's drone delivery coming soon!) All modern forms of optimization make waiting—and the time it takes—a problem.

It makes sense that late modernity would make waiting an enemy, because growth is one of its highest goals, if not the highest (even its *summum bonum*). Waiting has no place in the drive for growth. In late modernity, if you're not growing, you're declining—meaning if you're waiting, you're losing. When the church sees its essential issue as one of decline (negative growth), it seeks innovations that often move it far away from waiting. Waiting, even in the church, becomes wasting. But as we'll see, this only spins the immanent frame closed, compounding our problems by leading the church to think it is (or has to be) the star of its own story. This inevitably pushes the church to see itself as a competitor with the world, not a lover of the world.

Yet waiting is essential. In waiting, we can encounter the living God who is found acting in the world (even the modern world). Waiting is our disposition when we anticipate the event of God's in-breaking. Waiting is a profound theological and practical category for both the Younger's and Barth's pastoral theologies. While waiting at first blush seems hollow, which may be why we resist it, a deeper look reveals that it's bursting with dynamism.[12]

Waiting is dynamic when it comes to seeking a God who is God, because this kind of waiting is *attentiveness*.[13] It's no surprise that late modernity and its opposition to waiting has made attention the new staple of its economy. We are now living in an attention economy. The most sacred commodity in our digital age is no longer oil or other raw materials. It's attention. Companies such as Facebook and Amazon are worth billions because they own our attention.[14] They own our attention by keeping us from ever waiting, giving us the sense that we can have the world inside the speed of digital information. Yet, as most of us would testify, this lack of waiting doesn't seem to make us more alive or even more connected to the world. Despite what Facebook executives might wish, their goal to keep us from waiting by always directing our

12. Jürgen Moltmann, who also was inspired by the Younger Blumhardt, adds, "When we wait together with earthly creation for the coming of the Holy Spirit, we are awaiting both things: liberation from injustice and violence, and liberation from time and death." *The Source of Life: The Holy Spirit and the Theology of Life* (Minneapolis: Fortress, 1997), 114.

13. For the Younger, attentiveness is equal to watching. He discusses waiting in *Action in Waiting*, 43–44.

14. And if you're Amazon or Facebook you can track and collect that data, selling it to others at a high price.

attention makes us less connected to life. Their digital tools are now weapons used, maybe over and against their desire, to breed hate in and for the world.

There is no reason to wait when the immanent frame is spun closed. If the assumption is that the immanent frame is closed from all transcendence and divine action (from any encounter with the nongivenness of reality), then waiting can only be imagined as lazy dullness. Waiting is a state to resent and conquer. But if the immanent frame is open and a good life in the world equals more than growth and possession, then waiting is an attentive looking outside ourselves (and particularly outside the church) for the act of God. Waiting is an attentive anticipation of, even preparing for, the event of God's arrival in the world.[15]

To wait is to be catechized, to enter a school that forms us to see the action of a living God. Particularly for the Younger, waiting is a school that teaches us to pray for the world, pleading for God to act for the world's salvation.[16] Prayer itself is waiting.[17] Waiting leads us to pray not for the church's survival but for the freedom, wholeness, and life of the world. Waiting becomes the most direct and practical way to hold the boundary between the givenness and nongivenness of reality. When the church attentively waits with and for the world, it seeks a God who is God by loving the world and praying for the world. To wait is to be alive. In waiting, we find life.

Saint John the Baptist is not leaking relevance or members or even dollars. It's leaking life. As it recognizes this leaking, being a late-modern institution, it seeks to speed up its action, optimizing its vision, finding some way to expend energy its members don't have by seeking new ways to win young adults' attention. But this only seems to leak more life more quickly. Only when Woz arrives with a request it *cannot* meet (particularly not in a having kind of way) is it forced to stop and wait. In this waiting, as we'll see, life not only ceases leaking but starts to return.

The Younger and Barth see waiting as crucial, but my guess is that our uneasiness with waiting remains. Perhaps we need to explore how waiting is connected to action. Barth's practical pastoral theology is built on waiting,

15. Barth speaks of waiting in a few places in *The Epistle to the Romans* (London: Oxford University Press, 1933), 151, 313.

16. Christian Collins Winn explains the Younger's understanding of prayer. See his introduction to *Gospel of God's Reign*, by Blumhardt, xxvi.

17. Barth also builds his later ecclesiology around prayer. See *Church Dogmatics* IV/1 (Edinburgh: T&T Clark, 1956). Waiting remains essential for his thought. As John Webster says about Barth's understanding, "Prayer is to be understood with equal force as 'a genuinely human action.'" *Barth's Moral Theology: Human Action in Barth's Thought* (Grand Rapids: Eerdmans, 1998), 173. He continues, "In a very important sense, then, Barth views prayer (and thus human moral endeavor) as directed towards 'God's own independent action'" (174).

and yet his practice as a pastor is to join the line, giving his voice to the protest for workers' rights. This seems like a contradiction. How are waiting and action connected?

Waiting and Apathy

The church is the church, most predominantly in the immanent frame, when it waits. Yet, as we've seen, even with our short comments about prayer, this waiting is an active passivity.[18] The church's *activity* is in its movement into the world, in its praying for the world. Once in the world, the church waits (its passivity).[19] This active waiting allows the church to be in the world, not to *have* the world but to truly *be* with the world. The church's move into the world is not a march for market share, resource gain, or even cultural influence. Inside the immanent frame, the church is only a disposable tool, or is forgotten altogether, when it is assumed it can *have* the world. That's the major problem with Naumann, in Barth's mind. Rather, the church moves only to *be* with the world, waiting with the world for God's coming action. The church can *be* in the world by going into the world to wait.[20]

This waiting is a hastening, as the Younger would say. It is active waiting, but it is nonetheless a waiting. The dialectical nature of this waiting keeps it from being confused with apathy. Inside late modernity and its drive to have, we're tempted to assume all waiting is apathy. But that can only be so if all action is for having. Apathy is a by-product of *having*, never *being*. Apathy is more rightly a hastening that has no place for waiting. When the energy for hastened action is spent and yet the need to *have* and *do more* remains, apathy is born.

Apathy arrives when you can't find the energy to keep acting. When the energy tanks are on empty and the spirit is fatigued from all the rushed action, a defeated despondency arrives, which imposes a sense of apathy. This is why life kept leaking from Saint John the Baptist, the gauge getting close to the level of apathy. The coming war between Sue and Bert would have

18. As Vladimir Lossky says, "Union with God cannot take place outside of prayer, for prayer is a personal relationship with God. Now this union must be fulfilled in human persons; it must be personal, conscious and voluntary." *The Mystical Theology of the Eastern Church* (Yonkers, NY: St. Vladimir's Seminary Press, 1976), 207.

19. John Webster beautifully stages a conversation between Barth and Luther on passivity in *Barth's Moral Theology*, 192–200.

20. Returning to the point made by Willie James Jennings in *The Christian Imagination* (New Haven: Yale University Press, 2010), a misguided theology led colonialists not to go into a strange land and wait, but to possess it and own it as property.

depleted all remaining energy, leaving the victor to inherit an energy-empty congregation teeming with apathy.

Modernity hates waiting because it fears it. This legitimate fear occurs because waiting unveils that the drive for having is misdirected in the first place. Waiting reveals that action cannot be understood as only, or in totality, the expending of energy. Waiting offers a much different understanding of action. With waiting, energy is understood to arise not from within ourselves but from a hope that is outside us. Waiting attentively seeks the arrival of an all-new action that can save us. Waiting rests squarely on hope coming from a horizon outside of us.[21] To go into the world and wait with the world is to actively embody hope for the world, to be present before the world as one who hopes. Apathy, on the other hand, has lost the hope that action as expended energy can make any difference, and yet one is trapped with no other way of acting.

Apathy becomes a heavy form of alienation. Alienation is activity accelerated to such a pace that you lose touch with your own, and even the world's, being.[22] A church that cannot wait, particularly in late modernity, becomes a church both bound within and perpetuating alienation. It becomes the church of Esau, existing only for itself and the religion it protects. Alienation wants nothing to do with waiting. Yet learning to wait frees us from alienation. Alienation whispers (or screams) that waiting is death. The Younger proclaims that out of the death of waiting comes true life of true life.

To the Picket Line, Not Just for Rights but for Life

At this point we can see the connection between Barth's pastoral theology of waiting for a God who is wholly other and his concrete pastoral practice of joining the line in the strike. Barth and the Younger are aware that being alive isn't just a choice for many in the world. Those to whom the Younger and Barth minister suffer under the structures of oppression. Neither of these pastors misses this actuality. Both are involved in the socialist movement because of that actuality. Yet Pastor Barth and the Younger believe that waiting is prophetic, because waiting refuses to see the world as only something to have

---

21. The Younger affirms this in *Action in Waiting*, 25–28.

22. For a discussion on and definition of alienation, see Hartmut Rosa, *Resonance: A Sociology of Our Relationship to the World* (Cambridge: Polity, 2019), 178–80. For more on how Rosa is defining *alienation* and for the richest articulation of alienation in philosophy, see Rahel Jaeggi, *Alienation*, New Directions in Critical Theory (New York: Columbia University Press, 2016); see also Amy Allen and Eduardo Mendieta, eds., *From Alienation to Forms of Life: The Critical Theory of Rahel Jaeggi* (University Park: Pennsylvania State University Press, 2018).

and people in it as simply tools for this having. Both Barth and the Younger are calling the church to move into the world. The church is moved into the world to share in the yearnings and needs of the world, waiting for God's coming ministry to the world. Yearnings and needs cannot be embraced in and of themselves unless we can wait, sharing in the humanity and suffering of the world. This kind of waiting is a form of resistance. It resists the death drives that impose themselves on the world. Waiting is how we love the world and seek God in the world. Waiting is how we resist evil.

But again, this is an active passivity—this waiting does something when it is truly willing to wait. Waiting enters the world in and through the logic of being. To wait is to seek life as being, not to seek growth as having. Waiting disconnects us from the lie that growth equals life, that expanding and expending is the only way to procure life. Waiting calls all the structures in the world to uphold life—not through *having more* but by *being with*. Therefore, workers must be allowed to wait, to find their being in rest.[23] Without the seventh day of waiting and resting, the human creature becomes deaf to the Word that brings being out of non-being. On the sixth day the human creature is spoken into being, not to have the world, but to be with God on the seventh day, resting and waiting with God in friendship.[24]

The alienating acceleration of *having* disconnects our actions from life by eviscerating waiting. It alienates workers from the action of their work. They need to run faster and faster, expending so much energy that they're too tired to live, too exhausted to even feel alive. When the seventh day is lost, the other six days no longer provide life. Yet, if we can remember the waiting of the seventh day, we're reoriented to time. It gives us the time to remember that we are alive, that we are creatures needing something more than the closed immanent frame to be. Waiting doesn't eliminate our action, but it does redirect our action. It gives us the space to ask the purpose of our expenditure of energy. Waiting invites us to connect our action again to life, to remember that we *are* indeed alive, found in a world that reaches out to us and invites us to reach out to it. It invites us to remember that life itself is a gift. As a gift, its source must come from some element of the nongivenness of reality.

---

23. "Moreover, like Luther, Barth draws attention to 'sabbath rest' as definitive of humanity. In the ethics of reconciliation, he notes that 'there is a resting of the Christian life in God,' picking up a theme from the ethics of creation where the 'renouncing faith' of the Sabbath theme is introduced as a way of accomplishing 'a clear delimiting and relativizing of what man could and should will and do of himself.'" Webster, *Barth's Moral Theology*, 173.

24. Matthew Boulton has given a beautiful discussion of Barth and the creation texts, moving toward friendship with God, in his book *God against Religion: Rethinking Christian Theology through Worship* (Grand Rapids: Eerdmans, 2008).

As a concrete example of this, think of Martin Luther King Jr.'s non-violent resistance, which was, at its core, a passive activity. It was a waiting with the world. Waiting at the front of buses and at diner counters actively articulated the *being* of African Americans in the South. These human *beings* needed rights, not for the sake of *having* some abstract rights but so their *being* could rest, so they could be alive in body, mind, and spirit. King believed that this waiting connected the movement with something transcendent. His vision of waiting was much more than an immanent strategy to *have*. The waiting of direct resistance was born out of the waiting called for by a God who is God. King's dream is a waiting that confesses that, because God is God, the world will turn and justice will come. The God of life, the God who gives the gift of the seventh day, will meet the world in its waiting.

For King, "the arc of the moral universe is long, but it bends toward justice."[25] He did not believe there was something inherent within history that does this curving. Contemporary intellectuals such as Andrew Marantz, stuck in the closed corners of the immanent frame, have critiqued King for this assertion that history bends toward justice.[26] Marantz and others dislike this statement of King's. They believe it is naive. But they fail to see that, for King, the God who acts in history bends history. It is not history that bends itself toward justice (the givenness of reality can never do this). Rather, the God who is wholly other and who comes to us from the nongivenness of reality bends history toward justice. God does this by making a way for our being to participate in God's own being.

King can wait, knowing that history will bend toward justice. He has faith that God acts in the world. We can participate in this action by loving the world through waiting with it. Our waiting is a loving confrontation with the world for the world to put down its obsession with having and just be. Barth says something similar in relation to the Younger, quoting him: "Blumhardt's meaning is that waiting, although turned inward at first, is in its essence revolutionary: 'Lord God, make new! Make us new!' To act—to 'wait'—means just the opposite of sitting comfortably and going along with the way things are, with the old order of things."[27]

----

25. Martin Luther King Jr., "Remaining Awake through a Great Revolution" (sermon, National Cathedral, Washington, DC, March 31, 1968), available at https://mocada.org/aiovg _videos/martin-luther-king-jr-revolution-sermon.

26. See Andrew Marantz, *Antisocial: Online Extremists, Techno-Utopians, and the Hijacking of the American Conversation* (New York: Viking, 2019), chap. 1.

27. Barth, afterword to Blumhardt, *Action in Waiting*, 221.

Sue's search online for "How do I find God?" led to a dizzying cacophony of noise and ultimately to a frustrating dead end. She knew it was silly to even search such a thing. But where else do you go in a late-modern digital age when you're perplexed? The excess of opinions and confusing posts sent Sue to check in with Facebook before putting down her iPad.

When she opened the site, there was something different on her timeline. A navy blue header box said "3 years ago" and under that "Your memories." Under the header was a picture of Sue and her friend Magda at the Chartres Cathedral taken just as the sun was setting. The picture reminded Sue of that eventful day.

Sue and Magda had survived Sue's Picasso meltdown and spent the following day at Orsay Museum with a wonderful late-afternoon coffee at the Shakespeare and Company bookstore. Magda had an MA in English literature. She'd written her thesis on the lost generation—those 1920s American writers, such as Ernest Hemingway and F. Scott Fitzgerald, who had relocated to Paris after the Great War. When not in Gertrude Stein's flat, their hub was Shakespeare and Company. Sue and Magda spent a few hours taking in the busy vibe of those writers' old haunt, loving every minute of imagining themselves in the 1920s.

Before dinner they bought train tickets to Chartres for the next day. They planned to spend the morning taking in one of Europe's most beautiful gothic cathedrals, just an hour train ride outside Paris. The plan was a morning tour, lunch, and back to Paris for a late-afternoon tour of the Pantheon before crossing the Luxembourg Garden for dinner at their favorite restaurant, Georgette's. All went as planned, until they got back to the station for their return trip to Paris. In classic Parisian style, the conductors, without notice, had walked out, going on strike. The trains were now at a standstill with no clue as to when they'd run again.

Magda rolled with the inconvenience. Sue didn't. Luckily, they discovered that a local hotel was taking van loads of people back to Paris. They got seats, but on the third trip. They were now stuck in Chartres for the next six hours. Sue was frustrated. She was annoyed she was stuck waiting for a van with no other way back, and she was disappointed they would miss out on dinner at Georgette's.

With few options, they decided to return to the cathedral. Needing a place to sit, they figured it was as good an option as any other. Magda walked the perimeter of the grand building, reviewing the stained glass again, checking panels against her guidebook. Sue just sat, too agitated to do anything but stew in her frustration. She needed some space lest another Picasso-type meltdown ensue.

She sat and sat. She told herself the agitated stories about where her energy should be spent. She tortured herself with "should be." She told herself she should be anywhere but here, in this cathedral, in this little town. That wasn't the plan. Her exasperated narrative was interrupted when a small group of people sat four pews ahead of her. She watched them pray and embrace. Though unable to understand French, she could still understand their pathos. Watching them caused something to shift in Sue. She stopped propelling her imagination forward and just sat, allowing herself to just be in time, not race through it.

Eventually, the space started to do something to Sue. Her frustration disappeared. Her anxiousness left. She found that she was just there, just breathing and being. Calm. After an hour of just waiting and resting, she felt something reach for her. It came upon her with compassion and promised peace. It was full. It was a gift. She felt mainly gratitude for being there in that space, and for just being alive. In waiting, with the frustration gone, she felt found. It was one of the more holy moments of Sue's life. She ended up sitting there for four hours. She was waiting, not for minutes to be peeled away but to rest in a kind of fullness of time. In the fullness of time, the gifts of the world were given to her. She could simply be in the world, not possess it. She found herself thinking about her son and granddaughter. She prayed for them: she found herself praying—something that was not easy for her.

Inside that memory, Sue realized that she did know how to help Woz find God. She wondered how she'd forgotten about that experience. She wondered why it hadn't framed her life as much as it should have. The immanent frame was powerful enough to crop out such deep happenings. She somehow had become too busy to let that experience form her. But now that Woz had arrived, she decided she wouldn't forget it again. She realized what they needed to do to help Woz find God. Woz didn't need to actively find God. *He needed to wait for God to find him.* Sue had found that out in the cathedral. God found her. If Saint John the Baptist was going to help Woz find God, they'd need to come together with him and wait.

But Sue had no idea how she'd communicate this to Woz or to the Bible study. She was more comfortable crafting business plans for the church space or even talking to potential buyers for the church building. Narrating holy moments and speaking about how God finds us was way outside her comfort zone. It took a few weeks.

11

Waiting Sucks but Resonance Is Life

At the next Bible study, Woz arrived wearing a ripped T-shirt and a bright smile. Sue watched him intently throughout that evening. She expected to see a kind of hurriedness in him, a kind of consumer expectation. Woz had asked for help finding God, and the Bible study had implicated the congregation in helping him. But now here they were, with no real direction on how to do it. After all, how, from within the givenness of reality, do you take a young man into nongivenness? How do you help a guy like Woz (or anyone, for that matter) find a God who is God? You can't!

Sue had tacitly known this from the beginning. But this made her all the more concerned that Woz would demand this help in finding God. She worried that he would want the three easy steps or else leave. That's what she would want if she were Woz. If you come looking for a service, you expect some satisfaction.

But Woz didn't seem to have this expectation. For the next three weeks, he just showed up. He didn't say much during the discussions, but he laughed a lot. His laughter became infectious. The third week he arrived early, toting coffee and donuts he'd procured from the coffee shop where he worked. "Not-quite-day-olds," Woz proudly called them. Woz was his most animated before and after the Bible study, talking and laughing with all the older people.

At the end of the third week, Woz finally said something during the discussion. It started when Herbert Grapp, a man in his early eighties, said, "I'd like to make sure we thank God for Woz. How nice that you brought the coffee and donuts tonight. It's great havin' ya here at church, bud."

Woz blushed, his skin matching his beard again. Woz then returned, "Thanks, Herbert. That means a lot. But I'd also like to thank God for you all. Being with you all reminds me so much of my grandma. It hurts a little bit."

His smile was warm, but a slight grimace followed.

He continued, "It hurts because I miss her so much. It actually, honestly, hurts a lot. But in a good way, you know? The last few years my grandma really was my closest friend. I don't know if she told you all, but I'd had some problems . . . oh . . . you know, with substances. I discovered the only way to stay away from the stuff was to stay away from my old friends. So when I came to live with grandma, she was it. She was pretty much my only friend. And being with you all reminds me of her, and makes me miss her like crazy."

They prayed. Sue relaxed.

The text for the Bible study the following week was Luke 2. They ate more of Woz's "not-quite-day-olds" and read about Mary and Joseph bringing the infant Jesus to the temple. Woz seemed content but not engaged. The biblical text explains that there was a righteous man named Simeon who'd been waiting in the temple, clinging to the promise that he would see the Messiah before his death. Simeon had been waiting and waiting to see God's anointed one. Finally, after all the waiting, Mary put Jesus in Simeon's arms and the old man spoke of salvation coming to the world.

As they read the story together, it reached for Sue. She'd read it before, but this was the first time *it* was reading *her*. It took her back again to France. For the first time she decided to tell the group what had happened in the Chartres Cathedral. In speaking it to others, she felt more like she was reliving it. The meaning of the event became even more deeply formative as she told it to her community. Sue felt the event making its way deeper and deeper into her being. It felt like unearthing a beautiful stone path grown over by grass and weeds. This pathway led her deeper into life.

Experiencing a deep sense of connection, Sue found boldness. Sue wasn't shy, but she usually kept her opinions to more concrete matters like budgets and business plans. But here she was leading her community theologically. Sue turned to Woz and said, "And I think this is how we can help you. A few weeks ago we promised we'd help you find God. Personally, that threw me into a crisis. I realized I had no idea how to find God. But now I think I do."

Everyone in the group leaned forward, hanging on Sue's every word, shocked that Sue was talking like this. "I think Simeon's story and my experience in Chartres help me see how we can help you find God. What I realized is, *we can't*! We can't find God! But if we wait, really wait together, I think God will find us. Simeon doesn't find Jesus. Jesus and his parents find Simeon. I think how we can help you, Woz, is to wait with you for God to reach out to you."

Waiting for Something

The church cannot be the star of its own story, because its primary action in the world is to wait with the world for God to come to the world (not to the church). The church finds life only in and through the life of Jesus Christ. Like Simeon, it can find Jesus only by waiting (Luke 2).

Waiting, as Simeon shows, is always *for* something. Waiting is only truly waiting—in the dynamic way discussed in the previous chapter—when we recognize that waiting cannot stand alone. It is not an independent activity by itself. Waiting without *waiting for something* is a contradiction. Waiting needs to be *for* something. No one just waits. As contingent historical beings, we always wait *for* something. What we're waiting for often unveils what we believe gives our life meaning and purpose. All waiting is for something, even if that something is not defined. Even when someone is asked "What are you waiting for?" and she responds, "Nothing," she doesn't really mean nothing. She means nothing *specific* or nothing *worth mentioning*. Or it leads to a recognition that she's not actually waiting and she should get going. If she is waiting, she's waiting *for something*—like the restoration of her energy, or the bus to arrive, or the new episode of *Better Call Saul* to drop. Waiting always needs a corresponding direction. To wait without waiting *for something* is a prison.

As philosopher Michel Foucault has taught, punishment in modernity inflicts itself on minds, not bodies. In antiquity, for instance, a thief was punished by receiving a beating. Maybe, if he was part of a harsher society, his hand was cut off. He paid for his crime through the flesh of his body, not by taking his time. Modernity has supposedly outgrown this (or, better, hidden it). Modernity, instead of punishing the body, inflicts its penalty on the mind. The thief is forced behind bars where his body isn't necessarily beaten (at least not legally), but his mind is legally tortured by being unable to act.[1] He has to "do time," which means he is forced to wait for no real purpose except to eventually be released from the waiting itself. It's hard to live a good life when all you're waiting for is to start living again. It's hard to wait when all you're waiting for is an end to the waiting, to start taking steps of your own volition again.

As Andy says to Red in *Shawshank Redemption* when planning his escape from the prison, "Get busy living or get busy dying." But "get busy" is the key. This classic line from cinematic history reveals a normative commitment

---

1. For discussions of mental illness issues that come from prison time, see scholars Tricia Rose, *The Hip Hop Wars* (New York: Basic Books, 2008); and Imani Perry, *Prophets of the Hood: Politics and Poetics in Hip Hop* (Durham, NC: Duke University Press, 2004).

of late modernity. Inside the immanent frame and its focus on commerce and consumption, the purpose of waiting has been eroded—it's been made only natural and material. To keep these flat reductions from torturing us, making all of modern life a prison, we need to keep busy. Getting busy becomes way more important than waiting in late modernity.[2] Getting busy, as opposed to waiting, is now the sign of living. All people have to wait, of course, but supposedly the freer you are, the less you're forced to wait.[3] Those who *have* more wait less.

This contrast between "getting busy" and "waiting" in relation to prison life mirrors another popular cultural text, Regina Spektor's song "You've Got Time." This theme song for the Netflix show *Orange Is the New Black* offers haunting insights on the necessity of getting busy in late modernity. This theme is particularly poignant in Spektor's line, "Taking steps is easy, standing still is hard." Standing still is incredibly hard, even crippling to the human spirit, because waiting is cut off from some end. When there is nothing significant to wait for and yet you're kept from getting busy, as in prison life (or during a global pandemic), you're tortured. Spektor's lyric is directed toward those in prison, but just like the line from *Shawshank Redemption*, it says something important about late modernity.[4]

Late-modern people cope with the reductions of transcendence in the immanent frame by taking steps, by staying busy. Erich Fromm has shown us how and why (see chap. 9). Fromm explains that taking busy steps, while a legitimate strategy in late modernity, nevertheless risks a taxing alienation. But this taxing alienation of constant steps (and now your Apple Watch or

2. Getting busy was also a 1990s euphemism for having sex, usually in a kind of fast hook-up style, which fits my point. In a reductive modernity, getting busy just with activity or free sexual encounters is a way of finding meaning or even a kind of effervescence. Inside the immanent frame, waiting has no value because there is no transcendent reality to wait to encounter. But life can still feel full if you just get busy—making money, winning recognition, or hooking up. Sex is the frontier where waiting is excommunicated, made prudish, and considered to be a boring loss of living.

In the early twenty-first century there was a return even inside the immanent frame to waiting. The rise of yoga and meditation and mindfulness practices were the most direct examples. But these practices were much different from their original religious forms. In religious forms you did these practices to wait for something outside yourself to meet you. Inside late modernity your waiting actually becomes a way of coping with your busyness, preparing workouts (e.g., yoga) to ensure you are the windshield, not the bug, of a busy late-modern world. These practices become about the project of the self, meaning they're less about waiting and more about strategies for self-fulfillment.

3. For more on this, see Root, *The Congregation in a Secular Age* (Grand Rapids: Baker Academic, 2021), chaps. 2 and 3.

4. Foucault's point is that our form of punishment is embedded in our modern sense of power. Our prisons reveal something about our goods, goals, and purposes.

Fitbit will count them!) is better than acknowledging the hollowness of the things we're told to wait for. We stay busy because it keeps us from having to face the fact that what we're waiting for is cold and lifeless, thin and vapid. Better to face the risks of alienation and exhaustion from all the busy steps than to stand still and face the vacancy of late modernity. Standing still too long will mean waiting, and not as just as a pause in action but as a disposition of being in the world.

Two Kinds of Waiting: Toward Having and Toward Being

Late modernity may hate waiting, but it can never completely escape it. It *uses* waiting for the advantage of getting busy in having the world, as Fromm would say. Late modernity uses waiting to build hype for the release of the next iPhone or next year's Coachella. Waiting isn't a way of being in the world; it's a way to build momentum to race into the world and *have* more of the world. Ultimately, modernity refuses to make waiting a way of being in the world. Waiting is only a pause to make the busyness of *having* more eclectic (or to give a quick breather to soon get back to busyness). Again, following Fromm, all waiting has a *for*. The question becomes, Is that waiting an annoyed pause (a revving of the engine) *for having* the world? Or a way *for being* in the world?

Late modernity struggles with this latter way. We have a hard time with the thought of waiting as a way of being, because such waiting demands we give ourselves to something outside ourselves. Waiting as a way of *being* (the second way), as opposed to a pause in *having* (the first way), is to release control. To wait as a way of being is to be dependent on something that is not you. To get busy, to always be busy, is to give us a sense of control, which we often equate with freedom. To stand still and wait for the arrival of something outside us, on the other hand, is to surrender our freedom of taking hurried steps to have what we want in the world.

This second way of waiting gives us the freedom not to *have* the world but to *be freely in* the world, by waiting with and for the world. For most people in late modernity it's easier to just stay busy taking steps, because it feels better (until it doesn't). Even misguided and misdirected steps feel better than stopping and surrendering yourself to something outside yourself that you must wait for. (YOLO—"you only live once"—is the confession that mitigates the guilt of these misguided/misdirected steps.) The immanent frame seems necessarily closed when waiting is conceived only in the first way, only for pausing in having the world. In the rush of movement, in the drive to get busy, we lose any sense of a nongivenness to reality, making the immanent frame appear obviously closed. But things are different when we wait *for* as a way of being (the second way). In this second way we don't escape the immanent frame or try to live outside it. We remain modern people, but as modern people we nevertheless wait. This second way of waiting produces openness to the possibility that there are elements of reality, even in the immanent frame, that are nongiven.

The way to inhabit the modern world, and yet be open to the possibility of encountering a God who is God, is by waiting. This is the concrete way of *being* in the world, and in turn being for the world. Waiting is never a way of escaping the world or closing down the world. It is a waiting with the world for a God who is God to act in it. This is a deeply pastoral, even concrete, concern. And it says something important to the church in our own day, something Sue is moving Saint John the Baptist toward. As the storm clouds of decline gather around congregations like Saint John the Baptist, it's much easier for denominations, and their consultants, to push for steps. They imagine that the church needs busy steps. The church needs busy action plans. The church needs to speed up by taking steps to survive. But taking steps is easy, to echo Spektor's song, though it concedes to the closed immanent frame. The church, like the rest of late modernity, copes with the flatness of reality by staying busy in reality. We keep ourselves from standing still long enough to recognize that our busyness is vapidness. But to stand still intentionally, to wait as a way of being, is a gallant move of strength and courage, most particularly in late modernity. To wait is to open ourselves to something outside ourselves. To wait is to seek for the nongivenness of reality to come to us as the revelation of Jesus Christ. Like Simeon, we encounter this Christ by first waiting as a way of being. The church must first be still and wait. In waiting, we know that God is God (Ps. 46:10).

More on the Two Ways

The above discussion reveals a substantive difference between waiting for time to pass so you can get busy having the world and waiting for a baby to be born and therefore be in the world in a forever different way. There is a difference in waiting for the opportunity to have the world and waiting for the arrival of a gift and promise. This difference in waiting naturally holds to different senses of time. In the first way of waiting, time is vacuous and vacant. In the second, time is full and replete.[5] When Silicon Valley tries to

---

5. Modernity has chosen (and worked to instill) a hollow and empty sense of time. Not for any nefarious reasons necessarily, but because modernity is infatuated with speed. Modernity's

innovate beyond waiting, understanding waiting as a problem to be solved, it assumes that all waiting (because it's a delay in *having* something new or novel) is unnecessary. This is because of the view that time itself is empty of any sacred significance. Therefore, it's best to make the time of waiting as short as possible (and maybe avoid it altogether by giving us ways to *have* in the waiting).

Sue actually had an experience of both of these ways of waiting and their sense of time within forty-eight hours of each other. Her waiting in the Chartres Cathedral, while initially rocky, took her into the fullness of time. The time was fertile. This waiting connected her to life. Waiting as a way of being in time attached her to the world around her. She felt a relational bond to the people praying in front of her. She became connected to the space, drawn into its beauty, feeling truly *in* the space.[6] She felt linked to the history of pilgrims who had entered the space long before her. She felt drawn to her son and granddaughter across space back home in the US. Waiting in the Chartres Cathedral, time became full. *It was full of relationships.* Relationships with space, people, and mystery gave time a deep sense of sacredness. The waiting was active (or "hastened waiting," as the Younger calls it), because the waiting allowed her to recognize, and pulled her more deeply into, her relationship with the world. This waiting gave her *Weltbeziehung*, as the Germans would say: "world-relations." Inside these relations Sue was unequivocally swept into life. Life itself is a relational dynamic wherein waiting is participation and participation is waiting. Life is not rushing; we feel less alive when we're busy. Life is waiting, just being, inside relationships.

Yet, less than forty-eight hours later, Sue was pushed into the other kind of waiting. As she walked to her gate in the Charles de Gaulle Airport, she learned that her return flight home was delayed. The gate agent announced, first in French, to a groan—which alerted Sue that this was bad news—that her flight was delayed three hours thanks to a maintenance issue. Sue was again waiting. But on this occasion, time wasn't soaked with life but dull as dust.

While the Chartres Cathedral was a place of connection and relationships, the airport gate was the opposite. It was a nonplace *place*. It was a place formed to feel like no real place. It had no real character and lacked

---

power is its ability to speed up time. Time is much easier to speed up when it is hollow of divine consequence or moral priority. I've discussed this all at great length in *The Congregation in a Secular Age*, chap. 9.

6. Willie James Jennings says that his drive is to connect the Christian imagination to space (and land) again. Our relation to time plays a big part in getting to what Jennings rightly seeks. Jennings says, "Space here is both a relational practice and that which is created by a relation between Israel and Gentiles." *The Christian Imagination: Theology and the Origins of Race* (New Haven: Yale University Press, 2010), 272.

any signs of history. Waiting in nonplaces is painful because these spaces exist not for the sake of connection but to be specifically avoided. Yes, connections and relationships can be forged in such nonplaces, but it's much harder. And these connections are made with people who seem at first to be objects without history or interests or lives inside their own relationships. Such nonplaces encourage us to see people as furniture, art as distraction, and music as pacification. People are not there to wait for something that comes out of the dynamic of relationship. They are in a forced pause, and often deeply annoyed because of it. People in such spaces have an edge to their anticipation, not peace in their waiting, and therefore often no love for the world. They just want the waiting to be over. Waiting in such spaces can only be experienced as an inconvenient hindrance moving toward a frustrated rage. We often feel less connected to the world in the waiting rooms of doctor's offices, car dealerships, and airport gates. In these spaces we can only wait as an inconvenience, where we are waiting *for* getting loose from such spaces and returning to getting busy living. Waiting without relationship to the world is a vacuous waiting, where time is experienced as lost and waiting as a waste of fiercely guarded time.

We now have some further texture to our two ways of waiting. There is a kind of waiting that connects us to the world, a waiting that is for being in the world. And there is a type of waiting that does not connect us to the world. If Saint John the Baptist was going to help Woz find God by *waiting* for God to find Woz, then moving into this waiting that is a way of being— this waiting in which time is full of relationships to the world—would be essential. The best way to name this kind of waiting, and to help us better see what it looks like in a place such as Saint John the Baptist, is to turn to Fromm's protégé.

Building to Resonance

The birth of a new scholarly project is not always easy to spot, but there's something quite beautiful about it. It's like seeing a tributary form off a river from ten thousand feet, or seeing a beautiful strong branch coming off the trunk of a tree reaching for the sky. Or it's like seeing the exact moment that an organism gets its DNA to become its own species, if it were possible to observe such a thing. Scholars are like this. No scholar is made ex nihilo. We all take parts of our intellectual DNA from the inspiring thoughts of others. But it's rare to see so specifically where this birthing happens. It's uncommon to see the specific pages that produce a new project.

In this case, we can see that three pages from Erich Fromm's *To Have or to Be?* under the heading "Activity and Passivity," became the birthplace of a new scholarly project. These three pages were the seeds from which a great new tree grew. To switch the metaphor, it's from the smooth stones of these three pages that Hartmut Rosa has built a castle. Rosa has turned those three pages into a thousand pages (that's without exaggeration). But without those three pages from Fromm, Rosa's brilliant project would have never been. Of course, Rosa has expanded, deepened, and added to the implications and reach of Fromm's ideas. Rosa spent those thousand pages crafting a rich theory all his own.

From Fromm, his elder in the Frankfurt School, Rosa sees busyness, or what he calls "acceleration," as the problem of late modernity.[7] Rosa shows that acceleration stretches into all parts of modernity, both culturally and structurally. We feel the pace of our lives increasing, just as the economy functions and stabilizes itself by acceleration, seeking constant growth. Rosa's early contributions lucidly articulated this acceleration, showing in detail what Fromm hinted at: in modernity, activity has been made into busyness, and this accelerating activity breeds deep forms of alienation. Rosa, more than anyone, has powerfully shown that modernity means the speeding up of time. This speeding up, this getting busy, desynchronizes us. It brings inequality into the economy, frays democracies, warms the environment, and pushes human psyches into states of anxiety and depression.[8] Rosa's early work warned that getting busy has its consequences.

Rosa's early work wasn't quite the bombshell exploded on the playground of social theorists that Barth's *Römerbrief* was to theologians.[9] But it had an indelible impact on both academic thought and the larger public conversations about European society. Rosa was dubbed the "slowdown guru" in the German media, but he was uncomfortable with this label. To him, the alienation inherent in modernity couldn't simply be mitigated by getting a little (or even exponentially) less busy. The conundrums and contradictions of modernity were too immersive to assume so.

7. If Fromm is considered a late-first-generation Frankfurt School thinker, Rosa would be third generation, following the mammoth impact of the second-generation thinker Jürgen Habermas. Axel Honneth also needs to be mentioned. Honneth, as one of Habermas's most established students, stands between Habermas and Rosa.

8. To make this point, Rosa and many other continental thinkers have drawn on Alan Ehrenberg's brilliant text, *The Weariness of the Self: Diagnosing the History of Depression in the Contemporary Age* (Montreal: McGill-Queen's University Press, 2016).

9. The phrase "exploded on the playground of the theologians" comes from Karl Adams, introduction to *A Unique Time of God*, by Karl Barth (Louisville: Westminster John Knox, 2016), 5.

Like Barth, Rosa didn't seek to be unmodern, taking a sledgehammer to modernity's foundations. But he did challenge some of the core propensities of modernity. To give Rosa Charles Taylor's language, as we have done with Barth, he saw that conceding to the closed structures and spins of the immanent frame couldn't release us from the alienation that modernity produces.[10] The immanent frame needed to be opened.

Rosa resisted being called the "slowdown guru" because he didn't think a simple slowdown inside a closed immanent frame could help. The alienation imposed by late modernity's speed would prove too much. This alienation disconnects workers from the means of their production, and it stretches even deeper in a late-modern consumer society. When modernity makes action the expenditure of energy to have the world, we become alienated from the world. Modernity seems to love the world by wrapping it tightly in immanence, telling it to dream no more of transcendence. But modernity actually hates the world by making it into a disposable object. We are alienated from the world because the world is made into a thing.

Pastor Barth returned to transcendence even in modernity by confessing that there were indeed elements of reality that are nongiven. This (re)turn to transcendence was not an escape from the world (if it was, why march with the workers?). Rather, Barth believed this transcendence was the only way to embrace and love the world. Drawing a bold line between the givenness and nongivenness of reality allows the world to freely *be* the world (not a thing to have). For Barth, a world that can freely *be* the world can freely *be* addressed by the living Word of God. The closed structures of the immanent frame are dependent on making and keeping the world a thing able to be had. (In this dead world, it appears obvious that God is dead, but the truth is that the world, not God, is dead in modernity.)

Rosa recognized that he needed to get more constructive. The fact that modernity's problem was an accelerated speed didn't necessarily mean the answer was slowing down. A slowdown without a shift in aims would be

10. It is much easier to give Taylor's language to Rosa than to Barth, most obviously because of historical sequence but also because Rosa has been in dialogue with Taylor since the days of his dissertation. Rosa wrote his dissertation on Taylor's understanding of human action. Central to Taylor's understanding, which has never left Rosa, is that human beings' acts are always in relation to some expressed or inexpressible commitment to the good. Rosa makes the commitment to the good life central, differentiating him from the more Marxist-committed Frankfurt School scholars. This hallmark of Rosa also properly gives him a sense that the immanent frame—or modernity itself—is open. Rosa is shy in claiming any faith commitments. He is nothing like Karl Barth in this regard. But he does recognize the importance of faith in a God who acts. He made this clear in a personal conversation I had with him in 2019—though without offering much detail.

counterproductive. The waiting we needed would need to be aimed toward a horizon outside the obsession to have the world; otherwise it would make little difference. We really needed a different conception of action, a different way of experiencing the world itself. Rosa's next project picked up on Fromm's *being*-mode of acting, turning those few paragraphs into four hundred field-defining pages (see his book *Resonance*).[11]

Rosa's work showed that our understanding of action needed to shift from being an expenditure of energy to *have* the world to being a hastened waiting that allows for the action of *being* in relationship with the world.[12] All relationships that give life are for being together, which produces (rather than depletes) energy. The energy it produces we call *life*. Being in relationships, which are bound in the *being* form as opposed to the *having* form, is experienced as being alive. Rosa explains in this new project that a relationship that is for being together, which produces the energy of life, is best described as resonance.

Beyond Alienation

The antidote for alienation is not slowing down, pausing your acceleration and refueling to reenter the rush of having. Rather, the treatment for alienation is resonance. The church, by waiting for God, finds itself in a hastened waiting, as the Younger would say. It is a waiting filled with action. This waiting (the hastening that is bound in the waiting) is *not* a desert but is teeming with life, filled with—or full of—relationships of resonance. The church waits by actively being in relationship with the world, by being a community of resonance. The church thereby doesn't so much *do* something as *be* something.[13]

Saint John the Baptist is in the crisis of *being* unable to help Woz find a God who is God. They must wait for God to find them. But this waiting is not inactive, not a slumped cocoon of boredom or listlessness. Many congregations are in such a state, just waiting to die. Recognizing this, denominations and consultants prescribe a heavy dose of activity to *have* the resources necessary

11. In a long section on page 698 of *Church Dogmatics* IV/3.2 (Edinburgh: T&T Clark, 1962), Barth points to something like resonance.

12. For more on this, see Hartmut Rosa, *Resonance: A Sociology of Our Relationship to the World* (Cambridge: Polity, 2019), 116–17.

13. John Zizioulas says something similar: "The Church must cease to be looked upon primarily as an institution and be treated as a way of being. The Church is primarily communion, i.e., a set of relationships making up a mode of being, exactly as is the case in the Trinitarian God." *The One and the Many: Studies on God, Man, the Church, and the World Today* (Alhambra, CA: Sebastian, 2010), 15.

to survive, a prescription that is laced with the logic of having, thereby enclosing the world in immanence. Their prescription has the opposite effect from what they wish, more quickly killing the congregation by further depleting the congregation's energy. Or it shames the congregation for not expending the energy they simply don't have. If this approach is not implemented carefully, it makes the denomination or consultant a harsh debt monger, seeking to collect energy where there simply is none.

———

When Sue told Woz they would help him find God by waiting with him, Woz responded with a big grin and an okay. And the waiting began. Everyone in the Bible study committed to invite everyone in the congregation to expect God to find them, and to ready themselves for God to come arriving. Every Wednesday night Bert reminded them that this was what they were waiting for. They were waiting for God to find Woz. And then . . .

12

Waiting Is Living

The Church and Resonance

Then they lived. They read the Bible and prayed. And in equal measure they laughed and ate donuts. Woz started taking Herbert to his doctor appointments like he'd taken his grandma. They became friends. Bert and Helene cleaned out the basement storeroom, to great satisfaction. Sue decided to research Saint John the Baptist's stained-glass windows. After telling the community about her experience in the Chartres Cathedral, she really *saw* those windows for the first time. She felt a connection to them that she never had before. She put together a presentation on the men who were lost in the war and the women who paid for those windows. It reconnected Saint John the Baptist with its past and the neighborhood around it. It reconnected some with their own heritage. Children of old members now long deceased were invited to hear again or for the first time the stories of their past. The congregation, and specifically the Bible study, met, prayed, and broke bread (or at least "not-quite-day-old" donuts). They did this all as their way of waiting for a God who is God.

Both Sue and Bert took on the high responsibility to keep reminding the congregation that they were waiting for a God who is God. They talked about God and directly spoke to God in prayer as they waited for God to arrive. Inside the immanent frame it's easy for attention to decay in waiting. The need for leadership is high. Yet leadership should not cajole the community to expend energy (the assumed model for leadership) but should beckon them to stay attentive in waiting, just as Jesus asks Peter and others in the garden of Gethsemane (Matt. 26:36). The congregation needs to be reminded that they are waiting as a way of seeking. That waiting is a form of action; this seeking cannot be assumed as the expenditure of energy, because this kind of seeking cannot *have* what it seeks. Rather, the only kind of seeking that can encounter a God who is indeed God, who transcends the givenness of reality, is to wait. This is what the Younger taught Pastor Barth. And it's deeply practical.

Because Woz sought the *being* of God, he had to wait for this God to *act*. Waiting was the substance of seeking. Waiting is seeking. My concern is that, facing decline, most church leadership sees waiting as the enemy of survival, because they have assumed, along with modernity, that the only human action that counts is the expenditure of energy. The goal is to do something, to expend some energy, to survive. But the only human action that can save us is to wait.[1] Only waiting as a form of seeking readies us for an encounter with a God who is God. Waiting is the heart of faithful seeking.

This assertion that waiting is seeking, and therefore waiting is the only way to be the church, seems counterintuitive, because modernity has convinced us that human action (any kind of seeking, particularly inside the driving wants of the market) is the opposite of waiting. Human action entails getting busy. Any human action worth its salt, modernity asserts, includes the expenditure of energy. But such a stance moves us into *having-mode*. This having-mode turns both God and the world into objects to possess (when God and the world can be possessed, the church decides it must—it has no other choice than to—be the star of its own story). Yet God cannot be possessed, and therefore in this having-mode we seek *not* a God who is God but only a pathetic religious object. When pastoral practice and congregational life are linked to a form of action that expends energy, the best the church can offer the world is religion.

In turn, though we might be able to possess parts of the world, the more we adhere to this logic of possessing the world, the less we feel like we're in it. The having-mode alienates us from life by telling us to possess the world, burning us out on expending energy to have the world. The more we seek the world by speeding up to have the world, the more we're alienated from

---

1. We could even say that waiting is the concrete shape of our response to justification. The justifying act of God calls us into following the living Christ by waiting with him in the garden, and waiting with the world for his return. There is a strong connection between waiting and sanctification. To put this in Lutheran parlance, there may be a third use of the law, but the core content is to wait, to be formed into one who waits with the world, being one who exchanges the action of expended energy for the resonance of waiting.

living by being estranged from being with the world, being fully in the world as we wait. The form of human action that seeks to have the world loses the world. In *having-mode* we forget that we are creatures in relationship with the world, which we need in order to be. We forget that only in the world—while living and finding life in the world—do we encounter the God who is God, who so loves the world as Creator of the world. We seek the living God by waiting for this God to act, not to act in the church but to act in the world that God loves. Waiting, as a way to just *be* in the world, proves to be a gift.

The church that seeks God by waiting attends to its relationship with the world. It does so by hastening, by acting, by actively embracing the world, by seeking to be in right relationship (in the *being-mode* as opposed to the *having-mode*) with the world. Woz, Herbert, Bert, Helene, and Sue don't wait by doing nothing, as if put in carbonite like Han Solo, but by living. They wait by praying and reading Scripture. They wait by entering the world, to be with and for it. They enter the world by being in friendship and service, by contemplating art and remembering history. They wait by seeking life in and for the world.

Life cannot come or return by focusing on expending more energy. It comes through relational acts of being with the world.[2] This being with the world is best described, Rosa believes, as resonance. Resonance is waiting action. It is the sense of being in relationship with—connected to—something outside yourself. Resonance is always for the sake of *being* put in, or participating further in, relationship. Waiting is opening the space for encounter. Resonance describes what it's like to be encountered—to be found inside the gift of a relationship with the world while waiting. The church waits in a state of resonance, not a state of inertia.

Don't Get It Twisted

To name "resonance" as the quality of the church's waiting, however, risks misunderstanding. "Resonance," particularly in English, insinuates a kind of effervescent state of high emotion. Some may misunderstand resonance as bound in an overly emotive experientialism. By that rubric, a Hillsong service or night four of a middle-school-camp-crying-worship-gathering would be

2. At a purely reductive biological level, life can indeed come from the expenditure of energy. The sex act can be simply and only assumed to be one (or both) human animals expending energy, releasing the sexual energy. But this seems to turn sex into an operation that loses spirit. For human beings, sex seems better (both more pleasurable and more fulfilling) when it's done not in the having-mode of the release of sexual energy but in the being-mode of commitment, connection, and union with another.

the height of church life. But this would misunderstand resonance and Rosa's intent in developing it. Resonance is not without emotion. Nor would I want to disparage a Hillsong sing-along or a good camp cryfest. There can be a quality of resonance in these. Yet resonance cannot be reduced to only an emotive experience.[3]

Rosa, as a sociologist, is concerned not so much with emotion as with action.[4] We must continue to remind ourselves that, for Rosa, resonance is not an emotion but a form of action. Particularly as a critical theorist, Rosa understands resonance to be a form of action that confronts and critiques modernity's dominant view of action. If, as Erich Fromm taught us, late modernity asserts that action is the expenditure of energy, then resonance is an alternative form of this action that allows waiting to be dynamic. Resonance, more than simply emotive expressivism, is dually a critique and a constructive proposal for understanding human action.

As we delve further into this alternative form of action, it's my contention that the church will be unable, even with its best desires and efforts, to escape the reductions (and hidden false norms) of late modernity and its immanent frame until it reconceives its own action,[5] and does so theologically. Resonance seems to be a step forward. The church will keep trying to spend its way out

3. Rosa never references Barth, but he does discuss Schleiermacher. Though Rosa is not that interested in theology (though German theologians are interested in his work), nevertheless Schleiermacher is his theologian of choice. At a certain level this makes sense. However, what I'm exploring is whether Barth's flipping of Schleiermacher on his head isn't also congruent with Rosa. Rosa is careful to claim that resonance is not primarily an emotional state. It includes an emotional state but can't be reduced to that. Rather, as I'll unpack, resonance is a word-event. To me, this resembles how Barth flips Schleiermacher's desire to embrace the world. But unlike Schleiermacher, Barth disentangles this from an emotive sense of dependence and shifts it into a more concrete relational experience of word and response that is still embodied and deeply in the world. Much work is needed to unpack how Rosa is using Schleiermacher and how Barth is flipping Schleiermacher. But the purpose of this note is to acknowledge that point and to invite interested readers to develop it further.

4. Of course, it's never as clear-cut as the disciplinary line makes it. Rosa never wavers from his sociological and philosophical commitments. But these do give him a concern for emotion, particularly as emotion is related to the good life. Rosa fits with other sociologists like Eva Illouz who, even more than Rosa, has sought to think about emotions within the concerns of sociology. See her *Consuming the Romantic Utopia: Love and the Cultural Contradictions of Capitalism* (Berkeley: University of California Press, 1997).

5. I'm not alone in thinking this. Radical Orthodoxy and particularly John Milbank has made a similar assertion. In his classic *Theology and Social Theory: Beyond Secular Reason* (Malden, MA: Blackwell, 2006), Milbank shows how modernity's views of action have imposed a reductive, even nihilistic, ontology onto us. He asserts that the church would be better off returning to an Augustinian ontology and form of action. I have some sympathies for this argument. However, in concrete practical form it becomes reduced to a return to liturgy and church practice that stands in opposition to modernity. I'm exploring something different.

of its decline until it recognizes that this propensity to spend its energy and therefore speed up rests on a self-defeating form of action that has little room for divine action. When action is equated as expenditure of energy, the immanent frame is closed and reality is given *in toto*. As long as you have the energy, you can have it all! Yet, as we'll see, resonance as a form of action upholds, and necessitates, otherness. Resonance, as a form of action bound in (noninstrumental) relationships, must confess that there are elements of reality that are nongiven and *cannot* be possessed. Resonance is a form of action that centers on connection, solely for the sake of connection. Rosa explores this kind of human action where relations are an end (a way of being), not a means to having the world. Because there truly is otherness, which can only be known through the other's own free action, the immanent frame remains open.

When we're stuck in the false form of action (having-mode), we imagine that the only way to stabilize the congregation is to find ways to expend energy to *have* resources. But this method accepts a malformed shape of action and one that stands in direct opposition to a theological vision that sees God as God. In other words, the church cannot be free from the reductions of the immanent frame until it lets go of modernity's reductive conception of action. With resonance, Rosa gives us an alternative to this modern form of action.

Resonance as Affection

Instead of seeing resonance as emotive experientialism, it's better to understand it as a mode of relations, even as a word-event (which I'll delve further into below).[6] Of course, resonance is felt. You feel connected and therefore alive. There is emotion to resonance, but there is also affection. It's not just feeling something that matters. Because this is a form of action, we must be drawn to something. This being drawn to something is engendered by affection. Resonance is a form of action that is moved by affection. Like a parent with a child, we wait with our child, finding our affection grows for the child. Our affection never fails to call us into all kinds of action for the child and the world she lives in. Resonance is a form of action that waits by seeking affection for the world. God's own action, even in the ultimate act of sending the Son, is prompted by affection. God so loves the world that God acts in

6. Rosa doesn't necessarily develop this or even acknowledge it himself, but for me this assertion that resonance is a word-event seems to link him somewhere in his intellectual DNA with a Reformation dialectic. It's as if Luther has entered ever so slightly into his thought. To me this also connects his project to the early Barth, who was also affected by this return to Luther and the Reformation commitment to the Word as a dynamic reality that shapes both conceptions of divine action and theological anthropology.

the world by sending the Son (John 3:16) to be in the world to wait. The Son waits ("the Son can do . . . only what he sees the Father doing," John 5:19), attentive, seeking affection for the Father and the world the Father loves. From this waiting attentiveness, affection produces action.

Rosa gives us a form of action—even from a sociological and philosophical perspective—that is built on a love for the world. Affection has emotion, but more than that, affection is being drawn out into participation in life itself. Woz feels alive as he acts to help Herbert. Herbert feels alive as he receives a ride and conversation with a new friend. Bert and Helene feel alive as they work together to clear the storeroom. They feel a deep sense of satisfaction as they finish and assess the transformation their action has made to a space, recognizing a new connection to the space and one another.

All forms of human action have some kind of feeling attached to them.[7] Human action never lacks emotion, but it is affection that draws out action, while never destroying the necessity to wait and be with and for. In resonance the emotive experience is a sense of connection engendered at some level by affection. This affection moves you outside yourself to recognize your relation to the world. The source of this sense of connection is not your own self-enclosed affect. It is the *encounter* itself. It's the sense that your action moves you, out of affection, to share in the being of the world. Your action moves you into *being* in friendship or into *being* of use, turning chaos into order in a storeroom. Resonance is a relationship with something outside you that you now find yourself related to and therefore feel connected to. Resonance is felt as an atmosphere of affection that frames a mode of relations. It's what you experience in a deep conversation. This transforms waiting into anything but a boring, escapist waste of time.

Resonance and Suffering

Even if we're clear that resonance is not an emotive expressivism but a mode of relations engendered by affection, it still seems open to another critique, which must be addressed lest resonance be of little help to our practical ecclesiology and ministry.

The second critique is that resonance, even as a mode of relations, seems utopian and naively optimistic. For instance, it's one thing to call it resonance

7. To not feel can signal big problems. For instance, psychopaths have no feelings around the actions of killing someone. They don't feel it to be wrong; they don't feel anything. It's true that not all actions lead to feeling; some rote behaviors have little emotion. But I still have a little. It feels good or tedious to take my dog on a walk.

when Woz helps Herbert. But can we call it resonance when he grieves the loss of his grandmother? As a form of action that is a mode of relations-with-the-world, resonance at first blush seems unable to see the world as it is, particularly in its ability to recognize suffering, loss, and pain. Resonance seems to be a form of action (a form of relations) that has little room or toler-ance for suffering. After all, it attends to connections and union. Therefore, it is logical—though wrong, as we'll see—to assume that resonance cannot tolerate suffering. Resonance may not be emotive expressivism, but feelings of sadness and loneliness would seem to short-circuit resonance. By this way of thinking, in a practical way, the congregation acting in the mode of resonance would need to guard against anyone who brings negative emotions, eliminat-ing those people from the community (which unfortunately does happen, but not because of resonance).

But such an understanding of resonance proves incorrect. It falls into the same trap as the first critique that wrongly collapses resonance into an en-closed emotional state. Concrete suffering and the "negative" emotions that surround it don't destroy resonance; actually, they can create it. Saint John the Baptist changes because Bert finds Woz in the sanctuary after his grandma's funeral. Bert's encounter with Woz is resonance. It connects them to one an-other; it's a form of action that has its aim in *being* with. When Bert shares in Woz's grief, loss, and fear (all so-called negative emotions), a true relationship forms. Like Jesus with the rich young ruler, Bert leaves his encounter with Woz loving him (Mark 10). From that moment of resonance—from within that short relational connection born from Bert's action—Woz comes to the Bible study, assuming the Bible study can help him on his quest. Woz assumes this because he has experienced the connection of resonance inside his suffering.

Resonance is a form of action that can directly accompany suffering and bear "negative" emotion.[8] When action is assumed to be merely the expendi-ture of energy rather than to be for resonance, the space—or even tolerance—for suffering and "negative" emotion is obliterated. When the church sees action in the having-mode of expenditure of energy, then all "negative" emo-tion is a direct drain on the precious reserves of energy. The goal of this kind of action is not necessarily relations but the possession of resources (even relationships are turned into resources). Energy spent on negative emotion, which witnesses to concrete events of suffering, is energy regrettably diverted and wasted from being spent on having the world, not being in relation with the world. Only action in the being-mode, as opposed to the having-mode,

---

8. Rosa adds to this in Hartmut Rosa and Christoph Henning, eds., *The Good Life beyond Growth* (London: Routledge, 2018), 49–50.

can make a place for suffering. And without a place for suffering, there is no way to find the God who is God (as we'll see below).

When we're clear that resonance is *not* an enclosed emotional state but a mode of relations, then, as Rosa says, "'negative' emotions such as sadness or loneliness can lead to positive resonant experience."[9] This is exactly what happens to Woz in the sanctuary following the funeral. But here too we should be careful. Rosa doesn't mean that these "negative" emotions are positive. He isn't glorifying suffering. He means that experiences of suffering, and the "negative" emotions associated with them, can produce a mode of relation (it can produce a being-with that is full of life). They are "positive" not in the sense of being good in themselves but in the sense of mathematics (e.g., a positive number). They are positive in the sense of being able to yield relations. It isn't a positive thing that Jean has died and Woz is in grief. But from a moment of encounter in shared grief, a relationship is born between Woz and Bert. In resonance, relationship can be generated in and through suffering. "Negative" emotions such as sadness and loneliness *can* be the locale of resonance.

Rosa uses the example of a statement such as "The film was so good, I was bawling." Such statements "are not semantically nonsensical but rather express a common fact of experience."[10] They express a fact that shared suffering can produce a deep sense of relational connection, giving us a fuller love for the world. There is a fullness in the sadness that comes upon us as we listen to a beautiful piece of music and grieve love lost. The sadness of hearing those notes somehow takes us deeper, relating us more fully with life. To be sad in an encounter with a piece of art doesn't take life from us but opens us up to the dimensions of living. Our sadness connects us more deeply to life. "There's beauty in breakdown," as the band Frou Frou sings. This kind of action is resonance.

Yet when action is understood as an expenditure of energy to have the world, suffering and negative emotions possess *no* possibility of yielding relationship. Suffering and negative emotions become insatiable and lifeless, and there is no possibility of beauty even in the ugliness of the breakdown. Suffering in the having-mode has no positive quality at all (it is only a negative number). Resonance as a being-mode of action can relate to the world, binding itself to the world in and through the world's suffering because it's a waiting moved by affection. Resonance, therefore, can forge connection out of suffering. Theologically we've often called this reality of relations born

9. Hartmut Rosa, *Resonance: A Sociology of Our Relationship to the World* (Cambridge: Polity, 2019).
10. Rosa, *Resonance*, 168.

through suffering "ministry" or "to minister to," believing it the heart of God's own action in the world.[11]

This sense that suffering can host a deeper connection to one another and to the world itself is something Martin Luther saw long ago. Attending to suffering, waiting for God in suffering, doesn't produce disgust for the world, nor hatred for life, but love for the world and its beauty that comes even in its ugliness.[12] Sharing in suffering produces a resonant relation to the world that can deliver a shocking paradox of joy in being alive in the world.[13] The eyes of faith see beauty and joy in the suffering of the cross. From the cross comes an all-new relation to the world. From the suffering of the cross comes the freedom to be in the world and to love the world for itself.[14] Being freely justified, Luther asserts, means we are free from the having-mode (having to do works to save ourselves) to enter the joy of the being-mode (being in Christ). There is nothing to do but be in and with the world, waiting for God who is God to come to the world. There is nothing to do, no *having* action needed to save ourselves. We are now free to *be* in the world and love the world, acting for the world as our way of waiting for a God who is God to come to the world. Resonance is a form of action that moves us into the being-mode, and therefore, paradoxically, resonance is a form of hastened action born from affection that is at the same time waiting.

Resonance as Conversation

Against this backdrop, we can say that resonance is best understood as a form of action that comes in the shape of a word-event.[15] Resonance is a conversation with the world. It seeks not to possess (have) the world but to act in the world in a way that both addresses and is addressed by the world. In

11. For more on this sense of ministry, see my *Faith Formation in a Secular Age* (Grand Rapids: Baker Academic, 2017), part 2; and *The Pastor in a Secular Age* (Grand Rapids: Baker Academic, 2019), part 3. See also my *Christopraxis* (Minneapolis: Fortress, 2014).

12. For more on this, see Mark C. Mattes, *Martin Luther's Theology of Beauty* (Grand Rapids: Baker Academic, 2017).

13. Though Rosa doesn't mention it, there appears to be *theologia crucis* at the heart of resonance as a form action.

14. See Luther's famous *Freedom of the Christian*, in Martin Luther, *Three Treatises* (Philadelphia: Fortress, 1943).

15. Though this needs more development, I believe this shows Rosa's inherent connection to the thought worlds of Protestantism. There is so much similarity between Taylor and Rosa, but when one does some mining it's clear that Taylor has many inherent frames that are fundamentally Catholic. Rosa has these same frames, but they appear to be Protestant. Of course, this distinction would make sense: Taylor is a Quebecois Montrealer. Rosa is a German teaching at Jena and living in the Black Forest.

resonance, we feel spoken to by something outside us. Like a good conversation, action as resonance doesn't deplete our energy; it produces more energy. It actually makes us unconcerned for energy by drawing us far beyond worry for resources. We may feel tired after a long conversation, but we also feel full, rarely depleted, because we've experienced a tangible connection. The relational connection produces its own energy, giving amps to each subject in the discourse. In such conversations our own actions connect us to something bigger than us that nevertheless fully includes us. This sense of inclusion and yet encounter with otherness is what Rosa wants to describe as resonance.[16]

Rosa explains that the Latin etymology of "*resonance* is first and foremost an acoustic phenomenon—'re-sonare' meaning *to resound*."[17] Resonance is a form of action that is a reverberating word-event. This acoustic analogy is helpful for a few reasons. First, it shows that resonance is not a word-event in the sense of necessitating actual words or even cognitive abilities.[18] We've all felt spoken to by a piece of music, an ocean breeze, an infant's smile, or a kind dog. Second, the acoustic analogy helps us recognize that resonance as a form of action in the shape of a word-event (a conversation) produces a connection without enmeshment, domination, or cut-off. Conversations that lack mutuality are exhausting and therefore lack resonance. When we sense the conversation is not free of instrumental objectives (making the conversation a means to an end), when the conversation is for winning our vote or convincing us to buy a product, we feel our energy stolen. In such moments we may not enter the discourse for instrumental purpose, but we may leave

16. There is a connection here between Rosa's conception of action and Eberhard Jüngel's theological anthropology. Jüngel builds his theological anthropology on word-event, asserting that human beings are first hearers, which squares with the waiting of Barth and the Younger. Jüngel understands better than most the importance of the Younger to Barth. See Jüngel, *Karl Barth: A Theological Legacy* (Philadelphia: Westminster, 1986). John Webster's thought also has some connection here (see his *Barth's Moral Theology: Human Action in Barth's Thought* [Grand Rapids: Eerdmans, 1998]). Webster, through his concern for ethics, attends to Barth's understanding of human action. Webster gets at Barth's view of human action by placing it in conversation with Luther. He then turns to Charles Taylor. What Webster doesn't do, which I'm trying to do with limited space above, is use Rosa as a way to connect Barth and Taylor. Rosa has a deeply implicit Lutheran anthropology in him and a direct connection to Taylor. These intersections need much more space than I have.

17. Rosa, *Resonance*, 165.

18. Of course, right at this point Barth's concerns about *analogia entis* rush to the surface. I'll ask the interested reader to hold these concerns and wait until the next chapter, where I'll pick up some of these issues using a conversation on Barth and Mozart. This coming chapter will start to move the whole project in a christological direction, which I hope will assuage some of these concerns. I remind the reader that I'm not seeking to offer a piece on Barth but a piece that, while consistently drawing from Barth, seeks to answer larger questions of a practical ecclesiology inside the immanent frame of late modernity. Therefore, I don't feel overly concerned about being completely consistent with Barth in every way.

it unable to evaluate the conversation in any other way. We say to ourselves, "That was a waste of time," meaning that was a waste of the resources of my energy. That was energy that won me zero having. We feel this because our otherness, as a mutual dialogue partner, has been overlooked. Yet when we experience something that speaks to us—with or without words—we do so by encountering this interlocutor as other, recognizing our own otherness, made aware of the other's and our own being.

To show this, and to draw further from the Latin etymology, Rosa uses a tuning fork as an example. When a tuning fork is vibrating and it meets another fork, this other fork will also begin to vibrate. The vibrating action of the one fork leads the other fork to come to life and vibrate as well. But this other fork vibrates, at least at the start, at its own frequency. It is allowed to have its own voice, if you will. It is brought to life, but never by losing its own unique pitch. Eventually, if the two forks stay in communion, the freedom of the mutual responsive resonance will result in a synchronous resonance.

Eventually the two tuning forks will join frequencies and become stronger, but not by expending energy in *having* a louder frequency. The stronger frequency is produced by harmony, not competition. The power of the action of resonance is bound in the mystery of plurality and unity. Resonance's power is in harmony. Its power is in its weakness, as Paul would say (2 Cor. 12:9). Harmony, not victory, is resonance's transformational power. Action as the expenditure of energy creates its power in an opposite way. Its power as a form of action rests not in harmony but in the singular victory in competition. The great tragedy of late modernity is that the church (at least in its practical shape) has assumed that the only form of action available to it is the expenditure of energy in the having-mode. The church has seen itself invariably in competition with the world. Or the church has considered it necessary to adopt modernity's strategies of competition in the having-mode to survive, racing for capitalist business approaches over the waiting of theological contemplation.

Yet resonance is a much different form of action than the competition inherent within the having-mode of action as expenditure of energy. In resonance the agent doesn't have to produce their own energy from within themselves. The energy that feeds the action of resonance is delivered by the harmony of the union. In competition the energy is produced within the actor or by the resources owned and possessed by the actor. It's the actor's genius or bank account or fame or reputation that produces the energy. No wonder the church feels both depleted of energy and frantic to get more.

In resonance, energy is found within relationality. Energy is found through the event of an encounter with otherness, not through the possession of

resources. The conversation—the word-event—creates the energy in resonance. And it's always as gift. The actor finds this energy not through skill
or victory bound inside themselves but through a waiting to be addressed.

Pastor Barth has argued that faithful human action is a response to God's
wholly other Word. For Barth, human action is not obliterated (though I suppose it would be if human action were reduced to the expenditure of energy
in the having-mode). Rather, human action is drawn into God's own Word
as a resonant response.[19] Human action as response has a deep efficacy and
is not obliterated by the divine word. Human efficacy can only be assumed
to be splattered like a bug on the windshield of Barth's theological imagination if human action has been equated with the expenditure of energy to
have the world.

Drop the Echo Effect

Pastor Barth's succinct evaluation of liberal theology was that it thought it
was speaking of God but was only speaking of humanity in a loud voice. In
other words, the problem with the late-nineteenth and early-twentieth-century
theological establishment was that it assumed its echo to be the content of
theology. Pastor Barth's early thought (all the attention to a God who is God
and the givenness/nongivenness of reality) attempts to free the church from
the echo chamber of a theology that deafeningly succumbs to the immanent
frame.

Rosa too has no patience for echoes.[20] The cold beams of the immanent
frame seem particularly shaped as a cavernous space that creates echoes. Once
the furniture of meaning, virtue, and ritual have been removed by modernity,
a particularly echoey space is created that we must now inhabit. In this echoey
modern space there is the danger of assuming all relationships with (and in)
the world are nothing more than the echo of our own wants. Modernity has
an acute intrinsic risk of making all otherness into the same,[21] into objects
to possess and have. Modernity's dominant form of action as expenditure of
energy causes this. Inside the echoey immanent frame there is always the peril-
ous danger that true discourse with otherness will be lost in the cacophony
of the echoes of sameness.

---

19. For a much longer discussion on human action in Barth, see Paul Nimmo, *Being in Action: The Theological Shape of Barth's Ethical Vision* (Edinburgh: T&T Clark, 2007). For my
own articulation of Barth's sense of action, see *Christopraxis*, chap. 6.

20. See Rosa, *Resonance*, 167.

21. This shares some of the language of Emmanuel Levinas, *Totality and Infinity* (Pittsburgh:
Duquesne University Press, 1961).

Rosa is clear that resonance is not an echo. It is not something locked within the self that pacifies or authenticates the self. It's a form of action that leads to otherness, not sameness.[22] Resonance is always a direct experience with something truly other. Continuing with his development of resonance as word-event, Rosa says, "An echo lacks *its own voice*; it occurs in a way mechanically and without any variance. What resounds in an echo is never a response, but only ever oneself."[23] Resonance is a form of action that is fundamentally a (noninstrumental) relationship. Resonance is dependent on a true encounter with something other. All true relationship (whether human-to-human, creature-to-creation, or divine-to-human) must take the form of differentiation that allows for word and response. This differentiation keeps one from swallowing the other and therefore allows for discourse. Both sides in a relationship of resonance must speak with their own voice, never parroting or echoing the other.

Resonance is a view of human action that can attend to seeking for a God who is God. Resonance, like Barth's theology, is bound in the commitment that reality cannot be foreclosed in givenness. Rosa boldly states, "Resonance implies an aspect of constitutive inaccessibility."[24] Resonance contends that there are parts of existence that are inaccessible. Resonance is a form of action that depends on elements of reality being nongiven. Resonance, in a profound way, encounters this nongivenness. For Rosa, as much as for Barth, there are indeed elements of reality that are nongiven. Rosa says further, "Resonant relationships require that both subject and world be sufficiently 'closed' or self-consistent so as to speak in their own voice."[25]

Resonance, as a form of action, remains distinct from the mere expenditure of energy. Action as the expenditure of energy seeks to have the world and therefore needs to have little or no concern for closedness. Every boundary must be crossed to have more resources. "Good" action as the expenditure of energy always hurries over boundaries in order to possess. In contrast to resonance, the expenditure of energy welcomes echoes as the reverberating expanse of one's own voice.

Yet to shift our view of action toward resonance allows us to release action from being conceived as getting busy. We can wait—we are even forced

22. Rosa further discusses otherness in *Resonance*, 447–50.
23. Rosa, *Resonance*, 167 (emphasis original).
24. Rosa, *Resonance*, 174. Bonhoeffer in *Sanctorum Communion* (Minneapolis: Fortress, 1963), 66–68, says something similar about relationships. He articulates beautifully that relationships are always determined in and through the dialectic of openness and closedness. There is no relationship without closedness.
25. Rosa, *Resonance*, 174.

to wait—inside the action of resonance. Waiting inside resonance isn't just a pause, break, or refueling to get back to getting busy having the world. Rather, inside resonance, waiting is action that upholds the boundaries of otherness. Waiting is an attentive participation in respecting the boundary of the other. Waiting is expectant listening to be addressed. Waiting is an active way of honoring and confessing that there are parts of reality, parts of every level of discourse (inside all word-events) that are closed. Waiting is the concrete form of action as resonance, and, as paradoxical as that sounds, this is so because waiting is the only way to respect and still encounter otherness.

The emphasis of Pastor Barth's theology, up until at least the publication of *Römerbrief II*, is to remind the church of this closedness. The church is called to wait, not in inertia but as action, as the active way of seeking a God who is God. There can be no encounters with a living God who is God, escaping our own echo, until we confess that God is wholly other. The church waits as a confession of this closedness, making its waiting a seeking for a resonant encounter with a God who is indeed God. Waiting is the way to inhabit the immanent frame without succumbing to its echo. Waiting is the paradoxical way of action in the immanent frame that fills the immanent frame with the new possibility of encountering God's otherness.

Closedness Meets Openness

Here we uncover a dialectic in Rosa's articulation of resonance. This dialectic has a touchpoint with Barth's own dialectical thought. Resonant relationships require closedness so that otherness is upheld. But this boundary of closedness does not cause aloofness or withdrawal but instead encounter and connection. Over the boundary of closedness comes the free encounter of openness. Inside the confession of inaccessibility there is true encounter. The closedness makes the openness of encounter possible. Rosa is giving us a kind of vision of transcendence at the human-to-human or person-to-world level of action inside the immanent frame. Like Rosa, Barth's bold assertion of God's closedness makes a way for God's action inside the immanent frame.

Resonance contends that the other, while needing to always remain the other, can be shared. Resonance is the action of the relationship that encounters openness out of closedness. Resonance is a form of human action that seeks for relationship across the givenness and nongivenness of reality. The openness that comes out of the always-respected boundary of closedness can only be received as a gift. I never *have* a relationship; I can only *be* in a relationship. Within resonance, a relationship can never be a tool or operation but only an event of encounter.[26]

Just as waiting is how we respect the closedness, waiting also becomes the way we receive openness. The encounter with the other is a form of relational action that waits for the sake of being with the other, receiving the other's word as gift and responding in gratitude. Waiting is the shape of resonance because resonance cannot be controlled. As event, resonance is elusive; it is a gift coming from encounter with another who is closed to us. Openness is only openness (a revelation, if you will) because it comes out of closedness. We wait as a way of respecting the boundary of closedness but also as the concrete way of receiving the event of openness. The boundary between the givenness and nongivenness of reality must be drawn boldly not just to keep God other, and therefore closed, but so the church can truly be open to receiving an encounter with this living God (who is so much more than religion). Pastor Barth emphasizes God's elusiveness as a way of preparing, even in modernity, for a real encounter with God's openness.

The only appropriate way to receive a gift is to wait. You can never rush to have a gift, but you are asked to wait, to be, and to receive the gift. Even in a conversation it's the waiting that produces, or better receives, the openness. It's the waiting, the pauses and pregnant stillness in a conversation, that leads to the event of encounter. The person who cannot shut up in a conversation can never receive the gift of the openness of the other. The openness of a conversation is dependent on waiting to receive that which comes from respecting the closedness. Waiting dually upholds closedness while receiving openness. Waiting is the primary shape of resonance, because it confesses the elusiveness of such resonant relations (closedness), while at the same time witnessing to a gift of encounter that brings transformation (openness).

In the same paradoxical nature of closedness and openness, resonance is elusive and yet transformational. The openness of resonance puts me in the world in a different way, transformed, because resonance is a mode of being in relationship. My transformation, however, is not produced from within my own power but comes as the profound by-product of the relationship. Transformation is an event of *being* changed. This *being* changed cannot happen through the expenditure of energy but only by receiving an encounter of openness from the other side of closedness. Action is stripped of its transformational quality when it's understood as only the getting busy of the expenditure of energy. Inside the having-mode of action, transformation is lost, because a depth of open encounter is not possible. Transformation,

26. These themes connect my whole theological project, from first publication to this one.

by definition, must be an encounter with something outside me that changes me, relating me to the world (leading me to *be* in the world) in a different way. Inside the action of waiting, as the upholding of both closedness and openness, transformation is near. Or we could say that, because resonance is action that is both elusive and transformational, dependent on both closedness and openness, its most concrete form is to wait.

Waiting as Strong Evaluation

If we understand waiting as a concrete form of action called resonance, then there is one more element to this that we must discuss. This element proves important for the church. Rosa explains that resonance is "only possible where we act in accordance with our strong evaluations, where our cognitive and evaluative maps converge with our being or behavior."[27]

Rosa borrows the concept of strong evaluation from Charles Taylor. Taylor contends that any conversation (whether with or without words) that is more than noise or nicety operates out of an implicit or explicit strong evaluation. We always live out of some map (shaped by narratives) that we use to evaluate our actions and others' actions done to us. We use these narrative maps to discern whether our action, or that done to us, is good. Because we are conversational creatures (language animals), Taylor believes we're fundamentally evaluative beings. We are beings who are in the world always making strong evaluations. We are not just a bundle of instincts and behaviors; we are mindful bodies who act by evaluating what is good and what is not.

Rosa's point is that we experience the dynamism of resonance when an action correlates with our strong evaluation. A rock, a beetle, or a tiger can't experience resonance. A tiger can experience satisfaction, even enjoyment. But a tiger can't experience resonance, because it can't map its action onto a strong evaluation. Only humans can do so.

An action is resonant when it has a joyful or painful association with a strong evaluation. When your son hugs you after a long day of tension and says, "I love you," it's a profound encounter of resonance because the action meets up with your strong evaluation, unveiling in actuality (the act) what you know in your being (your strong evaluation that what's important is your relationship). This correlation between action and strong evaluation can also happen out of the "negative" emotions as well. James Loder tells the story of being bedridden after the death of his father, overcome with depression. His strong evaluation was dark. By chance he picked up Emil Brunner's *Man in*

27. Rosa, *Resonance*, 170.

Revolt. He says he didn't so much read it as recognize something in it. He said to himself, "So that's what's wrong," feeling swept up into transformation.[28] This too is an example where action accords with a strong evaluation ("something is wrong"). It is an experience of resonance because what's encountered meets, deepens, and redirects a strong evaluation.

If waiting is to be a resonant form of action and something more, or fuller, than a dull do-nothing-ism, then waiting must always be connected to a strong evaluation. Or we could say it this way: the church can wait faithfully only when it does so out of a strong evaluation. The church's waiting must be for a reason. It must have a moral or evaluative horizon. We wait for something good, for the very act of God to arrive and find us. To wait for nothing is not faithful waiting. For waiting to be an action (of resonance) there must be a strong sense, or a narrative-shaped map, of why we wait and what we wait for.

Catechesis becomes necessary in waiting resonance. Saint John the Baptist prayed and read the Bible as its acts of waiting. Its congregants took on these practices as a way of continuing to shape their strong evaluation. This transformed the waiting into faithful action, not the antithesis of action. Without this strong evaluation of what waiting is (good) for, waiting becomes just a despondent form of disobedience. The need to articulate what makes waiting good is the impetus not only for catechesis but also proclamation. Preaching is waiting, which is attention to the community's strong evaluation. Preaching as an action that attends to strong evaluation can bear the beautiful weight of resonance.[29] In study, prayer, and preaching, we are able to wait as the communal experience of resonance. Our waiting is attentiveness to our strong evaluation. We even come to know our strong evaluation in and through the actions of resonance.

---

28. This story is discussed in Dana Wright and John Kuentzel, *Redemptive Transformation in Practical Theology* (Grand Rapids: Eerdmans, 2004), 10–15. Of course, Loder's work is all about transformation. There are interesting connections between Loder's thought and Rosa's. Rosa's transformation dimension of resonance could be deepened by Loder's thought. In turn, Loder's thought could be freed from some of the structuralism and Parsonian sociology by a conversation with Rosa.

29. I can highlight one important ramification: it seems empirically proved that topical sermons that connect to faith in daily life are more meaningful to people. This has led some to argue that the church needs to preach only such sermons while leading others to disparage topical or series-based preaching. But both sides miss something more profound. The topical sermon does run the risk of being a strategy to win congregants' energy, pushing the sermons into a self-help cadence. But the other side fails to see that unless the sermon makes some connection to a strong evaluation, moving toward resonance, it is meaningless. Proclamation that makes no impact on strong evaluation is not proclamation in the dynamic of word and response.

For Saint John the Baptist, the strong evaluation that framed their waiting was that God is a God who acts to find us. They waited not as a stale void but as a way to move deeper into their strong evaluation that God will arrive even inside the immanent frame. We wait as expectant action. We wait by acting in the being-form of resonance.

American Protestantism misses, in all its drive for change and innovation—in all its calls for the church to get busy—that the crisis the church faces isn't a lack of willingness to expend energy nor a lack of wanting to accrue resources with an expenditure of energy Rather, its crisis is a vapid strong evaluation. Most congregations have little sense of what their action means, little explicit sense of a strong evaluation that binds them together. Denominations and consultants exacerbate the problem when they seek to solve the church's problems by giving them new strategies to expend energy. Denominations and consultants have failed to reflect on what action is in the first place. Too often denominations and consultants push the congregation to get busy, not recognizing that such action is defeating and debilitating without a direct connection to a strong evaluation. The congregation needs, and the church is called, to wait as the very way of bringing its action and strong evaluations together. This coming together of action and strong evaluation is best described as resonance.

What the search committee was looking for in a new pastor shifted. Saint John the Baptist had always assumed that they needed someone to help them *have* the resources they needed to survive. Now Bert recognized that what was most important was that the new pastor would be someone who could attend to the relationships as the congregation's way of waiting. But these relationships could only be attended to as faithful waiting if the pastor could continue to help shape the congregation's strong evaluation. There needed to be continued attention on the congregation's imagination to wait in anticipation, living out of a strong evaluation that God is God, whom we find by this God finding us.

Bert started moving in this direction as the search for a new pastor was retooled. He focused on texts like Peter's dream and encounter with Cornelius (Acts 10) and David's selection as king (1 Sam. 16). Bert didn't necessarily make the knowledge of the text itself central, trying to transfer information to the group. Rather, Bert made the calling that confronted Saint John the Baptist the focus. He assumed that these stories could speak to and shape the congregation's response to Woz's quest and their commitment to help him. This challenge became the lens through which they read the text and understood their own future. Bert said to the group, "So our job as a church, or at least as this Bible study, is to help Woz find God. And we've all admitted we're not sure how to do that. So let's read this story and see what it shows us."

As they did, with just as much importance, they focused on the quality of their shared life together. They attended to their relationships. Waiting, as we've said, isn't a vapid, dull do-nothing-ism. It's full of relationships of resonance. Waiting is far from a stalling tactic—it becomes the very substance of the church's action. Resonance is a form of life that makes the world, and the God whom we encounter in it, the subjects of the church's story. These relationships that fill our waiting mostly happen organically. The challenge for leadership is to see those relationships, point them out, and give further occasion for such relationships to blossom.

Woz had been driving Herbert Grapp to his doctor appointments for a few weeks. One Wednesday night, before Bert launched into the study, Woz said, "Hey, have any of you seen Herbert's workshop?"

About half the group recalled that Herbert was a woodworker. There were actually a number of pieces Herbert had made over the years throughout the church, most prominently the beautiful crosses on the end of each pew. Most had forgotten this. Woz's question led some to remember that Herbert had this skill.

"Yeah," Woz continued, bobbing his head in excitement, "he's super good. I saw a bunch of cool stuff he's still working on."

Even if somewhere deep in their subconscious they had remembered that Herbert was a woodworker, no one had known he was still doing projects. And Herbert wasn't the kind of guy to talk about himself.

"The coolest stuff is the guitars and banjos," Woz added.

Though Herbert regularly attended the church, no one remembered that he had once worked for a company that made guitars. All of this had unfortunately been lost. The congregation had lost the story of Herbert's life in its rush to survive by having resources. He never left, but the congregation left him, taking its mind off him, assuming that a relationship with him had little value in collecting resources. Now the Bible study was getting the opportunity to see Herbert afresh through the lens of his relationship to Woz. In a beautiful way, Woz was giving them back a relationship with Herbert, freeing Herbert from their rote assumptions about him.

Woz continued, "Did you guys know Herbert's got like forty guitars and banjos, and has at least two or three in process?"

"Well," Herbert jumped in, "it's much slower with my arthritis."

"Do you play?" Sue asked, a little embarrassed that she didn't know the answer. She'd known Herbert for over thirty years.

"Does he play?!" Woz excitedly interrupted. "He played with Johnny Cash in '67!"

"Well, Woz is being a little excitable," Herbert added with both pride and embarrassment.

"No, I'm not!" Woz said, overflowing with animation. "It's so cool; he's got pictures of it and everything in his shop."

Herbert tried to explain. "Johnny Cash visited our little factory and tried some of our guitars. I made one of the guitars he chose. He offered to play a few songs and invited me to play along with him. It was a one-time thing. A photo op."

The group had had no idea. No one had ever heard that story. No one had remembered that this man who had come twice a week to church for decades was a woodworker who still made instruments.

"Do you *still* play?" Sue asked again.

Woz interrupted again: "He does! I had two of my buddies from trivia come by his place last week and he played a bunch of Johnny Cash songs. Herbert is awesome."

Ignoring Woz's adoration, Herbert responded, "Yes, but not as much because of the arthritis."

Everyone was rendered silent. The room felt full and connected. After the few beats of silence, Woz jumped back in, now a little calmer. "It really was so cool. I grew up listening to Johnny Cash. My dad was old school and loved that old country and western stuff. The first song I remember that really touched me, that I was like wow, was 'Sunday Morning Coming Down.' I was like five or something. I have such deep and sad memories of my dad when I think of that song."

Everyone nodded and sat in silence, thinking of a similar song.

Woz, even more muted and reflective, said, "That's what was so cool about playing with Herbert. It really meant a lot to me."

"And to me," Herbert added quickly. "I hadn't played with other people in over a decade." He turned and said, "Woz, I didn't tell you this, and I can't believe I'm telling the group now, but when you and those boys left, I cried. It just was so good to play with some folks."

Woz and Herbert shared a look.

Resonance seeks more resonance—never as a means to accrue resources in competition but as the gift of shared life held together by relationships of affection.

Sue quickly added, "Can you play for us?"

13

When Mozart Goes Straight Into
and Through You

Like Woz, Karl Barth was five or six years old when it hit him—something mysterious in a song. According to Barth it was one of the most significant moments of his life. In one way or another, though Barth doesn't reflect on specifically how, it directed the rest of his life. And as with Woz, it was a moment with music connected to his father.

As we've seen, in his direct pastoral period, Barth was always orbiting around or seeking to escape the orbit of his father. In his student days and first pastoral experience in Geneva, Barth was seeking to propel himself outside the orbit of his father, to escape the gravity of the atmosphere around Fritz. Yet upon entering the vacant space of liberal theology and floating in its zero-gravity atmosphere, Barth saw the necessity, particularly in the pastorate in Safenwil, to return. But he needed to return in his own way. Pastor Barth's early thought is fueled by the necessity to reenter the atmosphere of his father's faith, but in a different way.

It shouldn't be surprising, then, that the most important and lasting experience of Barth's early childhood happened in relation to Fritz. This experience impressed itself deeply on the being of Karl Barth.[1] Barth is

1. Here I focus mainly on how this event relates to Barth and resonance. I don't have space to explore how childhood is a fertile spiritual time. I've explored some of this in *The Congregation in a Secular Age* (Grand Rapids: Baker Academic, 2021), chaps. 15 and 16. A tracing of childhood experience and theological construction would be an important project.

most commonly known as the theologian of God's wholly otherness *and*, though this is often assumed to be only tangentially related, the great lover of Wolfgang Amadeus Mozart. These two seemingly distinct pieces of Barth's outlook are stitched tightly together by his relationship with his father, which has often been missed. As elements of Barth's outlook, they may not be as unrelated as is often assumed.

Toward the end of his life, Barth explained that his love for Mozart occurred as an event. Like lightning striking the ground, or Barth's own view of revelation, his love for Mozart came upon him like a sudden event of encounter,[2] like an arrival from another world. This event, striking at the age of five or six, ignited something in Barth that accompanied him for the rest of his life. Barth testified to this event by starting, as with his theology, with a return to his father.

Fritz was very musical and particularly had the skill of improvising on the piano. He passed the time by playing little pieces. Yet one day was unlike all the others. When Karl was five or six, Fritz started playing, for no particular reason, something by Mozart. Those first notes were like a flash of lightning hitting little Karl straight in the chest. Reflecting on this moment late in his life, Barth said, "I can still picture the scene. He began a couple of bars from *The Magic Flute* ('Tamino mine, what happiness'). They went right through me and into me, I don't know how, and I thought, 'That's it!'"[3]

Wait, what's it? What is Barth talking about? In remembering and retelling this encounter, it was Barth, with his own hand, who put the "That's it!" in quotation marks with an exclamation point. The quotation marks signaled that this "That's it!" is exactly what his five-year-old self proclaimed upon hearing those bars of *The Magic Flute*. This was the direct dialogical response he gave to the event of this encounter.

"That's it!" appears to bear the weight of eureka. The statement has a kind of epistemic quality. But what kind of epistemological breakthrough could a five-year-old who's mesmerized by his father's piano playing have? Was Barth, meaning to or not, making himself into a kind of Mozart?

---

2. It is a shame that childhood and children have not been more central to theological reflection, especially for theological positions that see eventfulness and revelation as important. Childhood is a form of human experience framed by eventual encounter. You learn to be in the world through such events. Bonhoeffer, I believe, saw this, and this was one reason he desired for his *Habilitation* to be on children. However, he was told this was not possible. So he instead wrote *Act and Being*. For more on this, see my *Bonhoeffer as Youth Worker* (Grand Rapids: Baker Academic, 2014).

3. Barth, *Letzte Zeugnisse* (EVZ-Verlag, 1969), 17, quoted by Eberhard Busch, *Karl Barth: His Life from Letters and Autobiographical Texts* (Philadelphia: Fortress, 1975), 15.

The Mystery and Genius

In the early days of modernity (in the late eighteenth century), when the buildings of mystery were severely hobbled and were now being taken out in pieces from the center of the European imagination, a child arrived. In a world that was seeking to immunize itself from mystery, a great mystery stood before Europe. A child, no older than six or seven, played his instrument like a virtuoso. He was so little and yet so good. The sound was amazing, the quality of his performance far beyond his years. It was as if God himself had touched the boy with a gift. This small boy, in tailored adult clothing, was more skilled than most all of the court musicians across Europe. The great mysteries of the late medieval ecclesia may have been coming undone, but as they were, little Mozart reminded even the most hardened rationalists (like Voltaire himself) that a mystery called "genius" still existed. The immanent frame would come. There was no stopping it. But it could never be finally sealed closed, because the genius of the likes of Mozart seemed otherworldly.[4] This genius reminded the West that there were at least some elements of non-givenness to reality.[5]

Is five-year-old Barth's "That's it!" also the sign of a genius? Is little Karl accessing the epistemic depths known only to weathered critics and long-bearded philosophers? Like little Mozart, is little Karl outstripping the skills of men ten times his age? I don't think so. Barth is much too humble and self-deprecating to assume so. Not to mention that the boy who testified "That's it!" did *not* dazzle European courts or slip away to the temple to debate rabbis. No, young Karl punched other boys in the stomach and stole their lunch money. Barth is not equating himself with Mozart. Yet when he hears Mozart for the first time at five years old, he proclaims "That's it!"

Eberhard Busch, who relays this story in his biography, ends the discussion with Barth's words: "That's it!" The next paragraph assures the reader that young Barth was no Mozart, and Busch goes on to discuss Barth's militant and belligerent childhood character. The "that's it!" is left behind with no further discussion or interest. And as far as I know, no other scholar has found it worth exploring. I suppose it's assumed that five-year-olds—whose names are not Mozart—don't know much anyhow.

Yet they may know more than we think. It's left to us to see.

4. Paul Johnson in his biography of Mozart highlights this. See *Mozart: A Life* (New York: Viking, 2013), 7–10.

5. Piero Melograni adds to this in his biography, *Wolfgang Amadeus Mozart: A Biography* (Chicago: University of Chicago Press, 2007), 12–14.

What's the "That's It!"?

If five-year-old Barth is not an epistemological virtuoso, then what is "That's it!" referring to? His five-year-old self doesn't make the statement as a solution to an equation.[6] Nor is he searching for personal answers, trying to catalog his favorite music. "That's it!" isn't a reference even to a preference. He's too small for that. He isn't thinking, "That's it, that's my favorite music, that's what I'll build my identity around. I'll put all Mozart's posters on my wall, join his street team, and buy some old concert tees on eBay." "That's it!" doesn't refer necessarily to the quality or character of the music or its performer.

Those bars of *The Magic Flute* went right through little Barth, going into his very being. He said, even as an adult and one of the great theologians of church history, "I don't know how." This was an event that surpassed all epistemological categories. But though surpassing all knowledge, it was a sure encounter. Barth, even as a five-year-old, was certain he'd encountered something real. It's no wonder that in 1919, at age thirty-two, Barth would be sure that some elements of reality were nongiven. The experience of a five-year-old being overtaken by the profundity of a sound like no other framed the vision of the thirtysomething pastor.

Before his phrase "That's it!" Barth used two other phrases in explaining the event of encountering those bars of music: he said they went "through me" and "into me." These phrases point to emotion. He felt something in the music. The music vibrated the being of his five-year-old self. Barth may have been opposed to making the center of theology an emotive ex-perientialism, as Schleiermacher did. But he was not the kind of Reformed theologian who was opposed to feeling, choosing a stiff wooden disposition over laughter, humor, and a good smoke. Barth was a pastor and theolo-gian who felt (and in 1919 those feelings were a deep sense of friendship and annoyance, loyalty and betrayal!). The music comes into Barth's little being, and he feels full.

These other phrases ("through me" and "into me") also point to some-thing deeper, something more than feeling. "They went right through me." This five-year-old was moved to love something. He felt something, but this something called him out to something else. Listening to those bars, little Barth was overcome with affection. This affection was not directed toward himself (it went through him!), nor was it directed toward Mozart (as if he was swept away by a celebrity).

6. If this were true, I guess it wouldn't make Barth necessarily another Mozart but another Jean Piaget. Piaget (1896–1980), a fellow Swiss national, was the Mozart of naturalism. He did a number of studies, publishing them in journals, when he was only a child.

Rather, the affection that came over him, going through him—even as a five-year-old—was a love for the world. Those bars swept up little Barth, connecting him to the world, moving him to love the world. This was the moment; this was the first direct and conscious embrace he had of the world. Little Barth stood next to the piano watching his father play. The sound that met him took him, connecting him to something beyond him. Barth remembered those bars from so long ago, and he testified to their beauty by proclaiming "That's it!" because that was the very moment he fell in love with the world.

The Love Affair

This love for the world never left Barth. Both his early and his mature theology always centered on a God who is God who loves the world. For Barth, the world was always lovable in itself. Mozart's music is the soundtrack to this love. The uncompromising theologian, who shouts of God's complete and utter distinction from the world, also fell deeply in love with the world. Barth's bold line of God's otherness has often been wrongly understood as an escape from or hatred of the world. It's the opposite. And Mozart is proof.

Barth was so in love with the world that he could name the time and place it happened: that time when something went straight through his five-year-old being as he listened to his father play those bars of *The Magic Flute*. Barth can never be assumed to hate the world—or even modernity, for that matter. Barth could never wish for modernity's obliteration or regret modernity's birth, because it was early modernity that created Mozart. Mozart is the muse, who took a little boy by the hand and connected him to the world, teaching little Barth to love the world in freedom, joy, and sorrow.

Mozart and his music became, from that moment, a medium for Barth. But we should be clear that Mozart was *not* a medium for God, but *only* a medium for loving the world. When little Barth heard those bars, he recognized that they were playing him; they were playing through him, touching him and moving him. But more than moving him, they were moving through him, sending him deeper into the world to love the world. This sounds like what Rosa describes as the action of resonance.

For Barth, Mozart is the muse that he needed his whole life—particularly inside the human devastation of the two world wars—to maintain always a deep affection for the world. We called this resonance—this action of deep affection that includes emotion, which comes upon us elusively as something other than us, transforming us and yet connecting to the world. Little Barth was testifying to the action of resonance when he said it "went into me" and "straight through me." Little Barth felt the world playing him. He experienced the world as freely in play. Pastor Barth could contend that waiting is the faithful way of encountering the living God who is God, because waiting in the world is not a desert of inaction but a resonant space of play. Waiting is playing with and in the world.

The early twentieth century was not a period of play.[7] Hellscape trenches, devastating inflation, and fascism aren't typically triggers for play. But without play it becomes impossible to love the world, to encounter a resonant connection, receiving the world as a good gift. Without play the world is seen only as a thing to have, not to *be* with and love. And without loving the world it becomes impossible to encounter the God who is God for us in Jesus Christ who comes into the world for the sake of God's love for the world.

Masters of Play

In a Sunday newspaper article in 1955, Barth playfully says, "I . . . have to confess that if I ever get to heaven, I would first of all seek out Mozart and only then inquire after Augustine, St. Thomas, Luther, Calvin, and Schleiermacher."[8] At first read, this is a shock. How does Barth explain this? How does the guy who spent nearly all his waking hours from the middle of the 1920s until the day the newspaper article appeared in 1955 mastering Luther, Calvin, and Schleiermacher say he'd first go seeking to find Mozart? Why is Mozart first? Barth explains by saying, "Our daily bread must also include playing. I hear Mozart—both younger and older—at play. But play is something so lofty and demanding that it requires mastery."[9]

Mozart must be found first because Mozart taught Barth to love the world by inviting Barth into the serious business of true and free play. Mozart is the frame of reference for faithful human action. Barth never directly connects this, but he seems to insinuate that faithful waiting is playing. The congregation that waits (to connect us back to the previous chapter) is *not* in a stagnant place of inertia, impatiently looking at the clock and anxiously tapping toes to pass the minutes. Rather, a congregation that waits is a community of friends in play.

The congregation plays together as its way of waiting. The congregation waits with the world by inviting the world to play, by taking joy in the fact that the world is a place where play can inhabit. The world needs the church

---

7. Maybe the 1920s, but that was soon over.
8. Karl Barth, *Wolfgang Amadeus Mozart* (Eugene, OR: Wipf & Stock, 1986), 17.
9. Barth, *Wolfgang Amadeus Mozart*, 17.

to pray for its daily bread, entering picket lines for workers' rights. But, just as important, the world needs the invitation to play.

It's odd that in our time those furiously fighting for justice (predominantly Twitter users and particular pastors or Christian thought leaders) lack so much humor. Their earnestness is so hot it dries to dust any irony. There is no doubt that fighting for the world to have its daily bread is important, but never in a manner that forgets the importance of play (even with our political enemies).

Play reminds us that even those we struggle against are human, deserving a place in the world to play as much as we do. Without play we can work for the world without loving the world (which seems to be a danger in mainline Protestantism).[10] Without play our action is captured by the having-mode and turns into ideology. Our ideas, or our party's ideas, become more important than concrete persons. Play is important because it's a (maybe *the*) form of action that escapes the having-mode of expending energy and instead seeks to encounter persons. Sue's question to Woz and Herbert was deeper than she knew. She asked, "Can you play for us?" This question embodies the shape and direction of the church's waiting with the world for the God who is God. The church waits faithfully for God's coming by asking one another, by asking the world, "Can you play for and with us?"

Play as Mastery

Yet Barth's quote from 1955 reveals that there is another dimension to play. Barth sees a beautiful kind of dialectical nature inherent in play, which is represented in Mozart himself and which is why Barth indicates he'll go seeking first for Mozart in heaven. Barth is *not* just captivated by how Mozart plays but by how this play moves him, without expending him, into mastery.

Mozart masters his craft not in the having-mode but in the being-mode.[11] Being in such resonance with his music creates a near-transcendent kind of proficiency in Mozart. Such a profound proficiency doesn't produce but obliterates pride. Mozart, through the resonance of play, becomes so proficient at his craft that he feels played by the music more than playing it. This kind of mastery can only create genuine humility.

The inherent energy in playing his music, in feeling his music playing him, drives Mozart to master his music. Not to have it. Not to control and own the

10. It's right here that *ressentiment* is born and grows.
11. I contend that Mozart is the example of faithful human action in Barth's mind. Practical theologians who assert that Barth is uninterested in human action (see Don Browning, *A Fundamental Practical Theology* [Minneapolis: Fortress, 1991]) have missed the place of Mozart.

music, but to *be* found by it, to be connected through it to the world and its beauty. Mozart desires for the music to speak to him, moving him deeper into an encounter of loving the world as his music also plays him. This drive to play with the world and love the world produces mastery. Mozart is a virtuoso, but not because he expends the most energy to have the ability and control the music. He's a virtuoso because he gives himself over to being freely in the world, loving the world by playing with and for the world. Mozart is a master not because he plays his music best (the having-mode) but because his music so beautifully plays him (the being-mode of resonance).

We so often have things backward in late modernity. We tell young musicians and athletes that the hardest workers will master their craft. We tell the young musician or athlete over and over again that if he wants to be proficient (one of the best!) he'll have to work the hardest on the field or in the rehearsal room. We tell her that if she wants to be proficient, she must expend the most energy, picking one sport or instrument and spending every waking hour in drills. Yet this is only half true (it's a concession to the closed immanent frame that says the hardest workers achieve the most mastery). The proficient artist or athlete will indeed log the most hours in practice. But the master is rarely moved by the drive to have proficiency. Instead, the master finds herself being swept up into proficiency, into the beauty of the piece or the flow of the game.[12] The true master will log the most hours not because she is driven by having proficiency and the awards and acclaim that come with it, but so she might *be* more deeply in love with the world. The true master, like Mozart, will spend the most hours because the play itself will speak to him, connecting his being to the world. Mozart's mastery is the height of beauty for Barth because Mozart has no desire to have the world. Mozart's drive for mastery is always in the being-mode. His drive is born from the desire to be freely in the world, being played by the world.

Mozart becomes Barth's medium to love the world because Mozart plays.[13] Mozart is always playful. But his playfulness, while never becoming something other than playful, is so lofty and full it moves Mozart to mastery. Mozart's playful love for the world requires him to master his instruments, to play until his fingers bleed. This requirement comes not from within the actor's expenditure of energy but from the free relationship the playful actor has

12. We call this being "in the zone," which is a kind of resonance in play. The greats like Mozart or Michael Jordan seem to be able to connect to the world, entering a form of action called resonance in their craft more easily than others. This is what makes them great.

13. Paul Louis Metzger offers a nice discussion of Barth and Mozart, particularly on play. See *The Word of Christ and the World of Culture: Sacred and Secular through the Theology of Karl Barth* (Grand Rapids: Eerdmans, 2003), 204–10.

with the world. Play produces such a free and open love for the world that the actor who plays seeks mastery—seeks a kind of excellence.[14] The player plays, seeking to master the chords until her fingers bleed, to allow something to come into her and go straight through her. That something is not the power of possession or domination. It's resonance.

In 1955, Barth is imagining his own *Church Dogmatics* as a form of play that demands mastery. Barth has mastered the writings of Luther, Calvin, and Schleiermacher. But in heaven he must seek Mozart first because Mozart taught Barth to play. Mozart showed Barth that mastery itself doesn't happen when you seek mastery. It happens when you seek resonance. Mozart and his playful love prevent Barth's theology from becoming a stale, usable object. Mozart masters his music by allowing his music to always be free, permitting it to encounter him again and again. Mozart masters his craft through resonance, not control.

Mozart must be found first in heaven, before Luther, Calvin, and Schleiermacher, so that Luther, Calvin, and Schleiermacher are allowed to remain other, able to keep their own voice and speak.[15] Mozart is first because he's taught Barth how to be a theologian in the mode of resonance, allowing Luther and Calvin to live and speak to him. Mozart taught Barth that to master something is humbly to let it *be* free, giving it space for its own voice to speak to you. Barth wants to play Luther and Calvin, but not as an echo of Barth's own speaking. As with Mozart and his music, Barth desires for them to freely speak to him, for Barth to play them by letting them go "right through [him] and into [him]."[16] Mozart is the first one to be sought in heaven because he shows Barth how to do theology in the mode of resonance.

But even this kind of mastery, which sweeps us up into resonance (the being-mode of relation to the world), isn't just an attitude. There's a shape or content to it. It must be joyfully suffered. Barth learns this from Mozart (or at least sees and appreciates it in him). We could say it this way: Not only

14. We don't have time to take these thoughts into a conversation with Aristotle, Luther, and justification. These thoughts on play as *a* or *the* form of human action are ripe for a discussion on justification. The way play moves into mastery also seems to shift in a unique away from the Aristotelian perspective that Luther (and some of Eberhard Jüngel's work, such as *Theological Essays I* [Edinburgh: T&T Clark, 1989]) is opposed to. There is a rich conversation of how play, justification, and sanctification relate here.

15. To me, a sign that Barth is seeking to do his work in a resonance mode is his strong desire to not turn his own theology into a school. Barth doesn't want to make Barthians; he wants to say something true, to playfully master his theology in such a way that it speaks of something real and true in the world, just as Mozart's music does. Barth does not want to *have* Barthians; he wants his theology to move others into *being* in the world in such a way that they encounter the God who is God.

16. Busch, *Karl Barth*, 15.

does Barth see an inherent dialectic between play and mastery, seeing how true play can produce a drive for mastery that escapes the having-mode. He also appears to see a deeper or more fundamental dialectic in play itself. In Mozart, Barth recognizes how play as a resonant relationship with the world is kept from falling in on itself by being dialectically coupled with limits. Mozart is the playful master (he has mastery) because he bears—even welcomes—limits. This too is something Rosa taught us: without closedness and elusiveness, resonance cannot be. Resonance requires limits.

Play Has Its Limits

Barth is moved by how, for Mozart, limits and restriction become places for play, creativity, and life. In remembering the bold line between God and the world, between the given and nongiven elements of reality, we can find ourselves in play. In limits we can embrace the world as a place to play in waiting. Living with limits (and waiting) doesn't flatten and restrict the world. This is the devastating lie of consumerism and neoliberalism and its idolatrous form of human action as the expenditure of energy: they claim that there is *no limit* to having and growing. These realities claim that the good life is living beyond limits. But this only produces a hatred for the world, possessing and using up the world for the sake of growth, pushing us to eliminate the limit of rest that allows the world to be so that we can have more of the world. To honor limits is to love the world, by giving the world the freedom to be the world, to be embraced as a place of play, joy, and rest (waiting!). God imposes a limit on the world (keeping it always the world), giving it the freedom to playfully *be*.[17] When the church waits, it loves the world by respecting the world's limits.

Respect for limits, and the limit being the catalyst for creativity, is what Barth sees so beautifully in Mozart. Barth says that by "imposing limits, [Mozart] tells us how everything is. Therein lies the beauty of his beneficent and moving music."[18] Mozart, Barth explains, shows us that there are limits to both happiness and suffering. The world cannot be the world without seeing and experiencing both. The world cannot be loved as the world if we refuse to see it as it is, recognizing the limits to both happiness and suffering. There are limits to both the heights of happiness and the depths of suffering.

---

17. Bonhoeffer works this idea of limit in Genesis, asserting that the tree at the center is the limit God imposes on humanity as a way of allowing humanity to be freely human and God to be God. Sin enters the world when the human beings deny the limit. See *Creation and Fall: A Theological Exposition on Genesis 1–3* (Minneapolis: Fortress, 1997), 85–87.

18. Barth, *Wolfgang Amadeus Mozart*, 34.

For instance, it's an abstraction and refusal to love the world to cast the world as a utopia, a place where happiness can grow and expand, and expand and grow some more. To risk overstatement, we could say that Disney World cannot be the world and cannot love the world. Under its glossy shine, it hates the world.[19] Disney hates the world because it seeks to be a consumerist escape from the real world.[20] Disney hates the world because Disney cannot live with a limit to happiness. For Disney, happiness is limitless, which means it cannot, and refuses to, see the suffering of the world. Happiness, like the neoliberal growth economy that worships it as the highest good, sees no limits to growth.[21] You can always wish for more and more happiness. But too much happiness is like too much cake; it eventually makes you sick, too sick to embrace the world as it truly is. Happiness must have its limit for us to love the world and be free to play within it.[22]

Suffering too must have its limit. Entertainment and art that is produced in the society with supposedly limitless happiness is, in turn, limitless in its anxiety over suffering (dark dystopian novels and TV shows abound today, as do reports of rising depression and opioid use).[23] Late-modern people live with the terror that their own personal suffering, or the suffering of the world, is limitless. After all, if happiness is supposedly limitless, why wouldn't suffering also be? Few of us would admit this, but we nevertheless live with it buried in our consciousness, leading to huge amounts of anxiety and depression in our Western societies. But to see no limit to suffering is also to hate the world. Those who have been overtaken by the anxiety that suffering is limitless have lost all humor, sadly having no time to play, seeing the world itself as no place to play. While they are alive, they see no reason to live. *This is not to blame any individual.* These are the ramifications of a culture ignoring (and building societies) in opposition to limits. The loss of limitations produces an honest hate for the world and life in it.

19. The movie *The Florida Project* beautifully and painfully shows this to be true.

20. For more on Disney, see Vincent Miller, *Consuming Religion: Christian Faith and Practice in a Consumer Culture* (New York: Continuum, 2003).

21. For more on this kind of economy and its deep problems we seem unable to solve—mainly because we have built forms of the good life that oppose and cannot stomach limit—see Tim Jackson's incredible book *Prosperity without Growth: Foundations for the Economy of Tomorrow* (London: Routledge, 2017).

22. I discuss happiness and its limit more in *The End of Youth Ministry?* (Grand Rapids: Baker Academic, 2020), chap. 4.

23. Another example is that in the 1980s, at a time when consumerism was pushed further and further into our society as a way for happiness to grow without limit, forms of music spoke of limitless suffering. The genre of metal was the yin of limitless suffering to the yang of pop's limitless happiness. For more on this, see Donna Gaines, *Teenage Wasteland: Suburbia's Dead End Kids* (New York: HarperPerennial, 1992).

What Barth deeply appreciates about Mozart, making him Barth's medium and muse in loving the world, is that Mozart always holds to limits. Mozart's music lives. It speaks of happiness and suffering, but it never gives in to either one as limitless. This allows Mozart's music to embrace the world, to play with and for the world, to cry and laugh with the world. The limit is grace. This limit that keeps either happiness or suffering from being limitless is a gift. It's the grace of being able to live in joy *and* longing.

The dialectical movement that speaks of happiness and suffering without being swallowed by one or the other allows the world to *be*, allowing us to be in relationship with it, loving it. Limits, as Rosa teaches, are always the context for relationships of resonance. Mozart's music is Barth's medium into loving the world by upholding the limit as boundary. Barth says, "No, Mozart was not . . . an optimist (not even in his most radiant major-key movements, not in his serenades and divertimenti, nor in *Figaro*, nor in *Cosi fan tutte*!). But no, neither was he a melancholic or a pessimist (not in the small or in the great G-Minor Symphonies, not in the D-Minor Piano Concerto, nor in the 'Dissonance' Quartet, nor in the Overture to and the Finale of *Don Giovanni*!)."[24]

The limit that engenders the dialectic of happiness and suffering is clear. This limit allowed Mozart to speak honestly and lovingly of the world. Barth continues, "What [Mozart] translated into music was real life in all its discord. . . . In Mozart there are no flat plains but no abysses either. He does not make things easy for himself. But neither does he let himself go; he is never guilty of excess."[25] Mozart's genius is in the limit.

The limit is so important that Barth pushes the necessity of limits further. Barth imposes a further limit on Mozart as his way of loving him.

Mozart as Unrivaled: The Limit to Revelation

While Mozart is Barth's medium and muse into loving the world, Barth limits Mozart from being any kind of medium into revelation itself. Barth loves Mozart too much to make him bear that weight. Yet more needs to be said about Mozart's particular ability to serve as a medium to move Barth into love for the world and how this contrasts with revelation. We can consider this by hearing from Barth again. Seeing this playfulness within a dialectic of limits in Mozart, Barth says, "In Mozart I hear an art of playing as I hear it in no one else. Beautiful playing presupposes an intuitive, childlike awareness of the essence . . . of all things. . . . When I hear him, it gladdens, encourages, and

24. Barth, *Wolfgang Amadeus Mozart*, 34.
25. Barth, *Wolfgang Amadeus Mozart*, 34.

comforts me as well. Not that I want to utter even one critical word against anyone else. But in this sense I can offer my testimonial to Mozart alone."[26]

It's odd that Barth is so fully committed to Mozart, seeing him as having *no* rivals. Barth tried in his 1955 newspaper article to not throw shade on others (Barth had matured since 1919 and his tact had caught up with his genius). But even in 1955 Barth couldn't help saying that Mozart to him is the best. But this is odd in relation to the rest of Barth's life. Barth had a deep appreciation, not only professionally but also personally, for the Christian tradition. Barth was what we'd call today a "church nerd." The art in his house witnesses to this. Climbing the stairs of his final home in Basel you can spot pictures of the great theologians of the tradition lining the walls. But even so, these theologians would have to wait as he rummaged through heaven looking for Mozart.

It's difficult, if not impossible, to include Mozart as a great composer in line with the Christian tradition Barth so admires and remains committed to. Neither Bach nor Beethoven serve as Barth's medium. Bach's connections to church life, particularly Protestantism, and worship are much more clear. Mozart, on the other hand, is a lukewarm (at best) Catholic, more connected to his Masonic lodge than any church. Mozart is more interested in writing opulent operas than Christmas concerts. Nevertheless, this is the conductor that Barth loved, and not *solely* for aesthetic reasons. Of course his love included the aesthetic, but Barth had specific reasons why he passed over Bach and Beethoven and embraced the ecclesially uninterested Mozart. Mozart allowed the world to freely be the world. Barth says, "Mozart's music is not, in contrast to that of Bach, a message, and not, in contrast to that of Beethoven, a personal confession. He does not reveal in his music any doctrine and certainly not himself. . . . Mozart does not wish to say anything: he just sings and sounds. Thus he does not force anything on the listener, does not demand that he make any decisions or take any positions; he simply leaves him free."[27] The great theologian of God's otherness, the great reviver of Protestantism, the man who eats and drinks the Christian tradition, embraces Mozart, who had little direct interest in the church and little concern for faith, as his muse and medium, because of freedom.

If you were to sit at Barth's desk in the home office in his final house in Basel, you'd see to your right two doors. One leads back to the stairs with all those pictures of theologians. The other door opens to a small room filled with books that served as the office of his collaborator Charlotte von Kirschbaum.

---

26. Barth, *Wolfgang Amadeus Mozart*, 17.
27. Barth, *Wolfgang Amadeus Mozart*, 37.

Above one door is a picture of Calvin. And above the other, at the same height, is a picture of Mozart. These pictures represent a dialectic, with a bold line between the two sides in the dialectic. The pictures indicate that Barth lived and worked out of this dialectic.

Calvin reminded Barth of God's freedom. There were no mediums to encounter the living God other than God's own act given to us in Jesus Christ, the Scriptures that testify to him, and the Word that is preached of him. And yet, whether completely fair or not, Calvin is not remembered as a great lover of the world. His Geneva seemed to be quite the opposite.

Over the other door Barth placed Mozart's picture, at the same height as Calvin's, as testimony that it was Mozart who served as Barth's muse in embracing and being embraced by the world. Calvin reminded Barth that God is God. God loves the world. Mozart reminded Barth that he was alive, that the world was good and wonderful in itself. The world reaches out for us, seeking to play with us and move us. The sin that binds the world isn't in the world's life, but in the way sin seeks to destroy and smother life. Calvin and Mozart could *not* be more unlike. And yet Barth, as pastor and theologian, needed them both. John Updike says it poignantly: "Karl Barth's insistence upon the otherness of God seemed to free him to be exceptionally (for a theologian) appreciative and indulgent of this world, the world at hand."[28]

Mozart freely loved the world for its own sake, freely embracing his music not for some other end but only for itself. Mozart's music was itself his relationship to the world. He played music to be connected to the world, to encounter life, and to *be*. Barth loved Mozart, seeing him as a muse, because even as a five-year-old, Barth was taught by Mozart to love the world for itself—not for any purpose or goal that the world could be made into. Calvin (and Luther) gave Barth the language he needed for God's freedom. But Mozart gave Barth the experience of what this freedom tasted like in the world. Calvin allows God to be free. Mozart allows the world to be free. Barth's pastoral theology brings these freedoms together by drawing a bold line between them, waiting for the free God to act in the free world.[29]

Barth will act in the world while waiting, a way of faithful living as waiting (as pastor and theologian) in the resonance mode. Mozart is Barth's doorway into resonance. This is startlingly clear in another newspaper article from Barth. In this piece from 1956, Barth writes directly, in a playful manner, to

28. Updike, foreword to *Wolfgang Amadeus Mozart*, by Barth, 7.
29. Barry Harvey offers a nice discussion of freedom in relation to limit. See *Can These Bones Live? A Catholic Baptist Engagement with Ecclesiology, Hermeneutics, and Social Theory* (Grand Rapids: Brazos, 2008), 263.

Mozart himself. Barth says, "What I thank you for is simply this: Whenever I listen to you, I am transported to the threshold of a world which in sunlight and storm, by day and by night, is a good and ordered world. . . . With an ear open to your musical dialectic, one can be young and become old, can work and rest, be content and sad: in short, one can live."[30] This is the rich expression of waiting as resonance, of action in the being-mode as opposed to the having-mode. Mozart connects Barth's action in relation with the world. Mozart shows Barth how to relate to the world.

Just outside that door under Mozart's picture there was a record player. Every morning, Barth would play Mozart as a way of escorting himself back from sleep into the world, awake to love the world, to experience being alive, so he could be open to the vision of a living God who acts as God even in the immanent frame. Each day Barth prepared to do the joyous act of being a theologian by grabbing the hand of Mozart to be taken into resonance, to be placed back into relation with the world. In relationship with the world, Barth was ready to say something about the God who is God, who acts to be with and for this world God loves.[31]

Finally, Back to "That's It!"

We return now to the beginning of this chapter, with an open question that was never answered. Five-year-old Barth hears those bars of *The Magic Flute* and they go into him and through him.[32] As we've seen, Barth was swept up into resonance, which gave him a love for the world that would never leave him. This experience of resonance gave him an inability to abandon modernity or believe a God who is God cannot act within it. Those bars caused Barth to understand the Younger's call to wait not as void of action but as a form of action, like waiting at the side of Fritz's piano to be struck by a connection with and a love for the world.

30. Barth, *Wolfgang Amadeus Mozart*, 22.
31. Busch discusses the record player and its importance in *Karl Barth*, 363.
32. Melograni may give us a picture into why *The Magic Flute* so deeply impacted little Barth and how it set him up to love the world and to embrace modernity, being inspired by *The Magic Flute* to be the great modern theologian he'd become. Melograni says, "Mozart is modern because he uses his music to liberate us from many irrelevant restraints. From that point of view *The Magic Flute* seems to be the work that best expresses the desire to liberate humanity. The golden flute that a lady-in-waiting of the Queen of the Night gives Tamino in act I, scene 7, is highly symbolic. That flute and the sounds that it makes express the essence of music—sounds that come from the world of the irrational but are nevertheless capable of accompanying Tamino, his bride Jamina, Mozart, and all of us into life and beyond life, toward the world of the unknown and toward a greater awareness." *Wolfgang Amadeus Mozart*, 252.

But what does "That's it!" specifically refer to? What does five-year-old Barth recognize, confess, and proclaim, even to himself? I believe "That's it!" refers to life itself. "That's it; that's a fullness of life!" Of course, little Barth is already breathing; he is biologically alive. He knows that. But that's not the *it* he encounters. What he encounters in those bars of Mozart is a direct relationship to life. He feels not just medically alive but played by life itself, just as his father plays the piano. Life comes to him from outside himself, going straight through him, because it is more than him, lodging itself deeply within him. Although more than him, it includes him. "That's it!" is five-year-old Karl Barth's response to his first conscious experience of resonance.[33] He is swept up in relationship with the world that is the encounter of being truly alive, of being spoken to by the world itself. Barth is a theologian of life. His dogmatic and pastoral foci come together in his concern for life that is bound in a relational encounter. We encounter the life of a God who is God when God relationally acts for us (as Jesus Christ). We find life in encounters with the world by waiting with the world, loving the world, as God meets us in God's freedom in the world.

To wait as the church is to love the world by participating in relationships of resonance, by inviting persons to play and testify, "That's it!" That's life! That's the gift of being alive! It's inside this gift of life that we wait together for a God who is God. The church that waits is alive.

———

Two weeks after Sue asked, "Can you play for us?" Woz was dragging some instruments into the room where the Bible study met. Woz had made a sign from an old sheet and some spray paint that read, "The Grand Return of Herbert Grapp, Now with the Misfits."

33. I say "conscious" because I believe that the relationship between a newborn and mother (or caregiver) is an event of resonance. And it's safe to say that Barth had this experience. Rosa discusses the child/mother relationship as resonance in *Resonance* (London: Polity, 2019), 888.

14

Pietism and Its Discontents

A Dialectical Escape from Individualism and Religion

The Bible study usually had about eight to ten people participate. That night the room was packed with thirty-five people. Members of the congregation who never came to the Bible study came to hear Herbert. They mixed with a handful of Woz's trivia acquaintances. Woz and two of his trivia teammates, who playfully called themselves the Misfits, joined Herbert as they together played a dozen or so old country and western hits. It was a hoot, but not without tears. Herbert spoke of his loneliness and played like a man who'd lived through many broken hearts. Herbert was amazing, more talented (and honest) than anyone had thought. Even at his age, and battling his arthritis, he could play, picking those strings like a savant. And his voice! It was soaked with hope and despair, or—better yet—hope born out of despair. No one had known he could sing like that. He sounded like a raspy version of Hank Williams.

The smiles and tears painted on everyone's faces testified to an encounter with life. The room was alive, not by the current of happiness but by the encounter with resonance. Happiness is a one-way street that allows for only the traffic of good times. It has no capacity for suffering and loss. Resonance, on the other hand, is fundamentally dialectical. Resonance claims that life is a relational connection that is bound in both joy and suffering, openness and closedness, immediate encounter and elusiveness—never one without the other.[1]

---

1. It claims that joy and suffering are themselves dialectical. Joy as compared to happiness is dialectical. Joy is found in moments of suffering. Happiness cannot be.

Saint John the Baptist was waiting for a God who is God to arrive. They had no ability to bring this God, no real way to find God. They could only wait, and while they did, they readied themselves by waiting in resonance, by freely loving the world. The concert had no real purpose. The point wasn't to parlay the expenditure of the energy into building the church by accruing more resources from the resources spent.[2] Rather, the point was just to be. They were there to be with Herbert, to celebrate him and, in turn, to be with the neighborhood, inviting whoever wanted to come and be together. The point was to come and seek resonance as friendship. It was an opportunity to wait in and through a resonant relationship to the world. This concretely manifested itself in celebrating an old man with a great gift, which his congregation had tragically forgotten in its rush to *have* a future.

For an hour and half that small room roared with laughter and tears, hooting and sobbing. So much life exuded from that room that Bert figured it could light the church building for a year, maybe the neighborhood for a month. You could feel the life racing through the veins of the church for weeks. It was as if the moment just kept vibrating against the walls of the church building, making its way out into the neighborhood. Even people at Teddy's Tacos were talking about Herbert and his Hank Williams skills. People both within and outside the congregation were asking for another Herbert night.

Bert was now sure that Saint John the Baptist had the one thing it had searched for with Luke, but could never find. Luke added to the member list, gave the church a slick rebranding, and increased the number of programs. But all this expending of energy couldn't create what the church was experiencing now in its waiting: life. Saint John the Baptist felt truly alive. Life came when they could wait and bear the dialectic necessary to encounter resonance. This life came about by attending to the world and seeking a God who is God to arrive in it. Leaning against a side wall, eating a not-quite-day-old donut, Bert had his own "That's it!" encounter. Watching Herbert and Woz, remembering their mutual but distinct suffering of loneliness, and seeing Sue, Helene, and so many others wiping tears of joy and pain, all of them lost beautifully in the moment, Bert said to himself, "That's it!" That's life.

This life didn't come from a strategy of growth to have resources. It came through waiting with the world. This life, and the action in it we've called resonance, always bears the marks of a dialectic. It relates to the world, not to

2. As I hope the reader will see, I'm not against resources per se, but resources cannot bear the dialectical weight of life and therefore cannot, in themselves, deliver the kind of life we yearn for. For the church, resources without a dialectical nature cannot bear the shape of divine action itself. Therefore, the best that resources can do is get individuals to commit to an institution and thereby secure religion.

have anything from the world but to be freely with and for the world. The dialectic keeps the bold line of the given and nongivenness of reality from being blurred. Waiting didn't produce boredom and a spirit of defeat. It produced the freedom to be. It created a spirit of openness to encounter otherness and to be drawn into affection for the world. In waiting, Herbert was no longer seen as an old man resistant to change or as too slow to help the church have the resources it needed for the future. Rather, Herbert was encountered as other, as a distinct person with a distinct story and gift to share.

This gave Saint John the Baptist life. Bert was aware that Saint John the Baptist still had financial concerns, and maybe it would never have a significant market share compared to other churches. Exponential growth was not in its future. But it could *no longer* be called a dying church. It may not have been growing in its expenditure of energy to have resources. But it was alive. It had life. Its waiting for God drew the congregation and its neighbors into "That's it!" moments of resonance. Saint John the Baptist was alive with something more profound: resonance. This life meant that they'd find one way or another to be.

From the night of Herbert's concert, Sue never again talked about merging with another congregation or selling the building. She threw away the card of the corporate real estate contact who bought churches to flip them into microbreweries. She even stopped talking about the fear of Saint John the Baptist's short financial runway. That runway was admittedly still short and encircled by high, unforgiving mountains, but it all felt far less worrisome, even less precarious. They had life, and that was enough.

Life as the Substance of Waiting

Decades after he left Safenwil to become a professor and then eventually a world-renowned theologian, Barth returned to Safenwil for a visit. On his return, he apologized to his former congregation, confessing that his pastorate had included moments of self-indulgence. His intellectual pursuits had at times gotten the better of him. He'd talk and talk and they'd look confused. Barth could have been more attentive to the needs of each of them, he confessed. In retrospect, Barth was harder on himself than he should have been. Letters and other documents show that he was a good and focused pastor. But October 9, 1917, may have been a moment when Barth's intellectual pursuits did get the better of him.

Barth decided his congregation needed to hear a lecture called "Religion and Life."[3] This lecture was an occasion for Pastor Barth to critique both

---

3. In this section I'm leaning heavily on Eberhard Busch, *Karl Barth and the Pietists: The Young Karl Barth's Critique of Pietism and Its Response* (Downers Grove, IL: InterVarsity, 2004).

pietism and liberalism, giving Barth a place to stand beyond them.[4] Maybe
as in our own time, Barth recognized that there were few alternatives besides
pietism and liberalism. In 1917 Barth was seeking both a personal and an
ecclesial way between them. It would be a dialectical way. But in the lecture,
Barth isn't as clear as he could be. (And why Barth assumed at all that his
congregation cared to hear such a lecture, I'm not sure.)

Barth may have been blind to his congregation's legitimate apathy. According to Eberhard Busch, in 1917 he'd been working hard to wrestle himself
free from pietism as much as liberalism. While pietism and liberalism stood
in fierce opposition, nevertheless they had (and still have) more overlap than
either camp would like to admit. Though seemingly enemies from two different worlds, a closer examination reveals that pietism and theological liberalism are related (and not just distantly). Pietism and liberalism are siblings,
maybe even twins with a grudge. Even today there is a well-worn expressway
for children of conservative pietists to become hyperpartisan liberals (more
on this below).[5]

There are two clear links between the pietism and the liberalism that Barth
knew. While pietism and liberalism may take quite different positions on
the authority of Scripture and the importance of the natural and the social
sciences, both are a religious response born in the house of modernity. Both
are birthed under the same roof. I suppose this doesn't make them siblings,
but it's the second link that reveals a strong DNA match: The second link is
that both are committed, in their own different way, to "religious individualism." Both contend that it is the individual who incorporates or commits to
religion, making individual meaning out of religion. The individual is the
driver of religious experience.

After 1915, Barth had no patience for this. Yet, even in his impatience,
Barth sees no problem with either pietism or liberalism giving attention to
modernity. Barth, too, seeks a theological position inside modernity and its
immanent frame. Actually, in Barth's mind, agreement on a modern starting
point gives some legitimacy to both pietism and liberalism (he's not the great
enemy of either). But for the goods of these two modern perspectives to be
harvested and not rot, producing a hideous stink in the church (which Barth
thinks both have done), they must be freed from their mutual infatuation

---

4. Fritz Barth also stood beyond both pietism and liberalism. For more on Fritz Barth and
his relationship to pietism, see Busch, *Karl Barth and the Pietists*, chap. 1.

5. It's just the shifting of one purity code for another. They leave the purity code that speaks out
against sex and cultural consumption for the purity code of language use and political correctness.
Both are incredibly bound in an expressive emotivism. It takes little time to spot many of these
ex-evangelicals on social media, working out their purity now in a different tune to the same song.

with individualism and religion. *Römerbrief I* and *II* were a frontal attack on both religion and individualism. In the lecture "Religion and Life" (given when Barth was writing *Römerbrief I*), religion found itself squarely in Barth's crosshairs.[6]

The lecture could have been more aptly named "Religion or Life." Barth places religion and life in opposition, because religion cannot bear the dialectic necessary for life. Pastor Barth is saying that we can have either religion or life (these points will be more nuanced in *Römerbrief II*, though religion will still bear the force of a heavy-handed critique). Barth knows which one he'll pick. Religion has little appeal. His encounter with life in his five-year-old "That's it!" through the dialectic of Mozart's music is too strong to be reduced to flat religion. Barth contends that religion, in both its pietistic and liberal forms, obscures and even attacks life by being unable to stomach the dialectic that is inherent in life. Religion is idolatry because (to give Barth the language we've developed above) it's a form of action in the having-mode. Religion thinks it can have God, contending that God is obtainable. But God is only obtainable in God's unattainability. Religion does not want a *living* God—who is alive in speaking both a yes and a no—it wants an object to use for its own individual meaning making.

Against this god who can be had, God shouts a great *no*, judging religion. Barth would develop this even more boldly in *Römerbrief II*. But even in 1917, it was clear that religion stood in opposition to life because, whether in its pietistic or liberal form, religion deceptively gives the individual the idea that they can have God. Religion, Barth—maybe too boldly—states, hates life because it imposes a form of action that seeks to have what cannot be had.[7] Religion hates life because it denies the fundamental dialectical nature of life, denying that life can be found only in wrestling with death and limit.

But in 1917 this wasn't as clear as it should have been. Barth was certainly opposing religion. But an articulation of life was far from present. Busch admits that this articulation of life "is a bit vague" in the lecture.[8] (That's an

6. Bruce McCormack offers a nice conversation on Barth's understanding of religion. See *Karl Barth's Critically Realistic Dialectical Theology: Its Genesis and Development, 1909–1936* (Oxford: Oxford University Press, 1997), 283–86.
7. For Barth, particularly in *Römerbrief II*, though religion stands against life, the human being cannot live without religion. This is a kind of Luther-like stuckness that demands divine act to save us. Religion is law and the law cannot save. Barth, though strongly critiquing religion, also contends that one cannot live without religion. He's just working hard to remind us that we cannot and should not—as both liberalism and pietism have done—replace God with religion. For more on Barth and religion, see Barth, *The Epistle to the Romans* (London: Oxford University Press, 1933), 230–32, 269–75.
8. Busch, *Karl Barth and the Pietists*, 29.

understatement!) It's darn confusing in its underdevelopment. It seems that the Barth of decades later does have at least this obscurity to apologize for. Busch says, "Barth simply answers: 'Life in the world and life in the Bible.' Was life thus a phenomenon that could be found both in the 'world' as well as in the Bible? How does Barth come to assume that life in the world and life in the Bible are congruent and that both phenomena oppose 'religion' and are superior to it? . . . Barth's own position is somewhat unclear and unsettled."[9] Not "somewhat." It plainly *is* both unclear and unsettled.

Interestingly, to get some clarity on what life is and how it relates to the world and the Bible, Busch does what we've done throughout this project. Busch returns to what Barth learned from the Younger.[10] Busch explains that the key to understanding Barth's conception of life is to see it next to the Younger. When we do, we can spot life's dialectical shape and its relation to a God who is a living God.

The Younger and His Discontent

It was Blumhardt the Younger who threw gas on Barth's burning unease with both pietism and liberalism's religious individualism. The Younger didn't start Barth's fire. Concrete pastoral ministry, the desire to make personal and intellectual peace with his father, and the bold steps into the socialist movement struck the match. But the Younger brought the fire to a roar, directing it in a particular theological direction. The Younger embodied the dialectic that Barth would come to embrace and develop into a rich edifice, something that, honestly, the Younger could not have done. When Barth met the Younger after Peter's wedding in 1915, Barth was meeting a man who, out of a deep unease, had made two significant turns. These turns, particularly the first, give us important insight in decoding what Pastor Barth means by life, and how we should see life as fundamentally dialectical.

The Younger's first turn was a bold move. The Younger was pietist royalty. He was the prince of the whole of the German Pietist movement. Being the

---

9. Busch, *Karl Barth and the Pietists*, 29.

10. Busch discusses life and religion, and his objective is to see where and how Barth moves beyond pietism. See Busch, *Karl Barth and the Pietists*, 26–30. He leaves the question about what life means open as he moves into a section on page 30 with the heading "The Influence of Christoph Blumhardt and T. Back." One of the contributions I'm seeking to make is to show that a way of reading Barth's theology as a fundamental pastoral theology is to read it alongside the Blumhardts, or to see the Blumhardts as practical, even empirical, verification that God acts in modernity. Reading Barth as a pastor inspired and pushed forward by the pastoral theologies in the practice of the Blumhardts gives an interesting way of connecting Barth to practical and pastoral theology.

son of Johann Blumhardt put the Younger Blumhardt squarely at the center of nineteenth-century pietism. In Württemberg, a hot spot for pietism, there was no name more sweltering than Johann Blumhardt. Casting out demons, healing travelers from around the continent, and leading a revival will do that. And Christoph (the Younger) was an eyewitness to it all. If you think your middle and high school years were weird, try being the Younger, spending your Tuesday talking with a demoniac.

But the Younger found none of this to be reason enough to rebel. The Younger had no animosity for the Elder and his ministry, just admiration. So the Younger was happy to follow in his father's footsteps, seeking ordination and eventually taking over his father's Bad Boll ministry. The Younger had seen enough miracles to know that God acts in the world. The Younger knew more than anyone that his father was no charlatan; these were indeed the acts of a living God. The ministry of the Elder and the Younger Blumhardt is Barth's empirical touchstone that God can and still does act, even in the immanent frame of modernity, as God acted in the world of the Bible.

Yet, as the Younger took charge of his father's ministry, a great discontent came over him. God became a commodity. God became something to be *had*. Pietism, in the Younger's mind, had fallen into a kind of spiritualism, locking itself in the having-mode of action. Particularly after his father's death, people came from across Europe seeking to *have* miracles and spiritual experiences. As the nineteenth century neared its completion, pietism was being sucked further and further into the logic of individualism. The Younger worried that the people wanted ecstatic religious experiences more than they wanted to encounter the living God. They imagined life individualistically. And the people had no patience for God's *no*, wanting only the *yes* of a god made into an object of religion. They wanted to *have* individual spiritual experiences, possessing an ecstatic form of religion, rather than to follow the God of life into the deaths of the world. They wanted these experiences to take them out of the world, not further into the world God loves and acts within. This being taken out of the world meant pietism in the end could only be a flat form of religion, serving individual wants more than the living God. What really worried the Younger was that pietism seemed so satisfied with religion.

Out of both frustration and a desire for reform, the Younger made a turn. He did not turn away from pietism necessarily. Rather, the Younger took a strong turn away from religious individualism and its addiction to ecstatic experiences as the verification for God's action (as the way to have or possess God as religion). To escape individualism and religion, the Younger turned toward a ministry and a theology born out of a dialectic.

An Interlude for Immanence

The immanent frame is a complicated construction. Things are never straightforward. I suppose cultural imaginaries never are. For instance, the immanent frame pushes mystery and divine action away from the center of our imagination. With these gone, some people, now stuck in a material and natural world, cannot stand it.[11] They yearn and thirst for something more.[12] They race for ecstatic experiences. As the immanent frame pushes mystery and the arcane from the center the arcane pops up on the edges, to the frustration of elites running the closed-world structures of modernity. For instance, thanks to the internet, in a secular age like ours it comes in the form of conspiracy theories (which both the Left and the Right share) and other end-time predictions.[13]

The more the immanent frame outlines all things as natural and material, the more the occult and other forms of hyperspirituality (or just plain conspiracy) pop up at the edges. They can never again have their place at the center, at least as long as the immanent frame is in operation. But the occult, hyperspirituality, and arcane knowledge of conspiracy will not just disappear. These ideas are renewed on the edges of the immanent frame (as a kind of weak counterweight that nevertheless needs to feed off the immanent frame to exist at all).

These realities must concede to the core logic of immanence. As a pointy little rock in the shoe of the immanent frame, and though hating the reductions of immanence, they still need immanence to exist. Even radically strange spiritual practices and occult behaviors must concede to a logic that fits the immanent frame. To even survive on its edges these realities need to fuse to certain proteins of the immanent frame's embedded logic. The immanent frame cannot, and will not, sanction or support such experiences, always seeing them as dangerously unusual (even disgusting). Nevertheless, these experiences and practices can find traction with some if they are fundamentally, at their core, individualistic and religious. Forming themselves as inherently individualistic and religious, even as strange as they might be in the shadow of the immanent frame, gives them a foothold in modernity.

11. Taylor believes most can't. But most find ways other than hyperspiritualities and arcane occult behaviors to infuse the immanent frame with meaning and significance. See his discussion of the nova effect in *A Secular Age* (Cambridge, MA: Belknap, 2007), 299–313.

12. Most non-elites do, finding it in sports, consumerism, political tribalism, etc.

13. For example, see one *Atlantic* article as an example of how in a world without mystery, conspiracy becomes a new immanent-frame return to the mysterious, the hidden, and the arcane. See Adrienne LaFrance, "The Prophecies of Q," *Atlantic*, June 2020, https://www.theatlantic.com/magazine/archive/2020/06/qanon-nothing-can-stop-what-is-coming/610567.

These hyperspiritual realities are individualistic in the sense of being the choice of solely an individual's will and part of this individual's own authentic pursuits.[14] As long as the agent is free in his or her own expenditure of energy, such realities are considered weird but tolerated. The immanent frame and its ethic of authenticity will say, "That's weird that you speak in tongues or practice black magic in your backyard, but if that's *your* thing I guess it's cool."[15] Late modernity has a much easier time with vision boards and *The Secret* than with Hasidic Judaism and the Amish. The former are free choices of the individual; the latter appear to restrict individual choice in calls for collective obedience.

But of course, it's not just the individualism that gives such realities their place. There is also a sense that while they are free individual choices, they are religious. These realities are religious in the sense of being a private or personal decision unrelated to public institutions and the structures of common life.[16] If they are religious or if they are a religion in this private sense, they have a place (including tax breaks in some countries), but only on the edges of the immanent frame. They are not at the center of life but pushed to the periphery. They will never be able to vie for the center of our cultural imaginary, never really be able to make claims about what it means to live in the world. The immanent frame would need to be upended for them to return to the center and to frame the structures and institutional shape of life.[17] As long as spiritualities and arcane pursuits are on the edges, playing by the rules

14. This is why, legally, the government is not allowed to sanction any form of religion but will come down on those labeled cults. Usually you need a law to be broken, like the stockpile of weapons, but the public support is bound in a sense that the individuals are being manipulated, not willfully choosing such spiritual religion. These cults are also dangerous because they don't play by the rules of modern religion. They demand more than modern forms of religion do—they demand more than just choice and association/participation.

15. What makes this okay or cool is not just a simple relativism but a rich kind of late-modern ethics. What's cool has to consider equal mutual regard and respond correctly to politics of recognition. It is not necessarily a free-for-all. Rather, my point is that there is reason to the open and loose "That's cool."

16. The reader should remember that religion is fundamentally redefined in modernity. It is no longer the most public of activities holding society together, as it was in the *ancien régime*. But inside modernity, religion shifts to a private affiliation that is separated from public institutional structures.

17. In *The Politics of Virtue: Post-Liberalism and the Human Future* (London: Rowan & Littlefield, 2016), John Milbank and Adrian Pabst wonder if one of the reasons for militant atheists coming to the fore is that they sense that religion is returning. They fight because the immanent frame may be at risk. It is also interesting here to think of Douglas John Hall's plea in the 1980s and 1990s for the mainline churches to embrace their disestablishment—in other words, to recognize there was no way or reason to try to find their way back to the center of society. Hall told mainline churches, now disestablished, to avoid religion and live. Hall was indeed a second-generation dialectical theologian, though it is Luther more than Barth or

of individualism and religion, they can exist in the immanent frame. Somehow, by playing by these rules, being subjected to the edges but nevertheless using individualism and religion to find footing gives these perspectives the hubris that they can *have* God through their individualistic experiences and religious practices.[18] The hubris of both pietist and liberal forms of religion is born from religion's avoidance of the core dialectic—neither deals with the real experiences of life and death.

When Rivals Go Bad

In the 1880s the great discontent arrived for the Younger. With his father's death, a new generation of pietists seemed obsessed with individualistic religion. They wanted individual healing and believed that religion, bound in certain technical practices, could force God to expend God's energy however they wished. God became a reservoir of power who assisted individuals in getting what they wanted—as long as they used the right religion. By the late 1880s the Younger's discontent was reaching its apex. The Younger sensed that something stank badly in Württemberg.

To illustrate this, let's shift from the late 1880s to the late 1990s. During my senior year at a historically pietist university, there was talk of revival. Other Christian schools had already welcomed so-called revivals. Yet the content of such an occurrence was vague. It seemed to encompass long periods of emotional singing, hand-raising, impromptu speeches of devotion ("I really . . ." "I'm just yearning for . . ." "I just know . . ." "I just believe . . ."), and *a lot* of crying. There'd been chatter about how our school too needed revival. We (as individuals alone, but nevertheless passionately) were to pray for this revival. If enough of us individuals prayed and really wanted it (and if the music was good enough), revival would rain down on us.

Sure enough, one early spring night at our Sunday evening vespers service, the downpour of tears came. The forty-five-minute vespers service lasted five hours. Many of us were confused. Not necessarily by the never-ending three-chord cry-fest sing-along, but by our own individualistic subjectivity. Was this emotional effervescence from God or from us? Did our prayers bring this or did our own wanting it? Was this a gift from God or something we were manufacturing? Was this *God* at all? And if so, why did God want us crying

Bultmann that mobilizes his thought. See Douglas John Hall, *The Reality of the Gospel and the Unreality of the Churches* (Philadelphia: Westminster, 1975).

18. McCormack nicely locates Barth's theology in opposition to individualism. See *Karl Barth's Critically Realistic Dialectical Theology*, 140–43.

for hours in a dark gym? If this pietist revival was hope and the invitation to life, why did it feel like being a hamster on a wheel?

After a few days of "revival," students started policing each other's practice. People ranked each other's religion, contending that revival would continue only if we were heartfelt and devoted in our religious practice. Students told each other, "We [we = individuals] really, *really* need to want this." The "this" seemed to be a form of deep expressive religion, absent any dialectic. Continuing this revival would require us to focus all our attention on our own worship procedures and our own individual selves. After three straight nights of crying and outhearing the Spirit from one another, some of us felt trapped. Those questions above rushed to the surface. The individualistic religion was sucking the life from us.

Many of us were feeling a discontent not dissimilar to the Younger's a century earlier. To cope with the unease, some doubled down on the individualistic religion, believing only more individualistic self-commitment would pacify the discontent of individualistic religion. For others, the hyperexpressivism eventually (even years later) pushed them to liberalism (whether in a mainline theist style or more atheistic style). Feeling embarrassed by what felt like emotional hysteria, the individualism of liberalism—with a more reasoned, levelheaded religion—welcomed them. The revival mainly left discontent in its wake. The lack of a dialectic, even inside religious passion, didn't seem to move us closer to a God who is the God of life. It flattened life into a rigid religious mold, making us overly concerned about ourselves. The discontent was real.

Ironically, the more devoted and invested the person is, the more acute the discontent seems. This is why it's remarkably common for devoted pietist parents to produce liberal children. In most mainline denominations, the most liberal pastors and leaders are the children of conservative pietist parents (who themselves had a time of devotion). Late-modern pietism seems to have a propensity for making theological liberals.[19] The irony is that though pietism opposes liberalism, seeing it as a ferocious rival, something inherent within pietism produces theologically liberal children.

This radical shift is easy because it exchanges one individualistic religion for another. Those who flip from a rigid pietism to a rigid liberalism almost always imagine their move as heroic. And while it may cost them dearly (I wish not to

19. Without these children who have said goodbye to pietism and evangelicalism to depart to the mainline, the mainline would have very little coming-of-age leadership. Right now the mainline is mostly getting its future leaders from discontented evangelicals. For over a generation the mainline has struggled to produce its own up-and-coming leadership. There are some homegrown leaders, of course, but not as many as there are refugees from pietism and evangelicalism. This is a major issue the mainline will need to face.

overlook that), it's actually not much of a departure. Pietism and liberalism are distinct from one another on many levels, but not at the substructure. Both rest their footings on individualism and religion.[20] They have different cultural and political visions and goals, but it's individualistic religion, in avoidance of a dialectic, that operationalized both.

In the late 1880s, it looked as though the Younger's discontent would push him onto the well-worn path of pietist children becoming liberal adults. The Younger looked as if he'd become a forefather to the many ex-evangelicals that populate Twitter in late modernity. But the Younger recognized that this would only be replacing one individualistic religion for another. Instead, the Younger decided to take a dialectical turn, which would deeply inspire Barth. Both the Younger and Barth see life as inextricably dialectical.

Into the Dialectic

The Württemberg pietism that followed the Younger's father was centered on releasing captives from evil forces as signs of God's kingdom come. I'll tell the Elder's story in more detail in the next chapter—it's wild and crazy, particularly for late-modern Protestants! But what's important now is to see that the Younger didn't abandon, revolt from, or deconstruct this commitment to releasing captives. Release from captivity by the victory of Jesus remained central to the Younger, as it was to the Elder. In his discontent the Younger actually recommitted to this. But in doing so, he also took on an emphasis different from his father's.

The Younger asserted that people were captive to, and needed release from, something not just subjective and individualistic but social and material as well. The Younger took a further step into the world, recognizing that a living God is a God who brings life to the world, dialectically bearing the world's suffering so new life might come. The Younger saw that those in the world needed release from the captivity of poverty and the dehumanization of factory work. They needed life. But this would come only by bearing the world's impossibilities—not by individual commitment or religious energy. To truly love the world meant not *only* proclaiming the means of healing but also bearing the suffering of loss and brokenness.

Recognizing this (as mentioned in chap. 10), the Younger entered the social-ist movement, eventually becoming an elected official of the Social Democratic

---

20. This is Barth's belief, according to Busch. Nancey Murphy believes this is true at the philosophical level as well. See her *Beyond Liberalism and Fundamentalism* (Valley Forge, PA: Trinity Press International, 1996).

Party (although he had turned away from the party by the time Barth met him in 1915; both turned first toward and then away from the Social Democratic Party, and then both made the more fundamental turn toward a dialectic). But this move into socialism was *not* a departure from pietistic religion for liberal religion. Unlike with Naumann, whom Barth met at Peter's wedding, this wasn't the exchanging of one individualistic religion for another. Naumann didn't think theological substance mattered much at all. What mattered was the embracing of religion as a way to help individuals make it through the war and allow the party to take power by capturing the individual's commitment. Remember that Barth basically spit out his beer in response to this at Peter's wedding reception (as discussed in chap. 10).

The Younger, on the other hand, entered socialism as an outgrowth of a particular dialectical theological commitment that opposed individualistic religion. This dialetical turn kept the brisk winds of the Younger's discontent from flipping the colors of his flag from pietist to liberal. Barth follows this dialetical turn in shaking himself loose from the individualistic religions of both pietism and liberalism to embrace life.

Life is birthed inside the tension of the dialectic. Barth heralds this. As a relation to the world in the being-mode, life *is* dialectical. Rosa, too, has taught us this. Rosa reveals that life is a relationship with otherness. And otherness can be encountered only dialectically (as open and closed, as near to hand and completely elusive).

Barth's own pastoral imagination between 1915 and the writing of the *Römerbriefs* is shaped by something akin to the three little bears. Barth comes to believe that Pastor Hermann Kutter is too bent on waiting for God, while Pastor Leonhard Ragaz is too fixed on practical forms of human action. But Blumhardt the Younger is just right. What makes the Younger just right *is not* a kind of weak concession of a third way or even a synthesis of both positions (an attempt at peacemaking by claiming they're both right). Rather, the Younger is just right in being more radical. What makes the Younger profound in Barth's mind is that the Younger is fully and unrelentingly dialectical. The Younger holds that waiting is acting, as acting is waiting, while acting is not waiting and waiting is not acting.

Barth sees that the turn that escapes the individualism of religion faces and embraces the dialectic, seeks God dialectically, and embraces life as dialectically structured. This is more than an intellectual position: it is the way of relating to the world, as the way to enter and receive life. Following the Younger and Barth, we're wagering that in the immanent frame, only a dialectical disposition to ministry and church life will escape the boney clutches of individualistic religion to encounter a living God, who gives life (out of death). The dialectic is the way to peer into the world, to recognize that the God of the Bible is still unveiling Godself in the immanent frame. The dialectic is the angle of vision that escapes the immanent frame's obstructions to see God unveiled in the world. The dialectic is the way to find life by losing it (Matt. 16:25).

The Immanent Frame

It's only a dialectical theology that allows us to remember that God is God, wholly other than us, and yet to encounter this God as living, waiting for this God by joyfully embracing life. The life is in the dialectic. It's through the dialectic that we're swept up into life. Rosa, phenomenologically, and Mozart, in his own music, witness to this. Life is freedom from being captured and reduced in the having-mode. But we can only escape the having-mode and find life by embracing its dialectical shape. Life is encountered dialectically, and the God who is life can only be known in a dialectical manner.

Barth, following the Younger, believes individualistic religion is ultimately lifeless, because it takes us out of the world—and into a dark gym of subjectivism where college kids sing three-chord choruses over and over again. It encourages a break in our relation to the world. When this relation is broken the free gift of being in the world is turned into a pursuit to have the world, seeking God outside the world through religion. When the church stops seeking the life of others in the world, it loses the God who is God, who brings life to the world. This is the heart of the Younger's discontent.[21]

The immanent frame pushes Protestant faith to the immanent frame's edges by making it a religion for individuals. The immanent frame discourages the church away from the world by making it feel tenuous enough to have to fight for its own life instead of the life of others in the world. The Younger enters into socialism to escape this modern Protestant ecclesial iron cage.

The immanent frame does this by pushing the church to the edges and making it into individualistic religion. During the dawn of modernity the dialectic was written out of the dominant forms of Protestantism. Cultural Protestantism could exist, even look similar to its radical form, just without the dialectic. Protestantism as a civic religion could be tamed enough not to bite the immanent frame. But to do the taming, Protestantism's dialectical teeth would need to be removed. What makes Protestantism radical is its dialectic. Without its dialectic, Protestantism is a particularly flat and

21. Hear this in the Younger's own words in Christoph Blumhardt, *Action in Waiting* (Farmington, PA: Plough, 1998), 54.

vapid form of religion, absent even bells and smells.[22] But to have its safe place in the immanent frame, Protestantism needed to forget (even dislike) the confession that life is found in death, grace in judgment, community in confession, justification in sinners, and that being lost is the only way to be found. Protestantism needed to forget a crucified God who promises life out of death—or indeed that the only way to find God is to look for God unveiled in those places in the world where God should not be found: death and loss.

Protestantism without the dialectic becomes just a wispy religion that the immanent frame can push to its edges and use as it wishes. It was not its loss of cultural power or pure doctrine that made Protestantism wispy (these confused interpretations are often offered today for the ills of Protestantism). Rather, in losing the dialectic, Protestantism loses the world.[23] Protestantism in its best forms strips itself of cultic concerns for the sake of seeking God in the world. What makes Protestantism radical and beautiful is not its cultic rituals or fresco ceilings but its claims that the living God is encountered in the dirty, lowly, and beautifully mundane places of the world. Protestantism claims that resonance is not bound in religion but in relating to the world. The dialectic gives us the vision to see that God is fully in and for the world, while being completely other than the world. This living God gives life to the world. The dialectic allows us to confess a God who saves the world, freeing the captives of death imposed by the world, by suffering and dying in the world because God loves the world. Without the dialectic God is made into the echo of our own voice, bouncing weakly off the walls of our self-involved churches.

To lose the world, as individualistic religion inevitably does, is to lose a living God (settling for only religion). To lose the world is to lose the steering column of Protestantism. Without the world, Protestantism is aimless because it loses the vision of a living God who acts for the sake of the world's life. A living God brings life, not necessarily to the church but to the world. It is only as the church is in relation to the world (in resonance with the world) that the church is able to find life. When Woz arrives (along with the Misfits),

22. Protestantism itself admits it's not a rich cultic religion, especially in its Calvinist and Anabaptist forms. There are no intricate frescoes or deep ritualized forms. Protestantism sought to have its weight not in its own distinct culture but in its dialectic that committed it to the world. Once Protestantism loses this dialectic—a profound actuality of contemplating that God dies for the sake of life, that God completely judges and completely justifies—then Protestantism becomes the most boring kind of religion possible.

23. This is basically Bonhoeffer's claim and constructive edge in his ethics. It's an ethics that asks, What is the will of God? And the will of God is always for suffering with, for advocating for, for even acquiring guilt to be with the world. Bonhoeffer's ethics is an ethics that returns Protestantism to the world and therefore to its dialectic. *Ethics* (Minneapolis: Fortress, 2005), 47–75.

entering an event shaped by the dialectic of confession and celebration, little Saint John the Baptist is filled with life. The dialectic allows the church to find its life by remembering (and confessing) that it can never be the star of its own story. The church finds its life by losing its life in life-giving, resonant relations with the world. The church finds life here because here, in the world, the God who is God brings life.

The world finds life by receiving the ministry of God, which always bears the marks of the dialectic. Life is discovered when the dialectic does its work, when God kills and makes alive (uncomfortable words that both Luther and Calvin use to express the necessity of the dialectic that has so often been pulled out of Protestantism). Inside this dialectic, individualism is judged and we are invited to remember that we are creatures who need relations to one another and the world. When God says *no* to all our religion and is found ministering life out of death in the world, we confess something new. In new relational encounters, we find new life. Life is inseparable from this dialectic. The centrality of the dialectic (the no of death and loss and the yes of new possibility) makes Mozart, more than Bach, a witness to life.[24]

This all means that the church, in both its vision of itself and its ministry to the world, must be imagined dialectically. Inside the immanent frame, the dialectic becomes the way to release faith and theology from religion and its imprisonment at the edges. The dialectic, as we'll see more in the following chapters, becomes the way inside the immanent frame to enter a lived and living transcendence.[25] Without the dialectic, Protestantism and its ecclesiology falls into individualistic religion. And transcendence becomes either flattened into religion (liberalism) or made into an individualistic ecstatic expressivism (pietism). The dialectic gives us a way of imagining transcendence inside the immanent frame, because—as we'll see—the dialectic is the shape of divine action itself.

Coughing Up the Dialectic

Individualistic religion has been the deadly virus infecting Protestantism inside the conditions of modernity. Barth doesn't create this dialectic (it goes back to Paul, Athanasius, and German mystics such as Meister Eckhart, Martin Luther, and the Younger, as we'll soon see), but Barth is the first, with such unrelenting

24. Here I'm drawing from Busch's discussion of how Barth sees life. Busch turns to the Younger in seeking to describe how Barth sees life in relation to pietism. See *Karl Barth and the Pietists*, 32–33.

25. Lived transcendence is a concept developed by Ray S. Anderson in his *Historical Transcendence and the Reality of God* (Grand Rapids: Eerdmans, 1975).

passion, to set the dialectic loose inside modernity and its immanent frame.[26] Barth becomes the great modern reviver of Protestantism. But *not* because he purifies its doctrines, fights for Protestantism's religious status, or converts individuals to its institutional structures. Rather, Pastor Barth is the reviver of Protestantism because, while deeply inside the modern immanent frame, he returns to the dialectical heart of Protestantism.[27] Barth recognizes that the dialectic is needed more than ever inside the immanent frame.

The immanent frame flattens all forms of Protestant faith, seeking to turn all Protestant faith into the individualistic religions of pietism or liberalism. Barth ventures that the only way of preventing this imposition and allowing Protestant faith to not be flattened into individualistic religion is to commit without relent to the dialectic. Protestantism can be revived (even saved from pietism and liberalism) only by returning to its lost dialectical core.

Letting go of this dialectical core is the great temptation that Protestantism faces in every generation. Every generation of Protestants is tempted to cough up the dialectic and exchange it for an individualistic and civic religion. Unfortunately, many generations have succumbed to this temptation, imagining it possible to do theology and ministry without the dialectic. This may never have been more true than in the German generations right before Barth in the nineteenth and early twentieth centuries, and maybe now again in the American generations of the early twenty-first century.

Unfortunately, coughing up the dialectic always seems to lead Protestantism into trying to be something it just wasn't built to be—a cultic religion bound in institutional power. Our practical ecclesiologies bear these marks of assumed cultic religious power. Until the world arrived in the form of Woz, Saint John the Baptist believed that its life rested in growing its resources and winning relevance. These objectives of resources and relevance had neither the vision nor the patience for the dialectic. It then becomes assumed that the church's life is *not* bound in its dialectical relations to the world but in winning in the cult of cool and building institutional stability.[28]

26. Of course, I don't assume that Barth came up with this ex nihilo. Others, such as his teacher Wilhelm Herrmann, had pointed to this, and the Luther renaissance in Berlin led by Karl Holl was bringing this dialectic back to the minds of a new generation (Bonhoeffer being one). But it was Barth who so creatively and without caution wheeled this dialectic in relation to modernity. Herrmann and Holl see the dialectic but try to synthesize it within liberalism and its religion. Barth sees that the dialectic can only really be if it judges and radically upends religion in its pietistic and liberal forms.

27. Here is a taste of the dialectic in *Römerbrief II*: "Faith is neither religion nor irreligion, neither sacred nor profane; it is always both together." Barth, *Epistle to the Romans*, 128.

28. It may be true that the dialectic cannot grow megachurches. If the objective is to be a huge church—run like a business—then coughing up the dialectic is perhaps a strategic move. The

The Dialectical Savant

There are a number of influences on Barth that move him in this bold dialectical direction. Yet no one more profoundly articulates this dialectical direction than Barth. You can see this particularly in reading *Römerbrief II*. On every page you're shocked by the unrelenting and mesmerizing dialectic in action. The book can feel so strange, because the dialectic is never ceasing. The reader is never given a breath from being slingshotted from one side to the other (from death to life, from impossibility to new possibility, from the church of Esau to the church of Jacob, and more).

The unrelenting dialectic has led readers from the very beginning to not know where to locate Barth. For some readers he seems too pietistic and to others antipietistic. To still others he appears liberal or antiliberal. Barth cannot be located in any of the places of individualistic religion, because following the Younger, Barth is using the dialectic as both the hammer to break all forms of religion and the crowbar to free faith from individualism. Barth's dialectical performance stands outside both pietism and liberalism. In *Römerbrief I* and *II*, Pastor Barth masters the dialectic, rebirthing it in modern theology as a way of seeking God in the immanent frame.

Even in modernity, Barth wasn't the first to take this dialectical turn in ministry or theology. As James Clerk Maxwell was to Michael Faraday in the study of electricity, or as Vincent Van Gogh was to Paul Gauguin in late-nineteenth-century painting, so Barth was to the Younger in theology. Decades before Barth turned to socialism as an expression of pastoral commitment, it was the Younger who embraced the dialectic as the way to seek life in the world by seeking the living God who is God. The Younger saw that Protestantism needed to return to the dialectic.[29] Like Maxwell and Van Gogh, who drew from the style of their predecessors and then mastered their

---

dialectic crucifies all means of trying to turn faith into religion. Huge churches most often have found a way to master religion, even in stripping away religion. The seeker-sensitive movement of the 1980s and 1990s (which still exists) thought it was stripping away religion. It did this not through the dialectic but as a marketing strategy, meaning it succumbed all the more to the individualistic. It made consumeristic Christianity into a cultic form of religion. This is where Protestantism becomes gross. Where the Catholic cultic forms are bound in mystery, ritual, and ancient practice, the Protestant so-called cultic forms come to match market economies. Hence, huge megachurches look and operate like malls.

29. Charles Moore discusses this dialectic in the Younger, saying, "As Leonhard Ragaz once put it in summarizing Blumhardt's thought, 'From religion to God's kingdom, from the church to a redeemed world, from me to God.' This all-encompassing vision ultimately led Blumhardt back to Bad Boll." Introduction to *Action in Waiting*, by Blumhardt, xxv.

style or thought beyond what their predecessor could imagine, so Barth was with the Younger.[30]

The Younger, as the prince of pietism, took a dialectical turn and escaped the traps of individualism and religion by turning to what he called *Sterbet*, to dying. In the late 1880s the Younger asserted that we can find life only in the living God, by being found by the God who lives by dying. It is only by embracing the dialectic at its deepest level (of life and dying) that we can escape the idolatry of religion built on the idol of the individual. To understand how this dialectic can shape our practical ecclesiology, the next chapter explores the Younger's pastoral embrace of *Sterbet*.

For the Younger, as for Saint John the Baptist, it is inside a "great pause" that the necessity of this dialectic becomes clear. By embracing the dialectic inside a "great pause," Saint John the Baptist finds life and is one step closer to the possibility of being found by God. But to see how, we have to examine how the Younger comes to see the importance of the dialectic through his own "great pause." The Younger is forced to pause and open himself to the dialectic of life out of dying, because Vetter Hansjörg died.

30. Barth speaks of the Younger's dialectical genius in "Past and Future: Friedrich Naumann and Christoph Blumhardt," in *Beginnings of Dialectical Theology*, ed. James Robinson (Richmond: John Knox, 1968), 44.

15

A True Ghost Story and the Birth of Watchwords

The Younger's discontent with pietism was growing throughout the decade of the 1880s. But the discontent turned into a crisis in 1888. The Younger described this as a "great pause."[1] The Younger taught Barth the importance of waiting and how waiting can be a form of action.[2] In 1888, the Younger does something very hard for late-modern people to do who find themselves in discontent—he waits. He pauses. He doesn't push into the having-mode. He simply pauses and leans into being. He leans into the loss of being.

The great pause wasn't welcomed. It was not a break intended to clear his head. Rather, the pause was deeply painful. The great pause fell on the Younger because Vetter Hansjörg had just died.

Vetter Hansjörg was the Herbert Grapp of the Blumhardts' ministry. The warm use of "Vetter," which means "uncle," shows how important Hansjörg was to the Younger. Uncle Hansjörg was the last living member of the Elder Blumhardt's Möttlingen congregation. It was in Möttlingen, in the early 1840s, that everything changed for the Blumhardts. The Elder had come to the congregation in Möttlingen in 1838. In those first few years of ministry

---

1. He said this in a report to *Vertrauliche Blätter* (a kind of newsletter to supporters). For this discussion, I'm leaning completely on Simon Zahl's brilliant text *Pneumatology and Theology of the Cross in the Preaching of Christoph Friedrich Blumhardt: The Holy Spirit between Wittenberg and Azusa Street* (London: T&T Clark, 2010), esp. 40.

2. Hermann Kutter had emphasized waiting, but he was not able to embrace the dialectical nature of waiting as action as the Younger did. This is what inspired Barth.

nothing remarkable occurred. The Elder was a faithful pastor, doing better than just plodding along, but there was nothing spectacular about his leadership or the congregation. Up until March 1842, the most exciting thing to happen was the Elder's involvement in the organization of a new hymnal. But that changed, and shockingly so, when a young woman, who just happened to be Hansjörg's sister, started manifesting the oddest behaviors. And I must warn you, it was odd behavior. What follows is a story of demons and possession. Your own immanent-frame-imposed alarms may go off. But if we can hang in there, we can learn something important.

The Story of the Elder

The young woman's name was Gottliebin Dittus. She lived with her two sisters and Hansjörg in a run-down lower apartment of a narrow house. The death of the children's parents had thrust them into poverty, forcing them into far from ideal living accommodations. But they soon found out why the rent was so cheap. The walls, not just in need of a paint job, began to knock and creak uncontrollably. Then sounds of muffled movements started coming through the walls. Soon Gottliebin started seeing things. At first, it was just shapes and light, but then, bang! She was thrust to the floor unconscious.

The immanent frame, while still under some construction, was in place and operative enough to lead Gottlieb's siblings to keep the haunting undercover. This was too odd a thing to tell anyone about. But Gottliebin's condition worsened. After being knocked to the ground, she fell ill and wasn't recovering. Finally, Gottliebin's siblings called for Pastor Blumhardt. The Elder was no vampire hunter or ghostbuster. When the Elder visited, he found Gottliebin in bed. She didn't even look at him when he said hello, ignoring his greeting. The Elder left figuring this was just an ill-tempered young girl.

Weeks passed and things got weirder, soon becoming uncontrollable. By April 1842, the Elder learned from Gottliebin's relatives that the poltergeist noises had become so loud the neighbors could hear them. And Gottliebin herself started seeing the figure of a woman who had died two years previously. She saw this woman carrying a dead child in her arms. This woman told Gottliebin she could find no peace and asked for a piece of paper, promising not to return if she was given one.

Like you are while reading this, people were freaked out but also deeply intrigued. Why does a ghost need a piece of paper? What kind of note does a specter need to write? The intrigue was almost as high as the terror. Gottliebin's relatives returned to Pastor Blumhardt for help. Giving him this new information, they wondered whether they should ask this ghost lady why she needed a piece of paper. The Elder now knew that this case was much more than a young woman with a bad attitude. But it was also something that didn't alarm the Elder enough to make him rush to Gottliebin's side. The Elder advised Gottliebin not to talk with the figure and to earnestly pray. Like prescribing cranberry juice for a slight urinary tract infection, the Elder figured that with this advice "the matter would go away by itself."[3]

But it didn't.

The Darkness Ascends

Gottliebin continued to see the figure. By mid-May the noises had increased. Eventually, after some investigation, objects were found hidden in the house: chalk, salt, bones, and coins wrapped in blackened paper. The Elder contended that these objects had been more than likely used in some superstitious incantation that sought healing. The Elder, not an anti-modern man in any sense, thought there might be some kind of scientific explanation.[4] The Elder investigated further, and from the information Gottliebin received from the figure, discovered a connection to Mr. Widow Weiss, the previous owner of the building where Gottliebin now lay haunted. The Elder was shocked "when he [found] that the spirit's account agree[d] 'to a hairbreadth' with the confession made to [Weiss] by the woman who died in 1840."[5] Weiss said this woman (who he said was of "ill reputation") had called for him as she was dying, telling him exactly what the spirit had told Gottliebin. This woman, who now seemed to be tormenting Gottliebin, had died the next day.

Through May things just got worse. On June 2—one day after the birth of Christoph the Younger—the Elder, the mayor, and some members of the village council arrived at Gottliebin's house unannounced. As they entered they were met by loud blows, like a strong wind. The Elder set some men at posts outside Gottliebin's room, telling them to pray. When they gathered around Gottliebin's bed and sang "In Jesus I Abide," an even more forceful blow occurred. They sent Gottliebin to a neighbor and investigated the room.

3. Dieter Ising, *Johann Christoph Blumhardt: A New Biography* (Eugene, OR: Cascade Books, 2009), 164.

4. Though, to be honest, in this age, even the scientific had a sense of occult allure. The Elder talked with some scientists who were working on hypnosis and the spirit world. Not something you can get tenure for today, but in the 1840s it was legit. For more on this, see Jason Josephson-Storm, *The Myth of Disenchantment: Magic, Modernity, and the Birth of the Human Sciences* (Chicago: University of Chicago Press, 2017).

5. Ising, *Johann Christoph Blumhardt*, 165.

Under the floorboards in the area of the blowing they found more blackened paper and a pot full of bird bones.

By late June things were getting even worse. On June 26 the Elder grabbed Gottliebin's hands, placing her fingers together, as she lay unconscious. The Elder then shouted in her ear, "Place your hands together and pray, 'Lord Jesus, help me!' We have seen long enough what the devil can do; now we desire to see also, what Jesus can do!"[6] Gottliebin prayed and found peace for the evening.

New Course toward Prayer

Only now did Gottliebin's situation move to the top of the Elder's list of pastoral duties! At one level this seems absurd. The Elder had seen enough creepy strangeness to keep me up for weeks, sleeping with the lights on for months. But at another level, this is not absurd at all. It shows the depth and maturity of the Elder's pastoral imagination. He never chased sensation, never became captive to any form of subjectivity. This kind of reserved pietism, the Younger contended, was lost in the late 1880s. The Elder never allowed evil to have nearly the power of God. As a good modern pastor, the Elder figured there were immanent ways to help Gottliebin. But those immanent methods now seemed exhausted.

The next evening the Elder visited Gottliebin again. This meeting confirmed without doubt that Gottliebin was possessed by a demon. The Elder himself became the target of the evil force's rage. Gottliebin "clench[ed] her fists and [made] threatening gestures" to him.[7] The Elder prayed; the convulsing stopped. But then Gottliebin communicated that she saw the woman again. And then, like a scene from a horror movie (think *The Exorcist* meets *The Village*), Gottliebin was overtaken again and a strange voice came out of her, speaking of violence.

It's here that the similarities with a Hollywood horror movie end. The Elder refused to don a cape and enter the ring to battle with the devil as an exorcist. "Blumhardt conduct[ed] no exorcistic ceremonies; he [did] not recite prescribed texts, such as the *Rituale Romanum*."[8] The Elder worried that to do so would be to concede to the superstition of religion. It was superstitious religion that had put Gottliebin, and even more the figure that haunted her, in trouble in the first place. Healing, the Elder believed, would not come from

6. Ising, *Johann Christoph Blumhardt*, 168.
7. Ising, *Johann Christoph Blumhardt*, 168.
8. Ising, *Johann Christoph Blumhardt*, 168.

religion but from a relationship of care (call it a kind of resonance). The devil hates the world because God loves it. Healing would come by reconnecting with her and reconnecting her to the world. It wouldn't be the violent wrestling with a demon that released Gottliebin. Rather, the Elder believed it would be the embracing of Gottliebin's humanity in love that would deliver her. The Elder chose not direct exorcism but pastoral care done in and through prayer as his modus operandi.

"Usually, [the Elder uttered] a free prayer and encourage[d] Gottliebin to pray also." As Dieter Ising says, "The result is that we see not an exorcism but the spiritual counselor accompanying the sufferer."[9] This approach meant that Gottliebin and the Elder had a long road ahead of them. There would be no quick solution.

They prayed together for the next year and half. Gottliebin's experiences of manifesting evil became freakier as the months went on. Blumhardt now figured there were many different tortured souls attacking Gottliebin. One speaker, a male voice coming out of Gottliebin, told the Elder that he was the owner of the house before Widow Weiss. Blumhardt decided to ask him why he could not find peace. The voice confessed that he had murdered two children and buried them in a field. The Elder told him to pray. He said he couldn't. The Elder asked him if he knew Jesus who forgives sins.

He answered, "That name I cannot hear."

"Are you alone?" the Elder asked.

The voice responded, "No!"

"Who is with you?"

Hesitatingly, the voice responded, "The Most Wicked One."[10]

The Elder decided it wasn't wise to allow them to speak from this point on. As Jesus did, he hushed them. If they would not be quiet, the Elder would leave and return later. Can you imagine the Elder returning home early and his wife asking, "Why are you back so soon? I thought you'd be gone until 6 p.m." "That was the plan, but Gottliebin's demons wouldn't shut up, so I left early."

Humor aside, Gottliebin's torment continued.

The Coming Victor

In March 1843, Gottliebin's circumstances appeared to be turning in the right direction. The ministry of prayer was slowly releasing her. But Gottliebin was

9. Ising, *Johann Christoph Blumhardt*, 169.
10. See Blumhardt, *Krankheitsgeschichte* (Göttingen: Vandenhoeck & Ruprecht, 1978), 42.

far from free. The culmination, and victory of freedom and healing, would not come until Christmas.

Like any pastor, Johann Blumhardt was in his busiest time of the year during Christmas 1843. He had four sermons, four Bible studies, confirmation, a baptism, and children's catechism to concern himself with between December 24 and 28. Not an ideal time to add fighting the devil to your to-do list. But so it happened.

Word came that Gottliebin's siblings were now also being tormented. Katharina, Gottliebin's sister, manifested a voice that claimed to be an angel of Satan. As they prayed, the demon screamed from the mouth of Katharina so loudly the whole village could hear it. Blumhardt shares in his own words what happened next: "Finally came the most striking moment, which no one can sufficiently imagine who was not eye- and ear-witness. About two o'clock in the morning the supposed angel of Satan bellowed, whereupon the maiden [Katharina] inclined her head and upper body far back over the chair rest with a voice that one might scarcely reckon possible for a human throat; the words were: 'Jesus is Victor! Jesus is Victor!' . . . Now it seemed that the power and strength of the demon were more and more broken with every moment."[11]

From this moment Gottliebin and her siblings were free. Gottliebin still had some health issues. But as the Elder Blumhardt prayed in the name of Jesus who is Victor, she was healed and recovered completely. Like the Gerasene demoniac in Luke 8, the assurance that indeed she'd been healed was that after the demons left her, she was found fully clothed and in her right mind. Gottliebin, like the demoniac in Luke 8, was back in relation with the world. Soon she began teaching kindergarten. And like Mary Magdalene did with Jesus (who had seven demons cast from her, Luke 8:2), Gottliebin followed Jesus by staying connected to the Blumhardts for the rest of her life. Gottliebin and her family, particularly Hansjörg, eventually became part of the Blumhardt family. Gottliebin became the personal teacher of the Blumhardt children.

The Watchword

After the experience of Christmas 1843 and the evil angel's cacophonic proclamation "Jesus is Victor!" these words became the center of the Elder's ministry. Everything now revolved around them. "Jesus is Victor!" became what the Elder Blumhardt called his "watchword." A *watchword* is defined as a maxim that encompasses an individual or group's most central belief

---

11. See Blumhardt, *Krankheitsgeschichte*, 75–76.

or aim. *Watchword* has its etymology in military use. The one on watch has the *watchword*, a kind of password that orientates the watcher and anyone he encounters to what the watcher is watching for. The watcher watches for something, but always does his watching on behalf of someone. The watcher with a watchword serves another. The Elder now saw his ministry as being on watch. The watchword was the shape of divine action he was leading his congregation into waiting to encounter. The congregation's watching was a way of loving the world by serving and ministering to the world.[12]

From March until Christmas 1843, the Elder felt that his ministry to Gottliebin and her family was to take his watch and pray. After the Gottliebin incident and receiving his watchword, the Elder contended that pastoral ministry was leading the church to take its watch in and for the world. On watch, those watching cannot seek to possess anything.[13] The watchers with a watchword must just *be* present watching, free from the having-mode of action. The watchword gives waiting its attention. The one on watch must be waiting for what she's watching for. She doesn't watch bored and disengaged but attentively watches with the watchword that directs and shapes her waiting and watching.[14] The church acts by waiting with its watchword, attentive to the world, readied and formed by the watchword to witness to God's action in the world.[15]

Before Woz arrived, Saint John the Baptist was adrift, even with Luke's work to give them a mission statement, because they had lost their watchword. A mission or vision statement is important for a congregation, but it can only be helpful if it is subordinate to (even crucified by) the congregation's watchword. A mission or vision statement is about the congregation. It can mislead the congregation, if it's not careful, into thinking the church is the star of its own story. A mission or vision statement without a watchword can become just an organized or efficient way of expending energy to have resources, moving the church far away from the being-mode of divine action and the encounter with resonance. A mission or vision statement without a watchword slides into a false form of human action.

12. For a nice discussion of where the Elder fits in relation to the Lutheran critique of Schwärmer (a kind of enthusiastic practice and perspective of faith that Luther found problematic), see Zahl, *Pneumatology and Theology of the Cross*, 103–7.

13. Johann Friedrich Zündel discusses the change in the Elder after Christmas. See *Johann Christoph Blumhardt: A Biography* (New York: Plough, 2010), 128–30.

14. The watchword is a direct way of fronting the strong evaluation we discussed in chap. 12.

15. Barth's ecclesiology very clearly revolves around witness. Many have discussed this: see most famously Darrell Guder's *Be My Witnesses* (Grand Rapids: Eerdmans, 1985). But what has not been as clearly laid out is how this attention to witness has some origin in the waiting and watching learned from Blumhardt.

A watchword, on the other hand, is a shared social imaginary for divine action itself. To be on watch is to live (find life) inside the dialectic. Being on watch is a form of action that is both passive and active, both waiting and hastening. The watchword engenders an attentiveness that draws the church into relations with the world, loving the world as it waits for God's sure act to come to the world.

Neither mainline nor evangelical congregations are in a crisis due to their failure to have or execute a mission or vision statement. They're in crisis because they've avoided a watchword. The pastor and leadership of many of these congregations have not provided a clear way of discerning, interpreting, and most importantly, expectantly waiting for God to act. The watchword forms the imagination and is the continual reminder to expectantly wait in attention for this action. The watchword gives the congregation a formative sense of the shape of divine action.

After the Gottliebin incident the Elder saw that, for the church to be the church, it must wait as it attentively watches with the watchword. The Elder's congregation in Möttlingen watched for "Jesus who is Victor!" They watched for the Jesus who was still acting in love for the world, bringing the world into a life with himself. The watchword reminds the church that its purpose is to wait and lovingly act by watching with the world for God's act.

For the Elder, the watchword was far from just a flat motto of ministry. It couldn't be seen as just another kind of mission or vision statement with theological gloss or buzzwords. A watchword has a much deeper origin. The Elder believed that his watchword came in the form of revelation itself. The mission or vision statement cannot take the church into the transformation it needs, because it has no direct connection with (and can encourage an avoidance of) revelation itself. A watchword, on the other hand, fundamentally differs, because it claims its source in the direct encounter with the living God. The watchword is in the shape of a congregation's direct, narrated encounter with the living Christ in the world. The watchword encompasses the congregation's encounter with the living action of Christ in the world (Christopraxis). The key to pastoral leadership is to front such stories of encounter so that the congregation may together embrace those stories as their shared watchword.

"Jesus is Victor!" is not a watchword for every congregation, but it was for the Möttlingen congregation. In direct immediacy, they encountered the living and acting Christ in the healing of Gottliebin and her family. "Jesus is Victor!" is the formative shorthand for the whole story of Gottliebin and the arrival of the living God who is God in the congregation's waiting watch. *The watchword is the local and concrete narration of the community's encounter with the living God who is God in the world.*

A mission or vision statement almost never has its origin here. Inside the immanent frame, the mission or vision statement is in bounds—it doesn't grate against the immanent frame—and therefore it's ubiquitous. The watchword is odd and almost unheard of in most congregations.

"Jesus is Victor!" as the watchword didn't come from the Elder's own imagination, a marketing firm, or a brainstorming session at Jackson Hole. No, this watchword came from direct encounter with Jesus's ministry in the world (Christopraxis). The watchword was the very phrase proclaimed by the angel of Satan as it left Katharina and released its grip on Gottliebin. These words testified in the most direct way to the ministering act of a living Jesus, who was ministering life even in modernity. The Elder experienced this directly.[16] The watchword "Jesus is Victor!" was the Elder's commitment that everything, in every way, comes back always to Jesus and his action with and for the world that his Father loves. "Jesus is Victor!" asserted that God's action cannot be pushed to the edges of modernity, for Jesus is the fullness of reality.[17] Everything the Elder did—every sermon he preached, every pastoral care appointment he kept, every meeting he ran—wasn't correlated to an organizational mission statement but to this watchword. Everything he did received its energy from this very encounter with "Jesus who is Victor!" Everything bore the marks of this watchword. Everything was about being in the world on watch, seeking for the living Jesus who acts as Victor, giving life to those in the world. Through the watchword, the Elder Blumhardt led his congregation by putting them on watch, waiting for the living God in the world.

Pastor Barth admired this deeply.[18] A church on watch, never wavering from its watchword, directly shaped Barth's own ministry in Safenwil. Even more, Barth admired how Johann Blumhardt never swayed from his focus on the living Christ who acts in the world. Barth saw in the Elder an (maybe *the*) exemplar modern pastor, who encountered the living God of the Bible inside what we'd call the immanent frame. Barth wrote Thurneysen just weeks after

16. This gives more shape to why I claimed early on in this project that there was a way of reading Barth as a pastoral theologian of Christopraxis. This reading demands seeing the strong links between Barth and the Blumhardts. The Blumhardts show Barth, both phenomenologically and theologically, the importance of claiming the continued ministerial action of Jesus even inside the immanent frame.

17. Bonhoeffer has a long discussion on Jesus as the real in *Ethics* (Minneapolis: Fortress, 2005), 48–61. This christological center that so impacted Barth and Bonhoeffer begins in the Blumhardts.

18. William Willimon points to how the Elder's watchword was also important to Barth. See Willimon, *The Early Preaching of Karl Barth: Fourteen Sermons with Commentary by William H. Willimon* (Louisville: Westminster John Knox, 2009), 141–44.

their 1915 meeting with the Younger to tell Thurneysen that he'd been reading Friedrich Zündel's biography on the Elder and how he found inspiration
on nearly every page.[19] Now deep in his own ministry in Safenwil, Barth told
Thurneysen how much he respected the Elder's unwavering focus on Jesus.
More particularly, Barth admired how this focus on Jesus was not in a closed
form. The Elder didn't have or possess Jesus. Rather, the Elder's watchword
claimed the revelatory encounter with the living Jesus in the world. The Elder's
watchword and its unwavering focus didn't put the Elder in opposition to the
world but in deep relation with it.[20]

This sense of the Elder's encounter with the very revelation of God inspired
Barth's pastoral imagination. Soon enough it would have its say on Barth's
theology as well. The Elder showed Barth how a Christology of a living, present, and acting Jesus can have a place in the immanent frame. Unlike Barth's
teachers, the Elder did not consider Jesus to be *the* moral exemplar but a living
person who, even in modernity, overcomes death with life.[21]

Barth doesn't mention it, but I would imagine that he was also moved by
the dynamics of a father and son in ministry. With Fritz gone, Barth wished
he could have shared with his father what the Elder and the Younger were
able to experience together. Reading about the Elder Blumhardt, having now
come to know the Younger, must have reminded Barth of his own father.[22]

Barth was so moved by the story of the Elder he'd eventually give him a
place in his anthology of the great nineteenth-century theologians. Though
the Elder was not known for any great intellectually heavy theological ideas
(and while Barth is often—wrongly I think—assumed to be a theological
snob), Johann Blumhardt made the cut. The Elder's place is secured not
by some theological system or great philosophical idea but by his unwavering faithfulness in ministry (showing again that Barth is more concerned
about the pastoral than is often assumed). Barth contends that the Elder's
genius, though maybe *not* based in his intellectual output, is found in his
watchword and its faithfulness to the lived encounter of the Jesus who set
Gottliebin free.

Returning to Gottliebin takes us back to the Younger.

19. See Barth and Thurneysen, *Revolutionary Theology in the Making*, trans. James D.
Smart (Richmond: John Knox, 1964), 30.

20. Barth discusses his deep appreciation in *Protestant Theology in the Nineteenth Century*
(Grand Rapids: Eerdmans, 2002), 634–35.

21. It is beyond this project to discuss this further, but there is a sense here that Barth is
putting together Blumhardt the Elder and Wilhelm Herrmann, his teacher in Marburg.

22. There is some slight connection between Barth and the Elder Blumhardt. Before the
Elder took his Möttlingen congregation, he taught at a missionary school in Basel. Fritz would
have been too young to take courses under the Elder, but the Basel connection is important.

Gottliebin's Ministry

The Younger's first teacher was Gottliebin. Christoph Blumhardt was as closely connected to Gottliebin as anyone. From when the Younger was but a toddler until her death, Gottliebin was a central part of the Younger's life. Gottliebin loved him as her own child, and he loved her as a kind of second mother. Until her death, Gottliebin stood as a sure testimony that God acts in the modern world, that indeed "Jesus is Victor!" If we had a detailed account of the life lived after the healing by the Gerasene demoniac in Luke 8, this was what Gottliebin was to the Younger. In the months right after Gottliebin's healing, the Blumhardts invited her into their home. This led to many others coming and staying with them, all looking for prayer and peace inside the confession that "Jesus is Victor!" People from all over Württemberg came, and then those from far beyond. They began streaming into the Blumhardt home looking for prayer, healing, and freedom from evil forces.

Eventually the Möttlingen house and village were too small, and a spa in Bad Boll became more accommodating for a ministry of pastoral care as prayer. Gottliebin became an essential part of the Bad Boll ministry, as much a member of the Blumhardt family as anyone. Her most direct ministry was to the Blumhardt children: "She exercise[d] a spiritual influence upon Blumhardt's sons and many visitors."[23] The Younger may have followed his father's footsteps into ministry, but it was Gottliebin who ministered to the Younger, forming his faith as much as his parents did.

Gottliebin and her experience shaped two generations of Blumhardt ministry. In one way or another, the ministry of the Blumhardts impacted many of the great German-speaking theological imaginations of the early and mid-twentieth century. Not only was Barth inspired by the two Blumhardts, but so too were Emil Brunner, Dietrich Bonhoeffer, and Jürgen Moltmann. The Blumhardts' ministry in Möttlingen and Bad Boll assured many, most directly Barth, that even in modernity, the God of the Bible acts in and for the world. This act is fully and completely God's, for "Jesus is Victor!"

From Gottliebin's release in Christmas 1843, the Möttlingen congregation was transformed, and with it the whole region of Württemberg. There were others, like Gottliebin, who followed the Blumhardts to Bad Boll. Gottliebin's brother Hansjörg was one of these others. Hansjörg was a member of the Möttlingen congregation before following the Blumhardts to Bad Boll. After the Elder's death and the Younger's taking charge of Bad Boll, slowly but surely those connected to Möttlingen and the original encounter with the

23. Ising, *Johann Christoph Blumhardt*, 176.

living God during the Gottliebin incident all passed away. Those who knew firsthand the narrative shape of the birth of the watchword were disappearing. Gottliebin's own death was very hard on the Younger. Now, into the 1880s, the Younger was far from a young man himself. In early 1888, with the death of Uncle Hansjörg, everyone who had had a direct experience of Gottliebin, his father, and the Möttlingen congregation was gone. With them all gone, the Younger's discontent peaked. The discontent was so heavy, the Younger was forced to enter a "great pause."

The Great Pause

Suffering these losses, and pushed into a great pause, *the Younger was given a new watchword for a new time.* A watchword is never simply imposed by a pastor or leader. It is only discerned from deep within a community. It is typically more than one person who frames the watchword, but it will be intrinsically bound in a community that is waiting in discernment. The watchword is humbly offered as a summation, without reduction, of the shape of the community's encounter with the living God who is God. With a watchword, the congregation is called on watch—or on watch, the congregation is given a watchword. The congregation is called to wait with this watchword, attentively being with the world, waiting for God's further action in and for the world.

What pushed the Younger into his great pause was his sense that his father's watchword had lost its shape. Without the direct connection to Gottliebin and the congregation's ministry to her, "Jesus is Victor!" became molded into something it wasn't. It became a slogan for individualistic religion. Disconnected from those who suffered in Möttlingen, "Jesus is Victor!" drew sensation seekers, vampire hunters, and many who sought to have God by learning how to control God's expenditure of energy.

With Gottliebin, the Elder, and now Uncle Hansjörg gone, the Younger saw how the watchword "Jesus is Victor!" could be, and was being, appropriated without or beyond the dialectic. This loss of the dialectic had badly misshapen the watchword. The watchword was now something other than the attentive waiting for the coming Jesus. It was being used as a slogan for the triumph of individualistic religion. It was now a phrase that told the individual that she (her "I") was powerful enough, if she personally and subjectively believed in Jesus, to *have* the world and control God. The Elder understood his watchword as the deep confession that God is God, acting, as the Bible witnessed, even in the immanent frame. But without the dialectic that was lodged in the historical experience of the Möttlingen congregation, "Jesus is Victor!" became a way of having God, flattening the otherness of God. Only the dialectic can keep human action from idolatrously flattening God's otherness while in turn making the experience of encounter important. The dialectic can both judge and affirm experience.

The Younger's discontent, which caused a great pause, was due to the loss of the dialectic that was so essential to his father's "Jesus is Victor!" watchword. There was an intrinsic dialectic in the Möttlingen and early Bad Boll ministry. It wasn't dwelt on. It didn't need to be. But it was there. No one who lived through the Gottliebin incident could imagine the watchword triumphalistically. "Jesus is Victor!" could never be assumed outside impossibility, loss, powerlessness, and despair. "Jesus is Victor!" was as much, if not more, a confession of impotence as it was of power. The Gottliebin incident gave no sense to the Elder or the congregation that human action was profound and powerful in itself. The long, two-year suffering of prayer, pastoral care, and powerlessness unveiled this truth, clearly instilling one side of the dialectic in all who lived through it. Remember that the Elder never rushed into Gottliebin's haunted apartment wielding liturgies as incantations, never puffed his chest, never went nose-to-nose with a demon, ready to arm wrestle the devil and his evil forces. Instead the Elder chose to suffer with Gottliebin, to form a deep relationship with her, to take the slow and seemingly weak act of praying for her. The Elder sought a form of action in the being-mode of resonance as the way of Gottliebin's healing. The Elder chose to bear the impossibility and wait for God. In humility the Elder refused a fight, walking out when the demons taunted him.

"Jesus is Victor!" was simply the other side of the dialectic of impossibility, of hope and freedom born out of despair and captivity. But you had to live through this to understand it. The Younger had to admit that with Gottliebin, the Elder, and now Uncle Hansjörg gone, the dialectic had been lost. The Younger himself couldn't keep the poles of the dialectic of "Jesus is Victor!" from tearing apart. It depressed the Younger that he couldn't. And more depressing still, there was no one left who had lived through this dialectic in the Gottliebin incident. "Jesus is Victor!" was no longer the heralding of a dialectic (hope in despair) of a God who loves the world by suffering for the world. By the mid-1880s it had become an incantation of superstitious religion. "Jesus is Victor!" became a charm that pietists were using to give them good luck and good individualistic and subjective feelings.

This drift from the dialectical nature of "Jesus is Victor!" had been happening for some time. But now all the eyewitnesses were gone. And the Younger had never felt so alone. The discontent about what had become of the watchword was painful and disorienting. So the Younger could only enter a great pause.

The New Watchword

Inside "the great pause," a new watchword came to the Younger. This watchword was born from within a new community in a new time. This watchword would renew the dialectic by more directly articulating the dialectic. And this had a significant impact on Pastor Barth! The dialectic was so strong in this new watchword that, unlike the Elder's watchword, it could never be confused as a slogan of a triumphal, individualistic religion. This new watchword, in fact, was needed in the first place to break pietism's triumphalistic commitment to individualistic religion and its idolatrous avoidance of God's dialectical action.

The Younger—following the Elder and inspiring Pastor Barth—intuitively believed (Barth would explicitly show) that it is only in and through the dialectic that we can encounter divine action in the immanent frame. Only the dialectic can avoid the immanent frame's sneaky ability to turn all forms of, and yearnings for, transcendence into immanent religious spiritualities. The Younger was intuiting that only a truly *real* (*lived* as opposed to noetic, mental, or intellectual[24]) dialectic could allow faith to be modern and nevertheless not reduced by modernity's proclivities for a flat immanence.

In the *Vertauliche Blätter für Freunde von Bad Boll 1889*, a kind of new year's report on the state of the ministry to the friends of Bad Boll, the Younger discusses how dark 1888 had been for him personally. The Younger discusses Uncle Hansjörg's death and how it had pushed him into depression for much of the year. But it was in this pause—in which he bore the despondency and sought God not outside the uncomfortable pause—that the Younger encountered a transformational breakthrough.

The Younger says to the friends of Bad Boll, the "pause [was ended by] a demonstration in me of the life of Christ, [coming upon me] like a light from the Savior. . . . That is why we now feel as if we are allied under a new banner, which reads: 'Die, so that Jesus may live!'"[25] *This was the new watchword.*

---

24. One could think of the difference between a real and a noetic dialectic as represented in Kierkegaard and Hegel. Both have a strong place for a dialectic, but nevertheless they stand as enemies (more correctly, it was just Kierkegaard who had hard feelings toward Hegel and his system). For Kierkegaard the dialectic is a real, directly lived dialectic. For Hegel it is the intellectual structure of history itself. It is a movement of *Geist*.

25. Christoph Friedrich Blumhardt, *Vertauliche Blätter für Freunde von Bad Boll 1889* (Bad Boll: 1889), 1:20–21.

Simeon Zahl adds, the Younger "continues to use this precise formulation for years, often written down in quotation marks, indicating that he probably viewed the watchword, and the message behind it, to be a direct revelation from God, not unlike the elder Blumhardt's 'Jesus is Victor!'"[26] The watchword, for the community at Bad Boll into the 1890s, shifted from "Jesus is Victor!" to "Die, so that Jesus may live!"

This new watchword was the renewing of the dialectic. In finding a new watchword, which was unmistakably dialectical, the Younger believed pietism could be freed from individualistic religion. The new watchword bore a dialectic that not only judged individualistic religion but also, like any good watchword, articulated the way to encounter the living God who comes to us as a God who is God. Let's explore these in order.

1. Flesh and False Action

The dialectic needed to be boldly highlighted and renewed because pietism had smuggled in a false form of human action. It had followed the dominant form of agency in modernity and therefore saw action as bound inside the having-mode. To break this obsession with the having-mode and to invite pietism and all Protestantism back into the being-mode of resonance, the Younger focused on what he called the *Fliesch* (the flesh).

The Younger associated human activity and its obsessions with the having-mode of action with "the flesh," echoing Paul (Rom. 8:7). The flesh was the self-actualizing obsession with an individualistic form of action, which believed the expending of energy could have, and therefore possess, the world. The Younger declared, "It is over 'the flesh' that Jesus must truly be Victor."[27]

This was a step both toward and beyond his father. Demonic power, the Younger asserted, was bound in the addiction to *have* the world as much as it was in the manifestations of haunting and creepy voices (Jesus's third temptation in the desert seems to point to this, Matt. 4:8–11). The Younger contended that Jesus needed to be understood as Victor over demons. Sure! But just as much, Jesus's victory was over the *Fliesch* that seeks to have the world, contending that salvation is bound in the expending of energy. Following his father, victory was important, but the step beyond the Elder was to be more directly dialectical by claiming that this victory was over a *Fliesch* that sought to possess the world, a *Fliesch* that didn't recognize its own impossibility and therefore couldn't *be* with the world and love the world.

26. Zahl, *Pneumatology and Theology of the Cross*, 40.
27. Zahl, *Pneumatology and Theology of the Cross*, 41.

This is a memo that those captivated by the white, American, middle-class prosperity gospel simply never received. Not recognizing that Jesus's victory was over the *Fliesch* that seeks to have the world, the American prosperity gospel became the sad outgrowth of a pietism that passionately averts itself from the dialectic. It took on the rhetoric of hating the world. Hating the world, the prosperity gospel dove headlong into a spiritualizing that unashamedly sought to *have* the world, going so far as to equate the having (even of cars and jets) with the victory of Jesus. The American prosperity gospel hates the world so much—because its form of action is locked so deeply in a spiritualized having-mode—that it has an unquenchable thirst to possess as many of the material treasures of the world as it can. The prosperity gospel's hating of the world ironically makes it a religious form of the *Fliesch* that wants to possess the world. (It becomes like a bad relationship in which passion is fueled by mutual hate—both choose to possess the other because they actually hate the other but confuse that hate for romantic attraction.)

The Younger spotted the earliest cells of this idolatrous theology in pietism. The new watchword, and its sharp dialectical edges, was the scalpel needed to cut it out of pietism (and all of Protestantism). Unfortunately the immanent frame has sung such an enchanting siren song of having the world that Protestantism is willing to allow its dialectical blades to be dulled. The Younger understood that the *Fliesch* (the having-mode) needed to be overcome so the world, and human action in it, would *be*. Only the being-mode would allow the church to be about life as resonance in the Spirit and friendship in being with and for the world without seeking to possess the world.

Yet this leads us into the second important element of the new watchword. The new watchword claims Jesus is Victor over the *Fliesch*, but how is this victory achieved? Victory itself must be understood dialectically. In other words, Jesus is only Victor because Jesus is defeated. Jesus wins by losing. This is the heart of the new watchword, "Die, so that Jesus may live." Jesus's victory is bound in taking on a form of action that appears to be the opposite of victory: dying. The new watchword infuses the dialectic so deeply in the sense of victory that the dialectic is unavoidable in this watchword. The watchword keeps the dialectic sharp and operating in the community. A dulling of the dialectic had been the problem with the Elder's watchword. Without living directly through the Gottliebin incident, or patiently dwelling in the layers of the pastoral narrative, there was a deep temptation for victory, for "Jesus as Victor!" to turn triumphalistic, to forget that Jesus is Victor by going to the cross and dying.

2. Dying as the Way of Divine Action

There is another German word that conveys much of the deep theological wells of the new watchword. Next to *Fliesch* (flesh), the Younger adds *Sterbet* (dying). The Younger believed that in dying or *Sterbet*, the false forms of action are broken. *Sterbet* broke false forms of actions, but as the center of the new watchword, it was also constructive. *Sterbet* (dying) was the shape of divine action. The dialectic does not simply call *Fliesch* to die. It goes much deeper. In developing his *Sterbet* watchword, the Younger returned to Luther's *theologia crucis*.[28] Luther taught that we can only know that this is indeed the God who is God because he arrives in the opposite. *Sterbet* uncovers the dialectic at the deepest level. It claims that God is a God who dies.

Sterbet is not simply another pietistic religious device for human religious betterment. Rather, it is the ontological shape of God's being (God's becoming) in the world. To encounter a God who is God means to die. Not because the human being is discardable but because dying (*perishing*, as Jüngel would say) is the concrete location where God chooses to be found. The shape of divine action is dialectical, for it is Jesus who is Victor. But Jesus is indeed Victor by doing, shockingly, the opposite of what appears victorious: by dying, taking death into himself, so the Father can act and turn all perishing into the promise of the birth of new life.

It is God, unveiled to us in Jesus Christ, who enters *Sterbet*. Jesus is Victor because he dies. Jesus in toto is the dialectical man. The Younger says that to encounter the life of this living Jesus who dies, we too must die. Only in this dying to all the having-modes of action can we live. Only in a form of action that dies can we fully and completely embrace life and be. Even Hartmut Rosa, as a social theorist, points to something like this. Resonance is a form of life that embraces the dialectic of closedness and complete otherness. Therefore, it is able to face dying. The dialectic is now singing in the Younger's new watchword, and Barth will wager, from 1916 and beyond, that this dialectic is a hymn more profound than the siren song of the immanent frame.

The new watchword "Die, so that Jesus may live!" is *not* a functional or mechanistic statement. It is hermeneutical. Dying doesn't *make* or *cause* Jesus to live. This would be idolatry at the height of the having-mode of action (which both fundamentalist and liberal theologies have at times fallen into in their own ways). Rather, the Younger, following his father, has a deep sense of Jesus's free action in the world (which deeply influences Barth). We've called

---

28. For a discussion of the Younger's connection to Luther's theology of the cross, see Zahl, *Pneumatology and Theology of the Cross*, 55–59.

this Christopraxis, a sense that Jesus lives and freely acts in the world even now. For the Younger, Jesus is the fullness of God who is God. Jesus is the unveiled God before us and therefore is not dependent on us or our action to live.[29]

What the Younger's new watchword seeks to proclaim is how this Jesus who lives comes to us. The new watchword shouts that his coming is fully and inextricably dialectical. Jesus is unveiled as true God of true God by taking on the opposite. By dying, he is the dialectical God/man. The watchword heralds "Die, so that Jesus may live!" not as a magical way to revive Jesus but as the hermeneutical locale for recognizing and encountering what cannot be seen or encountered. The God who is truly God comes dying so that we can participate fully in life. Through the Spirit, we participate fully in the being of Jesus (by being in Christ), who is the resurrection and the life (John 11:25).[30]

Inside the dying of the world, inside the cries for ministry in Egypt, the God who is God acts, entering dying so we can *be* alive (Exod. 3:7). Human beings can only see, know, and participate in the life of this God—who is so fully a God who is God by dying—by loving the world so much we enter into its (and our own) dying. This dying is not a concession but the very location to encounter the God who is God. It's only through the dialectic, bound in God's own being, made known through God's act, that we can encounter a God who is God even in the immanent frame. The immanent frame cannot know the God who is God. The immanent frame always tries to push God to the edges, because the immanent frame cannot deal with dying.[31] Unable to face dying, it cannot be dialectical and therefore cannot escape a form of action that kills and alienates the world it claims is only and finally natural and material. Because the immanent frame cannot be dialectical, it struggles mightily to support life. Alienation, in all different kinds of manifestations, seems a much more constant and consistent outgrowth of modernity's immanent frame than life.

---

29. The language of "unveiled" is more Barth's than the Blumhardts'.
30. I've discussed this as theosis in *Faith Formation in a Secular Age* (Grand Rapids: Baker Academic, 2017), part 2.
31. Taylor discusses how the exclusive human flourishing of the immanent frame can do well with many things. But it doesn't do well with dying. Taylor's point is that the core moral codes of the immanent frame have ignored or opposed dying. Terry Eagleton draws out Taylor's point, saying, "As Charles Taylor remarks, 'modern humanism tends to develop a notion of flourishing that has no place for death.' [*A Secular Age*, 320] Christianity, by contrast, a faith which turns on an executed body, places death at the centre of its vision, in the belief that there can be no flourishing without confronting it." *Culture and the Death of God* (New Haven: Yale University Press, 2014), 143. See also J. J. Valberg's *Dream, Death, and the Self* (Princeton: Princeton University Press, 2007).

Ramification of the Sterbet

In using this new watchword, the Younger reminds his community that faith is the gift to recognize the dialectic and find life inside the dialectic. Inside the confession and direct experience of dying, we find the fullness of life. Therefore, we can encounter this God who is victorious in Jesus Christ only by following Jesus Christ to the cross and dying. Die, the Younger is saying, *not* so you can control God, expending God's energy as you wish. Your own sacrifice cannot bring God or do anything for God. But die all the same, entering the dialectic of seeking God in places where God cannot be found.

Dying is not a form of masochism for the Younger. Nor is it a form of doctrinal religion. Dying is a direct way of living. It is the form of waiting. It's the very shape of watching with the world out of deep love for the world. Dying is living, for the Younger, because it is the freedom to be, to be living by dying, dying as the way of living. Die so that you can find God who finds you in your death experience, bringing life out of death. Die, the Younger says, so you can live, so you can witness in your waiting to a God who so loves the world that God, through God's Son, dies that the world might live (John 3:16). The Younger says, "People have made Jesus the founder of a religion. No! He is the bringer of life."[32]

The Younger saw that the bondage in which his congregation found itself was not demonic in the form of possession. His congregation was in demonic bondage for its willingness to leave those in the world bound in the concrete bondage of poverty, meaningless work, and racism. These realities stand in direct opposition to God, mocking the statement that "Jesus is Victor." The Younger's response was to die, taking on the form of Jesus not by expending energy but by sharing in being.[33] The congregation needed to enter into the death experience of all those in the world, bearing the death experience as the way of having eyes to see the living Jesus who is ministering life to the world.

The Younger entered into party politics, becoming a ranking member of the Socialist Democratic Party for the sake of dying, for the sake of *Sterbet*. The Younger entered into the dying of others by his willingness to serve

32. Christoph Blumhardt, *The Gospel of God's Reign: Living for the Kingdom of God* (Eugene, OR: Cascade Books, 2014), 33. This quotation gives a beautiful sense of how the Younger understands dying. He says, "People think that Death is something dead. No! Death is a bacteria; it is alive and finds soil everywhere in which to propagate itself. It kills not only the body but often, long before this, spirit and soul. Death is something 'alive,' and this life of death is something you need to recognize more and more. I will not say too much about it. Perhaps some of you have felt something of this for a long time already. It is something each one must feel and come to know for himself. I can only hint at how much is alive that comes from death." Christoph Blumhardt, *Action in Waiting* (Farmington, PA: Plough, 1998), 135.
33. For more on this, see Zahl, *Pneumatology and Theology of the Cross*, 48–49.

others, waiting with others for God who dies to deliver God's promise to turn all dying into living. This is a kind of sacramental manifestation of new life coming to the world. In dying with the world, the church participates directly in the new life of the world.[34]

Yet Christoph Blumhardt eventually discovered in the party—as mentioned above—that it too avoided all *Sterbet*. Like the church, the party had become too enamored of the closed, antidialectical structures of the immanent frame. The party wanted its own life more than the life of the world. The Younger knew that, crushed by a world idolatrously caught in the having-mode, the only way for those in the world to live was for the congregation to die. The church needed to stop striving to survive, thrive, and secure its own resources and relevance. The Younger would remind us that the church can never stand up against the demonic powers of poverty and racism until it is willing to die. For only in dying (in the dying of Jesus) is the victory of life itself born.

Saint John the Baptist can find God only by dying. They must reach out to the world, embrace the world, and wait with the world. Only in dying to the need to be the star of its own story can the church live, finding the encounter with the living God who dies as life.

The Younger recognized that this *Sterbet* theology of ministry would not lead to a great growth strategy for the church. Rather, as Zahl says, the Younger "follows his father in articulating an ecclesiology of a 'little flock,' a faithful remnant who still seek the Kingdom when most of Christianity has lost its way."[35] This little flock would remain little because it was formed around the dialectic. But little and dialectical, this little flock would be alive because it dies. And because it dies, it would be full of life.

————

In the waiting and living—in waiting as living—Saint John the Baptist found its watchword. The watchword didn't come through the Bible study. They didn't know they were supposed to be looking for a watchword. Rather, the watchword found them. It was serendipitous and transformational.

34. Zahl discusses the Younger's sense of life in *Pneumatology and Theology of the Cross*, 102–4.

35. Zahl, *Pneumatology and Theology of the Cross*, 47.

16

Getting Real
with a Dialectical Demand

Sue had now been giving tours of the sanctuary's stained glass for almost six months. She was surprised that people kept requesting to see what the congregation had overlooked for years. The search for a new pastor also continued. It had slowed down, but only from its original inappropriate pace. The committee had originally wanted to hire someone by the fall, thinking they had to strike fast. They had feared that if they couldn't get someone while Luke's busy glow of relevance was still shining it would be hard to find anyone who would want the call.

But that anxiety had now melted away, disappearing when they started helping a pilgrim find a God who is God. It evaporated when, through Woz, they entered the world to love the world by being with the world. They were waiting with Woz and the world for this God to arrive. This somehow gave them peace to be a faithful small flock. They still needed a new pastor, but this waiting had ushered them into life. That was enough. That was blessed. Herbert's music and the stained-glass tours had become a sure sign of that life. Bert had settled into preaching, and the lay leadership was more than seeing the congregation through.

The fall turned into winter, and winter started to show signs of its own end. Things were now well into 2012. The search for the new pastor was moving forward, momentum was building, but with an easier spirit of discernment and patience. Woz had now been part of the Bible study for months. He made it to Sunday morning worship every once in a while, missing more weeks than he made. But to everyone's surprise, he signed up for the winter service weekend. Woz had everyone laughing all weekend as together they painted Habitat for Humanity houses, played music, and prayed.

Young adult Woz and elderly Herbert sat next to each other most of the weekend, laughing and joking like two middle school boys. They played their guitars late into the night. Helene finally yelled at them at 1 a.m. on Sunday to shut up. Herbert busted out in mischievous laughter. He told some folks at breakfast that he hadn't felt that naughty, or alive, in years. "It felt so good to get in trouble! My concert and now this! It's been quite a year for this guy," he told them, to their delight. Herbert spent most of the rest of the day fighting to stay awake. Woz giggled at him as he did. They were thick as thieves. It gave everyone great joy to see this true friendship.

———

The Bible study remained Woz's major touchstone. One week in late winter, Sue told the group about what she'd found in the church basement. No one knew more than Sue about Saint John the Baptist. She particularly knew everything about its finances, both present and historical. But giving tours took her deeper into the past stories of the congregation. It started as a purely utilitarian exercise. You need good stories to lead good tours. It didn't take long for her to find a treasure. She told the Bible study of old handwritten sermons, meeting notes, and typed testimonies given by each woman who had seen her husband or son placed in the stained glass.

Marjorie Myer, the oldest living member of the congregation, had alerted Sue that this material existed. Marjorie had been part of the church since she was a child, growing up with Jean, Woz's grandmother. When Marjorie told Sue about the special services for each stained-glass panel, Sue figured it would be impossible to find the old paperwork, if it existed at all. Yet, to Sue's great surprise, she found sermons, meeting notes, and more from those special services. It was meant to be, all thanks to Bert and Helene cleaning out a closet that hadn't been touched in decades. They had had no idea why they did that job, but it was now playing a small but important part in the story Saint John the Baptist was living out.

The Bible study was fascinated as Sue told some of the stories she'd learned about the women and the testimonies they'd given. It was a particularly holy moment of resonance when Sue pulled out a handwritten testimony by Jean, Woz's grandmother. It was dated March 18, 1947. Woz could only cover his mouth in astonishment as Sue held it up. Tears gathered in Woz's eyes as Sue talked about how she had found it. Sue asked if she could read it. Woz nodded, and there wasn't a dry eye in the room.

The whole group died with Woz, entering his death experience, swept up into a moment of resonance as Woz was given a glimpse into his own history. The letter from young Jean bled with pain as she lost the man she loved, leaving her with a small child. But she also wrote of God's provisions and God's nearness: "I've found God nearer to me in these moments than my own breath. I was a churchgoer before all this, but now I know God and his Son more than ever before. I know him, because I experience him getting me through this awful time. As Pastor Happenstad says so much these last few years, 'What is lost is found. When we grieve and cry out in loss, Jesus finds us. Jesus is the finder of what's lost.'"

This moment shifted things for Woz. Things had shifted once before when he bravely came to the Bible study and asked for help in his journey to find God. But Woz was starting to see that God was indeed finding him. Woz sat in silence for a minute looking at the ground, his hand trembling a bit.

Finally Woz said, "As my grandma was fading those last few days, she kept telling me to find God and his Son. Or at least I thought that's what she was saying. I think she was actually saying that now I'd find Jesus. I thought it was the meds messing with her tenses. I kept telling her that I wasn't sure I could go on without her. That she really was all that I had. I had only stayed sober because of her. I kept telling her that I needed her. And she'd say, 'You'll find Jesus.' I thought she meant go find God, get God in your life. So that's why I came here. But now I think I see that what she meant is with me losing her, with the pain of not knowing if I could go on without her, I'd find . . . I'd be found by Jesus. She wasn't telling me to go find God. She was telling me that now that I would be lost, Jesus would find me. I needed to come here to see that."

Woz was recognizing that if he let himself be lost, he would be free to be found. He had never done that before. He'd felt too much loss in his life. He'd tried to hide from it, tried to stay busy doing other things, afraid he'd never be found. But now, thanks to the humble community of the Bible study and Saint John the Baptist as a whole, Woz saw more clearly what Jean was saying.

"What's amazing," Sue added, "is that these phrases—'What's lost is found,' 'When we grieve and cry out in loss, Jesus finds us,' and 'Jesus is the finder of what's lost'—are everywhere. Each woman's testimony is different and unique, but each one says something very close to those words in their testimony. And Pastor Happenstad's sermons are filled with it, particularly between 1943 and 1953. For a whole decade he preached about it. Some part of the phrase even shows up in meeting minutes."

———————

This was Saint John the Baptist's watchword, and it had remained so until the mid-1960s. The watchword was renewed as the community changed. In the early 1960s beloved Pastor Happenstad retired. Pastor Reynolds followed. By the mid-1960s the congregation had become involved in the civil rights movement. Notes and sermons that Sue found revealed that this commitment was born out of the same confession and watchword that Jesus is the finder of what's lost. In the late 1960s the last stained-glass panel went up. It depicted Dr. King walking toward Chicago. You can clearly spot the year, 1967. For generations, the church had been confused about why Dr. King was walking toward Chicago, not Selma or Montgomery. And why 1967? The Chicago riots during the Democratic National Convention, which revealed the deep fissures in the country, didn't happen until 1968.

The notes in one of those dusty boxes cleared up the mystery. Sue discovered that a busload of folks from Saint John the Baptist went to hear King preach at Mount Pisgah Missionary Baptist Church in Chicago on August 27, 1967. That day King preached his famous sermon with its refrain: "God makes a way out of no way." The refrain was born out of what King called his "kitchen table experience,"[1] in which he heard God say these words to him. The words came as he recognized that out of his own power, out of the expenditure of his own energy, he couldn't produce what was needed for the bus boycott and for the people of Montgomery. King realized that the having-mode was bankrupt, even with the most righteous of intentions. Through a direct Word from God, not unlike the Blumhardts, King moved toward a dialectic. He came to realize that the action that brings freedom and justice is not in the having-mode but the being-mode.[2]

"When there is no way, God makes a way" became King's watchword. The last stained-glass window and the documents, sermons, and letters that Sue found showed that it became Saint John the Baptist's watchword too. The group had been so inspired by the sermon and the way it connected to "Jesus is the finder of what's lost" that they made it into the last stained-glass window in their sanctuary. Pastor Reynolds often used the two watchwords together: "Jesus is the finder of what's lost; God makes a way out of no way."

1. For more on this refrain and experience, see Rufus Borrow's important book, *God and Human Dignity: The Personalism, Theology, and Ethics of Martin Luther King Jr.* (Notre Dame, IN: University of Notre Dame, 2006), 104–5. I've also used this story of King in *The Pastor in a Secular Age* (Grand Rapids: Baker Academic, 2019), chap. 11. I obviously have a soft spot for this story, but I reuse it here because it so wonderfully shows the potential of a watchword that is fully and completely dialectical and therefore significantly shapes the imagination and action of those in the immanent frame.
2. King's nonviolent resistance is, at its core, action in the being-mode.

Yet by the mid-1980s something tragic had occurred. These watchwords were assumed to be unimportant and therefore not in need of renewal or even remembering. It was assumed that congregations instead needed mission statements and plans for building programs. With the loss of the watchwords, the congregation started to lose its life. Not because it lost relevance and resources, but because it lost the dialectic by losing these watchwords. In losing the dialectic, Saint John the Baptist couldn't wait for a God who is God. They were deceived into thinking that life was only possible in the having-mode of accruing resources and relevance. This drive to be a church in the having-mode disconnected them from discerning the living Christ and moved them somewhere far from resonance.

"When there is no way, God makes a way, by God finding what's lost." Bert repeated it over and over. Bert had become a civil rights lawyer because of King's inspiration. He had never known that this church had framed its imagination around King's own watchword. He just kept repeating it. Everyone in the Bible study nodded as he did. "We need to remember that," Bert said. It was similar to Josiah being given the law after it had been forgotten, lost, and rediscovered by his workers in the renovation of the temple (2 Kings 22). Bert felt that they were given back their congregational watchwords. He felt both joy that they'd been returned and anguish that they'd been lost in the first place.

Bert knew that whomever they hired to be the next pastor would need to help them as a congregation enter the world with this dialectical watchword to discern God's action in the immanent frame. Of course, Bert would never have said it like this, but he knew it in his bones. The challenge was how he would say it to the committee and candidates. If someone were to tell the committee the story of the Blumhardts, they'd show the person the door, incredulous about all the demon talk. Even being told they needed a pastor who could help the congregation find its watchword would seem odd. Bert didn't know how to explain what he was discovering in a way that didn't seem weird.

Barth and the Weird Evangelist

There seems to be a little bit of guilt by association. When one tells late-modern, contemporary people the story of the Elder, they usually dismiss him. The Elder's experience with demons is too weird for most mainline and centrist evangelicals. Yet, when those same people are told that Karl Barth loved the Elder, was inspired by his pastoral example, and devoured his biography, they tend not to know what to do with Barth. The Barth of *Church Dogmatics* seems so doctrinal, so academic, so reformed—not one to be enamored of pastoral demon jousting. Some might wonder whether Pastor Barth was susceptible to a kind of spiritual voyeurism or pastoral haunted-house tales.

To assuage these concerns, we have two interesting letters that Pastor Barth wrote to Eduard Thurneysen. Both are dated in 1916, one on November 15, the other five days later, on November 20. It had been a year and a half since Peter's wedding and their conversation with the Younger at Bad Boll. In that year and a half Thurneysen and Barth had searched for a new theological center for their pastoral work. In the summer of 1916 Barth started filling his notebooks with reflections on Romans (*Römerbrief I* was being birthed). In early November, the pietist evangelist Jakob Vetter (not to be confused with Vetter Hanjörg) came to Safenwil preaching salvation by the blood and freedom from the demonic. And Pastor Barth abhorred him![3]

Okay, that might be overstated. Barth had dinner on two occasions with Jakob Vetter, hosting him in Barth's own home. Overall, Barth seemed to like him. He found him personally to be far less annoying than his preaching and overall theology. To Barth's surprise, Vetter was even generous with praise for Barth's sermon that Vetter had had occasion to hear. How Vetter could like it, Barth wasn't sure, because it appeared clear to Barth that their theological commitments were quite different.

Barth writes to Thurneysen that this experience assured Barth that the new pastoral theology they were after was something different from pietism. If liberalism had its dead end, as they had together discovered in 1915, then 1916 showed that pietism did too. Barth says, "If *this* [the preaching and ministry of Jakob Vetter] were 'pietism,' we would never again believe that there was even the slightest point of contact between us and the pietist."[4]

Barth says that Vetter is psychologizing in its worst form. Vetter, like the Elder, speaks of awakening, but this waking is formulaic and stiff. There are levels of resisting the Holy Spirit, for example. To break through this resistance, Barth says Vetter's method was to claim that "the blood of Christ flows as medicine for the soul, and finally everything comes to a climax in appeal to the 'awakened.'"[5] This "awakening" offered by Vetter included four

---

3. Bruce McCormack discusses the Jakob Vetter experience in *Karl Barth's Critically Realistic Dialectical Theology: Its Genesis and Development, 1909–1936* (Oxford: Oxford University Press, 1997), 136–37.

4. Barth, in Karl Barth and Eduard Thurneysen, *Revolutionary Theology in the Making*, trans. James D. Smart (Richmond: John Knox, 1964), 40 (emphasis original).

5. Barth, *Revolutionary Theology in the Making*, 40.

things: (1) a visit to an after-meeting in the chapel, (2) prayer on one's knees, (3) an invitation to buy a little book, and (4) a subscription to the magazine *Tabernacle Gathering*.

And if that's not bad enough, the jaws of hell are always open, threatening the listeners with demise, leading to a hate for life and the world, Barth believes. Pastor Barth colorfully adds, showing how much he thinks such a ministry and the pastoral theology that mobilizes it leads to hatred of the world, "And over it all brooded an atmosphere of fear as though the ship were sinking and there were no rescue ship for most people anyhow."[6] After a week of hearing Vetter's sermons, Barth responded with a Sunday sermon that proclaimed that "the kingdom of God on earth begins with joy." Vetter complimented Pastor Barth, but at dinner that evening, Barth (his sarcastic edge now returned) tells Thurneysen, "The man of God set me right by describing the conditions which must precede such joy in the soul."[7] You can see his eyes rolling.

I Loved and I Hated

Now that his frustration with Jakob Vetter is clear, we have a question for Barth. We could playfully put it in the form of one of Barth's favorite verses. It's a verse he returns to again and again in the second half of *Römerbrief II* ("I have loved Jacob, but I have hated Esau," Rom. 9:13). Our question for Barth is, "Why did you love the Elder Blumhardt and hate Jakob Vetter?" It seems a bit arbitrary for Barth to choose one over the other. Both are pietists (at times even enthusiasts). Both confront demons. Both speak of revival, healing, and awakening. Both have ministries outside the standard congregational form. So why does Barth admire the Elder, seeing him as a sage, and yet only painfully tolerate Vetter, seeing him as a fool?

There are two reasons, which connect directly with our discussions in the chapters above.

1. Joylessness in the World

First, as Barth's sermon shows, he thinks Vetter, and more so his pastoral theology and practice of ministry, is joyless. Ever since Mozart's *The Magic Flute* went straight into and through little Barth, he encountered the fullness of life. He saw that life itself was experienced as joy. Even in suffering (even

---

6. Barth, *Revolutionary Theology in the Making*, 40.
7. Barth, *Revolutionary Theology in the Making*, 40.

in the necessity of the centrality of suffering), life is always a beautiful gift. For the theologian, pastor, and Christian, theology is lived by embracing the world in joy. The gospel is good news, joyful news, to the world. For Barth, this can never be forgotten. Pastor Barth refuses to produce, or even entertain, a theology that is not a ministry of joy, of living, of resonance. Suffering and the cross must be central so that joy, as the fullness of life, might be known.

Vetter he hates because in Barth's mind, Vetter is joyless, his message dire. But Barth loves the Elder because the Elder embraces life. The Elder lives, filling his congregation and then Bad Boll with laughter and life. He loves children. The Elder proclaims his watchword in and with joy. The watchword "Jesus is Victor!" is such good news that it leads the Elder to embrace life with both hands, singing songs of celebration. The Elder always celebrates joyfully. Barth loves the Elder because the Elder loves the world.

Barth always seems drawn to people who love life. He always has a soft spot for those who embrace the world. This is so much the case that for a moment Barth is even open to Vetter. Barth tells Thurneysen in the November 20 letter, "It must be said that *personally* [in contrast to his practice of ministry] he is most certainly an agreeable religious man." Yet to be called an "agreeable religious man" by Barth is like being called the smartest idiot. It's a backhanded compliment. The kind of people Karl Barth wants to hang out with least are *agreeable* (he's rarely agreeable himself) *religious men*. Nevertheless, Barth, for a quick minute, is drawn to Vetter through his laughter. Barth tells Thurneysen, "In private conversations there was something friendly about [Vetter] and especially a certain good-humored laughter that won me to him."[8] But that good humor ended in private conversation, evaporating as Barth witnessed Vetter's practice of ministry.

Through his ministry, Barth perceived that Vetter actually deeply hated the world. Vetter used his gospel not to more fully embrace the world but to escape it. Vetter wanted salvation as an escape from the world. The Elder, in loving the world, wanted a salvation that gives life to the world. Barth recognized, even in 1916, that his theology and practice of ministry could not be appropriately modern without embracing the world, even joyfully loving the world. For Barth and Thurneysen, who were looking for a theology of ministry that was inside and yet not reduced by immanence, Vetter was either antimodern or maybe even too bound in modernity (a classic conundrum of conservative Protestantism).

This leads us to the second reason that Barth loved the Elder, and Vetter he hated.

8. Barth, *Revolutionary Theology in the Making*, 40.

2. Lost Dialectic

To understand this second reason, we're confronted with other questions: Why can the Elder joyfully love the world while Vetter cannot? Why, in Barth's mind, was Vetter defeated by modernity and yet the Elder—who at first glance seemed so much like Vetter—could find a unique way to be faithful inside modernity?

The difference became the narrow ground that Pastor Barth stood on between liberalism and pietism. As Barth says in the November 20 letter to Thurneysen, the experience with Vetter sadly assured Barth that pietism is no home for the kind of theology that he and Thurneysen were seeking in their pastoral ministries. The ground that Barth found between liberalism and pietism, a ground that could allow for a theology to not be washed over and eroded by the immanent frame, was fully and always dialectical.

Barth loved the Elder but hated Vetter because the Elder's practice of ministry was fully dialectical while Vetter's was not. If we follow Rosa and his convincing argument that resonance is structured dialectically, we can even say that Barth loved the Elder because his dialectical watchword allowed him to love the world. And Vetter he hated because Vetter had no dialectic and therefore could not love the world. Vetter saw salvation not as bound in and for the world, but as an escape from the world. Because the Elder embraced the dialectic in joy, he could enter into the being-mode of action, opening his community to waiting for a God who is God in resonance. Vetter, without a dialectic, could see the gospel only through the lens of the human expenditure of energy, becoming caught in the having-mode. He lost both the world and the Word of God in this drive to have.

Right after Barth told Thurneysen that Vetter's laugh had won him over, it all crashed down. Barth, flabbergasted, wrote of Vetter's antidialectical having-mode theology in his practice of ministry: "But the things, the things—that for eight days he kept proclaiming up there—these are really *not* the gospel but rather a quite bad form of religious mechanics."[9] In the very next sentence, Barth tells Thurneysen they must leave pietism behind for good.

What flabbergasted Barth was that it *appeared* that Vetter was devotedly committed to the gospel, even inside the modern world. He boldly gave religious steps to be committed to the Christian religion. But Barth saw this as idolatry—as a having-mode of action that is therefore a terrible concession to modernity. Vetter's theology and ministry failed to meet the immanent frame in a way that did not ignorantly play by the immanent frame's rules. Vetter had eliminated God's transcendence by placing God inside the immanent frame,

9. Barth, *Revolutionary Theology in the Making*, 40.

forcing God to respond to religious mechanics. Vetter seemed devoted, but he flattened the gospel to these religious mechanics, allergic to the dialectic because he had conceded to the immanent frame. The immanent frame rewards mechanical and functional operations, and such operations, whether knowingly or not, attack transcendence by capturing all forms of action in the having-mode.

Vetter had no place for the dialectic in his practice of ministry because the immanent frame opposes the dialectic. The immanent frame recognizes that the dialectic exposes the immanent frame in its reductions and shortcomings. Vetter's eight-day message was a concession to the immanent frame by allowing the gospel to be stripped of its dialectic and made into religious mechanics. Vetter had no impossibility borne for the sake of new life. There was no "God bringing a new way out of no way," no "when we're lost we're found." In its place, there were four mechanical steps that ended not with new life—not in the fullness of being alive, in encountering something going straight into and through you—but with a subscription to a magazine. If this wasn't a concession to the immanent frame, what was?

Already in 1916, Barth was sensing that a theology and practice of ministry without a dialectic becomes religious mechanics.[10] The nefarious problem with religious mechanics is that they eventually attack life. At some point the mechanics will demand more and more expenditure of energy to have more and more of their own immanent goods. This will cause you to further speed up, alienating you from life itself. Vetter's pietism, ironically but logically, had found a secure place inside the immanent frame because it matched the having-mode of action the immanent frame promotes as the only legitimate form of action. In late modernity, this kind of pietism uses many of the immanent frame's consumer rhetorical devices for its own religious gain. No wonder steps 3 and 4 in Vetter's mechanics included buying a book and subscribing to a magazine.

Religious Mechanics versus Christopraxis

This wrongheaded approach to ministry becomes even more problematic when we move into Christology. Religious mechanics that succumb to the having-mode of the immanent frame cannot witness to the living Jesus. They cannot attend to encountering and being encountered by a living Christ in action (Christopraxis). The immanent frame creates both liberal and pietist

10. It will take until *Römerbrief II* for Barth to precisely articulate the dialectic.

forms of religion where Jesus is a model or exemplar but not a living and acting person. Both liberalism and pietism, in different ways, have given up on
the resurrection and ascension as reality. The resurrection and ascension may
remain spiritual, doctrinal, or ethical constructs, but they are not real in the
sense of shaping reality itself, especially the reality of modernity. Because of
this loss of the real, both liberalism and pietism (again, in different ways) have
turned faith into religious mechanics—a spiritualized or ethically religious
way of acting in the having-mode. Both have done so to find secure footing
inside the immanent frame. Religious mechanics accept the immanent frame's
presumption that Jesus cannot act inside modernity. If liberalism or pietism
has a Christology, it's not connected to Christopraxis. The more we become
committed to religious mechanics, the more we lose a vision of Jesus's own
living personhood, turning Jesus into a lifeless logo of religion.

Barth loved the Elder (and the Younger) because they gave him a concrete
and pastoral vision of Christopraxis. The Blumhardts were practical theologians of Christopraxis.[11] Both Blumhardts avoided all religious mechanics
and sought only the living Jesus. Both boldly believed, shaping their whole
ministries around, the confession (even real experience) of Jesus's living action that continues in ministry even in modernity. Both Blumhardts encouraged Barth, particularly with their watchwords, to go into the world, loving
the world, seeking to find and follow the living Jesus who acts even in the
immanent frame.

What Barth discovered, slowly but surely, from 1915 (but more fervently
from 1919) until 1922, was that finding this living Jesus who acts in love for
the world is impossible without the dialectic, particularly within the immanent frame. This Jesus, who is the fullness of the God who is God, finds us in
ministry. He is taking what is dead and making it alive, giving the world life
in and through his own death. Vetter avoided the dialectic, choosing religion
inside modernity, which formed his practice of ministry outside an imagination for a living Christ.

The dialectic claims that as the immanent frame eclipses God's action,
we find God acting inside this absence (if we are brave enough to peer into
it, taking on the being-form of action). The dialectic seizes the immanent
frame's ability to eclipse divine action and turns that into the horizon of

11. There is a silent, often overlooked, school of Barth reading that reads him as a theologian of Christopraxis (the theologian who most directly does this is Ray S. Anderson). Yet this
school—most particularly Anderson—reads him in relation to specific contemporary ministry
issues. There is little genealogical work that is self-reflective about this school of reading. I hope
that this work shows that this Christopraxis reading has its origins in the early Barth and his
connections to the Blumhardts.

God's presence acting in the places where God should not be found—the cross and all death experiences, such as Woz's loss of his grandmother. The very locations that modernity struggles to deal with, most directly death, become the location of God's acting life. Jesus is the living dialectical man. As the fullness of God, Jesus bears the dialectic, living the dialectic in his being, showing that indeed Jesus is true God of true God by perishing, turning perishing into the living location of God's ministering presence. When Jesus is lost, he, and all of humanity with him, is found. Out of the "no way" of an executed Galilean, God makes a new way, overcoming Jesus's perishing with the new promise of life.

Barth's theology, as it developed through the twentieth century, has been seen at times as unrelentingly Christocentric. A common critique is that his Christology becomes so prominent that it eclipses the Spirit. Yet, if we trace it back to his pastoral ministry and his admiration for the Blumhardts, we can see that his Christocentrism was not operationalized for stiff doctrinal reasons but rather came about for ministerial purposes inside modernity. Pastor Barth learned this Christocentric (call it Christopraxis) focus from the direct pastoral ministries of the Blumhardts. The Blumhardts showed Barth a way of confessing and witnessing to the action of the living Jesus who is Victor by dying even in the immanent frame. The dialectic is the hermeneutic needed inside the immanent frame to discern Jesus's continued ministry as the witness to and encounter with a God who is God. This is a ministry that bears the dialectic for the sake of loving the world.

A dialectically shaped practice of ministry and theology can be modern and yet not succumb to the closed reductions of the immanent frame. The dialectic is the shape of divine action itself, represented most clearly in the act and being of Jesus Christ. The dialectic as the shape of divine action is beautiful because it both judges the reductions of the immanent frame and makes profound space within modernity to encounter the living God.

Woz was discovering that Jesus had found him. Not by overtaking him, mechanically imposing himself on Woz's will, possessing Woz's own energy and having Woz for Jesus's own mode of power. Rather, Woz discovered that when he was lost—in grief, in doubt, in restlessness, and in yearning—when he turned this lostness over to the community that loved the world by suffering with the world in the name of Jesus Christ, Jesus himself found Woz, ministering to him. Jesus was *really* present. Jesus's real presence was encountered, ministering life out of death. There are no mechanics here, only relationships of encounter. Only the freedom to be together (to be in the being-mode), finding resonance with the world as we encounter the actual living presence of Jesus Christ in and through these relationships.

Jesus, as the dialectical man who is both fully divine and fully human, dies and therefore is Victor. It's in our dying, the Younger contended, that we experience the living Jesus. This occurs not because our dying is blood magic, making Jesus appear. Dying is the concrete, and therefore real, way to wear the humble robe of the dialectic. It gives us the vision to see the living Christ whose Father so loves us that Jesus enters all the deaths in the world, sharing in them so that they might be turned from nonevents of meaninglessness into locales of God's presence, even into events of resonance.

Inside the immanent frame, only the dialectic positions us on the road to Emmaus, able to encounter the living Jesus lovingly ministering to us by hearing our lostness, and sharing his word of salvation with us (Luke 24). Only a living Jesus can free us from religious mechanization to live, sharing in our narratives of loss and in a meal of resonant friendship. Jesus's own dying is the victory over the having-mode of action. God chooses to so love the world that God in Jesus Christ bears the full violence of the having-mode. The resurrection appearances reveal that Jesus has overcome the having-mode by meeting each disciple in the being-mode. Jesus appears not with a to-do list and operational plans to possess the world. He arrives with words for renewed friends (John 20:11–18). His touch overcomes doubts (John 20:24–29), and his words are not of owning the world but of feeding little sheep in and through the open wound of personal failure (John 21:1–14). Jesus appears as the Victor over dying to offer friendship, forgiveness, and ultimately (and cosmically!) participation in his own being.

The postresurrection appearances are signs and testimonies of the form of action that is in Christ. They testify that the having-mode has been overcome by the being-mode of action. The church's foundations are set in this being-mode, in Peter's feeding of little sheep.

Through the dialectic of dying and now living through dying, Jesus offers the world, by the Spirit, the invitation to be in Christ. Jesus invites us to be in the world, free to love the world by being free from the having-mode of action, to now be in him, to take on his own being-mode of action of love, peace, and transformation through the Spirit.

The Real Dialectic

Without the dialectic that has its origin and continuation in the being of Jesus who lives, the immanent frame gives us a God who is not God. Without the dialectic, God can only be an object obtainable through religion. Modernity and the immanent frame are more comfortable with such a God. Barth pastorally turns to a *real* dialectic, bound in the *real* presence of an acting Jesus Christ (revelation), as the way of returning to a God who is God. A dialectical

Christopraxis is the way to witness—in the sense of both seeing an occurrence and giving a public statement—to the God who is God even in modernity. These thoughts oppose both the theological and the pastoral environment of the time to such a degree that Barth needs two shots at describing this dialectic. For all his genius and skill, Barth often needs two tries before his thoughts and writing are clear. On the second try, Barth really finds what he's trying to say.

This is nowhere truer than in *Römerbrief I* and *Römerbrief II*. In *Römerbrief I* Barth was trying to carve out the narrow space between liberalism and pietism that he and Thurneysen were trying to find for their ministries. He was trying to return to a God who is God. He sensed that the dialectic was important. But only after giving the lecture at the Student Christian Movement conference in 1919 (just months after *Römerbrief I* was released; see the beginning of chap. 9 above) and having further conversations with others who pointed Barth to Plato, Kierkegaard, and Dostoevsky was he able to unleash the dialectic to do its work.[12]

The dialectic gives us a pastoral vision for how to encounter the living God of the Bible in the immanent frame and in turn keeps the reductions of the immanent frame from turning God into something other than God. The dialectic is how modern people, even in a village like Safenwil, can encounter the nongivenness of reality while always remaining nongiven.

Barth's objective into the 1920s and during his final few years as pastor in Safenwil—which led directly into the rewritten *Römerbrief II*—was to tease out the shape and reach of this dialectic. The need to do so was the impetus for the rewrite.

When the Noetic Meets the Real

German theologian Michael Beintker has done his own teasing out of *Römerbrief II*, finding two operating dialectics within it.[13] The first he calls a noetic dialectic, the second a real dialectic. *Noetic* describes a mental or intellectual activity. This first dialectic is a form of thinking. *Römerbrief II* was done in a noetic dialectical fashion. Every thought comes to the reader in dialectical shape. For the pastor to *think* the faith inside the immanent frame,

12. Heinrich Barth turned Karl Barth to Plato and the given and nongiven elements of reality. Thurneysen encouraged Barth to read Dostoevsky and Kierkegaard.

13. Beintker's research is found in his book *Die Dialektik in der 'dialektischen Theologie' Karl Barths* (Munich: Christian Kaiser Verlag, 1987). For this discussion I'm drawing on Bruce McCormack's discussion on Beintker in *Karl Barth's Critically Realistic Dialectical Theology*, 10–13. Beintker discusses four dialectics, three of which are real dialectics. In what I say below I hit on all three. But to be honest, I find the three, while important, blurry. A direct dialogue with each might be more confusing than helpful. Therefore, following Beintker, I'll just stick with what he discusses as the overarching real dialectic of time and eternity.

her best bet is to do so dialectically. She must place every "theological state-ment . . . over against a counter-statement, without allowing the dialectical tension between the two to be resolved in a higher synthesis."[14] This way of doing theology into the late 1920s, 1930s, and beyond became what Barth is known for. It's much better to call the theology that Barth and others were doing "dialectical" than "neo-orthodox."[15]

This attention to the noetic (way of thinking) dialectic as if it were the only dialectic has led many to see Barth as impractical and pastorally ambivalent. Some even paint Barth as a twentieth-century Protestant scholastic. But this can only be assumed if we foreclose on the first dialectic, seeing the dialectic in Barth's thought not as multivalent but only and finally as noetic. Missing the multivalent shape of the dialectic leads to the misguided assumption that Pastor Barth is more concerned with developing a noetic dialectic for academic theology than with a real dialectical (*Realdialektik*) theology for the practice of ministry.[16] This is a mistake.

The other dialectic that Beintker finds even more prominent in *Römer-brief II* is a real, not a noetic, dialectic. Barth's attention to the *Realdialektik* makes his early theology so rich and pastoral. The noetic dialectic is pre-ceded, dependent on, and made profound by the real dialectic. Only the real dialectic, not the noetic, can confront the reductions of modernity. The real dialectic is a kind of bony fish that cannot be swallowed by the whale called the immanent frame. A purely noetic dialectic can be swallowed up as easily as a minnow, making little difference to the whale. The whale finds the noetic neither appetizing nor important. But the real dialectic confronts the whale and yet cannot simply be swallowed whole by the whale. Barth sees the real dialectic, and the noetic's subordination to it, ringing so clearly in the ministry of the Blumhardts. This real dialectic proves to be a much different way of doing ministry and theology in modernity.

What's So Real about It?

Our next step is to ask, What does it actually mean to call it a *real* dialec-tic? Real is not being contrasted with fake here. Neither of Barth's dialectics

14. McCormack, *Karl Barth's Critically Realistic Dialectical Theology*, 11.

15. This remains true even after Barth's Anselm book (*Anselm: Fides Quaerens Intel-lectum* [London: SCM, 1960]) and his more analogical approach, though I'm convinced by McCormack's argument (in *Karl Barth's Critically Realistic Dialectical Theology*) that the analogical shift that moves away from the dialectical is overstated.

16. Those exposed to Barth's 1920s theology saw this. In his first teaching posts, he was assumed to best fit practical theology. He had been a pastor for ten years, and the real dialectic had significant practical theological implications.

is fake. Rather, the *real* here means *really lived* or *really experienced in the world*, as opposed to a construct of thinking. Real is contrasted with abstract or theoretical. But this raises another question we need to face: If a noetic dialectic operates in the mind or intellect, where specifically does a real dialectic operate? To say that a real dialectic is *really lived* or *really experienced in the world* is to say that it specifically operates in relations. To call a dialectic "real" means that the dialectic is experienced objectively in real, even concrete, relationships. A noetic dialectic is an operation of the mind; a real dialectic is in the shape of a relationship of encounter in the world.

Rosa has taught us that the being-mode of action is best thought of as resonance. As we've seen, resonance is not solely an effervescent feeling but rather a form of relations. This form of relations that is resonance is bound, even for Rosa, in a real dialectic.[17] Rosa vividly points out that concrete and lived relationships in and with the world, which are resonance, can only be as encounters with true otherness—that is, dialectically. This encounter with true otherness *is* a real (lived) relationship in dialectical form.

Pastor Barth's real dialectic is concerned with the real relations of God with the world. The real dialectic is the very way of perceiving the real relations between God and modernity, the human agent and God's Word, and much more. This dialectic is *real* because it's concerned with concrete and lived relations—particularly between God and the world. The real dialectic is the impossible possibility of a relationship between sinful human beings and the God who is truly God. The real dialectic is the means of accessing such a real relation between a God who is God and sinful humanity, who is addicted to the having-mode of action. These relations, as long as they remain always dialectical, are how human agents encounter a God who is God in the immanent frame.

Such *real relations* (between sinful humanity and the God who is God) make up the direct environment Barth seeks to explore theologically. This direct environment of real relations means it's the pastor, not the academic theologian, who is our primary concern. The pastor's primary habitat or environment is that of real relations in the world. The pastor is tasked with the impossible possibility in modernity of speaking of the living God who is God inside the immanent frame.

This sets the table to more directly discuss the *Realdialektik* running through the hot, pulsing veins of *Römerbrief II*.

17. This project in many ways was born from seeing this real dialectic in Rosa and wondering if it was possible to relate it to Barth—and what would happen if I did. This whole project is really a thought experiment in the alchemy of thinkers. It mixes Barth with Rosa, all with the hope of making some gold that might help the church in its ministry.

The Real Dialectic in Action

For Barth in *Römerbrief II*, the *Realdialektik* is best stated as the *infinite qualitative difference between time and eternity*. The utter distinction between, and yet possible relation of, time and eternity is the real dialectic. Barth borrows the description of this real dialectic as the *infinite qualitative difference between time and eternity* from Kierkegaard. Kierkegaard wielded it against the Danish religious establishment. As a recluse, Kierkegaard threw this dialectic like stones at the nineteenth-century Danish Lutheran Church for its concessions to an immanent-bound religion. Barth follows Kierkegaard, not as a rancorous agitating philosopher but as a pastor. We'll see the importance of his pastoral concern soon. But first, a little bit more on how Kierkegaard understands this dialectic and why Pastor Barth embraces it.

Kierkegaard glosses this dialectic as "God is in heaven and you are on earth, you stupid idiots!" (Okay, the "stupid idiots" part isn't in the quote, but Kierkegaard as much as means it.) This real dialectic should be obvious to the Danish church. Every human being (at least in corrupt Christendom, Kierkegaard thinks) should feel this dialectic in their being. The real dialectic is that time and eternity stand in opposition, meaning there is no relation between what is bound in time (humanity) and what is eternal (God). There is *no way* to have and possess God, no way to free ourselves from time (not even with a truckload of having-mode actions). The inability to recognize, and more so confess, the infinite qualitative distinction between time and eternity means that even human religious structures and patterns, which are bound in time, cannot live in any delusion that they can build a staircase, even a stepstool, to heaven. This is impossible, and God says, "I hate, I despise your festivals, and I take no delight in your solemn assemblies" (Amos 5:21), because they've been made into idolatrous projects of religion, used to hide from the *Realdialektik*. The infinite qualitative distinction between a God in heaven and humanity on earth means there is no point of contact between them that can be initiated by the human side, no natural linking point that can be molded and controlled by the having-mode of action. The one side of this real dialectic is the utter impossibility of any form of human action working itself out of any of the constraints and existential pitfalls of time itself.[18]

The immanent frame tries to ignore or deny this real dialectical experience of the qualitative distinction between time and eternity. People inside the immanent frame work very hard to live without concern for or interest in the

---

18. Stanley Hauerwas has a nice short discussion on the eternity–time dialectic in *With the Grain of the Universe: The Church's Witness and Natural Theology* (Grand Rapids: Baker Academic, 2013), see 160–61.

relationship between time and eternity. But because this is a real dialectic, it is, as we said, a bony fish that cannot be digested by the immanent frame. The real dialectic between time and eternity can be successfully ignored in the immanent frame until it inevitably can't. It can be ignored until you're diagnosed with stage 3 lung cancer or you realize your kids have grown up so fast. Or maybe until you're laid off or you find yourself just plain choking on the sawdust of late-modern meaninglessness. But even if modernity can work to ignore this real dialectic for a period, the pastor cannot opt out of direct confrontation with this real dialectic. Even outside modernity the overarching real dialectic of the relationship between time and eternity is a struggle. Now inside the immanent frame, this real dialectic, which the pastor must bear, is a crisis.

The Barth of *Römerbrief II* believes the pastor has no choice. If she wishes to be a faithful pastor, she must bear this real dialectic. She must minister under its weight. It is the real dialectic (not the congregation's decline and lack of resources) that should cause her to toss and turn, interrupting her sleep. The pastor must claim again and again that time and eternity are unrelatable. And yet (and yet!) without losing the total unrelatability, she must proclaim, and help her congregation participate in, the miraculous actuality of time and eternity's real relation, which comes out of its impossibility. This dialectic is *real* because it's located in lived relations. This lived relation, which is the context of the real dialectic, is both time and eternity's impossibility, and yet impossible possibility, of encounter.

As we've said, Barth's early theology is sometimes called a theology of crisis, because Pastor Barth saw no way, nor any reason, to avoid this dialectical crisis. The only constructive possibility for theology and ministry under the weight of immanence is to embrace and suffer this crisis of the real dialectic. Inside the immanent frame, we can never escape crisis. But inside the crisis, the strict dialectical difference between time and eternity, between a God who is God and humanity, can miraculously find a relation. The relation has its meeting at the location of the crisis itself. In the preface to *Römerbrief II*, Barth says that he's seeking to "keep . . . [the] difference [of time and eternity] constantly in view in both its negative and positive significance."[19] Barth continues, "The relation of *this* God to *this* human being, the relation of *this* human being to *this* God, is for me both the theme of the Bible and the sum of philosophy."[20] I would add, and I think Barth lived it, that this relation is at the heart of ministry and pastoral leadership!

---

19. Karl Barth, *The Epistle to the Romans* (London: Oxford University Press, 1933), 10.
20. Barth, *Epistle to the Romans*, 10 (emphasis original).

The italics in that quote from Barth are original and important. The italicized *this* is meant to highlight that this relation is real and lived. It is a real encounter between God and humanity.

The relation of *this* God to *this* or *these* human beings comes into real relation—but only at the level of the crisis. The real dialectic of time and eternity finds that eternity is encountered in time, by *Sterbet*, by dying. In dying, in our experience of the crisis of dying, we find ourselves in a deep relationship with the God of eternity who brings new life out of God's own crisis of dying. The infinite qualitative difference between time and eternity is bridged, relating time and eternity, in the God/man. Jesus Christ, who is eternal God, dies in time so that time itself might be taken into eternity.

The church serves the world by living under this real dialectic.[21] The church confesses its suffering in time. Through the church's suffering, the church confesses the real encounter and participation in the life of the eternal God. This eternal God dies out of deep love for the world. By dying, God miraculously (unfathomably!) places dying within the realm of eternity. Because God the Father knows the dying of a beloved and the beloved Son dies, dying itself is now forever transformed. It's *not* the void of real relation. It is fertile with the real ministering relationship of God to humanity, of eternity to time. Now where there is death in time, God brings life. For death itself, as the cruel master of time, is bound within the eternal relationship of the Father to the Son in the Spirit.

Preaching

One reason that Barth has been discarded by many practical and pastoral theologians is that the two dialectics have not been differentiated. In fact, against the early Barth's wishes, most have assumed the noetic dialectic has priority over the real. As we've shown, it's the opposite. While both dialectics are important, the real dialectic has precedence over the noetic. But few who have sought to connect Barth's theology with the practice of ministry have allowed the distinctions in these two dialectics to shape their perspective. The ramifications are significant. When the dialectic is imagined (either intentionally or not) as solely noetic, the *only* real, viable form of practice is a kind of doctrinaire preaching, and in turn the whole of ecclesiology is seen as almost completely for this kind of preaching (though interestingly Barth's own ecclesiology doesn't go here in *Church Dogmatics* IV/1).

21. Hans Urs von Balthasar discusses this further in *The Theology of Karl Barth* (San Francisco: Ignatius, 1992), 103–4.

Inside this preaching-centric approach, the pastoral task is really nothing more than preaching in a pseudoacademic or fully academic form. The idea is that ministry equals releasing or even imposing the noetic dialectic on your people. In my mind, even Eduard Thurneysen himself falls into this trap. His book *A Theology of Pastoral Care* essentially asserts that pastoral care is preaching.[22] I don't want to disparage this. There is something true and important about it. But there is also something misguided. To start, it misses that the noetic dialectic is subordinate to the real dialectic. The noetic dialectic alone cannot meet the challenges of the immanent frame. Just making more good preachers who can more sophisticatedly mobilize the noetic dialectic will not do. Good preaching alone is not enough to witness to God who is God in modernity.

Rather, because the dialectic is primarily real, and real means an environment of relations, the practical implications for the pastor and for our ecclesiology are pushed into a relational direction. The pastor doesn't just preach the noetic dialectic; the church is not just the house of this way of *thinking*. Rather, while the pastor will need to preach in the shape of the noetic dialectic (I'm not against this), her primary calling is to attend to the concrete ways her people live under the real dialectic, encountering the absence and presence of the living God in and through their relationships.

The pastor's first job and the church's first way of being in the immanent frame is to move away from the having-mode to the being-mode. Under the real dialectic the church is first for being together, being a place of confession, being in prayer, and being in celebration of life through narratives of loss and hope.

The pastor must not just noetically preach but also form a community whose members relate to each other and the world in resonance—because the dialectic is real. In bearing the real dialectic together, and with the world, we really—not just mentally or intellectually—encounter the living God. It's not in noetic preaching primarily that we encounter the living Christ (Christopraxis) but in and through our relationships of ministering to one other, sharing in each other's real dialectic.[23] This emphasis doesn't downgrade or eliminate the noetic; it appropriately locates it, placing it under the real dialectic.

---

22. See also Andrew Purves for an example of a very good thinker who seems unable to keep the dialectics apart, giving a kind of doctrinal coldness to his practical perspectives. Purves and I are very close on so many things. However, it seems to me that he focuses more on the noetic dialectic, while I only wish to grab the noetic because of deeper attention to the real dialectic. See Andrew Purves, *Reconstructing Pastoral Theology: A Christological Foundation* (Louisville: Westminster John Knox, 2004).

23. This is a core difference in those who read Barth in the Christopraxis school. For us, the locale of revelation is not simply in the operation of the noetic dialectic but inside the encounter

The watchword becomes important because it fuses the two dialectics while ordering them correctly in practical pastoral and ecclesial actions. The watchword needs to be always in noetic dialectical shape (it needs to preach and be preached). But it is preached only because it's born out of the encounter with the living God in and through the real dialectic and because it is used as a hermeneutical lens to discern God's continuing action inside the real dialectic. Only inside bearing the real dialectic is the church able to discern God's own free action for the world in the immanent frame.

———

It was in the confession of the real dialectic that Woz was moved to ask the saints of Saint John the Baptist to journey with him. The real dialectic of losing his grandmother in time, yearning for an answer to his many experiences of death and loss, moved Woz and Saint John the Baptist into relationship. Woz began to see that time and eternity were being bridged for him through experiencing the real dialectic as the hermeneutic for divine action, taught through the watchword. The little flock—with few resources, lacking funds, and with aging members—was able to participate in the miraculous impossible possibility of *this* God who is truly the eternal God relating to *this* human being named Woz. Saint John the Baptist's ability to do this didn't rest in its skill or vitality but in its bravery to invite a lost young man to confess his lostness. Saint John the Baptist had no power to find Woz. Only the eternal God is able to find lost persons in time, inviting them to be found in participation with God's own eternal being.

———

It started with a rattling cough. Woz heard it for the first time when he was returning a guitar that Herbert had lent him. Within three days, Herbert was hospitalized.

---

of relationships of ministry in the real dialectic. Because the real dialectic is about relations, the conception of revelation is bound in relations.

17

Deepening the Dialectic

Avoiding Sledgehammering the Ceiling

Woz was MIA. He'd been missing in action for a while. No one had heard from him since Herbert was hospitalized for pneumonia. Bert had called and left a detailed message. He told Woz that Herbert was in a bad way. Herbert had asked for him and wanted to see him. But there was nothing. Woz missed Bible study, and no one could reach him. He had never missed a Bible study since he had started coming after his grandmother's funeral, back in the summer. Woz joked that he owed them those not-quite-day-old donuts, even when he felt like taking a break. But now there were no donuts and no Woz. His absence was a throbbing deficit. And its connection to Herbert seemed obvious. In the next few days Helene called countless times. Sue texted. Finally Bert went searching.

Bert made his way to Teddy's Tacos on trivia night. Woz might have missed Bible study, but Bert figured he'd never be absent from trivia night. But he wasn't there. Woz's team told Bert they hadn't heard anything from Woz for a while either. Woz normally dropped into Teddy's a couple of times a week, grabbing a taco for lunch or dinner. Grabbing that taco, Woz often gabbed with Teddy, his old high school acquaintance, about new music or, to Teddy's amusement, Woz's new investment portfolio. But Teddy, too, told Bert that Woz hadn't been in, not even once in the past week.

Bert drove to Woz's place. He knocked and looked through the windows. There was no motion. But a few lights were on, so Bert decided to wait, sitting on a wobbly old kitchen chair on the dusty 1930s porch. It badly needed a coat of paint. Bert could spot multiple coats that had been painted on top of other coats over the decades. It smelled like dust and oranges.

About forty minutes later, Woz came biking up. When he reached the porch, the dusty orange smell was covered by what Bert was pretty sure was weed. Woz's eyes were red. At first Bert figured it was the weed, and it might have been. But soon Bert realized how much pain Woz was in. It had been a week of tears, Bert figured.

Woz was distant at first. But when Bert caught his eye and said, "I know how hard this is," Woz's distance retreated and Bert saw the same honest, hurting guy he'd met for the first time in the sanctuary after his grandmother's funeral. Woz told Bert he didn't think he could do it all again. He couldn't lose someone who'd become so important to him. The loss of Grandma Jean still hurt too badly. Hearing about Herbert's hospitalization felt too much like the same, adding to this pain. So Woz had gone back to hiding, cutting himself off from everyone, retreating into himself. The pain made him wonder if this journey for God was a waste of time.

Bert listened. Then Bert reminded Woz of their watchword. "If it wasn't for you, Woz," he said, "we as a church would never have gotten back to looking to find Jesus in what's lost, because out of no way is where God makes a way. Remember that, Woz?"

"I know," Woz said. "It's been running through my head. I just thought the hard stuff was behind me. I thought those words were for making sense of what happened, not for preparing for what was going to happen."

"But that's life, Woz. This is living. It hurts, but there is a beauty in it all."

Bert and Woz talked for another hour, and the next day Woz visited Herbert.

Woz indeed found Herbert in a tough spot. He was covered in tubes, wrapped in a blanket, and fighting to stay awake. Even so, he was happy to see Woz. Woz apologized for not coming earlier. Herbert told him he forgave him. But Herbert did need a few things from him.

Herbert started by telling Woz how much he'd come to care for Woz over the last few months. He told Woz he planned to beat this pneumonia, but if he didn't, he wanted Woz to have all his guitars. Woz teared up, knowing how much those guitars mattered to Herbert.

Herbert continued, "I never had a child. But even when I was too old to ever have one, I just foolishly thought I'd give my guitars to my kids or grandkids. But lying here, I realized I wanted you to have them. Playing with you has been the best part of the last ten years for me. You got me playing again, and that's been so good."

Fighting back the tears, Woz could only nod to show that he'd take them if it came to that.

"But I need one more thing from you," Herbert continued. "I need you to pray for me."

"Okay, but I should probably get Bert or Helene to come do that. I mean I can be here and stuff, but they'd probably be better—"

"No," Herbert interrupted, "you're my friend and I want you to pray for me."

"Honestly, Herbert, I'm not real sure I'm the praying kind of person. I mean I've come a long way in my journey, and I do think Jesus has found me, but honestly I'm not sure prayer does anything."

"That's okay," Herbert responded. "I believe. You pray and I'll believe. I just need a friend to pray for me. Will you pray for me?"

"But I don't even know how to pray," Woz said.

Herbert told him to pray the watchword, to just be with Herbert and wait for God, to tell God that they were together waiting for God to act. So Woz did pray. And he came back three or four times a week to pray for Herbert. Then they talked and laughed. When Herbert transitioned to a long-term-care facility, Woz continued to come and pray for Herbert.

One day Woz met Teemon, who was having coffee with Herbert. Teemon's room was a few doors down from Herbert's. Teemon was closer to Woz's age than Herbert's. He'd been in a terrible car accident, with months of recovery. By chance, Herbert and Teemon had met in physical therapy and hit it off. They liked talking about old cars. When Woz arrived, Herbert introduced him to Teemon, saying, "This is my good friend, Woz. We play music together and he comes here and prays for me."

Teemon grabbed hold of the "prays for me," repeating it as a question: "He prays for you?"

Woz just nodded his head, his teeth appearing in a half smile. Then to both Herbert's and Woz's surprise, Teemon said, "Would you pray for me too?"

Woz shrugged and found himself saying, "Yeah, sure."

From that point on, Woz never stopped praying. He came to realize that indeed Jesus had found him. Woz saw that, having been found, now as part of the church, he was called to enter the world to pray for the world. He had once been the embodiment of the world coming to Saint John the Baptist. He still was, but he was also now the church, part of this community that loved the world by waiting with the world and praying for the world. Woz found himself rooted deeper and deeper in the community through prayer.

Woz discovered, and Bert with him, that the church existed to embody the being-mode of action as resonance in the form of prayer. Over the years as Woz learned to pray, so too did Saint John the Baptist. The disposition of prayer directly reminded them that they were not the star of their story, and yet inside this story they had action to take. This action of prayer embodied the being-mode by forming them to be a people who waited for a God who is God. Prayer was the direct way of embracing the real dialectic, seeking God in what is lost, trusting God to move in the "no way." Praying the watchword was the noetic dialectical way of confessing the real dialectic and opening them—even in the immanent frame—to the living and acting dialectic man, Jesus Christ.

An End and a New Beginning

Karl Barth had been the pastor of the Safenwil congregation for ten years. The year 1921 seemed like a good time to move on. In no way was an academic position presumed to be the next natural step. A nonacademic position seemed more obvious. Barth was invited to consider other congregations in Basel and Bern (moving beyond the village). He was even asked to consider standing for election to the Aargau Great Council, transitioning into political life. Barth called this later invitation "a great temptation." Not because he found it unseemly but because it appealed so much to him. If you were making bets in 1921, Barth seemed more likely to leave pastoral ministry for politics than academics.

But just when Barth was pondering another pastorate or a political life, the academic world came calling. A new chair in reformed theology had been established at Göttingen, with funding directly from American Presbyterians. Barth was surprised to be asked to consider it. He was still working on *Römerbrief II*. But *Römerbrief I* had caught the attention of the professors and pastor in charge of filling the new chair. Barth's surprise revolved around the fact that neither *Römerbrief I* nor the coming *Römerbrief II* had any real dialogue with Calvin or the Reformed tradition proper. Barth, perhaps overstating, claimed that he had very little understanding of the Reformed tradition at all back in 1921. Yet Professor Karl Müller and Pastor Adam Heilmann, who were driving the committee, were drawn to Barth's clear passion for Holy Scripture, as was so evident in *Römerbrief I*. Feeling out of his depth, but also feeling a sure sense of call, Barth quickly accepted the offer.

On October 13, 1921, Barth again left Switzerland for a German university. This time not as a student but as a professor. This time not as a young, inexperienced bachelor but as a father with growing children and a decade of pastoral experience. This time not in defiance of his own father but carrying a piece of his father with him. Karl lugged Fritz's desk across the border with him. He'd use it for the rest of his life, writing most of his thousands of pages on it. The desk still sits in his office in his last house in Basel.

In Göttingen, the desk would become an anchor. Not only did the desk powerfully and beautifully tether Barth's mind and spirit to his father, but in those first years, Barth's body was almost literally tethered to the desk. He realized quickly that not only did he need to write out all his lectures for the first time (an overwhelming task for any new professor), but worse, that he didn't have the background to teach the subject matter he was called to teach. To rectify this, he'd need to spend huge amounts of time reading the material for the first time, lecturing on it hours later.

The first few years were brutal. Barth says of that period that he was "almost always on the night shift. . . . More than once, the lecture which I gave at seven o'clock in the morning had only been finished between three and five."[1] It was exhausting. Barth adds, "I had to find my way through the fog like a poor mule, still hampered above all by a lack of academic agility, an inadequate knowledge of Latin and the most appalling memory!"[2]

All this catching up was grueling, and Barth didn't make things easy on himself. After a year or two of teaching specifically Reformed theology and being assumed to be more of a practical theologian, Barth pushed to be allowed to teach a section of dogmatics. This took political maneuvering within the faculty. But it was soon decided that in spring 1924, he'd have the opportunity. Of course, this added even more to Barth's reading load. In May 1924, anchored to his father's desk, seeking, before the break of dawn, to scrape a new dogmatics lecture out of his brain, Barth stumbled into another breakthrough. Drinking from the tradition with the force of a fire hose, Barth saw a dialectic he had not recognized before.

The New Dialectic

As we saw in the previous chapter, dialectical theology can exist inside the immanent frame without being reduced and flattened by the closed spin of

1. Barth, *Briefwechsel Karl Barth-Eduard Thurneysen, 1913–1921* (1973), 81, quoted by Eberhard Busch, *Karl Barth: His Life from Letters and Autobiographical Texts* (Philadelphia: Fortress, 1975), 127.
2. Barth, *Briefwechsel Karl Barth-Eduard Thurneysen, 1921–1930* (1974), 134, quoted by Busch, *Karl Barth*, 127–28. I personally take comfort that Barth curses his memory. It appears that the fallibility of memory is something every scholar with a large reading load laments, and it means, at least for me, that I can ease my own hypochondriacal fears and assure myself that my own lack of memory is normal and not a neurological condition.

immanence. We saw that this dialectic is multivalent. The dialectic is both noetic and real. Or perhaps better, it is noetic, a way of thinking, because it's primarily real. Paul is operating out of a noetic dialectic by describing a real dialectic when he says, "[God's] power is made perfect in weakness" (2 Cor. 12:9). For Barth, the noetic dialectic is always subordinate—filed under—a real dialectic. The real dialectic has precedence over the noetic dialectic.[3]

This real dialectic isn't just a way of thinking. What makes this dialectic real is its environment. The environment of a noetic dialectic is the mind or intellect. The real dialectic is located in the environment of relationships, and it orders relationships appropriately. The real dialectic allows us to recognize that God is God. Eternity can be in relation with time by entering time—even the time of the immanent frame. The eternal can encounter us in finite time. But finite time can never, by definition, invade eternity and allow eternity to remain eternity. Therefore, being clear about the dialectic allows for the distinction of time and eternity (God remains always the eternal God), while also allowing for the eternal God to enter relations with finite beings in time, unveiling God's eternal being to them in time (we call this revelation).

But following this real dialectic means that we, as finite beings, suffer the qualitative distinction between time and eternity. We suffer as beings bound in time. We suffer the impossibility of saving ourselves from time. We seek some way that time and eternity can be bridged, confessing that only God can do the bridging. We're judged for our sinfulness in time, needing the salvation of eternity. Through the rewrite that would become *Römerbrief II* Barth sees multiple ways of naming this real dialectic, but all of them are framed within Kierkegaard's existential dialectic of the infinite qualitative distinction between time and eternity. The cross itself becomes the singular mathematical point of the revelation of eternity in time.

Yet, in May 1924, as Barth read more deeply into the tradition, he discovered that there was another real dialectic to consider. Barth saw a different way of theologically describing this real dialectic, freeing himself from the existential philosophy that undergirded *Römerbrief II*. This newly discovered real dialectic is more incarnational and christological, as opposed to existentially located.

This second real dialectic that Barth stumbled upon in his reading at Fritz's desk is what the church fathers called "enhypostatic/anhypostatic Christology." This second dimension to the real dialectic can add to the pastoral theology and lived ecclesiology we've been working out for the immanent

---

3. This means, when worked out, that ministry always has precedence over theology; the minister or pastor has precedence over the theologian.

frame, but only if we can get a handle on what these strange words and their confusing prefixes mean.

It's All Greek to Me

The Cappadocian fathers in the fourth century, out of great theological creativity, reworked the Greek word *hypostasis*. For thinkers before them, like Aristotle, *hypostasis* meant *being* and was basically synonymous with *ousia*. Yet the Cappadocians saw that there were different qualities to being.[4] Some things just were and others were (or were becoming) because of the event of relations. Italian physicist Carlo Rovelli uses the example of the difference between a rock and a kiss to make this point.[5] A rock just is. The constitution of its being isn't born out of a relationship.[6] But a kiss, Rovelli explains, only *is* through a relational encounter. A kiss is something, but not something outside of two persons in relationship. There is no way outside of persons in a relationship (of action) to have (for there even to be) a kiss. You can't subtract the persons and keep the kiss. A kiss cannot exist outside of persons in relationships of action.

In working out the trinitarian formula, the Cappadocians claimed that God is one ousia (or being) and three hypostases (or persons) who are in relation. The Trinity, like a kiss, is three persons so fully and completely in the action of the being-mode that they are uniquely and singularly one, while always remaining three. The Godhead is like a kiss. It's the three persons in relation, in the full and complete action of the being-mode. In the same way, there is a unique and singular hypostatic union in Jesus Christ. In his unique and singular person there is a union of divine and human natures. These natures are not constituted by the logic of percentages, as with the ingredients of a cocktail. Jesus is not 65 percent human and 35 percent divine. Rather, the distinct, yet united, and single natures of Jesus are like a kiss. In a mutual kiss, particularly of passion, there isn't a percentage, as if partner A could contribute 58 percent of the kiss while partner B contributes only 42 percent.

---

4. John Behr provides a nice discussion of hypostasis and its meaning for the Cappadocians. He points to how complicated the issues around this are in the patristic tradition. See *The Nicene Faith: Formation of Christian Theology* (Yonkers, NY: St. Vladimir's Seminary Press, 2004), 2:306–10. Trevor Hart also provides important context and connects hypostasis to Barth in his *Regarding Karl Barth: Toward a Reading of His Theology* (Eugene, OR: Wipf & Stock, 1999), 15–22.

5. See Rovelli, *Seven Brief Lessons on Physics* (New York: Riverhead, 2016).

6. Of course this is all a matter of perspective. A rock is ultimately the relationships of force, sediment, and time. But Rovelli knows this and is trying to make another point.

If this kind of division were discernible, it wouldn't really be a kiss. A kiss that could be spliced into percentages isn't a kiss. Rather, in a mutual kiss of passion, the kiss *is* made by the full union of both partners' 100 percent participation. The hypostatic union of the divine and human natures in the singular being of Jesus Christ is like a kiss—it's a full 100 percent involvement from both sides. In Jesus Christ there is a hypostatic union, a union of the fully divine and fully human natures in the person of Jesus. In Jesus alone the divine and human natures kiss.

This Cappadocian theological anthropology (which most of the Eastern theologians affirm) would claim that human beings too are hypostatic.[7] We are persons.[8] We have our being in and through relationships in the being-mode of action. We have our being only in and through encounters and connections with others. In opposition to the currents of Western modernity, this hypostatic anthropology claims that we are not fundamentally individual wills or subjects. We are persons who have our personhood in and through relationships that are outside us that nevertheless make us. Human beings are therefore open for union at the divine and human levels. But this hypostatic constitution of the human being, and the hypostatic union of Jesus Christ, are two *fundamentally different* realities. Human beings seek union with and for the sake of being hypostatic—being persons. But Jesus Christ uniquely is the singular being of union. His natures are in hypostatic union. Only Jesus finds his personhood in the eventful encounter and full union of the divine and human natures—both natures keeping the union one hundred percent. The salvation of all other hypostatic creatures, and the restoration of all things, is dependent on the hypostatic union of this singular person, Jesus Christ.

When the church fathers peered more deeply into this hypostatic union of this singular person, they saw a dialectic. This dialectic—for the likes of Basil, Gregory of Nyssa, and before them Athanasius—did not encourage them to abandon the world but to embrace it, not to despise life but to treasure it. Peering into this hypostatic union at play, they, and more specifically Cyril of Alexandra, saw the enhypostatic/anhypostatic dialectic. And looking over their shoulders from Fritz's desk, Barth saw it too.

---

7. Vladimir Lossky discusses this hypostatic anthropology in *Dogmatic Theology: Creation, God's Image in Man, and the Redeeming Work of the Trinity* (Yonkers, NY: St. Vladimir's Seminary Press, 2017), 82–85.

8. Alan Torrance in his important book *Persons in Communion: Trinitarian Description and Human Participation* (Edinburgh: T&T Clark, 1996) discusses hypostasis in depth. He brings together many different perspectives (see 227–90). Torrance draws from John Zizioulas, who discusses hypostatic anthropology in *The One and the Many: Studies on God, Man, the Church, and the World Today* (Alhambra, CA: Sebastian Press, 2010), 30–35, 140–48, 405–7.

The Enhypostatic/Anhypostatic Dialectic Meets the Time/Eternity Dialectic

What Barth sees as he looks over the shoulders of the church fathers is that this enhypostatic/anhypostatic (en/an) dialectic is as real as the eternity/time dialectic he borrowed from Kierkegaard, but more directly rests in the very being of Jesus Christ. Kierkegaard was not shy in talking about the God/man and showing the importance of the cross. But, Barth had to admit, it became a little dire and drab. Kierkegaard's rage could border on, or at least be confused with, a disdain for life (e.g., Søren refuses to marry Regine even though he loves her). Later Barth called Kierkegaard "the melancholy Dane." Something in Kierkegaard's stark dialectic didn't compute for Barth. It was hard to reconcile Kierkegaard's melancholy with Mozart's *The Magic Flute*.

Then in 1924 Barth started to see that if one failed to rethink the real dialectic in and through the en/an dialectic, waiting as a form of action (as resonance) could be lost. To love the world and embrace life, the real dialectic would need to be rethought. Barth saw that if he stayed with the melancholy Dane and the eternity/time *Realdialektik*, he'd have to exchange Mozart for Beethoven. That wasn't an option! And it wasn't because the real dialectic embedded in Mozart did something different from or beyond fronting the existential. It spoke of the transformation of life for the sake of life. It spoke of resonance. This transformation of life, as the embracing of the good gifts of life, could only be recognized as salvation.[9]

Yet ultimately what Barth saw, peering over the shoulders of the church fathers and into the *Realdialektik* of en/an, was a way to more richly articulate his deepest pastoral concern. As we explored in the previous chapter, Barth named this concern in the preface to *Römerbrief II*. The en/an, as we'll see, allowed Barth to more fully describe "the relation of *this* God to *this* human being,"[10] which he saw as the very theme of the Bible and the most difficult, but essential, task of the pastor and theologian inside the immanent frame. The en/an dialectic allows Barth to soften his prophetic deconstructive cadence, exchanging it for a full and more constructive christological rhythm. But this new rhythm is no less radical. Now in the university, Barth was not relaxing his focus on the encounter with a God who is God through the living/acting

9. Bruce McCormack nicely discusses the shift from the time/eternity dialectic to en/an in *Karl Barth's Critically Realistic Dialectical Theology: Its Genesis and Development, 1909–1936* (Oxford: Oxford University Press, 1997), 264–66. Robert W. Jenson discusses this shift in one of his earliest books, *God after God: The God of the Past and the Future as Seen in the Work of Karl Barth* (Indianapolis: Bobbs-Merrill, 1969), see 70–74; and again in *Alpha and Omega: A Study in the Theology of Karl Barth* (1963; repr., Eugene, OR: Wipf & Stock, 2002), 79–80.

10. Barth, *Epistle to the Romans* (London: Oxford University Press, 1933), 10.

Jesus Christ in the modern world. Barth was seeking, as much as before—if not even more so—the *real* encounter with the living God.

The *Realdialektik* of en/an allows the real encounter with the living Jesus Christ to be imagined beyond the singular point of the cross and its eschatological unveiling (allowing for a much richer articulation of Christopraxis, as we'll see below). The *Realdialektik* does its work by locating the site of revelation. It points to a specific environment where Jesus Christ is unveiled. This specific pointing out is always a humble confession but is nevertheless necessary, particularly inside the immanent frame. Without locating the site of revelation, faith has no source in Jesus Christ, but becomes only religion, flattened like a pancake by immanence. Both editions of *Römerbrief* (but more so *Römerbrief II*) find this site of the unveiling of Jesus Christ (revelation) in the cross. The cross (and resurrection) is the eschatological event that brings eternity into time, brings the eschaton into the now. It is *now* for Jesus himself, and through him promised to all humanity.

Barth never abandons this site of the cross (nor do I). But he now sees that without adding the *Realdialektik* of the en/an, things can become too narrow, potentially attacking life or inviting an escape from life. And even more dangerous, without attention to the en/an dialectic, the pastoral and ecclesiological necessity for transformation and participation in the life of God can be missed, allowing for its own kind of slide into religion. Moving to the en/an dialectic broadens the site of revelation from the cross to the whole of Jesus's incarnational life, providing a richer articulation for how the human being, bound in time, nevertheless participates in the eternal life of Jesus Christ, who is eternally before the Father while being completely and fully human. The en/an allows for a transformational participation in revelation that nevertheless keeps the strict infinite, qualitative distinction in place.

Even with all this said, we still need to unpack what the enhypostatic/anhypostatic *Realdialektik* actually *is*. I've taken steps to show how it adds to the *Realdialektik*. I've tried to show how the en/an is even given priority as a *Realdialektik* over the *Realdialektik* of time/eternity. Now we need to understand more precisely what the en/an actually is. But first we need to see how it adds to and deepens the *Realdialektik*, by relocating it.

Why the En/An Needs to Come before Time/Eternity

The *Realdialektik* of time/eternity is experienced directly by humanity in its dissonance. In our own finitude and limitedness, we suffer the constraints of time. And yet we long for eternity. We are even willing to sin to overcome time and make our own way to eternity (as if that's possible). But this only produces in us, and the world as a whole, a having-mode of action that leads to the expenditure of energy to get ourselves to some kind of eternity we can possess (which will always be bound in immanence). But this is impossible, meaning we end up *not* with life (the witness of eternity) but as depleted, exhausted, and alienated (thrust into the dark shadow of time). Jesus Christ, as the unveiling of God in time, becomes the only way to appropriately embrace this dialectic and find life inside the dissonance of this *Realdialektik*. Inside the dissonance of this *Realdialektik*, borne by Jesus Christ, the relation of *this* God to *this* human being can occur, even in the immanent frame (the concrete relation of the *this* is what the immanent frame obscures).

While brilliant in its existential (and even eschatological) description, the *Realdialektik* as time/eternity offers little on the soteriological depth of Jesus's entering of time as the eternal one. The soteriology it provides allows for saving from the dissonance and constraints of time, but it doesn't as fully and expansively embrace life. In other words, what Barth sees in 1924, now reflecting on a decade of pastoral ministry, is that the real dialectic of time/eternity is substantive in its articulation of human dissonance, but not articulate enough in its relation to Jesus's own act and being and his call to live in and love the world. The real dialectic of time/eternity tells us very little about the real dialectic that the church fathers saw in the being of Jesus Christ.

The fulcrum of the dialectic in time/eternity is the human existential experience. But the church fathers see a real dialectic embedded in the very being of Jesus Christ himself. And it's in this dialectic that our salvation rests.[11] Barth has come far in showing how a dialectical theology can speak of the *this* relation between a God who is God and human beings. But now Barth sees that it all needs to be taken a step further. The real dialectic needs to have its weight not in existentialism but in Christopraxis. The *Realdialektik* of time/eternity may front revelation inside the immanent frame (this is an incredible contribution), but it has not adequately been able to describe why the encounter with this revelation in the dissonance of the time/eternity dialectic is the salvation of life (is participation in the very being of God).[12]

To do this, the fulcrum of the *Realdialektik* needs to be shifted from the existential to the christological, or from the dissonant experience of the being of humanity to the very being of Jesus Christ. As we'll see, this post-1924 move

11. Keith Johnson adds to this in *The Essential Karl Barth: A Reader and Commentary* (Grand Rapids: Baker Academic, 2019), 279–80.

12. For more on en/an, see Bruce McCormack, *Orthodox and Modern: Studies in the Theology of Karl Barth* (Grand Rapids: Baker Academic, 2008), 209–12.

into en/an is not Barth's fetishizing of doctrine or dogmatics. It's the way to more deeply articulate the shape of Christopraxis inside the immanent frame.

So, finally, we can ask, What is this real dialectic that the church fathers see in Jesus's own person? What does all this *en* and *an* talk refer to?

What's So En? And What's So An?

The primary *Realdialektik* is the en/an, which stands above the time/eternity dialectic. Remember, what makes a dialectic real is not its opposition to something fake but its description of actual or real relations. The en/an is the description of the real relation of humanity to the person of Jesus Christ, and the person of Jesus Christ to the eternal God. Let's start with the en, seeing what difference this makes for our practical ecclesiology and pastoral imagination.

Starting with En

As one side of the dialectic, *the enhypostatic union claims that Jesus Christ as the second person of the Trinity is found en (in) flesh.* To know or encounter this living God made known in Jesus Christ is to know him in the flesh of humanity. The enhypostatic union claims that flesh—real and lived humanity—is the location of relation between God and the world. This real taking-on of humanity is universal. Jesus Christ has taken on *not* a hybrid or a suprahumanity but the very same universal humanity of each and every one of us. In this shared humanity, God encounters the world. To quote from Genesis, the enhypostatic union claims that Jesus Christ is true "bone of [our] bones and flesh of [our] flesh" (Gen. 2:23). There is no distinction in his flesh. He is our true brother. He is the one just like us. Jesus is fully and completely human, fully and completely sharing *en* (in) our humanity. Jesus then is universally bound to all human beings through his free act to *be* completely *en* (in) our humanity. This has important ramifications, particularly for our practical ecclesiology and pastoral theology.

The enhypostatic pole means there is no other form that human persons must take to encounter the living Jesus Christ but finally and fully our own humanity as it is. There is no necessary expenditure of energy to take another kind of form than the being of our own humanity. If it is true that we are in the form we need to be to be with God, we are closer to being released from the having-mode of action, exchanging the expenditure of energy as the purpose of action for a resonance in life. The enhypostatic union as God's complete identification with us in and through the humanity of Jesus Christ means freedom (as Luther would say) to be (as Paul Tillich would add) truly human ourselves (as Bonhoeffer would assert). The relation of *this* God to *this* human being comes finally and completely in the form of humanity itself. We are human when we are in resonant connection with the world. This incredible gift makes salvation possible, a remarkable kind of salvation that gives us back life in the world. This gift of Jesus completely sharing our form as the form of salvation means there is no reason to rush to have the world by expending energy to become something we're not. Instead, we can be, acting in the world in the being-mode, because God in Jesus Christ has so fully acted for us that Jesus Christ has enhypostatically become fully and finally human.

This means that Jesus meets us not when we escape our humanity and possess the world (even in his name). Jesus meets us when we live truly human lives, embracing life and the resonant encounters in the world, like Barth with *The Magic Flute*. There is no need to escape life, because Jesus is fully and completely human. The fact that Jesus lives and moves in the world (and is not bound in some spiritual state or in propositions of religion) means living in the world is the very place where we are met and embraced by God. This highlights further why the church cannot be the star of its own story and can only be the church by being with and for the world.

The enhypostatic reality asserts that a church that truly wants a relationship with Jesus Christ will find—or be found by—the living Christ by being in relationship in and with the world, loving the world *not* by expending energy to have the world, seeking resources and relevance, but by sharing in life by finally and completely being with the world. Resonance is a concrete form of human action in the being-mode that witnesses and participates in the enhypostatic reality of Jesus's incarnate life.

It's within human life, not just in the midst of an existential crisis, that we encounter the living God. The enhypostatic pole, as one side of the real dialectic, means that we encounter the living God in and through the real encounter of human persons in relationship. The enhypostatic union means true relationships (that move past the having-mode to just be) are the concrete location of God's unveiling in the world (more on this in the next section).

Even in an immanent frame, the concrete place where people testify to encountering the presence of the living Christ is in resonant actions of relationships, which avoid the temptation of expending energy and instead just be. The *en* makes relationship with humanity (being with and for the hypostatic other) the direct locale of revelation even in the immanent frame. Because God in Jesus Christ has completely and fully assumed humanity as the real enhypostatic side of the dialectic, relationships with human beings can never be reduced to the having-mode and made into instruments for relevance or for the sake of resources. Humanity is too precious (God completely taking on humanity's form) to be objectified in any form, allowing humanity to be free for the being-mode of life and action. If relations of human persons are in the being-mode, as opposed to the having-mode, they witness to a real relation of Jesus's own hypostatic being in his enhypostatic union with all humanity.

This is just what Woz discovers in his relationship with Herbert (and Teemon too). In turn, it's just what the Bible study, and through them the whole congregation, is able to experience when it is freed from the having-mode to act in the being-mode. When they choose to just be with Woz, they're not made into a less thriving church, losing ground. They are made *more* alive. They remain vulnerable institutionally, and always will be, but nevertheless they're filled with the Spirit of Life. They are participating in the enhypostatic reality of Jesus Christ himself, who freely and completely takes on humanity for the sole sake of being with and for humanity.

In Jesus's own being, in Jesus being with and for the world, humanity (all flesh) is completely assumed by God. To be human—to share in humanity—is to share in the hypostatic life of God. Woz finds that Jesus has found him when he bears the dialectic of time/eternity, when he faces his loss instead of hiding. But what makes this transformational, and assures him that it is Jesus who finds him in his dying, is the sharing of cohumanity.[13] It is the experience of being ministered to by Bert and Helene. Woz is found by a God who is God, not because Bert and Helene had a perfect strategy of action to expend energy and capture Woz's loyalty (winning his future action). Rather, what was transformational (call it even converting) was the being-mode that led them to just be with and for Woz, to simply share in his life and journey with him as friends. It's friendship in and through the ministry of shared suffering, which is the direct manifestation of this enhypostatic reality, that transforms Woz.

Woz's discipleship is inaugurated not when he masters some informa-tion or signs a contract (not when he expends energy for the church in the having-mode) but when he both receives ministry from and gives ministry to Herbert and Teemon. In relationships that give and receive ministry, we participate directly in the enhypostasis of Jesus, who takes on—completely, universally—the flesh of all humanity, all for the sake of ministering life to humanity, loving the whole of the world. When Woz prays for Herbert, he is directly coming up against, and therefore following, the living Jesus, sharing in his enhypostatic being. Prayer with and for a fellow human being is the height of the enhypostatic reality. The church *is* when it's in Christ enhypo-

13. Eventually Barth will develop this into his anthropology. See particularly *Church Dog-matics* III/2 (Edinburgh: T&T Clark, 1958). See also Daniel Price, *Karl Barth's Anthropology in Light of Modern Thought* (Grand Rapids: Eerdmans, 2002).

statically by praying for the world, caring for the flesh of the world. Prayer is the ultimate form of action in the being-mode. Prayer is waiting while acting before a God who is truly God by completely and fully sharing in humanity. The church that is encountering the living Jesus Christ in the world takes on the shape of "relationships of prayer."[14]

But there remains a creeping concern: there is an unrelenting temptation inside the immanent frame to make God into an echo of our own voice. How then does the en/an dialectic overcome this modern temptation? It's the an-hypostatic pole that safeguards us from this flattening temptation, while also leading us more deeply into visions of transformation.

Moving into the An

So far we've discussed only one side of the *Realdialektik* that is bound in the person of Jesus Christ. This one side without the other can lead (and often has led) to a defeated form of ministry that claims that because God is in the flesh of Jesus, fully identifying with us, there is little reason to seek transformation. Jesus is just there, not doing much while present. But this misunderstanding misses the other side of the dialectic. If the enhypostatic union lifts up the full and complete humanity of Jesus Christ, claiming that Jesus completely shares in (*en*) our flesh, at the same time and with the same passion, *the anhypostatic side claims that Jesus Christ is without flesh.* He is fully God, eternally and forever the second person of the Trinity. If the enhypostatic union claims Jesus's universal and complete bond with all humanity, then the anhypostatic side claims Jesus's unique particularity. Unlike us, he is the Logos who is from the beginning (John 1:1), *being* from the beginning without flesh. The *an* claims that even in Jesus's complete and full identification with humanity, he is always and eternally the second person of the Trinity, true God of true God.

This anhypostatic side of the dialectic, in a radical way, keeps the qualitative distinction between the infinite and the finite, holding the boundary between the givenness and nongivenness of reality. But instead of seeing this line as drawn in the starkest of opposites and explained in the cadence of "You are on earth and God is in heaven, you idiot!" (which can so easily lead to a frustrated hatred of the world), we adopt a more dynamic incarnational perspective that allows us to take another large leap into loving the world and affirming life in it.

In this incarnational perspective, what produces the otherness is constituted in the humanity of God. The enhypostasis of Jesus's full and complete

14. For more on this, see Root, *The Relational Pastor: Sharing in Christ by Sharing Ourselves* (Downers Grove, IL: InterVarsity, 2013), chaps. 13 and 14.

humanity allows for the fullness of his divinity (anhypostasis) to enter and lovingly confront the world. Barth sees that the otherness of God cannot be reached and captured, because it comes in the form of its opposite, because it is veiled, and yet unveiled, in the suffering humanity of Jesus Christ. The boundary is kept between the God who is God and the systems/structures of modernity by the Wholly Other God being unrecognizably veiled in human form. Nevertheless, in this human form, by encountering this unique and singular humanity of Jesus Christ, we come up against the God who is God.

Jesus uniquely brings humanity into the being of God. He is able to do this because he is unlike all other human beings. While completely *en*, sharing in our flesh, he is also completely *an*, without our flesh, eternally the Logos present at the beginning, ministering creation into being. Through Jesus's humanity we are invited (and able) to participate in God's very life by sharing in God's humanity. While the enhypostatic union binds Jesus's being to all humanity, making humanity the form of being with Jesus, the anhypostatic side brings humanity into the very trinitarian being. We are not only *with* Jesus enhypostatically but also *in* him anhypostatically.

Thanks to the anhypostasis, there is now something human in God's very self. The second person of the Trinity as enhypostatic (as in the flesh) takes humanity (takes this flesh) anhypostatically into the uncreated realm. Humanity is given a place in God's own being, allowing us to participate in God's eternal life by and through the flesh of Jesus's own flesh that is shared completely with our own. The *en* and *an* bring humanity into the being of God. This humanity of God (the very title of one of Barth's most famous lectures, given September 25, 1956, and then turned into a book) allows us to participate *really* and truly in the being of God, by receiving the act of God in the being of Jesus Christ.[15] To participate *in* a God who is God is impossible. Finite creatures cannot share in the infinite being of God. But this impossibility is bridged, and becomes an impossible possibility, by the anhypostasis of Jesus's very person who becomes enhypostatic. As Hebrews says, he is our great mediator (Heb. 9:15).

Jesus identifies with humanity enhypostatically, and through his own humanity as the incarnation of the second person of the Trinity, he takes humanity into direct participation with God the Father through the Spirit. Through Jesus's anhypostasis, we participate in God, though we are never something other than human. We are in Christ, transformed through the anhypostasis into Christ. This being in Christ does not come in a form that is something

---

15. *Really* is emphasized to point to how this dialectic is real—it continues the realist or realistic commitment Barth has had from the beginning of his theological exploration.

other than human (thanks to the enhypostatic union, we don't become mini-gods or *Übermensch*). Nevertheless, while in the form of humanity, the hypostatic human being is made into Christ's form by Jesus's own anhypostatic being. By sharing in Jesus's life, we share in the life of God.[16] In the enhypostatic union, God shares in humanity completely and fully by God in Christ sharing completely in the human form. In the anhypostatic, humanity shares in the being of God, incompletely and provisionally, but really and truly, by being transformed into Christ.

The way to keep the immanent frame from flattening divine action is to embrace the en/an. The immanent frame attacks transcendence by making it nonhistorical, voiding events of encountering God in the world like those experienced by the Elder. The immanent frame often places a ceiling over the world, enclosing the world within itself. Barth recognizes that there is no way to climb to the immanent frame's ceiling, like a great trapeze artist with a sledgehammer, punching skylights into it.[17] The immanent shell makes it impossible for any form of human action to *have* its way and make the immanent frame unambiguously open to transcendence.

What Barth sees is that there is no reason to expend energy fighting to open skylights in the immanent frame anyhow. This doesn't mean that we ought to concede that transcendence and divine action cannot be encountered in the immanent frame. Rather, Barth sees that God himself, in God's fullness of being God who is God, is not on the other side of the brass ceiling, wishing we would break through. God has arrived in the world in God's full glory. But this glory of the God who is God is veiled "in a creaturely medium. [God] enters [the immanent frame in] 'the divine incognito.'"[18] This truth is what both the Blumhardts knew and uncompromisingly lived out in their ministries.

In this divine incognito, veiling himself fully and completely in humanity, God is beyond any and all have-able actions of modernity. God is able to *be* encountered, heard, and loved. In the veiled and yet revealed humanity of

16. Barth is very careful, as this develops, to not slide into theosis. I personally think this is too bad. There seem to be similarities between Barth's work and its dialectics and Maximus the Confessor's dialectic of the essence and energy of God. I've written at length about the necessity of the transformation in ministry to embrace theosis. See *Faith Formation in a Secular Age* (Grand Rapids: Baker Academic, 2017), part 2. Barth doesn't want to go that far, but his anhypostatic focus here moves him in that direction. See Bruce McCormack, "Theosis No, Participation Yes," in *Orthodox and Modern*; and Adam Neder, *Participation in Christ: An Entry into Karl Barth's Church Dogmatics* (Louisville: Westminster John Knox, 2009).

17. This metaphor of skylights is taken from Charles Taylor. Taylor believes that there are indeed ways to recognize skylights in the immanent frame, but he doesn't think we make them; they're inherent in the frame itself.

18. McCormack, *Karl Barth's Critically Realistic Dialectical Theology*, 327.

Jesus Christ, who remains alive (as the Blumhardts saw), the church avoids the reductions of the immanent frame. The church doesn't need to expend energy to make those skylights, winning the acrobatic resources to climb to that brass ceiling, innovating ways to hang windows on it. Instead, the church can embrace life in modernity. In loving the world through actions of resonance, the church embraces life by seeking to encounter the divine incognito. We come up against the living Jesus Christ, as the divine incognito, in our relationships of giving ministry to and receiving it from one another.

The enhypostasis means Jesus suffers with us. The anhypostasis means that salvation comes through this suffering. The enhypostasis encourages us to embrace life, finding God incarnationally in the resonance mode of life. But the anhypostasis reminds us that no finite life can hold God. While God identifies with life, God is transforming life, promising and leading the entire world into all-new life. To forever *be*. For our being itself is hidden in the being of God (hidden with Christ, Col. 3:3).

This anhypostasis points to a kind of mystical union. The relation of *this* God to *this* human being is a transformation into the being of the one who is both *this* God and *this* human being—Jesus Christ. This mystical union is not a way to escape the world. Rather, if we can call this a mystical union—which most of the church fathers do—we must not see it as a purely metaphysical operation. With our eyes never taken off modernity and the pastoral constraint of the immanent frame, participating in the trinitarian life is best seen as a word-event. It is an encounter of resonance, which—as Rosa has explained—is also fundamentally a word-event (resonance is hearing the world speak).

Participation in the being of Christ is the calling to enter the world in the being-mode of action that is ministry. We participate in the being of Christ by sharing in his action. This action is never the expenditure of religious energy, but instead the freedom to be with and for the world in resonance. Here is where the second *Realdialektik* returns. We are in Christ, transformed into Christ, participating in his anhypostatic being, by sharing in his action and ministering to those in the world who bear the dissonance of the time/eternity dialectic. When Bert bears Woz's pain and acts to be with him in it, and when Woz does the same for Herbert and Teemon, there is participation in anhypostasis, there is a living out in the world of the en/an dialectic through entering, with the world, into the time/eternity dialectical dissonance. The Blumhardts' two watchwords—"Die, so that Jesus may live!" and "Jesus is Victor!"—are the two sides of the en/an dialectic, which seeks the living Jesus in the world, ministering life out of the deaths of the time/eternity dissonance.

———

Why did Teemon want Woz to pray for him? Woz wasn't sure. But Woz's experience with Herbert had been formative enough for him to accept the invitation and enter into the ministry. The next time Woz went to visit Herbert, he arrived twenty minutes early and found Teemon first. Part of Woz hoped Teemon had forgotten about the whole prayer thing. Maybe they'd just talk for a while and that would be enough. But unfortunately for Woz's desire to avoid the awkwardness, that wasn't the case. Within minutes Teemon was ready to pray. Woz awkwardly did just what Herbert had taught Woz to do for him.

And when Woz said amen there was . . . nothing really, just an exchange of nods. Woz breathed out his awkwardness and leaned back in his chair. Teemon then explained why he wanted Woz to pray for him. It took Woz's breath away.

Teemon wasn't a big partier, but he'd indulged that night of the accident. He explained that he'd just been promoted, so he went out drinking to celebrate with some friends. He had a few shots with his beers. He knew he wasn't right to drive, but talked himself into it. He was only a few miles from his apartment. He had plans in the morning, and he wanted his car at home. An Uber seemed too inconvenient. It was only a few miles, he told himself. And he hadn't had *that* much to drink, he'd rationalized.

But in those few miles, hell reigned on earth. Teemon ran a red light that he never saw. He smashed violently into the driver's side of a Toyota Highlander. He was in and out of consciousness for the next few days. At one point Teemon was told he was being taken in for his third surgery. At another point, a police officer was asking him questions. Finally, when Teemon came to, he was told that he had a rod in his back and was looking at months of physical therapy. But that wasn't the worst of it.

The police officer arrived a few minutes later to inform Teemon that the woman in the Highlander, a mother of three children, had died at the scene. Teemon couldn't believe it. All the pain in his body disappeared as the acute shame and anguish began to strangle his soul. The officer told Teemon he had been too injured to do an official sobriety test on-site, but their best guess was that he had been drinking, and it could be confirmed in trial. Regardless, Teemon was being charged with manslaughter.

Teemon lived with this shock for days, the burden of it all breaking his back more than the accident. Coming to grips with going to jail was nowhere near as horrible as facing the fact that he'd killed a mother. Eventually the officer returned with the family. It was the woman's husband and oldest daughter. Teemon guessed the daughter was in her early twenties. The officer talked, but Teemon couldn't hear him. Teemon was transfixed by the daughter. Her brokenness was so evident, her grief so exposed. All else disappeared. Teemon didn't hear it, but he figured the officer had asked him something. Yet all he could do in response was look at the daughter and say, "Sorry. I'm so sorry."

She looked at Teemon, wiped tears from her eyes, and said words that changed him forever: "I forgive you."

Her words pierced him. They took Teemon's breath away. The father turned to the officer and said, "It looks to us like he's suffered enough. Getting another pound of flesh and destroying his life like he's destroyed ours isn't going to bring her back. We're not going to press charges."

The daughter touched Teemon's arm as she left, and out of her gaping wound, she said, "I'll pray for you."

Throughout the months of painful rehab, Teemon thought of the daughter praying for him. It broke him and somehow also brought him back to life. He started thinking a lot about prayer. He had dreams of crying in shame and being reminded again and again that he was forgiven and that he was being prayed for. He even had a dream, which felt so real, of someone, whom Teemon felt like he knew but couldn't identify, say to him, "All is made new in me." He had no idea what any of that meant, but it brought a tangible peace. Teemon eventually found himself thinking, "If she's praying for me, I should pray too." But he didn't know how. He didn't even know where to start, until the day Herbert introduced him to Woz and said, "Woz prays for me." Immediately Teemon knew that Woz was sent there for him.

———————

Woz told all of this to the Bible study. In sharing in the story of Woz's ministry, they were being drawn concretely and really into the en/an dialectic. They were most faithfully the church when they were in the world, praying with those in the world who were being met by the living Christ, drawn through the dissonance of time and eternity into an enhypostatic encounter of shared life that brought witness to the anhypostatic reality. Teemon's experience wasn't bound in the church. It happened in the world, even in the immanent frame. Saint John the Baptist was not the star of its own story. But the congregation was faithfully participating in God's story to unveil himself in the incognito/incarnational encounter, to which Woz now testified. The church could only share in and help interpret these experiences, such as Teemon's. The church is called to go into the world to love the world in the being-mode of action that at its core is prayer. The community lived (was given the life of the Spirit) through sharing in these en/an narratives, experiences of Christ enfleshed and also completely God. Teemon was not, and never would be, officially part of Saint John the Baptist, but in a real sense, he was. Woz's ministry to him brought him into the community, his person and story, and Woz's participation in his person through his story (Woz even being an answer to prayer) was a real manifestation of divine action (of the incognito of revelation) in the immanent frame.[19]

Woz had found Jesus, or—better—had been found in Jesus. He was taken up into the en/an dialectic by sharing in Teemon's personhood, receiving his confession, and participating in the living out of Teemon's reconciliation. Woz prayed for Teemon and received his story as a deep personal act. Woz's personal action—his agency in praying—both freely shared in Teemon (as a witness to the enhypostatic) and shared in the life of Jesus Christ, who heals and forgives (as a witness to the anhypostatic). Woz participates in Christ, in both poles of the en/an dialectic, by praying for Teemon, as Ananias does for Saul in Acts 9. Woz had found God not by escaping the world but by learning the being-mode of action through prayer and entering the world as a personal agent, receiving and giving ministry as participation in Jesus's own en/an life. Woz did this by recognizing his own life as a kind of Christoresonance that led him to love Jesus by loving the world.[20] Woz was alive because he was drawn into a lived transcendence made available by the humanity of God.

Saint John the Baptist too was alive. They were most acting like the church in the dual movements of being in the world: waiting with the world in prayer and being together sharing in the stories of God's arrival in the world. Saint John the Baptist's calling was to be in the world praying with the world enhypostatically, in tangible experiences of Christ. And they were also called to be proclaiming to the world that this one who Teemon met is Jesus Christ himself inviting Teemon and the world into the anhypostatic transformation of new life—what God does quite beyond and apart from us. In these stories of testifying to enhypostatic encounters, they were participating in anhypostatic transformation, proclaiming this to the world by sharing in the humanity of the world. It all started with Bert enhypostatically being with Woz, who was now drawing the whole community into the anhypostatic reality through his testimony of participating in God's own ministry.

Saint John the Baptist had life because it had the lived transcendence of God's encounter in and through personal agents acting with and for one another for the sake of being with one another. They too are free from the

19. Barth's ecclesiology ends with prayer, as does this one. Barth discusses this in *Church Dogmatics* IV/3.2 (Edinburgh: T&T Clark, 1962), 880–90.

20. *Christoresonance* is a neologism Erik Leafblad came up with in reading through this manuscript.

having-mode of action, released from seeking to borrow enough energy to spend in staying alive. They can now just be.

At the next search meeting for the new pastor, with three candidates before them, Bert shared thoughts like this. He wasn't sure he was communicating well. Of the three viable candidates before him, two seemed unlikely to lead them further in the direction God was moving them. Both were able candidates, but Bert didn't sense they could understand what the Woz-event meant for the congregation. As Bert was explaining this reservation, one of the other committee members interrupted and said, "Maybe it's you!" Bert stopped in his tracks, confused. "Maybe it's you, Bert! Maybe you're supposed to be our next pastor."

Saint John the Baptist didn't have the resources and relevance they once thought they needed. But they now had something more. They had encountered the revelation of the living God, who called them to wait. This waiting prepared them for direct encounter with personal agents such as Woz who were unveiled in the incognito of the God who is God. Saint John the Baptist was a church that was now alive because it was a church encountering a lived transcendence.

Bert had come to see that the expending of energy would never give Saint John the Baptist life (or faithfulness). Life would come only by participating in the life of the God who is God. Bert's surprising but sure call into pastoral ministry would help the congregation seek this living God. Even as the congregation struggled, they would trust that seeking the living God would see them through.

And that's enough! That's everything!

INDEX